Pricing—
The New CEO Imperative

Pricing— The New CEO Imperative

A Book from the Pricing Profession to the C-suite

**Edited by
Stephan M. Liozu, PhD**

Value Innoruption Advisors Publishing • Crown King AZ • 2021

Pricing—The New CEO Imperative: A Book from the Pricing Profession to the C-suite
Edited by Stephan M. Liozu, PhD
© 2021 Stephan M. Liozu. All rights reserved.

Published by Value Innoruption Advisors Publishing
PO Box 551
Crown King, Arizona 86343
USA
www.valueinnoruption.com

The Software Pricing Framework® is a registered trademark of Miller Advisors, Inc.

ISBN: 978-1-945815-08-9 trade paperback
      978-1-945815-09-6 electronic book

First printing

Design and composition: www.dmargulis.com

MANUFACTURED IN THE UNITED STATES OF AMERICA

In memory of Manu Carricano, husband, father, teacher, entrepreneur, and a great pricing expert who left us too soon.

•

I dedicate this book to all the hard-working pricing professionals who drive pricing and profit improvement programs with a passion. They play a critical role in their organization and they are often not fully appreciated and recognized. I want to salute their hard and important work!

Contents

SECTION 4: PRICING MATURITY AND CAPABILITIES

SECTION 5: PRICING AS A FORCE OF TRANSFORMATION

List of Figures

Preface

THE WORLD IS CHANGING quickly, and forces of disruption are upon us every year. The latest major crisis, the
COVID-19 pandemic, has severely disrupted the business world.
All consultants agree that the new or next normal will not be
the same. Business will be more digital, more connected, more
direct, more diversified, more real-time, and extremely fast. In
that context, companies will invest further in digital transformations, in direct-to-consumer business models, in additional
e-commerce capabilities, and in superior commercial excellence
programs. For all these programs, there will be a strong pricing backbone to extract value from their markets and to manage highly dynamic, data-driven transactions. Given that only 22
percent of Fortune Global 500 companies have dedicated pricing
teams, there's an imperative for CEOs and C-suites in general to
pay attention to pricing, to embrace pricing as a necessary function to drive efficiencies, and to increase investments in state-of-
the-art pricing methods, systems, and designs. The new normal
cannot be managed manually via pricing transactions and without proper strategic pricing capabilities. It's time for CEOs to

make pricing a source of competitive advantage and a strong profit lever.

This book is a collective effort from the pricing profession to the C-suite. It has 21 chapters organized in five main sections. I thank the following contributors:

- Bhupi Arora
- Mark Billige
- Camille Brégé
- John Bruno
- Gregor Buchwald
- Dave Burns
- Manu Carricano, PhD
- Gernot T. Dambacher
- Lindsay Duran
- Jered W. Haedt
- Nate Hamilton
- Andreas Hinterhuber
- Valerie Howard
- Ron Kermisch
- Mitchell D. Lee
- Vernon E. Lennon III
- Janene Liston
- Augustin Manchon
- Scott Miller
- Kevin Mitchell
- Georg Müller
- Terry Oblander
- Amadeus Petzke
- Jens Pfennig
- Ole Iacob Prebensen
- Frank Rautenberg, PhD

- Cavan Reinsborough
- Sonya Roberts
- Pierre Schaeffer
- Sho Shinohara
- Ranjit (Jit) Singh
- Gabriel Smith
- Mark Stiving
- Karen Lellouche Tordjman
- Bob Vezeau
- Dr. Andreas von der Gathen
- Joanna Wells
- Maciej Wilczyński
- Craig Zawada
- Frederico Zornig

A special thank you as well for my project team: Kristen Ebert-Wagner, in charge of editing (editor@ebert-editorial.com), and Dick Margulis, in charge of formatting, designing, and virtually setting up the book (dick@dmargulis.com).

This book is an initiative of the Coalition for the Advancement of Pricing (CAP).

Pricing—
The New CEO Imperative

Introduction

IN 2010, AS PART of my PhD research, I interviewed 11 senior leaders to understand their perceptions of pricing and how they potentially become involved in the pricing process. The answer was clear: they do not! Most paid no attention to the pricing process or to pricing decisions. I did find, however, a difference between top leaders in firms performing value-based pricing and those in firms performing cost-based or competitive-based pricing. This was an eye-opening exercise. I heard some of the most shocking statements by these CEOs: "I don't have time to pay attention to pricing. I get involved in margin discussions"; or "Pricing is a set of tactical activities that doesn't get discussed in the C-suite"; or even "We do 50 percent margin: why should I get involved?" At that time, as a CEO myself and being involved in our value-based pricing transformation, I wondered why these CEOs would give me such answers. So I decided to launch a wider survey of 557 CEOs to validate some of the findings. When asked to distribute 100 points of attention between cost-cutting, growth, and pricing, they assigned pricing only 16 points on average. Most of the CEOs' attention was given to cost-cutting priorities.

Fast forward to 2019, and now I'm the chief value officer of the Thales Group, promoting pricing and greater investments to our executive committee. I'm working closely with my boss, the CMO of the group and a strong proponent of the power of pricing. We'd positioned our approach with the support of Simon-Kucher & Partners (SKP), after an internal assessment of many business units, and after conducting six pilot projects with SKP and Boston Consulting Group (BCG), we had a highly structured approach and a rather well-documented ROI of what we'd done and a projection of what we could deliver to the group over two years given a serious investment in pricing consulting and systems. So, we went on a mission to convince our CFO, our COO, and other key executives in the group. Most of them understood our approach and understood the ROI of our actions, but we weren't able to secure the requested investments. It was mind-blowing. To this day, I still can't understand what makes it so complicated to justify pricing investments and to secure funds to deliver strong EBIT impact that other functions could never match. I concluded that something else wasn't clicking in our approach and that we had to do so something different. These executives are smart. They're well educated in finance and business operations. They manage investment requests each day. Why did they fail to see the benefits of pricing investments? I do not blame them. I admit that I was responsible for justifying the business case and that I failed at doing so. In the end, I'm the one who failed. This is when I decided to conduct another qualitative inquiry to explore exactly what was happening in the heads of these executives when they were presented pricing business cases.

Formation of the CAP initiative

To try to understand the phenomenon discussed above, I created the Coalition for the Advancement of Pricing (CAP), an informal group of pricing practitioners and thinkers dedicated to moving the pricing profession to the next level. The group lives on LinkedIn and was established as a noncommercial working group. CAP's first initiative was to launch this first qualitative inquiry conducting semistructured interviews with pricing executives and thought leaders.

About the research

I conducted 31 semistructured qualitative phone interviews with 31 pricing professionals at the end of 2019. The sample included CEOs of the top five pricing management software companies globally, six heads of the most relevant pricing consulting companies globally, 12 VPs or directors of pricing at significantly large companies, and eight C-suite executives (CEOs, CMOs, and CGOs). Interviews lasted 30 to 40 minutes. The data were transcribed, coded, and synthesized to produce key findings.

The interviews focused on understanding C-suite executive perceptions of pricing, on how C-suites in general prioritized pricing investments, and on how the pricing profession can better convince the C-suite to pay more attention to pricing. Once again, the key findings were highly informative:

1 The quality of the business cases and ROI calculations proposed by pricing leaders in firms are not always professional or business-centric. The proposals are often disconnected from other processes and functions in the organization.
2 Pricing investment requests often lack risk analysis and scenario planning. Pricing is perceived as a somewhat risky discipline, and top executives want to better understand the risks and rewards of these investments.

3 Top executives understand the propositions and believe the ROI calculations but lack confidence in their teams' ability to execute the projects well. They believe they lack internal capabilities and expertise needed to reap the benefits of the investments. They also don't want to hire a new team to do this work.

4 Pricing investments are often considered second priorities, although the impact of such projects is accepted. Organizations often have a holistic strategic transformation sequence, and pricing does not fit well into that sequence.

5 Because of the risk aversion of certain C-suite executives, they tend to try to influence the CFO and the CEO to stay away from pricing programs that could "poke the bear" and make customers very unhappy.

6 There are myths about pricing that remain alive and kicking in the C-suite. These myths reveal a lack of understanding of what pricing is and how it's evolved over the past 20 years.

These are the major themes that emerged from the 31 interviews. Armed with these insights, I decided to collaborate with some of the organizations involved in CAP to disseminate the findings through blogs, podcasts, keynote presentations, and the submission of several academic papers. This is also when the concept of this industry book was created. What if we pulled the energy and collective forces of the pricing industry and profession and wrote a book dedicated to the C-suite to address these findings?

A book from the profession to the C-suite

The main motivation of this book is to educate C-suite executives about what pricing is, its potential impact in the organization, and the capabilities needed to reach the zone of pricing excellence. This book is not intended to promote or sell any particular software solution or consulting service. It's a collective effort to bring together a new narrative for the C-suite, especially in the context of after the COVID-19 pandemic. In first quarter of 2020 and right in the middle of the crisis, I contacted the key players in the pricing space to pitch to them the idea of this CAP book. I'd interviewed many of the pricing executives in the past, and they quickly understood the need for greater coordination and professionalization of the pricing industry. Most agreed that this crisis presented a unique opportunity for the profession to position itself more concretely in the mind of C-suite executives. After two months of conversations with these pricing leaders, the book was put in motion in the second half of the year. The result of this effort is what you hold in your hands!

1 Strong representation from the software and consulting branches of pricing.
2 Support from the Professional Pricing Society (PPS) to ensure that the CAP initiative brings the expected impact to the profession.
3 Participation and contribution from some of the most progressive pricing practitioners and experts in the form of testimonials.

Of course, I wasn't able to convince everyone. Some organizations hid behind their corporate shields. Others plainly expressed a lack of interest. And some were too lazy to answer emails or to participate. That's part of the work of an evangelist: we keep plugging away! The goal was to achieve an acceptable level of industry representation and diversity of content. Mission accomplished: for the time since the formation of the pricing profession, we have a coordinated approach by our industry for the benefit of the C-suite. Pricing practitioners and vendors for the most part care about advancing the profession. They want to make sure that C-suite executives understand what pricing can bring to their organization, especially as they invest more in e-commerce, digital transformation, data analytics, and commercial excellence. The future of business is great. The future of business with a pricing engine is fantastic.

Structure of the book

This book has 21 chapters organized in five main sections.

- Section 1 focuses on addressing the myths of pricing as well as some of the lessons from pricing transformational projects. A team from Deloitte Consulting's Pricing and Profitability practice gets us started by addressing five myths about raising prices that every CEO should know (chapter 1). Chapter 2, by Andreas Hinterhuber, addresses the pricing myths that kill profits in firms. In chapter 3, a group of authors from the Bain Global Pricing Practice share with us some of the lessons from the C-suite on why pricing initiatives succeed or fail. In chapter 4, the CEO of Manchon & Company shares some lessons for the C-suite on how to make pricing a board-ready priority.
- Section 2 goes deep into the topic of pricing ROI and impact. I begin with a review of all documented nuggets of ROI by summarizing impact nuggets that C-suite executives can use as a benchmark (chapter 5). Chapter 6, written by Dr. Carricano, deep-dives into the topic of pricing power from an economics perspective. Chapter 7, by the Zilliant CMO, addresses pricing benchmarks and their impact on margins. Chapter 8 is a reprint of one of my papers focused on pricing power, published in *Business Horizons* in 2018. This section closes with

some international flavor and a contribution by the CEO of Quantiz on how they delivered one billion dollars of impact to their clients in South America (chapter 9). Considering the importance of giving a voice to the profession, I invited pricing leaders and pricing experts in smaller consulting firms to give us testimonials on a case study or an experience working with the C-suite.

- Section 3 is dedicated to testimonials and interviews. Chapter 10 is a collaboration between BCG and the Thales Group listing insights from their pricing journey. It's followed by an interview with Sonya Roberts, President of Cargill Salt, about their pricing journey (chapter 11). Chapters 12 and 13 offer a series of short testimonials by practitioners and experts from around the world demonstrating that pricing has no boundaries. I collected short narratives from Japan, Poland, France, Germany, and other countries.
- Section 4 highlights the criticality of pricing maturity and capabilities in the achievement of pricing excellence. This section presents a collection of chapters from INSIGHT2PROFIT, Impact Pricing, Vendavo, and Miller Advisors. Chapter 14, by the Chief Growth Officer of INSIGHT2PROFIT, highlights the importance of adopting a complete-solution approach to ensure pricing success. In chapter 15, Mark Stiving from Impact Pricing highlights the case for bridging the value gap in organizations. Chapter 16, by Mitch Lee, the Profit Prophet at Vendavo, focuses on managing commercial excellence through an economic downturn. In chapter 17, Scott Miller discusses best practices in pricing and offer designs for B2B digital solutions.
- Section 5, the longest section, covers the important dimension of pricing as a force of transformation. We know that most companies invest heavily in digital and organizational

development. We also know that the COVID-19 crisis was a serious earthquake in the business world and required many companies to do things differently. In chapter 18, a group of authors from the BCG pricing practice in France and Germany introduce the concept of bionic pricing to augment human intelligence. Chapter 19, from the co-CEOs of Simon-Kucher & Partners, covers how pricing and commercial agility can help companies survive the COVID-19 crisis. The next two chapters are dedicated to the topic of pricing in the context of digital transformations. In chapter 20, Valerie Howard writes about the need for pricing to be a force to increase digital selling maturity. Chapter 21, by Gabriel Smith of Pricefx, addresses how pricing, digital, and commercial excellence are tightly related in these days of needed recovery and greater technology investments.

I am privileged to have the book's concluding thoughts written by Kevin Mitchell, president of the Professional Pricing Society. He guides us through the evolution of the pricing profession and makes predictions about where the profession is headed. It's essential for top executives and members of the C-suite to understand the industry's roots. Pricing is no longer just a clerical and tactical function in firms: it's now a strategic function with dedicated professionals (CROs, CPOs, CVOs) active in the C-suites of the most progressive organizations. Kevin also highlights the need to keep pushing as a profession to convince more CEOs to pay attention to pricing and to invest in the discipline. There are many great resources available to go fast and bring short-term impact to the bottom line. In 2010 only 10 percent of Fortune 500 companies had a pricing team. This number now stands at 22 percent, so progress is being made.

Concluding thoughts

This book is rich in content, concepts, and methods. It's a quick way for CEOs and their C-suite executives to get up to speed and to find the nuggets necessary to make more intelligent investment decisions when it comes to pricing. It's also a guide for quickly learning the latest pricing concepts and how they can help companies reap the benefits of their digital and commercial excellence investments. The future of business is more connected, more real-time, more digital, and faster. As companies invest in more technology and more progressive organizational designs, pricing is front and center in the transformation. You need pricing when you automate the sales process (CPQ). You need pricing when you implement an e-commerce platform or direct-to-consumer technology (pricing scrubbing). You need a pricing engine when you diversify in recurring business models and launch subscriptions directly to your end users or through your trade channels (billing engine). You need pricing to optimize your deal desk decisions and launch creative bundles (price optimization). These technologies have evolved greatly and are readily available. Let's stop pretending that pricing can be managed manually by a group of clerical employees. More and more companies have vice presidents of pricing and analytics. Others have centers of excellence in pricing that guide their divisions to superior results. The profession pooled their resources to convince you in the C-suite to pay more attention to pricing and to guide teams to make better investment propositions. We aren't saying that every company should have a chief pricing officer in the C-suite. Nor are we saying that CEOs should get involved in every deal or transactions. Our goal is to promote pricing, the capabilities that are required to reach pricing excellence, and the impact of doing so. The impact can be achieved quickly by focusing on low-hanging fruit. But companies should focus on long-term transformation for sustainable contribution to the bottom line over time.

It was an honor to serve as project manager to make this industry book possible. Through my research and numerous conversations with the contributors, I've met a group of passionate individuals who have a strong passion for pricing. Most have a burning fire within to help companies be more successful and profitable. I've also met brilliant entrepreneurs who've dedicated their lives to developing new technology for the profession. I thank all the contributors and sponsors of this book. I want to officially recognize the sponsors who have supported CAP and this project financially:

- Boston Consulting Group
- Deloitte Consulting LLP
- INSIGHT2PROFIT
- Manchon & Company
- Miller Advisors
- Pricefx
- PROS Holdings
- Simon-Kucher & Partners
- Vendavo
- Zilliant

I have been formally in the pricing profession for the past 11 years. I've seen the great progress that pricing software vendors have made. I've heard of the many successful pricing consulting projects that have delivered millions of dollars to the bottom line. I've participated in numerous PPS conferences and heard many stories of successful pricing transformations with the support from the C-suite. And I've conducted many large-scale projects myself as a practitioner and a consultant. I'm passionate about pricing and about how pricing can drive profit in organizations. I don't consider myself a pricing expert: I'm a businessperson who loves achieving great profit levels while working on new technologies and adopting progressive methods. That includes value-based pricing, AI-based pricing, pricing optimization, bionic pricing, and many other methods.

If you're a top executive in a firm, a business owner, or a CEO reading this introduction, I ask you to read the whole book to learn about pricing and its impact. Then have a conversation with your executive committee about pricing and how it's managed in your firm. If you do have a pricing team, get to know them, and spend time understanding the tough role they play in your organization. Pricing isn't an easy job every day, and recognition does not come easily or often. I ask you to thank them for their hard work and to give them the latest modern tools to perform that work every day. You'll be amazed at their motivation to improve your bottom line. Thank you for getting this book and for reading it. Be bold and join the pricing revolution!

Abbreviations/acronyms used in this book

ACV	Actual captured value	**ERP**	Enterprise resource planning
AI	Artificial intelligence	**GE**	General Electric
BAFO	Best-and-final-offer	**GM**	General Motors
BCG	Boston Consulting Group	**HBR**	Harvard Business Review
BU	Business unit	**KPI**	Key performance indicator
CAP	Coalition for the Advancement of Pricing	**MVP**	Minimum viable product
CBCV	Customer-based corporate valuation	**PE**	Private equity
CFO	Chief financial officer	**PECO**	Pricing ecosystem
CIO	Chief information officer	**PIMS**	Profit impact of market strategy
CMO	Chief marketing officer	**PO&M**	Price optimization and management
CoE	Center of excellence	**PPA**	Pricing power assessment
COGS	Cost of goods sold	**PPS**	Professional Pricing Society
COO	Chief operating officer	**PVM**	Price-volume mix
CPQ	Configure, price, quote	**RFQ**	Request for quote
CRM	Customer relationship management	**RFP**	Request for proposals
CSR	Corporate social responsibility	**ROI**	Return on investment
CVM	Customer value management	**SaaS**	Software as a service
DTC	Direct to consumer	**SDR**	Say, do, and reinforce
DX	Digital transformation	**SKP**	Simon-Kucher & Partners
EBIT	Earnings before interest and taxes	**SMB**	Small and medium businesses
EBITDA	Earnings before interest, taxes, depreciation, and amortization	**TCO**	Total cost of ownership
ECV	Expected capture value	**VCG**	Value capture gap
EDLP	Everyday low price	**WTP**	Willingness to pay
EMAC	European Marketing Academy	**XaaS**	Delivery of anything as a service

SECTION 1

PRICING LESSONS AND MYTHS

The Five Myths about Raising Prices That Every CEO Should Know

Bhupi Arora, Senior Manager, Deloitte Pricing & Profitability Practice; Georg Müller, Director, Deloitte Pricing & Profitability Practice; and Ranjit (Jit) Singh, Partner, Deloitte Pricing & Profitability Practice

"Price is what you pay. Value is what you get."
—*Warren Buffett*

"Only children, fools, and cowards would allow
a company to treat them as if prices were set
by customers."
—*Mokokoma Mokhonoana*
(social critic and writer)

Overcome these myths to unlock your company's full margin potential

Business executives have an excellent opportunity to use the pricing discipline to improve their top and bottom lines. Unfortunately, most companies suffer from outdated pricing skills, oversimplified processes, and ineffective systems and tools, leading to missed pricing opportunities. Effective price management is all about addressing potential leakage points as a means of creating material margin growth.

The question for every enterprise boils down to this: "How do we ensure that we are realizing all the pricing value that we should for long-term success?"

Unfortunately, addressing the pricing challenges evokes fear and anxiety in many organizations, even when buoyed by good economic conditions that should instill confidence. And the anxiety only amplified during times of uncertainty.

In this chapter we discuss how taking a customer-centric view to pricing for value can lead to the results every company wants and demystify some of the myths around taking prices. What follows is a discussion of the five major objections to addressing the pricing challenge that CEOs are likely to hear from their organizations. See if any of these sound familiar!

The importance of effective price management

The times are dynamic and will only become more so. Now is the time to look at your pricing:

- Customer/consumer behaviors are shifting in an accelerated manner to digital platforms, upsetting current value models like convenience, safety, and transparency.
- Raw-material and input costs are continuing to become more volatile.
- Rapidly changing demand forecasts are increasing the complexity of managing production and inventories.

All of these are creating ongoing margin challenges for companies and changing customer expectations. In addition, the negative impact of ignoring pricing discipline is staggering. Results from hundreds of price management improvement projects show that companies add 3 percent to 5 percent of revenue to the bottom line through price management improvement (Deloitte Consulting LLP, Analysis 2020). Looking only at the bottom quartile of the Fortune 500 ranked by profitability, adding 3 percent to 5 percent of revenue to the bottom line equates to $94 billion to $156 billion of additional earnings for these companies (Deloitte Consulting LLP, Analysis 2020).

With such powerful results, executives must grab the opportunity to improve pricing. However, they may get a lot of resistance both internally and from the market on raising prices.

Unfortunately, experience from the field shows that five misconceptions block pricing progress at most companies. This chapter describes the five myths, explains pricing reality, and provides short case studies of how companies overcame those myths to achieve excellent price management improvements.

The five myths that paralyze price increases

In this chapter we address five common myths around pricing that often lead to deferred decisions, missed opportunities, and defeat in the marketplace:

- Myth 1: We are a commodity business; we cannot raise prices.
- Myth 2: Because we are a customer-centric company, we cannot raise prices.
- Myth 3: Our business environment is changing; we cannot raise prices during this uncertainty.
- Myth 4: As a B2B company, pricing is negotiated by our sales team; they control what we can get with price.
- Myth 5: Our customers are extremely sensitive to price; there is no way we can raise prices without losing business.

Companies that overcome the five myths can see dramatic benefits

Many companies have debunked these myths and have generated excellent results from increased revenue and improved margins.

Myth 1: We are a commodity business; we cannot raise prices.

Reality: Commoditization is a perceived notion; in reality, you can decommoditize any offer.

The *Oxford English Dictionary* defines *commodity* as any raw material that can be bought and sold. However, in the commercial world, the term has become synonymous with products/services that are unspecialized and that have zero differentiation. In our experience, one of the most common pushbacks that executives get from their internal teams around price increase revolves around this concept of "feeling like a commodity business" and subsequently the "market" dictating what the price point *must* be. If you've heard this, you've probably wondered whether this was just a convenient excuse or a legitimate concern.

Even though there may be components of your products that are less differentiated than your competitors' because of quality or performance standards set by the industry or by law, we believe you can decommoditize almost anything. We find that companies in this situation struggle to differentiate their products on the basis of product performance alone. What they miss out on are opportunities to create differentiation around all the other components that make a holistic offer, like availability, delivery, technical services, brand, shipment quantities, payment terms, customer engagement, and so forth.

Moreover, the "market" is made up of *your company, your competitors, and your existing and potential customers.* While the market may set the average price, companies set the transaction prices.

Unless you believe your competitors have access to specific information or algorithms you lack that are helping them set prices, there's no reason to believe the "market" is setting your price. Each transaction you have with your customers informs that market. The most successful companies are those that frame the value of their offerings in a way that customers find compelling, are easy to do business with, and connect with a customer's goals (Figure 1.1).

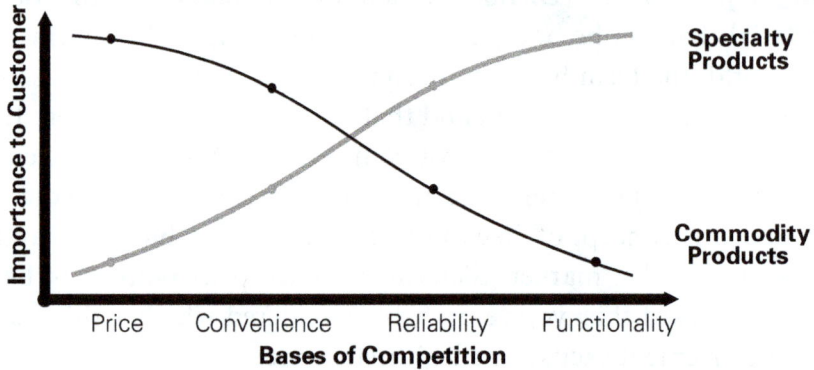

Figure 1.1. What your customer values will change over time.

Analysis shows that up to 70 percent of transactions at any given company are priced below the market price (Deloitte Consulting LLP, Analysis 2018). Price can be increased transaction by transaction using price-band analysis to pinpoint poor pricing decisions. A price band compares the price attained for a particular product or service across all salespeople and transactions. There are multiple price-band views, but this basic view often reveals actions that can be taken immediately to improve financial performance (Figure 1.2). Transaction prices that fall below the overall weighted average price (e.g., the market price) have the opportunity to be raised.

Case snippet. An industrial manufacturing company performed price-band analysis and found up to a 50 percent variance in the invoice price for the same product in the same region with the same competitors that was perceived to be a highly commoditized offering. After providing new price guidelines to salespeople, the company raised the median price by 12 percent. This improvement resulted in over $19 million in benefits while driving an increase of 1 percent in year-over-year volume.

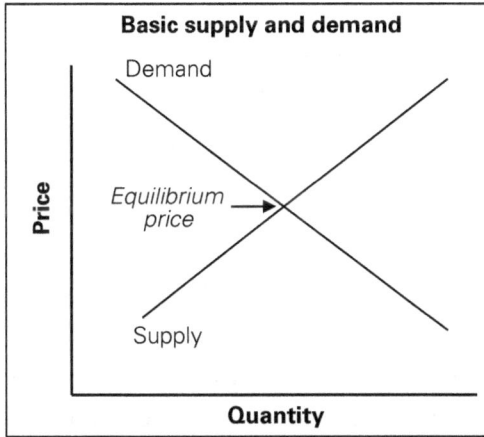

Macro view – price set by the market

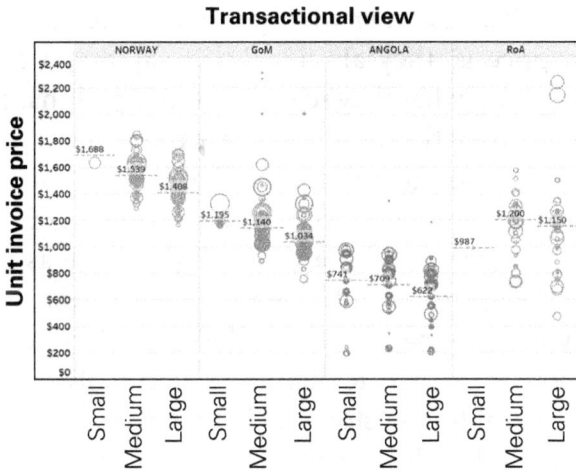

Micro view – price variability exists by transaction

Figure 1.2. The "market" rarely actually sets your customer's price.

Here are two things you should do today to address this myth:

- Sit down with your business and think about the real value your company/offering provides in the market today. Have *all* those elements been taken into account when setting and raising prices?
- Talk to five customers to understand where they derive value from consuming your product/offer versus a competitor's. Are you communicating and monetizing that value differential adequately?

Myth 2: Because we are a customer-centric company, we cannot raise prices.

Reality: A better understanding of how your customers buy your offerings, what elements they value, and their buying process and source of value can actually allow you to *raise* prices.

If you ever ask a customer whether they would pay more or how important price is, they almost always say they wouldn't pay a penny more than what they're paying today and that price is very important, perhaps the most important thing. But if you take price off the table and ask your customer what elements of your offer are most important, you can uncover the real sources of value around the product, service, and the value they provide as part of their product/service to their end customer (Figure 1.3).

Nobody wants to pay more, but the cost of business disruption is much more expensive. Sometimes successfully raising prices is just about reminding customers that your company needs to be profitable enough to be able to stick around to provide the products and services they desire.

Additionally, many companies fail to regularly examine and pursue price increases and then three to five years later realize

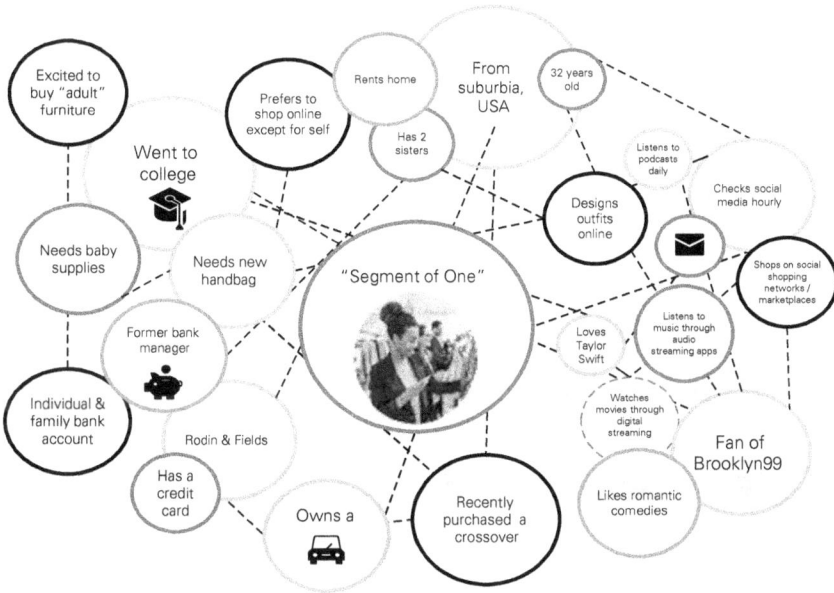

Figure 1.3. Your customer-centric vision does not mean focusing on price.

that they need to raise prices to cover their costs, and now they're looking at 25 percent price increases. It's important to train your customers to expect price increases. Better to do it in little steps along the way than in one big jump.

Everyone says they want to be customer-centric, but it costs money to change processes, become more digital, and be more responsive to your customers. And if you really want to be more responsive, you'd better be able to extract the value you create.

If you can connect your price increase to a new source of value, it makes the conversation easier. There used to be a simple model for this: if I can create more value (by being more efficient or finding additional levers that end-customers value), then I'll split the difference with my customers. All customers want companies to be thinking about how to create better value for them. This is what customer-centricity really means (Figure 1.4). It's not simply

Example: economic value estimation:
- Efficient pricing depends upon differentiation between competitors
- Prices can be set based on products' economic benefit

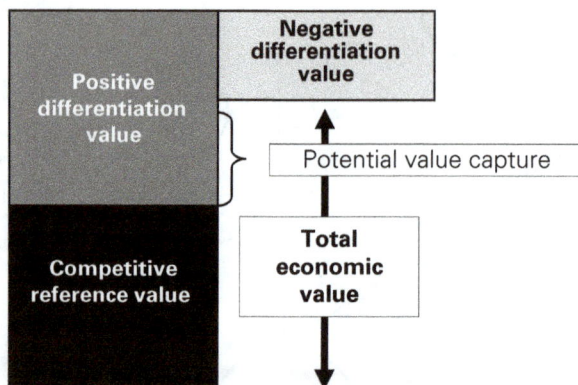

Figure 1.4. Understand the customer economic value you provide.

about replying quickly to an email or tweet. To bring your customers valuable innovations, you must also be incented (i.e., paid) to do so. Don't be afraid to state your position as clearly as that.

Case snippet. During the COVD-19 pandemic, restaurants were able to charge 5 to 30 percent more for delivery by understanding how customers began valuing safety, convenience, and availability much more than in the past and were willing to pay more.

Here are two things you should ask your sales team today to address this myth:

- How are our efforts to be "customer-centric" bringing direct value to our customers? Can we explain what we do in terms of how it generates value?
- How do we ensure that we are paid for that investment and that our customers understand that that is part of the value we provide?

Myth 3: Our business environment is changing; we cannot raise prices during this uncertainty.

Reality: Changing your business model is the *perfect* time to redesign how you charge for your value.

During times of uncertainty, whether a pandemic, a recession, or competitive threats, the tendency of most organizations is to "batten down the hatches" and ride out the storm. Unfortunately, this usually translates to a paralysis on doing anything new, and a doubling down on executing the old playbook—even though the market has fundamentally changed.

In some cases, the sense of paralysis is reinforced by external factors. During pandemics and natural disasters, governments often impose restrictions on price increases in the form of anti-gouging laws, limit customer traffic with stay-at-home orders, or slow the approval process for new business applications.

In times like these, it may seem like the worst moment to change prices. However, the idea that it's imprudent to change prices during times of uncertainty cannot be further from the truth. During times of massive change, the underlying market needs are changing more dramatically than ever before. And the businesses that serve these needs need to adjust.

Consider the example of a manufacturer of premium building materials. This company produced a premium wall covering that had many highly differentiated benefits—including water resistance and superior dimensional stability, among other attributes. It also cost 30 to 50 percent more than a more conventional version that lacked these added attributes. When the housing market tanked in 2008, demand for all building materials declined precipitously. Virtually every supplier in the industry reacted by discounting prices in a desperate effort to increase demand. The exception was this manufacturer of premium wall coverings. This company recognized that the remaining customers still building houses were generally those who had the financial wherewithal to weather the storm and, in fact, were not very price-sensitive at all. So in the face of the worst housing downturn in history, this building materials manufacturer raised prices and managed to significantly increase margins on the remaining sales they still had.

Another example comes from the grocery industry. During the recent COVID-19 pandemic, as unemployment rates surged and consumers faced significant economic uncertainty, grocery stores redirected marketing budgets from in-store promotions to profitable delivery capabilities to help address their margin pressures as the food inflation index rose by over 4 to 5 percent in the summer of 2020. How did they do it? Recognizing the value of anything frozen or shelf-stable, grocery stores eliminated many of the previously ubiquitous discounts and promotions, effecting a net increase in transaction prices, even if many regular prices remained the same. Instead, these monies were redirected to support supply chain efforts to address the increased consumer demand for homemade meals.

Finally, times of uncertainty open the opportunity to fundamentally reimagine a company's market offerings. For example, a leading car manufacturer recognized that during periods of great change, consumers are less willing to commit to 36-month (or longer) payment terms for a new car purchase—irrespective of the level of discounts offered—given that their household income may be hard to forecast over that time horizon. In response, this car manufacturer created a program whereby consumers could purchase a car using the conventional financing method of a long-term monthly repayment program—with a twist. Should the consumer lose their job and no longer be able to afford the monthly payment, they had the option to return the car to the dealership and be absolved of all remaining loan payments. This program was an instant success and allowed the car manufacturer to grow sales while the rest of the industry endured a double-digit sales decline.

Another example comes from the quick-serve restaurant space where a restaurant chain facing decreased demand due to COVID-19 reimagined itself as a grocery store. In addition to assembling sandwiches to order, the chain also sold the individual ingredients so that customers could make their own sandwiches at home and reduce their exposure to the outside world.

As illustrated by the above examples, when the sales environment changes, so do the things that matter to customers. It's essential to fundamentally rethink the core assumptions of your business during a downturn, challenge the orthodoxies that may have prevailed during better times, and ask: "What has fundamentally changed about my customer? How can I adjust my offering to better meet their new needs?"

The sellers that recognize the new reality, and respond the fastest, are usually the most successful at mitigating the headwinds brought on by a shifting business environment.

Here are two things you should do today to address this myth:

- Ask your teams "How well we are planning (and pricing) for uncertainty? What if more than 25 percent of supply or customer demand changed; how would we react?"
- Put yourself in your competitor's shoes for a day—ask "How would we disrupt ourselves, if we were trying to?" You might find the answers giving you surprising insights about uncertainty.

Myth 4: As a B2B company, pricing is negotiated by our sales team; they control what we can get with price.

Reality: The online buying process is completely changing customer's expectations for how they want to be treated, even in B2B (or B2B2C) environments.

B2B sales teams have always strived to "set" pricing as best as possible when negotiating with their customers on a deal-by-deal basis. However, the process for setting the "right" price has historically been shrouded in mystery ("What will they accept, and not be too upset about?"). This has led to a situation where the sales team becomes the gatekeepers of what you can or cannot do with pricing with your customers. How many times have you felt that you're at the mercy of your salesforce and can't direct them on what to do with pricing?

Salespeople have different styles that affect the price they offer—some sell on the basis of quality, some on price, some on value, and some on relationships—if you have that variability in your business, there are elements of what high-performing results look like on each of these dimensions that need to be shared.

Malcolm Gladwell, an author on human nature, famously theorized that to become an "expert" in your field might require 10,000 hours of practice. But can your business afford to have each member of your sales team spend that much time becoming an expert at pricing?

Even if sales will always involve a one-on-one negotiation with each customer, that doesn't mean your business can't embed strong processes and analytics to improve your likelihood of pricing success. Good salespeople embrace additional insights, processes, and structure that help them do their jobs better. There will always be an information asymmetry: your customer will always have more insight than you into what value your product provides them. So how can you provide more visibility of that value to your salespeople?

Moreover, sales as we know it is changing—B2B customers have gone from feature-focused (products) to buying solutions (products and services) to demanding value-laden end-to-end experiences. They're demanding better interactions across the discover-buy-use-and-renew life cycle, not just at the time of sale.

When it comes to sales, there is another myth to counteract: the notion that greater discipline in pricing will hinder salespeople. In fact, having structured policies and processes should help speed things up. If customers learn that salespeople will hold the line—rather than going back to check with a superior as the negotiation process stalls—they may be more likely to accept the initial price quickly, leading to a faster sale. When sellers develop clear policies around pricing and strong guidelines and support for their sales teams, those teams can be more successful at driving value in the long run (Figure 1.5).

Case snippet. A global manufacturer of industrial products was caught in an annual cycle of renegotiating customer contracts, such that over half the year was spent in drawn-out negotiations. Concerns about locking in volume often led to heavy discounting at the beginning and end of each contracting negotiation cycle. When the company decided to set new guidelines for their key customer segments and held the line on negotiations, they retained their customers to make value-based trade-offs—resulting in shorter negotiations and increased margins.

Here are two things you should ask yourself today to address this myth:

- Can you test and measure which sales reps are successful at managing pricing and value discussions with B2B customers over the long run?

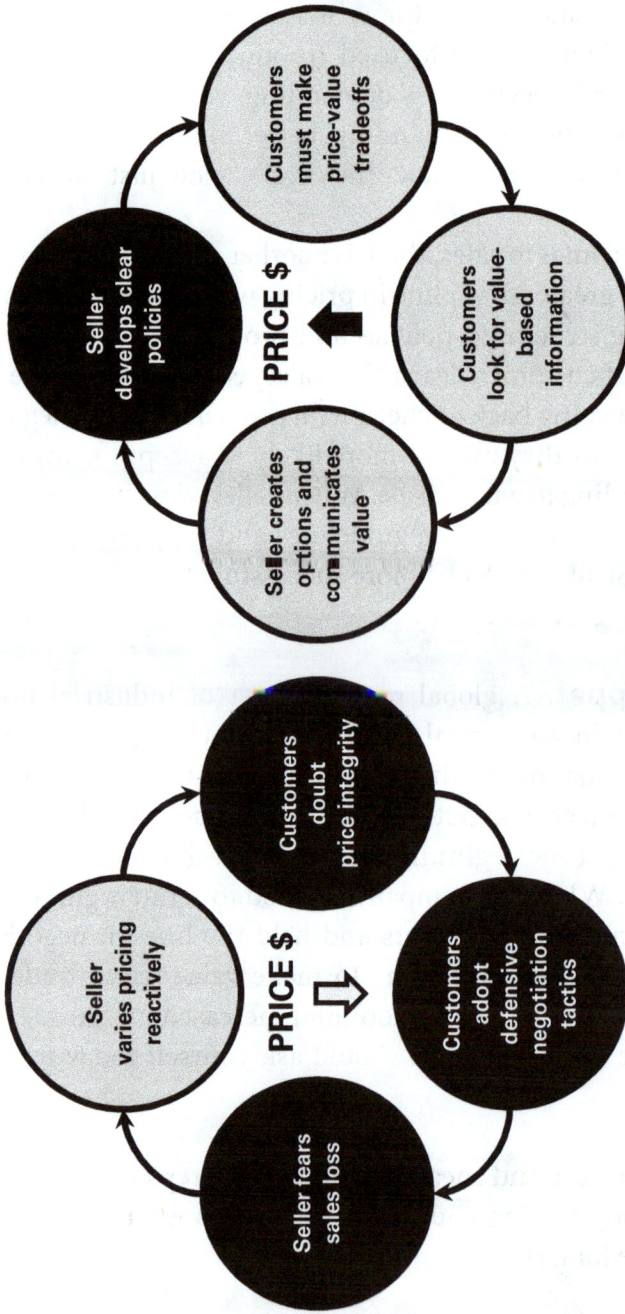

Figure 1.5. The vicious cycle of price negotiations—the good and the bad.

- What tools and information (and incentives) are you giving your sales teams to help them make more informed and value-driven pricing discussions with your customers?

Myth 5: Our customers are extremely sensitive to price; there is no way we can raise prices without losing business.

Reality: Understanding your customer's buying psychology can help overcome any perceived price sensitivities.

Under Myth 1 we talked about how the "feeling of commoditization" is mostly a perceived notion and not necessarily an inherent characteristic of certain products or markets. For Myth 5 we elaborate the statement to say that in certain situations, commoditization is real; however, it relates to the psychological state of the customer rather than to a physical state of the product or market.

A commoditized customer is one that exhibits limited expectations of a product's features and high sensitivity to any price changes. Customers in such situations have become convinced that any price change or increase is unwarranted because there are minor differences in features that do not translate to tangible and quantum changes in the value they derive from those differentiated features.

Although this may be true for some customers, we know it's not true for all. Most customers believe pricing is the most important consideration when choosing what to buy. Our challenge as strategic marketers is to figure out who's truly price-sensitive and who isn't. And then, how to address the needs of each customer.

If your customers are truly price-sensitive above all, you can unbundle your offer and create simple, basic solutions that remove additional costs. For customers who value other factors more than price, it's about offering the right choices and trade-offs to provide more value-added services (Figures 1.6a and 1.6b).

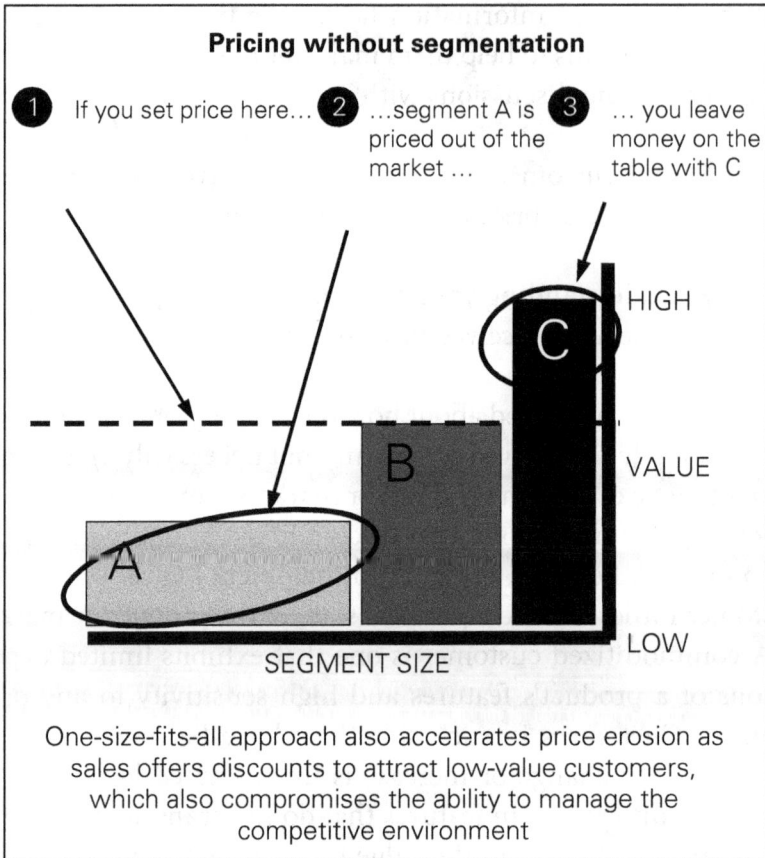

Figure 1.6a. Create tiered offers based on what customers value.

The success of any pricing effort also depends on how a business incentivizes its sales team. Focusing on volume at the expense of margin creates a salesforce that would rather sell a large deal with no profit than a smaller, more profitable deal. When strategic pricing decisions are made by the corporate pricing team, it's next to impossible to enforce them if salespeople are incented based on volume. Salespeople become customer advocates because it's easier to sell products and services at the lowest possible price.

Pricing with segmentation

Three techniques for segmented price setting: (1) Create tiered offers based on value (2) Find a price metric that aligns revenue with customer value (3) Implement policy-driven price fences to sell the same offer configuration at different price

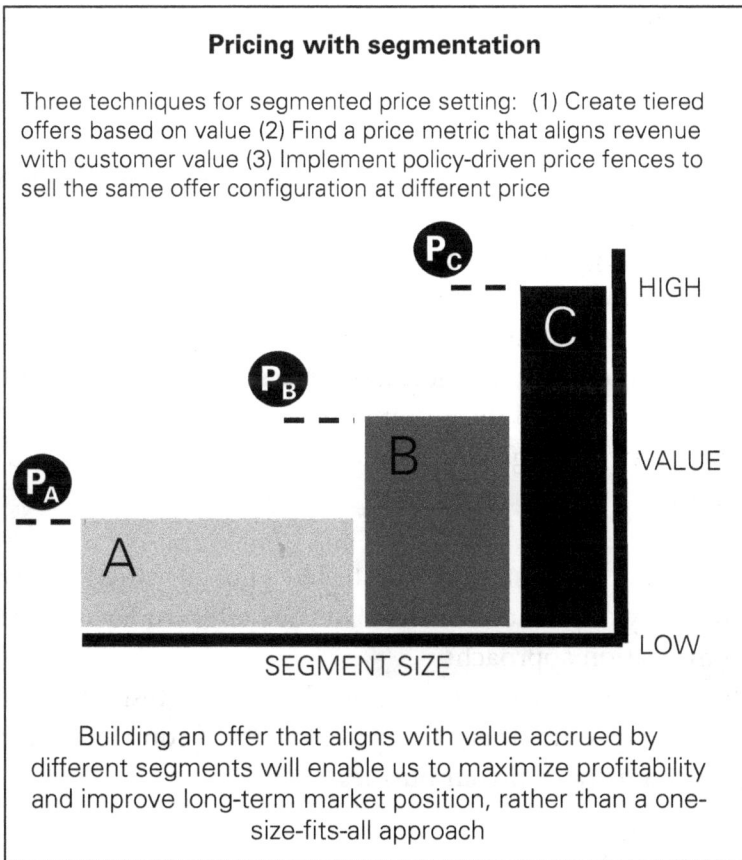

Building an offer that aligns with value accrued by different segments will enable us to maximize profitability and improve long-term market position, rather than a one-size-fits-all approach

Figure 1.6b. Create tiered offers based on what customers value.

While the most successful pricing companies have created wholesale changes to incentive structures, even companies that start small have achieved benefits. For example, some companies have introduced a "controllable" margin component in their sales incentive structures that equates to 25 percent of the overall commission. Controllable margin refers to the cost elements over which the salesperson has control, such as service, freight, expediting charges, or payment terms—in contrast to net margin, which includes elements beyond the salesperson's control, such as manufacturing cost, overhead, or labor.

Case snippet. The 900 salespeople at a $5 billion distribution company told the price management team that there was no way to raise prices because customers wouldn't accept higher prices. After realigning commissions with net margin and applying customer segmentation principles based on price sensitivity and offer design, those same salespeople delivered a 50 percent increase in net margin and achieved increased prices on 15 percent of deals, adding $45 million to the bottom line in nine months.

Here are two things you should ask yourself today to address this myth:

- When was the last time you tested and measured the price sensitivity of your customers? Do your offers today reflect that segmentation approach?
- How are your sales teams incented? Can you test a sales commission structure that includes elements of contribution margin in some part of your business?

Conclusion

Pricing is a lever that can be extremely powerful for driving sales and profitability in any organization. Unfortunately, it's also a topic that generates significant fear and loathing in most organizations. This fear often manifests itself in the five myths presented in this chapter—and builds into a set of barriers that lead to paralysis and inaction.

In our experience a few key principles are required to overcome these myths:

- Pricing needs leadership support from the very top. If the CEO isn't actively supportive of building pricing into a strategic capability, it will likely never happen.
- Getting good at pricing requires a portfolio of opportunities. Most organizations have a multitude of discrete margin management opportunities that can be addressed in a sequenced, prioritized manner. Doing this can generate a series of wins that build confidence that prices can be managed successfully.
- Pricing has to be a sustained effort. There's no "pricing season" whereby prices are set annually. Instead, getting good at pricing requires dedicated effort that is sustained throughout the year and allows an organization to respond in real time to market changes.

When an organization gets pricing right, it can be incredibly profitable. In our experience, organizations often realize gains of 2 to 3 percentage points simply from implementing better controls over discounting and enforcement of terms and conditions (Deloitte Consulting LLP, Analysis 2020). More comprehensive strategy refreshes often yield 5 to 10 percentage-point improvements in margins. Getting pricing right is one of the most powerful levers to growing sales, profits, and competitive advantage!

The authors

Bhupi Arora is a Senior Manager with Monitor Deloitte's Customer & Marketing practice and has around 12 years of consulting experience driving customer and pricing strategies, commercial excellence, and revenue management transformations across oil, gas, chemicals, consumer and industrial products, and other B2B sectors. Bhupi brings deep B2B expertise across the commercial value chain, helping clients identify and execute customer and pricing strategy programs that drive incremental revenue and profit growth. Bhupi has also authored multiple articles / white papers on the topics of dynamic pricing, CPQ / pricing technologies, B2B pricing, and profitability issues. Bhupi can reached via email at bharora@deloitte.com.

Georg Müller is a Managing Director at Deloitte, where he leads the Product, Pricing, and Commercial Spend practice and specializes in helping firms develop and implement profitable growth strategies across a variety of sectors, including direct selling organizations, consumer products, retail, distribution, apparel, and software. Georg co-authored the sixth edition of *Strategy & Tactics of Pricing*, the leading pricing book used in business schools, and conducts the executive development program for strategic pricing at the University of Chicago. Georg can be reached via email at gemuller@deloitte.com.

Ranjit (Jit) Singh is a leader in Deloitte's global Pricing & Profitability Management practice and has over 20 years of consulting experience assisting companies focused on organic growth in the industrial, automotive, consumer products, and retail sectors.

Jit has managed revenue growth and margin improvement engagements across multiple industries and has delivered engagements for global clients across the Americas, Europe, and Asia Pacific. His work includes developing disruptive pricing strategies, designing innovative value pricing, and building pricing organizations and capabilities, all to drive commercial top- and bottom-line growth. Jit can be reached via email at ransingh@deloitte.com.

2

The Six Pricing Myths That Kill Profits

Andreas Hinterhuber, Partner, Hinterhuber & Partners

PRICING IS THE MOST important driver of profits. Pricing is also, surprisingly, the area most executives overlook when implementing initiatives to increase profits. There is a reason: this research suggests that most executives implicitly retain a series of weakly held assumptions about pricing that ultimately are self-defeating. These pricing myths are that (1) costs are the basis for price-setting, (2) small price changes have little impact on profits, (3) customers are highly price-sensitive, (4) products are difficult to differentiate, (5) high market share leads to high profits, and (6) managing price means changing prices. This research shows how executives can overcome these misconceptions and implement sustainable profit improvements via pricing as a result.

Pricing: Guided by principles or driven by myths?

Pricing is, for better or worse, the most important driver of profitability (Schindler, 2011). Yet, pricing is not yet on most executives' agendas as a primary concern. Less than 5 percent of companies have a chief pricing officer (Hinterhuber & Liozu, 2014). For every company that has a chief pricing officer, such as General Electric (GE), there are dozens of Fortune 500 companies—such as BASF, Volkswagen, Nestlé, Sony, Toshiba, Bayer, British American Tobacco, and others—that do not. At the vast majority of companies, pricing falls between the cracks: everybody, from sales (in negotiating prices with customers) to marketing (in setting list prices) to finance (in defining payment terms) to controlling (in setting discount levels) to supply chain (in determining which customers are eligible for free shipping) to key-account management (in price negotiations with large accounts), is responsible for pricing. In the end, of course, nobody is.

How does this self-defeating behavior persist? The extensive research I conducted over the past five years (see "About the Research") suggests that senior and middle managers unconsciously cling to six pricing myths that kill profits. In this chapter I explore these myths in detail. And, conversely, I also show that an increasing number of highly profitable companies that incorporate well-crafted pricing strategies in their executive agendas have found ways to overcome these myths and increase profits.

So the key question is this: is pricing guided by sound principles or driven by myths? There are abundant examples of companies that fail or merely limp along because they fall victim to the pricing myths. One such dramatic case occurred at General Motors (GM).

A tale of two companies in the automotive industry

At GM, market share was the number-one goal of the company's executive suite. Legend has it that Rick Wagoner, the former CEO, wore cufflinks engraved with the number 29—the magical market-share objective. Bob Lutz, then vice chairman, justified aggressive discounting thus: "We had to keep the plant going and pump out vehicles to meet the market plan" (as quoted in Simon, 2007). Contrast this obsession with volume with the approach of another mass-market producer, Fiat. Sergio Marchionne, the CEO of Fiat Chrysler Automobiles, states, "Unprofitable volume is not volume I want. We have a very good track record for how to destroy an industry—run the [plants] just for the hell of volume, and you're finished" (as quoted in Linebaugh & Bennett, 2010, p. B1). Historically dominated by engineers and finance wizards, pricing at GM was heavily cost-based. Bribing customers to drive its vehicles off dealers' lots—in other words, discounting—became an integral part of the company's culture. In a press release following reports that some customers obtained more than US$10,000 in discounts despite company-wide attempts to cut back on the practice, a GM spokesperson comments, "It's to be competitive. You have to do something out there" (as quoted in Simon & Reed, 2008, p. 17). GM in the past simply assumed that the first purchase factor of customers was price, followed possibly again by price. Similarly, the company fatally (and fatalistically) assumed that cars were seen by customers as a commodity. As a result, GM stopped creating breakthrough customer value through innovation and made discounts from list prices the main selling point, inviting a series of profit meltdowns.

Only recently did GM finally come to grips with the importance of pricing, and executives enthusiastically started by changing list prices and discount structures.

Contrast this approach with the principle-guided approach to pricing of another company in the automotive industry, Continental AG, the second-largest automotive supplier globally, headquartered in Germany. Executives at the company understand that changing prices is the last part of any pricing initiative: Continental AG improves information systems, pricing processes and tools, incentive systems, and pricing capabilities. Most important, it invests significantly in improving the abilities of its salesforce to practice value-based selling: the salesforce, armed with relevant and resonating messages, is thus superbly able to demonstrate to customers why high prices are more than justified by higher value. The difference in profitability between these two companies is staggering. Both GM and Continental AG are in the automotive industry. The former went bankrupt, largely as a result of ineffective pricing; the latter is among the most profitable and valuable automotive suppliers globally, largely as a result of its disciplined approach to price-setting and price-getting.

The six pricing myths

I contend, as a result of this research, that a significant cause of GM's profitability problems—and, by extension, those of other companies lacking adequate pricing leadership—is a reliance on outmoded pricing myths that damage profitability; and, conversely, that an important cause of Continental AG's success is its rigorous attention to pricing: guided by principles, not driven by myths. In the next sections, I look at these myths, state the reasons for discarding each myth ("truth"), and provide insight on how to build a more viable pricing strategy after each myth is eliminated from practice ("key learning"). Figures 2.1a and 2.1b provide an overview.

The origins of these myths:
About the academic research and the managerial practices underpinning these misconceptions

Myths are widely held and unquestioned beliefs that lack scientific basis. The following, counterintuitive observation is important: the actions resulting from an erroneous reliance on myths produce desired outcomes. A scientific analysis, as opposed to a myth-driven analysis, will conclude that these outcomes are not optimal. Consider the following example (adapted from Denrell, 2008): an anthropologist visiting a remote tribe observes that, each morning, members of the tribe sacrifice a goat. This, so the tribe elders say, makes the sun rise. Because food is scarce in this poverty-stricken community, the anthropologist has a simple idea to alleviate the suffering: she proposes that the community refrain from sacrificing the goat for just one day to see if the sun will still rise. In response, tribe elders tell her, terrified, "In matters of life and death, we cannot afford to experiment."

This story illustrates the fundamental problem of misconceptions: decision-makers associate actions with a desired outcome and infer a causal relationship without attempting to understand whether alternative actions produce a superior outcome.

Similar forces are at work in pricing. Take the first myth, concerning the role of costs in pricing decisions. Before the birth of cost accounting, let alone activity-based costing, establishing accurate costs of goods was a nontrivial problem for executives. In an article in the *Harvard Business Review* published more than 75 years ago, Nickerson (1940) quotes

Before price cut

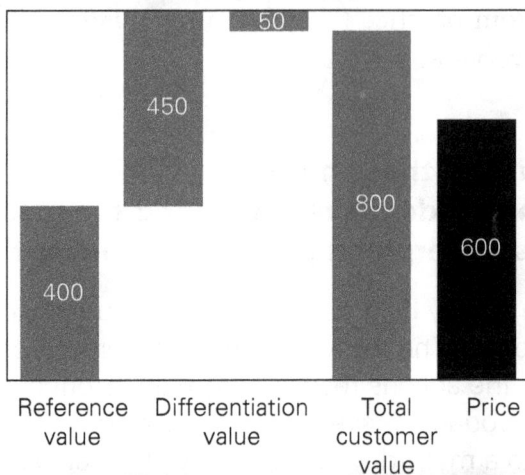

Reference value — Differentiation value — Total customer value — Price

(400, 450, 50, 800, 600)

After price cut

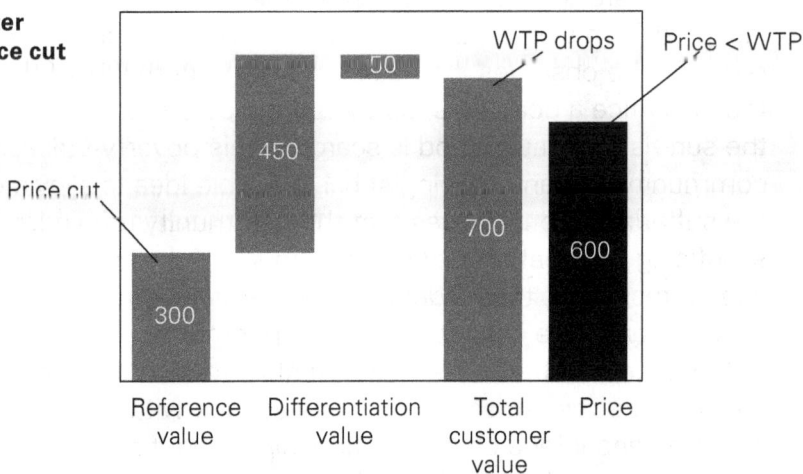

WTP drops — Price < WTP — Price cut

Reference value — Differentiation value — Total customer value — Price

(300, 450, 50, 700, 600)

The case of highly differentiated products: A price cut—€100 in the example—by the competitor representing the customer's vest available alternative reduces customer willingness to pay (WTP) for own product by the same amount: WTP after the price cut is €700; before, €800. Since the price of own product—€600—continues to be below customer WTP, there is no need to follow the price reduction. The best reaction may be doing nothing. Value communication is, of course, key.

Figure 2.1a. To follow or not to follow? The effect of a price reduction by competitors on own feasible pricing strategies.

Before price cut

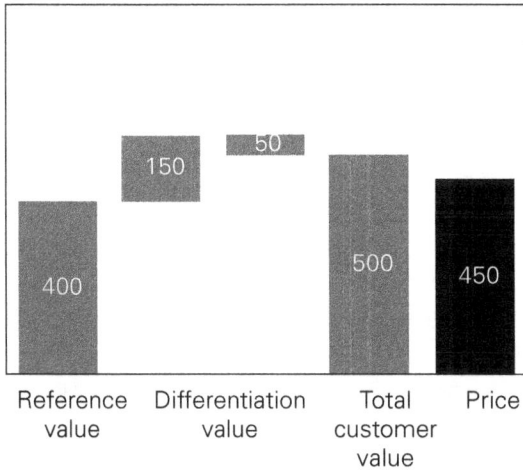

Reference value	Differentiation value	Total customer value	Price
400	150 / 50	500	450

After price cut

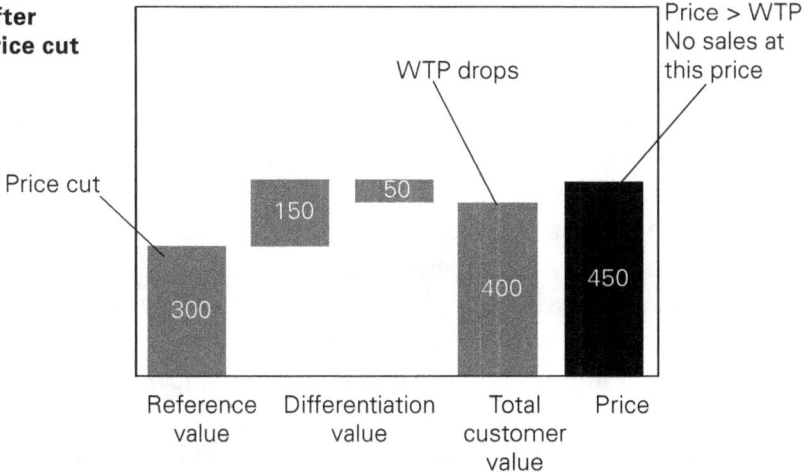

Price cut → (300) · WTP drops → 400 · Price > WTP No sales at this price

Reference value	Differentiation value	Total customer value	Price
300	150 / 50	400	450

The case of weakly differentiated products: A price cut—€100 in the example—by the competitor representing the customer's vest available alternative reduces customer willingness to pay (WTP) for own product by the same amount: WTP after the price cut is €400; before, €500. Since the price of own product—€450—is currently higher than customer WTP, the product is now overpriced. The best reaction is to reduce the price as well—from €450 to €350. Differentiation to increase WTP is, of course, a viable longer-term option.

Figure 2.1b. To follow or not to follow? The effect of a price reduction by competitors on own feasible pricing strategies.

an executive stating that "not more than 15% of shoe manufacturing companies have anything approaching an accurate
knowledge of their real costs" (p. 419). Nickerson also quotes
a management engineer—a consultant in today's terms—
suggesting that the true figure is at best 8 percent of companies. Nickerson attributes the high failure rates in the US
shoe industry at that time—more than one in six firms cease
business in the decade 1926–35—to a lack of understanding
of costs. In those early days of business, understanding costs
was an asset. Today, as this chapter illustrates, an obsession
with costs is becoming a liability. There are clear parallels
between the focus on costs and the sacrifice of the goat: in
both cases, decision-makers, unwilling to examine causali-
ties, do not even attempt to explore whether an alternative
action—setting prices based on customer willingness to pay
or doing nothing, respectively—will lead to improved outcomes. Decision-makers repeat past actions because of an
implied past virtue without attempting to understand causal
relationships and without attempting to examine whether
alternative actions produce superior outcomes.

The second myth concerns the erroneous belief that small
changes in price affect profitability only minimally. This misconception has a simple origin: ignorance. In a widely cited
article, Marn and Rosiello (1992) analyze financials of nearly
2,500 companies and report that a 1 percent change in price
increases operating profits by 11 percent on average. Subsequent studies confirm this finding: small changes in price
have a far bigger impact on operating profitability than similar
changes in other elements of the marketing mix (Hinterhuber,
2004). Nevertheless, despite robust evidence, managers
seem to ignore this fact. More precisely, managers behave
as if unaware of the impact of minute changes in price on
profits. The result? Pricing receives too little attention by top
management, salespeople are granted too much price negotiation authority, and profitability suffers.

Myth 3 concerns the allegedly high price sensitivity of customers. This myth originates from a false overgeneralization of one's own experiences. Managers are intensely involved in all stages of pricing—price-setting, price-getting—and know the prices of their own products inside out. Customers must be like themselves, or so the thinking goes. Academic research, by contrast, shows that managers as price setters tend to overestimate the price sensitivity of actual and potential customers (Hinterhuber, 2004). Contrary to managerial intuition, academic studies find that minor changes in price do not influence demand (George, Mercer, & Wilson, 1996; Han, Gupta, & Lehmann, 2001). Specifically, customers do not seem to notice price variances under 2 percent (Monroe, Rikala, & Somervuori, 2015).

Myth 4 suggests that products are difficult to differentiate. This myth stems from the microeconomic notion of perfect competition whereby buyers and sellers are numerous, entry is free, information is complete, factors are mobile, transaction costs do not exist, buyers are rational, and, finally, products are homogenous (Varian, 2014). All models are a simplification of reality. The model of perfect competition is a gross misrepresentation of reality. Managers should discard it. More specifically, studies across a number of industries showed that differentiation is possible even in highly competitive industries (Forsyth, Gupta, Haldar, & Marn, 2000).

Myth 5 is about the apparent benefits of market share. As elaborated in detail, this misconception stems from a dated research project of the 1960s advocating a causal link between market share and profitability. Subsequent academic research suggests precisely the opposite: the pursuit of market share is detrimental to profitability (Anterasian, Graham, & Money, 1996).

Myth 6 concerns the misconception that managing prices means changing them. This misconception emanates from the notion that management is fundamentally about realizing change: "Because business activity is economic it always attempts to bring about change" (Drucker, 1973, p. 66). Successfully managing pricing, by contrast, is not necessarily about changing prices. Todd Snelgrove, the chief value officer of SKF, a world market leader in industrial bearings, is adamant that the most important task in industrial selling is communicating value, not necessarily changing prices: "If you can't quantify the value of what you're offering, how do you expect a procurement person to do so? If your company creates value then you need to communicate that value, and I have found that if you can quantify it, procurement is more willing and able to pay for it."

In summary: The six misconceptions I discuss in this paper originate either from outdated academic research or from unquestioned managerial practices. These misconceptions—not unlike the myth of the goat sacrifice causing the sun to rise—produce results, but vastly inferior results than actions guided by scientific principles. This, of course, is true also for pricing: For pricing to act as a driver of superior performance, pricing has to be guided by scientific principles, as opposed to being driven by myths.

Myth 1: Costs are the basis for pricing.

Truth: Pricing has to be based on customer value.

Key Learning 1: Strive to understand and create customer value, which then serves as the main basis for pricing.

According to academic research, only about 15 to 20 percent of companies set their prices primarily based on customer value—the vast majority of companies use cost- or competition-based pricing (Nagle & Holden, 2002).

As an example, to companies aiming to grow via international expansion, the Australian Trade Commission presents cost-based pricing as the "traditional method" for calculating export prices (Austrade, 2006, p. 3). I have to be clear: the idea that only small enterprises or companies without direct contact to end users implement cost-based pricing is erroneous. Companies of all sizes and shapes make heavy use of cost-based pricing. Hugo Boss, the German luxury apparel retailer, reached global sales in excess of €1.5 billion while relying essentially on a "cost plus price formation" (Hake, 2009, p. 39). The company has since changed from cost- to value-based pricing—profits, prices, and sales have grown significantly henceforth. Nike, the largest US apparel company and among the 125 largest companies overall, had a cost-plus pricing model until about 2010: Nike "simply charged a margin over the cost to manufacture" (Barrie, 2014, p. 1). The company only recently changed its pricing model from cost- to value-based pricing. Don Blair, former chief financial officer, said, "One of the changes that we made over the last 5 years or so is really focusing on the consumer as we set price.... it's about the value equation that we're trying to create with the consumer" (as quoted in Nike, 2014, p. 11). Analysts attribute a substantial part of Nike's recent surge in profitability to this change to a customer value-based pricing strategy (Barrie, 2014).

Sixty years ago, Jules Backman (1953), a professor at Columbia Business School, observed, "The graveyard of business is filled with the skeletons of companies that attempted to base their prices solely on costs" (p. 148). This should be a wakeup call for executives.

Many companies have failed as a result of cost-based pricing, but cost-based pricing itself is not dead. Currently, few cutting-edge companies practice value-based pricing. At the same time, recent quantitative empirical research suggests that value-based pricing is the only pricing approach positively linked to profitability: cost- or competition-based pricing leads to lower profitability (Liozu & Hinterhuber, 2013b). In other words, executives are deeply in love with cost-based pricing and the accompanying sense of short-term security this approach provides—although we now well know that it kills profits.

Consider the following scenario. The amount that car companies charge for metallic paint, depending on car size, ranges from $600 to $1,500. In a recent research and consulting project with a global car manufacturer, we calculated incremental production costs for metallic paint at approximately $80 per car—a value, according to industry experts, typical of a midsized car in the global automotive industry. Cars must be painted anyway, and adding metallic pigments to an existing substrate of paints increases production costs only marginally. Then why do car companies not offer this optional feature at, for instance, $120? The reason is, of course, that savvy marketers understand that customer willingness to pay (WTP) is unrelated to production costs and depends only on customer perceptions of value. The creation of high customer value allows high prices, even if costs are literally zero.

The fundamental principle of pricing is this: there is no relationship between customer WTP and actual company costs. An understanding of WTP allows companies to charge prices that far exceed costs but that nonetheless keep customers satisfied. Instead of focusing on costs, executives should focus on understanding and increasing customer WTP. Costs are not as relevant for pricing purposes as most managers think. Costs provide the lower boundary for prices and therefore should be calculated. But only an understanding of customer WTP—that is, an understanding of the total value created for customers—can provide guidance on the upper boundary of prices.

I remind executives who cling to the apparent sense of security provided by cost-based pricing that it's better to be approximately right than to be precisely wrong. Costs are precise, but they're the wrong basis for setting prices. Value is subjective and perceived; it's less precise but is the only relevant basis for pricing.

Myth 2: Small price changes have little impact.

Truth: Small price changes have an extremely significant effect on company profitability.

Key Learning 2: Fight for pennies! Successful pricing means getting many small details on many small transactions right rather than aiming for the one big improvement in one big product or account.

Small changes in price, most executives seem to believe, do little to improve the bottom line. Nothing could be further from the truth. Current empirical research suggests that a 1 percent improvement in net selling prices increases profitability anywhere from 5 to 20 percent or more (Hinterhuber & Liozu, 2012). A simple example illustrates this point. For a company with a 10 percent operating profitability—for example, the average US industrial company today—a 1 percent improvement in prices increases operating profitability to 11 percent, a 10 percent improvement over current levels. For companies with lower levels of profitability, the effect of small changes in price on profitability is even larger: for example, for the brand Volkswagen, with an operating profit margin of 3.5 percent of sales in 2012, a 1 percent increase in price increases profitability by a staggering 35 percent. Even small improvements in pricing have a strong leverage effect.

If you're a senior executive, ask yourself how your sales managers typically react if customers suggest rounding down the price from, let's say, $10,219 to $10,000 or from €102.5 to €100. Do they give in and put the rounded price on the invoice, or do they stand firm and put the odd-numbered price on the invoice? This simple question could be the litmus test for your salesforce. If your average sales manager insists on the actual sales price, I congratulate you and the sales manager—well done! If she gives in, you need to do better. A CEO we interviewed commented, "It's interesting, but our Asian suppliers always insist that we pay our invoices down to the last digit and penny. Asian companies fight for every penny." In pricing, it pays to fight for pennies, and senior executives should teach their salesforces to do so. Todd Snelgrove (2014), the chief value officer of SKF, observes, "Give me a nickel every day. Find ways to convince the customers that we are worth a little bit more every day, and pretty soon these small sums will hit our bottom line in a big way."

Myth 3: Customers are highly price-sensitive.

Truth: Customers are frequently unaware of prices paid. In business markets, customers are more sensitive to total costs of ownership than to price.

Key Learning 3: Segment customers based on their needs, and address the price-sensitive market segment with a different value proposition than other, benefit-sensitive segments.

In consumer-good markets, customers frequently state that price is a key purchase criterion, but their behavior suggests otherwise. In a famous study, researchers examined the extent to which supermarket shoppers are aware of prices paid (Dickson

& Sawyer, 1990). They found that 50 percent of customers cannot correctly name the price of the item they've placed in their shopping cart just seconds before being interviewed, and that more than half the shoppers who purchase an item on sale are unaware that the price has been reduced. Dozens of subsequent academic studies examining actual purchase data reported substantially similar findings (for a review, see Jensen & Grunert, 2014). Even for frequently purchased products, more than 50 percent of customers have no idea whatsoever about prices paid (Gaston-Breton & Raghubir, 2013); among those customers who have at least some price knowledge, the majority tend to *overestimate* prices (Evanschitzky, Kenning, & Vogel, 2004). Finally, the category of shoppers that retailers dread most, the extreme cherry-pickers—customers shopping only on price and visiting specific retailers with the exclusive intent to purchase loss leaders—account for less than 2 percent of shoppers (Talukdar, Gauri, & Grewal, 2010). In conclusion, the behavior of most customers does not suggest that price awareness or price importance is high.

Conversely, this behavior contrasts with what customers themselves think they exhibit. When asked directly about their own decision criteria, many customers list price as a very important, if not the most important, purchase factor (Nagle & Holden, 2002). So, this is the first paradox of price sensitivity: in theory, when asked, customers are highly price-sensitive; in practice, when observed, they are not. The second paradox of price sensitivity is that managers think customer price sensitivity is high, whereas in practice customer price sensitivity is low. Numerous studies document that executives perceive customers as increasingly price-sensitive, deal-prone, and willing to switch to lower price offers as soon as the opportunity arises (Garda & Marn, 1993; Heil & Helsen, 2001; Reimann, Schilke, & Thomas, 2010). In reality, customers are habitual creatures, often exhibiting behavioral patterns with a generally much lower price sensitivity and price awareness than they themselves like to admit.

How can marketing and pricing managers deal with customers having highly malleable preferences? Rather than ascribing to customers a price awareness that even the most deal-prone do not possess, savvy marketers recognize that customers can be divided into distinct segments, each with its own needs and preferences. In the 1960s academics recognized that "the market" is an "unreality," consisting instead of highly distinct segments of customers having very different needs (Weir, 1960, p. 95). Market research is thus a necessary component of every pricing initiative: market research allows one to determine the nature, size, and composition of market segments and to estimate how many customers purchase mainly on price-based criteria.

My own studies with hundreds of companies suggest that the size of the purely price-driven market segment is unlikely to account for more than 30 percent of customers, and in many cases far less. I find that 70 percent or more of customers seek other benefits such as services, convenience, expertise, speed, quality, customization, and so forth. Once marketers determine the number of customers who want a product or service offering that goes beyond the lowest price, they can offer different product configurations at different price points. It is then a strategic choice of the company to decide to cater to purely price-driven customers, if at all. In many cases the answer, after a well-crafted marketing strategy, will be "no."

What about the differences in business markets' and consumer markets' perceptions of price? They are as distinct as night and day. In the former, executives are paid quite handsomely to be price-sensitive; in the latter, the sheer number of daily purchase decisions makes it nearly impossible to be fully informed of prices. Recent studies, however, suggest a pattern (Avila, Dodd,

Chapman, Mann, & Wahlers, 1993; Ulaga & Eggert, 2006): although price awareness is high in business markets, price is usually not the most important purchase factor. A recent study examines which factors account for industrial customers' decisions to award key-account supplier status to a given supplier over a set of alternative candidates (Ulaga & Eggert, 2006). The authors surveyed more than 300 senior purchasing managers and found that costs have the weakest potential to differentiate suppliers from one another (explained variance is 20%); conversely, the benefits created have a much larger impact on customer decisions to select a potential supplier as a key supplier (explained variance is approximately 80%). Customers in industrial markets are much more sensitive to benefits than they are to costs.

Furthermore, for many purchases in industrial markets, the initial purchase price represents just 10 percent of the expenses the customer will incur throughout the product's life cycle (Kapur & Dedonatis, 2001). Frequently, 90 percent of expenses are incurred after the initial purchase, for installation, maintenance, energy, repairs, operation, and product disposal. Rather than purchase price, industrial purchasing managers thus should be concerned about optimizing total cost of ownership (TCO). For many industrial purchasers, TCO is the most important purchase criterion, ahead of price (Plank & Ferrin, 2002).

Savvy purchasing managers clearly recognize that suboptimizing a component is necessary to optimize the whole. In other words, higher prices for component products may optimize TCO. Once B2B sales managers recognize that their customers are (and should be) interested in TCO, they have a chance to collaboratively identify opportunities for joint value creation or cost reduction to help their customers meet their own goals of a reduction in TCO. Despite its intuitive advantages, TCO is certainly not the most beneficial purchase criteria for industrial buyers. The most advanced industrial suppliers, such as SKF, quantify the total value their product offer brings to potential buyers: this value is the sum of quantitative benefits—revenue increase, cost reduction, risk reduction, capital expense savings—and qualitative benefits—brand, expertise, track record, process benefits (Hinterhuber, 2015a). SKF, for example, quantifies the total value of ownership to customers, a sum that includes the benefits of soft, qualitative advantages, in addition to those of hard, quantitative advantages (Snelgrove, 2012). The process of value quantification enables SKF to sell its products at a price premium over competitors that ranges from 5 percent to over 50 percent and still achieve high sales.

In sum, value creation and differentiation is possible and desirable in industrial markets to at least the same degree as in consumer markets. Few customers purchase on price only, both in B2B and in B2C.

Myth 4: Products are difficult to differentiate.

Truth: Even commodities can be differentiated.

Key Learning 4: Treating products as a commodity is a self-fulfilling prophecy.

Once executives assume that price is the most important purchase factor for customers, it's a very short step to treating products like commodities. Take a look at the US automotive industry. The reason both Chrysler and GM went bankrupt is simple: executives of both companies believed that the only way to persuade customers to take their cars out of dealer lots was through a bribe, that is, through cashback payments. "Cars are all alike—customers want a cheap car, and incentives will get customers to buy our cars," top managers at GM may have thought. These thought processes are clearly speculative; however, the annual polls on key purchase reasons conducted by the company itself suggest that, in the five years preceding bankruptcy, incentives were the most or second most important purchase reason for customers for three consecutive years (LaNeve, 2007). Although GM's legacy costs certainly contributed to its declining competitiveness, its main weakness was its inability to create meaningful product differentiation.

Once CEOs, marketing managers, designers, and sales executives begin treating a product like a commodity, the product quickly becomes just that—a commodity. Leading companies recognize that a commodity is, first, a state of mind; there is no product that cannot be differentiated.

Take the example of Shell. One would assume that the physical product of gasoline is a commodity. Not so Shell. In 2003 the company launched V-Power, a high-octane fuel that promised to bring Formula 1 fuel performance to ordinary drivers. In response to the advertising claim of both increased performance and reduced consumption, sales of V-Power increased rapidly. In 2010, seven years after market introduction, V-Power and other differentiated fuels accounted for 15 percent of all sales and helped Shell increase its market share over rivals. At a price premium of up to 10 percent over conventional fuel and with minimal incremental costs—as the company outlines during an investor presentation—Shell V-Power was hugely profitable (Routs, 2005). Rob Routs, Shell's head of downstream operations, said, "The important thing in retail—any kind of retailing—is that you keep on changing things; that you keep different customer value propositions, and you keep changing them all the time" (as quoted in Crooks, 2006, p. 12). Did the product indeed lead to lower fuel consumption and better performance? When a German journalist visited Mercedes, BMW, and Audi, the near-unanimous answer he received from car manufacturers was that engines are optimized for the fuel currently available on the market. A Daimler spokesman said, "The new gasoline does definitely not enhance the performance of our engines" (Beukert, 2003, p. 19).

The key insight of this case study is that even irrelevant differentiation creates customer value and increases customer WTP. All differentiation is based on perceptions. If customers perceive a product to be differentiated, it is differentiated—even though, on a technical basis, the actual differentiation may be minimal. This case also shows that differentiation is indeed possible and profitable also for products that could be perceived as commodities. But, then again, there is no such thing as a commodity, and senior executives should ban this word from their repertoire.

Myth 5: High market share equals high profits.

Truth: Market share and profitability are not correlated.

Key Learning 5: Strive for leadership in customer insight, not leadership in market share.

Jack Welch, the former CEO of GE, famously insisted that all business units be number one or number two worldwide or risk being closed or disposed of. This belief was the result of the famous PIMS (Profit Impact of Market Strategy) studies undertaken—in part at GE—in the 1970s and 1980s, which showed a positive relationship between market share and profitability (Buzzell, Gale, & Sultan, 1975). What was true then is bad practice today. Robert Buzzell (2004), the program's co-founder, declared in 2004 that PIMS was in fact "effectively out of business" (p. 478). Nevertheless, the obsession with market share is deeply ingrained in CEOs.

A cursory analysis of companies such as GM, American Airlines, and Dow compared with companies such as Porsche, Southwest, easyJet, DuPont, and others shows that there are just as many market-share leaders struggling (or approaching bankruptcy) as there are market-share laggards leading in profitability. Academic research strongly confirms that there is no relationship between market share and profitability (Anterasian et al., 1996).

Witness the airline industry: Kathryn Mikells, CFO of United Airlines, commented after the company's decision to shrink its fleet in order to focus on more profitable customer segments, "There is a willingness not to be wedded to things that have not worked well—like market share" (as quoted in Baer, 2009, p. 17). To be clear: even in industries with high fixed costs, the pursuit of market share erodes profitability. Savvy executives know that market share leadership simply does not matter: Jørgen Vig Knudstorp, CEO of Lego, said: "What matters to us is to be the best, not the biggest. We want to be the best playing experience for children, the best supplier to our retailers and the best employer" (as quoted in Milne, 2013, p. 17). Counterintuitively, even executives at Apple, a market-share leader in most of its categories, do not chase market-share leadership. Tim Cook, CEO of Apple, said: "Apple will not chase market share for its own sake, instead preferring to keep exciting its customers, and ensuring it can charge a decent profit for doing so" (as quoted in Bradshaw, 2013, p. 15).

Why is the pursuit of market share a killer of profits? An aggressive push for market share encourages discounting, which is detrimental to profitability. Market-share goals encourage CEOs to pay too much attention to competitors, thus distracting them from the only constituency that truly matters: customers. Rather than being masters of their own destinies, companies that blindly pursue market-share goals risk becoming slaves to their competitors' whims. As a result, customers are neglected and profits plunge.

Market share is frequently seen as a proxy for pricing power. This may explain why chief executives covet market-share leadership. The travails of bankrupt former number-ones such as American Airlines, Blockbuster, Suntech, and Polaroid suggest that market-share leadership, by itself, is not worth a cent. Pricing power stems from the ability to create products or services that address customers' latent needs, from understanding customer needs better than customers themselves understand their own fleeting desires. Superior abilities to create customer value sometimes translate into superior market share (see Apple, 2014, for example), but not the other way around (Hinterhuber, 2013b). Profits follow leadership in customer insight, not leadership in market share. Leadership in customer insight enables innovation, which in turn leads to pricing power.

How can companies achieve leadership in customer insight? Current academic research suggests two main approaches: ethnographic research and outcome-driven innovation. Ethnographic research is a method borrowed from cultural anthropology that relies on the systematic recording of human action in natural settings (Arnould & Wallendorf, 1994). Participant observation occurs via long-term immersion producing "thick" descriptions (Arnould & Wallendorf, 1994, p. 499). The objective is a credible, not necessarily an exhaustive, interpretation of activities aimed at explaining cultural variation. Main data sources are observations in context and verbal reports by participants that frequently and purposefully contain overgeneralizations and idiosyncratic accounts. This research method enables researchers to experience the specific, naturally occurring behaviors and conversations of customers in their natural environments. As a result, insight into unsatisfied needs may emerge. This insight can then lead to meaningful innovation.

Outcome-driven innovation relies on a combination of qualitative and quantitative research to uncover existing but unsatisfied customer needs (Hinterhuber, 2013a): researchers first interview customers in order to discover the tasks that customers wish to accomplish; each task is then broken down into a series of desired outcomes, that is, criteria that customers use to evaluate different solutions (Ulwick, 2002). Subsequently, researchers use quantitative research with much larger samples to prioritize these outcomes along the two dimensions of satisfaction and importance. Those outcomes that a large percentage of customers rate as both high in importance and low in satisfaction are defined as unmet needs. These outcomes can suggest ideas for breakthrough innovation (Hinterhuber, 2013a).

Myth 6: Managing price means changing prices.

Truth: Managing price includes improving systems, processes, skills, and the ability of the salesforce to communicate customer value. In many cases, this can be done without changing prices.

Key Learning 6: Managing price is far more complex, and at the same time also simpler, than changing prices and requires a true organizational transformation.

Managing prices, for most of the executives we polled, implies changing prices. Since changing anything—personal habits or business practices—is difficult, the prospect of changing prices, including explaining price changes to sales representatives and customers, is daunting for even the most battle-tested executive. A CEO of a multibillion-dollar B2B company asked, "We cannot change prices short-term; are you still suggesting we need to manage pricing?" Managing pricing is indeed what a CEO worth their salt should do.

Managing price is indeed possible without changing prices. In a consulting project with one of the largest global paper companies, sales representatives faced increasingly aggressive purchasing managers who had been instructed to treat the company's products as a commodity. These purchasing managers negotiated aggressively and threatened to switch to lower-priced suppliers unless sales representatives substantially increased discounts. The company faced a dilemma familiar to thousands of executives around the world: should the company reduce prices and forgo profits in the uncertain hope of maintaining volume, or should it maintain prices and risk losing volume and profits altogether? "Which option do you pick if both options stink?" the company's CEO asked.

My research and current best practices show that there is a further option, one too often overlooked. That is, a company should quantify the customer benefits of its own products and document that the quantified incremental value provided is greater than the price premium. In the consultancy project with the paper company, we equipped the entire salesforce with argumentation cards and value quantification tools, highlighting the unique customer benefits of the company's products and quantifying the incremental business impact of the company's products on the profitability of customers. What we found was that attributes that the salesforce generally takes for granted have dramatic customer benefits. For example, an improved paper consistency eliminates the need for inbound quality control and thus improves customer productivity; an apparently trivial feature such as exact sheet count reduces the amount of stock customers need to keep on hand and improves service levels to their own customers. Even for an apparent commodity such as paper, the analysis showed, value quantification is possible. As a result of using these argumentation cards, sales representatives now say to purchasing managers, "Yes, our paper has a price difference of around $100 per ton over our leading competitor. But this is not why we are here today. We can prove to you that if you invest $100 to do business with us, we will deliver to you quantified benefits of $450 per ton." The implied message to aggressive purchasing managers is this: "It would be an error *not* to purchase the premium-priced product: our product delivers an incremental ROI of over 300 percent [implying that the price premium of $100 delivers $450 in incremental cost savings]." As a result of this process, unwarranted discounts disappear almost completely, and the focus of the discussion with customers shifts away from price to the realization of quantified customer benefits. The company's profitability and customer satisfaction levels have soared since then.

Managing price is possible without changing prices. This is what SKF does superbly. Quantifying value to customers and communicating value to customers both increase customer WTP and reduce the need to discount, thus improving profitability. Of course, an analysis of customer perceived value will, in many cases, reveal instances where prices are misaligned with customer value. If the perceived customer value is substantially greater than current prices, there is indeed an opportunity to increase price without losing customers.

Why executives cling to destructive myths

Underlying these myths is the assumption that any longstanding practice must have value, otherwise it would disappear. In the words of George Stigler (1992), winner of the 1982 Nobel Prize for Economic Science, "Every durable social institution or practice is efficient, or it would not persist over time" (p. 459). This is not true. Bad practices persist for centuries. Slavery, for example, was legal until the late 20th century in the United Arab Emirates. Human sacrifice to end periods of drought is still common practice in India today (Kulkarni, 2013). I use these emotionally distressing examples to make one point: that certain practices have been repeated, even for centuries, does not legitimize them. Only the use of moral, rational, scientific thought can answer the question of whether an activity is worth pursuing or not. Executives have clung to these pricing myths simply because they have persisted over time. Rational, empirical analysis today suggests that the six practices described—implementing cost-based pricing, ignoring small variations in selling prices, deeming all customers price-sensitive, treating products like commodities, pursuing market-share leadership, and equating price management with changing prices—are a recipe for low profitability.

Exploring guiding principles of pricing excellence

Pricing is problematic for most executives because it is often left in the hands of ill-prepared junior sales managers while senior executives concentrate on what they perceive as momentarily more important drivers of success. This need not be. Senior executives can and should champion pricing in their organizations. Quantitative empirical research suggests that CEO championing of pricing improves pricing capabilities and firm performance (Liozu & Hinterhuber, 2013a).

Once executives have liberated themselves from the six myths explicated above, pricing will become a true driver of profits and customer satisfaction. Exploring guiding principles of pricing excellence requires that executives critically examine their own deeply held beliefs. This will lead executives to look at pricing in a radically different way. Michael Sandel (2011), a political philosopher, says this about the study of his field: "Philosophy estranges us from the familiar, not by supplying new information, but by inviting and provoking a new way of seeing. But, and here is the risk, once the familiar turns strange, it is never quite the same again."

This is probably valid also for the study of my own field, pricing: the risk of this exploration is that we may find further unquestioned truths in need of examination. Take, for example, the concept of WTP, which traditional marketing theory depicts as the inherent, albeit unobservable, property of goods or services and which should be measured with conjoint analysis and other approaches (Voelckner, 2006). Traditional marketing theory invites us to take an essentially passive approach—to measure what is already there and to derive profitable pricing strategies from this analysis. Not so leading companies such as Apple, which clearly view the concept of WTP as something that can be actively managed and influenced. How does Apple create WTP so that customers preferentially purchase its most expensive products and shun its entry-level products? The company uses an understanding of consumer psychology—the decoy effect. Figure 2.2 shows the prices of different iPad mini 2 WiFi-only models in 2014.

As memory size doubles, prices increase by an apparently much lower amount. Compared with the entry-level product, the most expensive product looks cheap. This is the decoy effect at work. Apple uses memory size to influence customer perceptions so that

Model	16GB	32GB	64GB	128GB
Price	$399.00	$499.00	$599.00	$699.00

Figure 2.2. Apple product-line pricing and the decoy effect. Apple, Inc., 2014, *iPad mini 2*, retrieved July 1, 2014, from www.apple.com/ipad-mini-2/specs/.

the most expensive product appears underpriced. The example suggests that an understanding of the psychological foundations of pricing allows companies to influence customer perceptions of value and price without actually lowering the price (Hinterhuber, 2015b). Put differently, the assumption that WTP is inherent in a product or service is a further misconception. WTP can be created.

A further example of a pricing misconception that savvy marketers will question is the idea that a price drop by a direct competitor requires a corresponding price reduction so that the apparently disrupted equilibrium is restored. This idea is wrong. This notion originates from the hypothesized existence of a "value equivalence line" (Leszinski & Marn, 1997, p. 100). The only scientifically correct response to a price drop by a competitor in "it depends"—whether a price cut by a competitor requires a reaction depends, first and foremost, on WTP: customer value. Demand elasticity needs to be considered only for products with a high WTP. Consider Figure 2.3.

For highly differentiated products, the best answer to a price drop by a competitor may be to do nothing. This principle is illustrated in Figure 2.1a: A price cut by the competitor reduces customer WTP for one's own product by the same amount; WTP after the price cut is €700, as opposed to €800 before. Since the price of one's own product—€600—continues to be below customer WTP, there's no immediate need to reduce the price. Given an inelastic demand, the best reaction may be to do nothing. Value communication is, of course, key. This may explain why Apple does not react to a price drop by Samsung, its closest competitor.

For weakly differentiated products, the best answer to a price drop by a direct competitor is, conversely, a corresponding price drop. Figure 2.1b illustrates this principle.

	Myth	Truth	Key learning
1	Costs are the basis for pricing	Pricing has to be based on customer value.	Strive to understand and create customer value as basis for pricing.
2	Small price changes have little impact	Small price changes have an extremely significant effect on company profitability.	Fight for pennies! Successful pricing means gettng many small details on many small transactions right.
3	Customers are highly price sensitive	Customers are frequently unaware of prices paid. In business markets, customers are more sensitive to total cost of ownership than to price.	Segment customers based on their needs.
4	Products are difficult to differentiate	Even commodities can be differentiated.	Treating products as a commodity is a self-fulfilling prophecy.
5	High market share = high profits	Market share and profitability are not correlated.	Strive for leadership in customer insight, not leadership in market share.
6	Managing price means changing prices	Managing price includes improving systems, processes, and skills and communicating customer value. This can be done without changing prices.	Managing prices is far more complex, and at the same time simpler, than changing prices; it requires a true organizational transformation.

Figure 2.3. A decision aid for responding to price reductions by competitors.

A price cut by the competitor representing the customer's best available alternative reduces customer WTP for one's own product: WTP after the price cut is €400, as opposed to €500 before. Since the price of the own product—€450—is higher in this example than customer WTP, the product is now overpriced. The best reaction is to reduce the price as well—from €450 to €350, for example. This may explain why Samsung reacts to a price drop by HTC or LG, two competitors from which Samsung is perceived as being only weakly differentiated. Differentiation to increase WTP is, of course, a viable longer-term option.

Defining the guiding principles of pricing excellence is a journey. In this sense, this exploration of pricing myths should be considered a first puck on the ice at the beginning of a very long game.

About the research

This research is based on a poll of over 450 executives attending open-enrollment and in-house workshops that I and my colleagues at Hinterhuber & Partners conducted over the past five years. As part of the workshop pre-assignment, executives answered a questionnaire consisting of open-ended questions on current pricing practices and strategies, on factors leading to current pricing practices and strategies, on strengths and weaknesses of current practices, and on other elements related to pricing strategy. In some instances we polled participants orally on these questions during the workshops and transcribed answers concurrently. Respondents in our sample are mostly from companies headquartered in Europe and the US, and are mostly from B2B companies; respondents work in marketing including pricing, followed by sales, finance/controlling, and general management. In terms of size, participants from small (<500 employees), medium-sized, and large companies (>10,000 employees) are distributed nearly equally. Respondents are from a very broad range of different industries with representatives from nearly all industries as defined, for example, by current Fortune Global 500 lists. We complemented this analysis with a rigorous literature review of cutting-edge academic research on pricing and marketing that included an analysis of pricing strategies at over 100 Fortune 500 companies from publicly available sources (e.g., conference presentations, analyst reports, investor presentations, consultation of specialized databases).

Acknowledgments

I wish to thank the Editor, Prof. Dollinger, and the anonymous reviewers for their constructive comments on earlier versions of this paper. Reprinted with permission from Andreas Hinterhuber, 2016, "The Six Pricing Myths That Kill Profits," *Business Horizons, 59*(1), 71–83. All rights reserved: Copyright Elsevier, 2016.

References

Anterasian, C., Graham, J. L., & Money, B. (1996). Are U.S. managers superstitious about market share? *MIT Sloan Management Review, 37*(4), 66–77.

Apple, Inc. (2014). *iPad mini 2*. Retrieved July 1, 2014, from www.apple.com/ipad-mini-2/specs/

Arnould, E. J., & Wallendorf, M. (1994). Market-oriented ethnography: Interpretation building and marketing strategy formulation. *Journal of Marketing Research, 31*(4), 484–504.

Austrade. (2006, October). *Guide to pricing for export* (Australian government white paper). Canberra, Australia.

Avila, R., Dodd, W., Chapman, J., Mann, K., & Wahlers, R. (1993). Importance of price in industrial buying. *Review of Business, 15*(2), 34–48.

Backman, J. (1953). *Price practices and policies*. New York, NY: Ronald.

Baer, J. (2009). United Airlines scales back its ambitions. *Financial Times*, April 15, p. 17.

Barrie, L. (2014). New pricing strategy pays off for Nike. *Just-Style,* July 24. Retrieved March 15, 2015, from www.just-style.com/analysis/new-pricing-strategy -pays-off-for-nike_id122400.aspx

Beukert, L. (2003). Edelsprit lockt Raser an die Zapfsäule. *Handelsblatt,* Düsseldorf, June 5, p. 19.

Bradshaw, T. (2013). Cheaper iPhone seeks to retain core values. *Financial Times,* August 27, p. 15.

Buzzell, R. (2004). The PIMS program of strategy research: A retrospective appraisal. *Journal of Business Research, 57*(5), 478–483.

Buzzell, R. D., Gale, B. T., & Sultan, R. G. (1975). Market share: A key to profitability. *Harvard Business Review, 53*(1), 97–106.

Crooks, E. (2006). Interview with Rob Routs: "You have to keep changing." *Financial Times,* October 23, p. 12.

Denrell, J. (2008). Superstitious behavior as a byproduct of intelligent adaptation. In G. Hodgkinson & W. Starbuck (Eds.), *The Oxford handbook of organizational decision making* (pp. 271–286). Oxford, UK: Oxford University Press.

Dickson, P., & Sawyer, A. (1990). The price knowledge and search of supermarket shoppers. *Journal of Marketing, 54*(3), 42–53.

Drucker, P. (1973). *Management: Tasks, responsibilities, practices.* New York, NY: Harper & Row.

Evanschitzky, H., Kenning, P., & Vogel, V. (2004). Consumer price knowledge in the German retail market. *Journal of Product & Brand Management, 13*(6), 390–405.

Forsyth, J., Gupta, A., Haldar, S., & Marn, M. (2000). Shedding the commodity mind-set. *McKinsey Quarterly, 37*(4), 78–86.

Garda, R., & Marn, M. (1993). Price wars. *McKinsey Quarterly, 30*(3), 87–100.

Gaston-Breton, C., & Raghubir, P. (2013). Opposing effects of sociodemographic variables on price knowledge. *Marketing Letters, 24*(1), 29–42.

George, J., Mercer, A., & Wilson, H. (1996). Variations in price elasticities. *European Journal of Operational Research, 88*(1), 13–22.

Hake, B. (2009). *Hugo Boss: The use of analytical tools to supplement pricing decisions.* Presentation at the 8th Strategic Pricing conference, Marcus Evans, September 10–11, London, UK.

Han, S., Gupta, S., & Lehmann, D. R. (2001). Consumer price sensitivity and price thresholds. *Journal of Retailing, 77*(4), 435–456.

Heil, O. P., & Helsen, K. (2001). Toward an understanding of price wars: Their nature and how they erupt. *International Journal of Research in Marketing, 18*(1–2), 83–98.

Hinterhuber, A. (2004). Towards value-based pricing—An integrative framework for decision making. *Industrial Marketing Management, 33*(8), 765–778.

Hinterhuber, A. (2013a). Can competitive advantage be predicted? Towards a predictive definition of competitive advantage in the resource-based view of the firm. *Management Decision, 51*(4),795–812.

Hinterhuber, A. (2013b). Letters to the editor: By itself, market share leadership isn't worth a dime. *Financial Times,* July 3, p. 6.

Hinterhuber, A. (2015a). Value quantification—The next challenge for B2B selling. In A. Hinterhuber & S. Liozu (Eds.), *Pricing and the sales force* (pp. 20–32). New York, NY: Routledge.

Hinterhuber, A. (2015b). Violations of rational choice principles in pricing decisions. *Industrial Marketing Management, 47,* 600–612.

Hinterhuber, A., & Liozu, S. (2012). Is it time to rethink your pricing strategy? *MIT Sloan Management Review, 53*(4), 69–77.

Hinterhuber, A., & Liozu, S. (2014). Is innovation in pricing your next source of competitive advantage? *Business Horizons, 57*(3), 413–423.

Jensen, B., & Grunert, K. (2014). Price knowledge during grocery shopping: What we learn and what we forget. *Journal of Retailing, 90*(3), 332–346.

Kapur, S., & Dedonatis, R. (2001). *The total cost of ownership vision* (White paper). Accenture, Dublin.

Kulkarni, K. (2013). Anti-superstition activist Narendra Dabholkar shot dead. *Reuters,* August 20.

LaNeve, M. (2007). *U.S. sales and marketing media briefing.* Presentation to General Motors investors, Detroit, Michigan, June 21.

Leszinski, R., & Marn, M. V. (1997). Setting value, not price. *McKinsey Quarterly, 34*(1), 98–115.

Linebaugh, K., & Bennett, J. (2010). Marchionne upends Chrysler's ways. *Wall Street Journal,* January 12, p. B1.

Liozu, S., & Hinterhuber, A. (2013a). CEO championing of pricing, pricing capabilities and firm performance in industrial firms. *Industrial Marketing Management, 42*(4), 633–643.

Liozu, S., & Hinterhuber, A. (2013b). Pricing orientation, pricing capabilities, and firm performance. *Management Decision, 51*(33), 594–614.

Marn, M. V., & Rosiello, R. L. (1992). Managing price, gaining profit. *Harvard Business Review, 70*(5), 84–93.

Milne, R. (2013). Lego brushes off toy sector gloom. *Financial Times,* February 22, p. 14.

Monroe, K. B., Rikala, V.-M., & Somervuori, O. (2015). Examining the application of behavioral price research in business-to-business markets. *Industrial Marketing Management, 47,* 620–635.

Nagle, T. T., & Holden, R. K. (2002). *The strategy and tactics of pricing: A guide to profitable decision making* (3rd ed.). Englewood Cliffs, NJ: Prentice-Hall.

Nickerson, C. (1940). The cost element in pricing. *Harvard Business Review, 18*(4), 417–428

Nike. (2014). *Nike FY 2015 Q2 earnings release conference call transcript, December 18.* Beaverton, OR: Author.

Plank, R. E., & Ferrin, B. G. (2002). How manufacturers value purchase offerings: An exploratory study. *Industrial Marketing Management, 31*(5), 457–465.

Reimann, M., Schilke, O., & Thomas, J. S. (2010). Toward an understanding of industry commoditization: Its nature and role in evolving marketing competition. *International Journal of Research in Marketing, 27*(2), 188–197.

Routs, R. (2005). Presentation to Shell investors, May 1, The Hague, Netherlands.

Sandel, M. (2011). *Justice,* Harvard Online Course, Retrieved March 1, 2015, from www.justiceharvard.org

Schindler, R. (2011). *Pricing strategies: A marketing approach.* Thousand Oaks, CA: Sage.

Simon, B. (2007). GM launches its last-chance saloon in family car market. *Financial Times,* November 15, p. 22.

Simon, B., & Reed, J. (2008). GM makes a U-turn over sales incentives. *Financial Times,* August 20, p. 17.

Snelgrove, T. (2012). Value pricing when you understand your customers: Total cost of ownership—past, present and future. *Journal of Revenue & Pricing Management, 11*(1), 76–80.

Snelgrove, T. (2014). *Quantifying and documenting value in business markets.* Professional Pricing Society online course, presentation available at: www.pricingsociety .com/home/pricing-training/online-pricing-courses /quantifying-and-documenting-value-in-business -markets

Stigler, G. (1992). Law or economics. *Journal of Law & Economics, 35*(2), 455–468.

Talukdar, D., Gauri, D. K., & Grewal, D. (2010). An empirical analysis of the extreme cherry picking behavior of consumers in the frequently purchased goods market. *Journal of Retailing, 86*(4), 336–351.

Ulaga, W., & Eggert, A. (2006). Value-based differentiation in business markets: Gaining and sustaining key supplier status. *Journal of Marketing, 70*(1), 119–136.

Ulwick, A. W. (2002). Turn customer input into innovation. *Harvard Business Review, 80*(1), 91–97.

Varian, H. R. (2014). *Intermediate microeconomics: A modern approach* (9th ed.). New York, NY: Norton.

Voelckner, F. (2006). An empirical comparison of methods for measuring consumers' willingness to pay. *Marketing Letters, 17*(2), 137–149.

Weir, W. (1960). *On the writing of advertising.* New York, NY: McGraw-Hill.

The author

Andreas Hinterhuber is a partner of Hinterhuber & Partners (www.hinterhuber.com), a consultancy specialized in strategy, pricing, and leadership, based in Innsbruck, Austria. He can be reached via email at andreas@hinterhuber.com.

3

Why Pricing Initiatives Succeed or Fail: Lessons for the C-suite

Ron Kermisch, Partner in Bain's Boston office and leader of Bain's Global Pricing practice; Dave Burns, Partner in Bain's Chicago office and leader of Bain's B2B Pricing product; and Nate Hamilton, Practice Vice President in Los Angeles

POOR PRICING PRACTICES ARE insidious—they damage a company's economics but can go unnoticed for years. For example, a major industrial goods manufacturer struggling with low profit margins traced much of the cause to a mismatch between its sales incentives and pricing strategy. The manufacturer was compensating sales representatives based solely on how much new revenue they generated. Reps thus had little motivation to protect price levels on any given deal, and most were closing deals at the lowest permissible margin.

As with this manufacturer, many business-to-business (B2B) companies have a major opportunity to improve their pricing outcomes. Over the past five years, my colleagues and I at Bain have analyzed why some pricing initiatives succeed and others fail. The insights may surprise you.

Roughly 85 percent of companies we surveyed believe their pricing decisions could improve. While most executives *say* pricing is a high priority, companies too often treat pricing initiatives as hyperanalytical or technology-driven, while neglecting the capabilities that enable the front line—sales, merchants, and the organization more broadly—to achieve better price outcomes day in and day out. Our research shows that, on average, large capability gaps exist in price and discount structure, sales incentives, use of tools and tracking, and structuring cross-functional pricing teams and forums.

What pricing leaders do differently

To understand what drives success, we studied a subset of top-performing companies, as defined by increased market share, self-described excellent pricing decisions, and execution of regular price increases. While different pricing capabilities may be important for a particular situation, the analysis showed that top

Percentage of respondents who strongly agree or agree	The best	The rest
Our pricing strategy maximizes returns at customer and product levels	76%	41%
Our incentives encourage prudent pricing	80%	42%
Our salesforce has the right tools and data	77%	40%

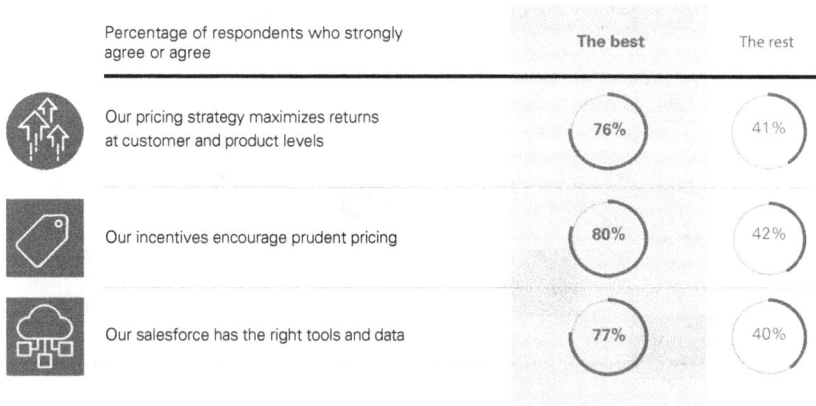

Note: Top performers defined as respondents who have strong pricing outcomes and have increased market share over the past two years. Source: Bain B2B Pricing Capability survey, 2018 (n=1,704)

Figure 3.1. Top-performing firms stand out on three pricing capabilities.

performers exceed their peers primarily in three areas (Figure 3.1). Top performers are more likely to

- employ truly tailored pricing at the individual customer and product level;
- align incentives for front-line sales staff with the pricing strategy, to encourage prudent pricing, through an appropriate balance of fixed and variable compensation; and
- invest in ongoing development of capabilities among the sales and pricing teams, through training and tools.

Our analysis also revealed just how much excelling across multiple pricing capabilities pays off. Among the companies that excel in all three areas, 78 percent are top performers (Figure 3.2). Let's explore why these three areas have such a strong effect on pricing.

Percentage of companies that are top performers, by capability

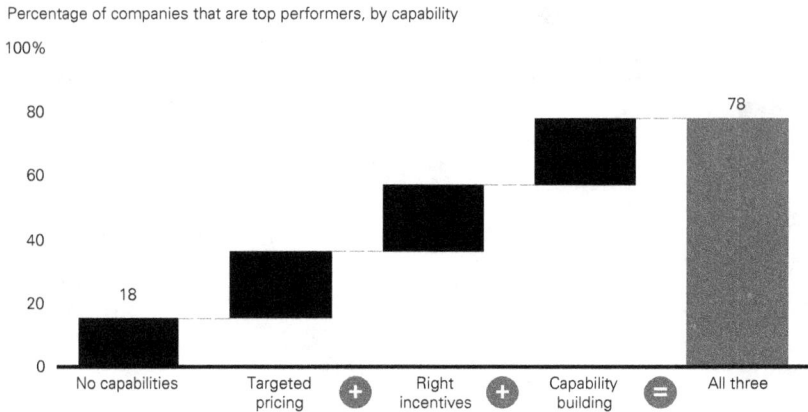

Source: Bain B2B Pricing Capability survey, 2018 (n=1,704)

Figure 3.2. Excelling in all three capabilities sharply improves pricing performance.

Pricing to the average is always wrong

One-size-fits-all pricing actually fits no one. Yet, it's not unusual for sales leaders to admit that "our ability to tailor prices at the customer and transaction levels is rudimentary at best" or that "we are not even aware of how much margin we make on deals."

B2C companies often address this need through constructs such as good-better-best, where they grossly divide their customer base into three segments. While far from comprehensive, this approach does enable companies to take more in price by charging more to customers willing to pay more and to hold on to share by preventing lower- and higher-end competitors from picking off their customers. And it does so in a way that is easily understood by customers.

The challenge for B2B sellers is the same. But B2B sellers also have a luxury that for at least a subset of their largest / most valuable customers, they can create very specific value propositions (and pricing). Advanced companies tailor their pricing carefully for each combination of customer and product, continually working to maximize total margin. They bring data and business intelligence to bear on three variables for setting target prices:

- the attributes and benefits that customers truly value, and how much value is created for them;
- the alternatives and competitive intensity in the market; and
- the true profitability of the transaction after netting out leakage in areas such as rebates, freight, terms, and inventory holding.

One North American manufacturer whose margins were highly dependent on raw-material pricing suffered from an undisciplined approach to pricing. A diagnosis allocated costs at the product and customer level to determine true profitability (Figure 3.3). That diagnosis provided the support needed to raise prices where appropriate in subsequent contract negotiations, leading to an average 4 percent increase. The company designated

Margin indexed to 100

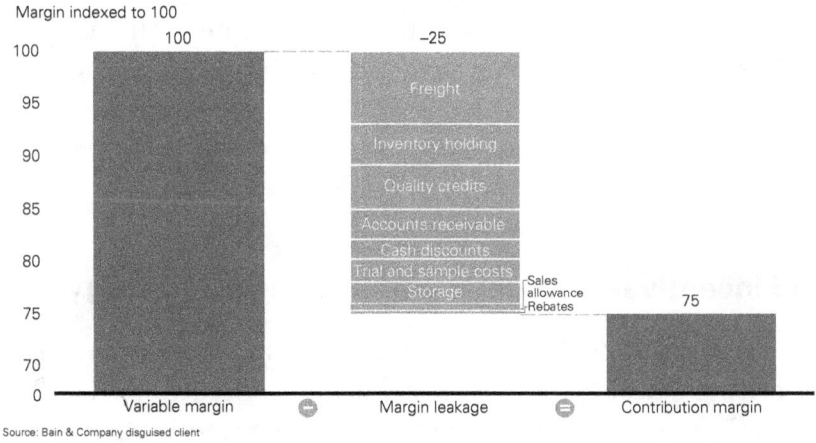

Source: Bain & Company disguised client

Figure 3.3. Identify the true cost of serving the customer at a transaction level.

an executive to own related margin opportunities and track the status and effect of each price increase. As a result, the company improved EBITDA by 7 points.

Another company—a pharmaceutical ingredients manufacturer—saw even more dramatic gains when they shifted from a "cost plus" pricing model to one that reflected their customers' needs. The manufacturer had a new product with COGS moderately higher than earlier products. The new product, however, provided a major operational efficiency benefit to many (though not all) customers—far greater than the moderate cost increase. The manufacturer was hesitant to introduce this product at a much higher price than the existing product, however, for fear that it would fall flat in the market and customers would stay with the existing product or, worse, adopt competitor solutions—and that all the money spent on product development, marketing, and so forth would have been wasted. After investing the time to understand the customer value and the competitive landscape, the manufacturer gained the confidence to price the new product more than 50 percent higher than it had originally planned. Then, to ensure successful execution of this strategy, the company developed and deployed clear value messaging and training for its salesforce. The results far exceeded expectations: in return for a slight decrease in volume purchased, the company realized much higher profits.

Bad incentives undercut the best pricing strategy

Managers often criticize sales reps for losing a deal, but rarely for pricing a deal too low, so reps learn to concede on price until the deal closes. Moreover, companies rarely reward sales reps for exceeding price targets, which means few of them take risks to push for a higher price. Misaligned incentives push deals down to the minimum allowed price (Figure 3.4).

Net price as a percentage of list price

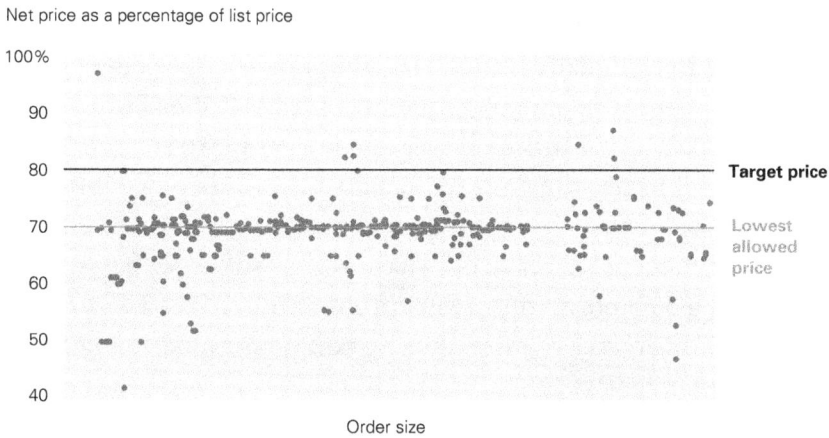

Source: Bain & Company disguised client

Figure 3.4. Sales commissions thresholds tend to depress deal prices.

The antidote is to align compensation with strategic goals and to enable field sales reps to see the effect of changing price on their own compensation. Their incentives should align with those of the company. In many cases, this requires maximizing price without sacrificing volume. Incentive plans benefit from following a few principles:

- Clarify the objectives—whether revenue growth, share gains, margin gains, or others—and the behaviors that will help meet the objectives.
- Make it foolproof. Help sales reps understand the payout calculation, simplify the quota structures and supplemental incentives, and make the upside for outperformance meaningful.
- Ensure transparency. Sales reps should easily see the effect of a deal's price on their personal compensation.
- Track the results, through regular review that flags areas where front-line staff might game the system.

Returning to the case of the industrial goods manufacturer described in the introduction, the company overhauled its incentive program to balance revenue and profit. It created a pricing tool to make the commission on each deal visible to sales reps—for instance, "if I raise the price by $2,000, I earn an extra $700." Sure enough, reps began to close higher-margin sales. These changes led to a 7 percent increase in prices, which added 95 basis points as part of a 350-point improvement in margin overall.

Not all incentives require altering compensation; *saving time* is a powerful incentive to encourage desirable sales rep behavior. For example, one software company notionally had 5 percent annual price increases on existing subscriptions, but these were usually not executed, because they required a salesperson to manually edit an annual renewal letter—many didn't bother. The company changed the process to generate the letters with the price increases already included. The salespeople could still choose to edit the letters back to the old price before they were sent—but relatively few did so. Simple process changes and "nudges" like this can have an outsized impact when they save reps time and routinize price execution.

Training, tools, and forums— often an afterthought—can have a big payoff

Top performers invest in building capabilities of the pricing team through training and forums for best-practice sharing. This runs counter to the norm at many B2B sales organizations, which give little or no formal training on price realization.

Further, most companies can raise their game by adopting foundational pricing software tools. For example, software solutions can provide front-line reps real-time pricing feedback on the characteristics of a deal underway, based on performance of historical deals. Whether in-house or from a provider such as PROS or Pricefx, pricing software still has only 26 percent penetration across surveyed companies, despite its proven value. Using dedicated pricing software is associated with 2.5 times stronger pricing outcomes (Figure 3.5).

The value of developing capabilities became evident to a specialty chemicals producer with lackluster margins. The company had hundreds of different products, each with different competitors, substitutes, and customer bases. Product and sales staff could not explain their pricing decisions and often resorted to a rule of thumb summed up by one product manager: "I estimate I can raise price by 4 cents per pound." Not surprisingly, she had raised prices by 4 cents per pound for four straight years, leaving money on the table.

By analyzing the various products and their markets, the specialty chemicals producer found pricing opportunities that enabled it to increase EBIT by 35 percent within two years. Just

Firms that use pricing software make better pricing decisions
"Our organization makes excellent pricing decisions and consistently prices at the right level."

Percentage of respondents who strongly agree

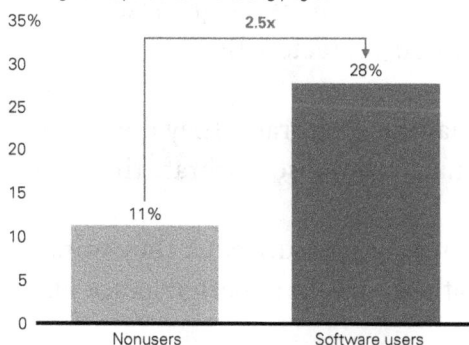

Yet only 26% of all firms use dedicated pricing software

Percentage of respondents

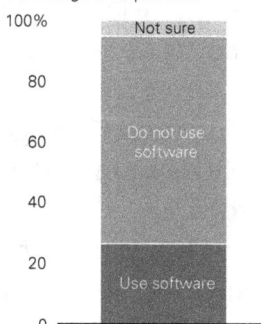

Source: Bain B2B Pricing Capability survey, 2018 (n=1,704)

Figure 3.5. Pricing software has low penetration despite its proven value.

as important, the company set out to raise its game on pricing capabilities. It created forums for best-practice sharing, trained product managers in fundamental pricing analysis, and trained salespeople to have better price discussions with their customers. New dashboards monitored progress toward pricing goals and flagged places where sales reps might be getting too aggressive. Finally, the CEO reinforced these measures by demanding that the product and sales teams report on pricing actions taken, as well as results, so that effective pricing remained a high priority. The company established itself as a pricing leader in its chemicals markets and continued to optimize margins, both by raising prices and by using price to repel lower-cost competitors without giving away too much.

How change-oriented pricing leaders can be effective champions for these capabilities within their organizations

What we discuss above—building capabilities and changing behaviors—requires true change management across the organization. And this is where senior leaders can make a real difference. When we look at companies that have the greatest success in these efforts, we see five common characteristics:

1 Senior leaders change what they celebrate. They don't just celebrate landing the "whale"; they also celebrate the pricing heroes.
2 They change their scorecards to measure what they want to change (e.g., price realization) and share performance up and down the org.
3 They create and talk about "lighthouse" success stories (individual sellers and sales leaders) to drive momentum.

4   They instill the importance of profitability management throughout the organization.

5   They embed and coach value pricing in the sales organization (training, mentoring, incentives)—more on this below.

How to engage with the salesforce to collaborate on these sorts of tools and prevent organ rejection

For many (most?) B2B businesses, pricing initiatives live or die on the front line. Engaging the front line early and often is critical to success. Leaders that do this well typically engage sellers early to understand how sellers operate today and their requirements and to identify where they are likely to object and resist change. They also complement all the pricing analytics with business knowledge informed by the sellers. This means working closely with sales leadership and sellers to create the analytics and ensure front-line business knowledge and feedback loops are designed into the recommendations. Last, they embed the "project team" with sales team members. This collaboration model enables the team to reach the right decisions and build organizational buy-in and adoption at the same time.

For example, a multinational appliance manufacturer had a major opportunity to improve its front-line discounting and rebate practices but required an overhaul of its pricing technology and processes to do so. Knowing the risks and "horror stories" of failed pricing technology implementations at other companies, the manufacturer had a change management plan from the very beginning of the program. Salespeople were deeply involved in the design and testing of the pricing functionality and user interface as part of cross-functional agile teams. Then, when it came time for launch, the company recruited a network of change sponsors in sales and other functions and invested in multiple rounds of training across the salesforce. These trainings not only covered how to use the new technology but also explained the strategy behind the new pricing guidelines and practical role-plays to practice applying the new guidelines to specific customer situations. A key component of the overall messaging to the salesforce was to emphasize the benefit they would get from the new system: an 80 percent reduction in quote approval time. The result was 98 percent front-line adoption, a significant improvement in price realization, boosted efficiency, and an under 12-month payback on the company's technology and consulting investment.

•

Regardless of a company's starting point in pricing, there's significant value in building out these capabilities. The three areas discussed here have proved to be the most important for upgrading tools, resources, and behaviors. That said, companies in almost all industries have underinvested generally across pricing. The episodic "pricing project" approach leaves companies well short of full potential. With meaningful margin upside at stake, managers cannot afford to continue pricing by guesswork or rules of thumb.

Implications for the C-suite and pricing

Our research shows that executives can dramatically improve the success of pricing initiatives in their organizations through three specific (and fundamental) actions:

- setting prices that are tailored to customer segments and products;
- making sure that the front line is incented to optimize pricing in line the pricing strategy (through an appropriate balance of fixed and variable compensation); and
- investing in ongoing development of capabilities among the sales and pricing teams, through training and tools.

In many ways these are much less complicated than more common efforts to deploy technology and pricing analytics.

The authors

Ron Kermisch (ron.kermisch@bain.com) is a Partner in Bain's Boston office and the leader of Bain's Global Pricing practice.

Dave Burns (david.burns@bain.com) is a Partner in Bain's Chicago office and leads Bain's B2B pricing product.

Nate Hamilton (nate.hamilton@bain.com) is a Practice Vice President in Los Angeles and oversees all of Bain's pricing efforts.

Bain & Company is a global consultancy that helps the world's most ambitious change-makers define the future.

Across 59 offices in 37 countries, we work alongside our clients as one team with a shared ambition to achieve extraordinary results, outperform the competition, and redefine industries. We complement our tailored, integrated expertise with a vibrant ecosystem of digital innovators to deliver better, faster, and more enduring outcomes. Since our founding in 1973, we have measured our success by the success of our clients, and we proudly maintain the highest level of client advocacy in the industry. For more pricing insights from Bain & Company, visit www.bain.com/insights.

4

Five Lessons for the C-suite on How to Make Pricing a Board-Ready Priority

Augustin Manchon, President & CEO, Manchon & Company

THIS CHAPTER DESCRIBES FIVE concrete lessons distilled from the most recent client work by Manchon & Company. Three unique principles are the key success factors behind all the projects described in this chapter. They have also been the competitive differentiators of Manchon & Company since its founding in 2009:

- Always ensure that the board, the CEO, and the sales officer are the three "equal" stakeholders from day one.
- Never settle for less than a world-class agile pricing analytical tool.
- Always leave behind self-sustaining pricing capabilities that make the client organization the number-one innovator in its industry for value creation and value capture (and ensure that the pricing director earns an ongoing seat at the top management table).

The client companies that form the case study basis of this chapter had the following characteristics:

- All pricing projects were conducted in the last four years.
- All led to the promotion of the pricing head from manager level to director level and/or to member of the executive committee within 12 months of the initial meeting (in one case there was a second promotion in the second year!).
- Pricing made it into the top two agenda items of the boards of all companies within six to eight months (and stayed a significant agenda item of their boards each of the following years).
- All delivered additional pricing-attributed EBITDA eight to 13 times the investment within nine to 16 months.
- All actually surpassed the bottom- and top-line impact that had initially been identified and committed as potential gains.
- One led to the preparation of an IPO.
- All case study companies are based in Europe: five are global multibillion-dollar corporations active in all continents; three are national champions with European operations.
- The majority are in mostly B2B industries; three are B2B2C. Two have significant B2C operations.

This chapter describes five proven ways that each, or in combination, ensured board interest, sponsorship, and funding for successful pricing quick wins and capability-building programs (Figure 4.1).

1. Start with the top board-level issues and make pricing relevant to each of them. Yes, each and every one of them.

The profession of pricing practitioners, management consultants, business book authors, *HBR* article researchers, conference speakers, and software vendors has consistently claimed for years that

Operationalizing segmentation

1 **Start with the top board-level issues and make pricing relevant to each of them.**
    Yes, each and every one of them.
2 **Use scenario planning to make pricing a source of resilience to survive the COVID-19 crisis.**
    Yes, all extreme future scenarios may require the same core set of pricing capabilities.
3 **Make the shareholder, the CEO, and the commercial officer cook together a more ambitious pricing project.**
    Yes, all three need to be in the kitchen from day one.
4 **Transform narrow pricing KPIs into a full "profitable growth" balanced scorecard.**
    Yes, it can be consistent from the sales floor to the boardroom.
5 **Make sustainability investments and corporate social responsibility affordable through creative pricing.**
    Yes, your customers will be willing to pay for most of those extra costs with the right pricing design.

Figure 4.1. Five proven ways to bring pricing into the boardroom.

pricing is the most powerful lever of profitability, collectively demonstrated that pricing projects deliver high ROIs, and made numerous business cases to C-suites to invest in pricing strategy diagnostics, pricing capability roadmaps, pricing tool implementation pilots, pricing cross-functional councils, and value-based selling training programs—and, indeed, the extended profession of practitioners, consultants, and vendors has grown by double digits annually .

However, chief value officers (to handle the number-one profit lever!) are still rare in the C-suite; most pricing managers and directors (with business cases that promise high ROIs!) are competing with a myriad of other corporate priorities also deemed strategic; defensive chief information officers push vendors into extended beauty contests between AI proofs of concept while Excel remains to this day the most used pricing "technology"; most chief sales officers continue to initially see the emergence of pricing departments or projects more as a threat to salesforce autonomy than as enabling them to meet their profitable growth targets.

Fortunately, more and more CEOs have seen the light: many are willing to explore and experiment, some realize that pricing could make or break the success of their short tenure, but few have succeeded in making pricing a core internal capability that does not depend on external PowerPoint presentations. Almost all CEOs of publicly traded companies still provide poorly prepared responses to questions asked by financial analysts and investors during their quarterly earnings call. A pre-COVID-19 Manchon & Company analysis of the minutes of 200 such earning conference calls shows that two-thirds included at least one question on prices or pricing. Even more telling, we've asked the CEOs of our prospect clients (both Fortune 500 and privately owned companies) at the start of our relationship whether they could name their head of pricing. Most had to ask around before answering! Some came to us with the response (apparently not embarrassing to them) that their "pricing department" was "the part-time responsibility" of an obscure N-4 position!

So, what's behind this paradox of poor reception to a message that should resonate immediately in the C-suite?

In our view, the problem is not the message itself but whom it's addressed to.

Most proposals and business cases are written with or by the pricing manager/director/VP, reviewed by a mix of functional heads of sales, marketing, finance, IT, and sometimes presided over by CEOs. Often, they are parties to competing investment proposals and project business cases.

A root cause of the challenge, as most members of the C-suite (and more generally of the senior management team) privately confess, is that the totality of their formal pricing education fits into a few hours of a microeconomics 101 course, back in their university years. Not their fault: pricing was (and still is) at best "taught" as a subtopic of foundational courses, as a tactical afterthought, or as one of the four P's of marketing. Sometimes a CEO will get excited after reading an article in the *HBR* or accidentally encounter one of the growing numbers of excellent pricing books. But how many pricing practitioners have managed to bring their CEO along to a Professional Pricing Society conference to invest in person one day of their life that could have been one of the best eye-openers of their careers? Pricing executive education and certification is fortunately helping progressively to fill that gap, but so far the vast majority of attendees come from below the C-suite.

So, if the C-suite isn't the right audience, who is?

We argue that pricing matters to the board directly and that it has to be made relevant and critical to the interaction between the shareholders and the CEO. When it does, pricing reaches its rightful place in the strategic priorities, fulfills the full potential of its profitable growth lever—and saves a lot of time and paper!

Too often pricing projects have been conceived in response to functional requests (product management, marketing, etc). Founding Manchon & Company was synonymous with proactively making pricing a priority for the board, not waiting for a need to be expressed.

The first lesson was to be aware of the top board-level priorities and to identify how pricing would be part of the solution. Some recent examples are shown in Figure 4.2.

As proved in those recent examples, relevance can be achieved in different ways. What's common is the high level of ambition and creativity.

One of the powerful ways that Manchon & Company managed to get pricing invited to the board has been, especially since the spring of 2020, through mastering the technique of scenario planning, first used for pricing in 2009 during the financial crisis.

2. Use scenario planning to make pricing a source of resilience to survive the COVID-19 crisis. Yes, all extreme future scenarios may require the same core set of pricing capabilities.

The recent crisis can be described as a combination of three shocks: on the demand side, on the supply side, and on the cash-flow side. The new normal forces all corporations to face many risks and uncertainties, ranging from very negative (closures) to very positive (demand surge). The temptations have been to use pricing in shortsighted ways:

- Many companies have wrongly interpreted the uncertainties on the demand side as a need for demand stimulation through aggressive prices, while the root cause was actually elsewhere.

Decentralized culture (fruit of past acquisitions) with historical reluctance to centralize decision-making →	A pricing shared-services unit was created **at the exclusive service of the decentralized geographic units, without central control but with board approval!** Quick wins and capability pilots led to full consensus for a consistent pricing governance in an organization hostile to centralization. The position of pricing director was created. Year 1: the pricing erosion was reversed (unique in the industry). Year 2: became a multiyear program to make pricing capability the leading differentiator in the industry. IPO in preparation.
Arrival of a **new CEO** without any expectation on pricing →	A pricing diagnostic (both a capability assessment and an analytical assessment) **challenged all established assumptions on growth and profit drivers** while validating each step of the way with historical management team
Need for **EBITDA turnaround** mostly based on cost reduction and growth initiatives —	We obtained directly from the board to transition the traditional price setting to **full pricing architecture overall including Terms & Conditions trade-offs and sustainability-related price communication**, systematic request of customer counterparts for each discount request, introduction of good-better-best pricing. Pricing was made by the board the biggest COVID-19 initiative. Year 1: double-digit millions of $ of EBITDA impact.
Revamp of analytics was in the works, Key Performance Indicators originally led by CFO and CIO →	Creation of a **pricing balanced score card** measuring all drivers of profit, growth, and innovation based on a single but modular visibility on performance, from board to salesforce level. The pricing scorecard became the overall company scorecard after inclusion of related KPIs, but still led by the pricing department.

Figure 4.2. Taking board-level issues and making pricing the relevant solution.

- Supply disruptions have led some to overstocking, in turn leading to untimely price promotions and price wars, accentuating
  preexisting deflationary trends.
- Absorbing supply shortages has also been exploited as
  price-gouging, with lasting consequences for customer
  perception.

The acceleration of digitalization and e-commerce has, among
other pricing-related consequences, expanded price transparency
in customer minds through easier comparisons on a larger set of
purchases.

- Unemployment increase and cash accumulation will likely
  lead to a K-shaped recovery, a combination of inflationary and
  deflationary price trends between industries but also within
  the portfolio of a single company.
- The government stimulus plans being implemented or being
  planned vary in magnitude, geography, sector, and timing.
  This is already contributing to significant international currency unbalances and foreign exchange (forex) fluctuations.
  For corporate-level pricing, this has exposed forex exposure
  unbalances between, for example, costs carried in euros and
  revenues invoiced in US dollars. Boards need to understand
  not just the future exposure but also how alternative pricing
  policies can be rolled out to customers, such as incentives for
  customers to strategically switch their invoicing from one currency to another.

Scenario planning is a discipline born in the military field and
popularized in the corporate world after the oil crisis of the seven-
ties. Manchon & Company began using this approach to address
the 2009 financial crisis and adapted it to the pricing field. Con-
ceptually, the traditional exercise has three mains steps:

- Identifying and describing several different external environments and extreme event scenarios: for example, V, W, L, or K price inflation scenarios both upstream (raw materials and suppliers) and downstream (competition and customers).
- Developing strategies and capabilities best suited for each scenario, taken independently from each other: for example, developing alternative revenue models and risk reduction price architectures, or alternative ways to pass exposure or power to customers.
- Prioritizing and bundling together core strategies and capabilities that are best suited for the widest set of scenarios or the most probable to occur, while putting in place leading indicators for the scenarios that are currently deemed unlikely.

After several pricing projects, we have extended the approach to five phases (Figure 4.3).

The following recent client stories show how adopting scenario planning was critical to inserting pricing into the board agenda:

- In one case, we were able to better distinguish between price elasticity and price cross-elasticity (involving product category cannibalization) leading to elimination of their traditional promotional strategy and to a full rethinking of their product offering. We needed the board to get it approved because of initial resistance from marketing.
- With two other companies, we made the case to the boards for radically transitioning from a traditional transactional pricing model to a subscription model or outcome-based revenue model (respectively) in order to better handle the volatility of future scenarios and develop adaptability to black swan events of the future.
- Following the revolution happening in the hierarchy of customer value and societal values, a fourth client company

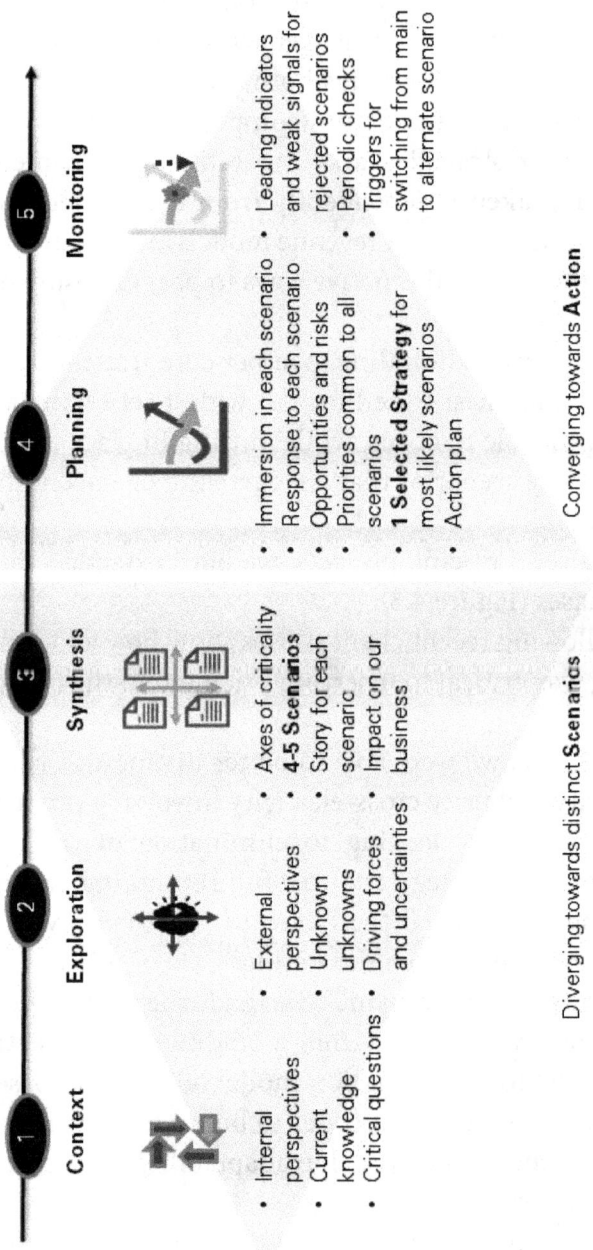

1	2	3	4	5
Context	**Exploration**	**Synthesis**	**Planning**	**Monitoring**
• Internal perspectives • Current knowledge • Critical questions	• External perspectives • Unknown unknowns • Driving forces and uncertainties	• Axes of criticality • **4-5 Scenarios** • Story for each scenario • Impact on our business	• Immersion in each scenario • Response to each scenario • Opportunities and risks • Priorities common to all scenarios • **1 Selected Strategy** for most likely scenarios • Action plan	• Leading indicators and weak signals for rejected scenarios • Periodic checks • Triggers for switching from main to alternate scenario

Diverging towards distinct **Scenarios**   Converging towards **Action**

Figure 4.3. The five phases of scenario planning.

revisited its entire crisis communication strategy through a better understanding of its value to customers and launched a vertical integration strategy, along with a financial model integrating the funding of customers' equipment. The whole scenario planning was coordinated by the pricing team, coached to be relevant to the board from the start.

More generally, instead of adapting or diversifying a revenue model, we consider disrupting the industry revenue model through pricing innovation. Yes, pricing can be the source of business model innovation instead of an output from it. For years the sources of pricing innovation have been about what unit to price (e.g., charging per hour of equipment functioning without interruption instead of charging for the sale of the same equipment). It has broadened since from product pricing to product-service bundle pricing to outcome-based pricing to usage-based pricing, giving rise to an ever-expanding subscription economy that permeates most industry sectors.

We have found that experimenting with subscription pricing, for example, often needs to be mandated by the board in order to overcome the natural resistance from existing management teams. The pricing director or the pricing coach are uniquely suited to lead the charge, in direct dialogue with a governance around the three C's.

3. Make the three C's (capital investor, CEO, and commercial officer) cook together a more ambitious pricing project. Yes, they all have a role in the kitchen.

Each corporate function naturally has a mix of reductive ideas about or even negative prejudices toward pricing: a limitation to growth (sales), a market sizing afterthought (marketing), a cost-plus-margin calculation step (product), the companion of volume and product mix in margin reports (finance), a benchmark versus competitor prices (competitive intelligence), yet another application tool to integrate into a legacy ERP or a sidekick to a CRM system (IT), a narrowly defined consulting project or proof of concept to fit a limited budget (pricing heads). Yes, sometimes even a pricing function may fail to see the big picture or may drop the ball too early.

Establishing a cross-functional pricing council goes a long way toward addressing the multiple ramifications of pricing within the whole organization and gaining approval for common-denominator opportunities. However, it does not, per se, address the dilution of power and conflict of interest that are encountered as soon as controversial trade-offs are considered. At that stage, who pricing is reporting to becomes critical but also whether the board and the CEO are engaged.

At Manchon & Company we are clear about this success factor: we only accept new work if at least two of the following three players are at the table on day one: shareholder, CEO, or sales head. We call them the three C's: capital investor, CEO, commercial officer. If only two are at the table on day one, we ask to meet the third player. Once all three are on board to address the topic of pricing (and that could take some negotiation), the next two parallel steps are the launch of a pricing governance and the access to the transactional data.

- The most effective pricing governance model requires two levels: decisional and operational. The decisional pricing committee will involve the three key players plus at least the CFO, the CIO, and marketing (when distinct from sales). The operational pricing committee involves representatives of all the functions concerned but at the most operational level, including some members that are often forgotten in traditional pricing councils: sales representatives, P&L owners, cost accounting manager, supply chain analyst, and so forth. The operational pricing committee investigates opportunities, validates insights, manages test pilots, proposes options, develops business cases, compares tools, and submits recommendations. The decisional committee meets less often, and its role is to review recommendations, compare options, assign resources and responsibilities, make final decisions, escalate to the board, rally the organization around the plan, and periodically review progress and alternative scenarios.

• The initial analytical work focuses on quantifying the range of value opportunities, measuring the spread of behaviors, assessing the gap versus best-practice pricing capabilities, developing a capability-building roadmap, creating a pricing balanced scorecard to monitor future progress, enabling future drill downs on individual transactions and value levers, building impact scenarios, and recommending a pricing tool for the salesforce.

Back to the three C's: they are the ones who will, with the help of the decisional committee, establish the right mix of quick wins and capability-building roadmap that are relevant to the board's key issues. Too often pricing diagnostics get lost too early in a huge scope of analyses and opportunities. Having the three C's at the table from day one ensures the relevance of the *what* and the *why*, the funding of the *how much*, and the feasibility of the *how, who*, and *when*. Traditional pricing projects either decelerate after the preliminary phase or have their scope of impact spread over a long period, whereas the configuration presented here has proved to ensure a mutual commitment between the shareholder, the leader, and the implementer.

Beyond the efficiency and effectiveness effects described above, we've observed that the strategic effects are over time the most notable. After hardly a few months, we've observed that the board typically begins to task the pricing governance team with the primary role in tackling more structural and strategic questions such as business model renewal, crisis management, postmerger integration, and scenario planning. In fact, the most frequent complaint by the pricing head is, after a few months, no longer "I wish I got more attention and support from top management!" but instead "I wish we are given more time in between all these frequent board meetings where pricing is on the agenda!"

4. Transform narrow pricing KPIs into a full profitability scorecard. Yes, it can be consistent from the sales floor to the boardroom.

You get what you measure. In pricing, the extra challenge is that the behaviors you want to influence and the impact you get are multiple in nature, in audiences, in timing, and in how directly pricing can take credit for an improvement (Figure 4.4).

It's therefore critical to develop a pricing scorecard that balances the direct and indirect impacts in a modular way so that both the board and all levels of management have a common view of the truth without, at first, necessarily focusing too much on what can be attributable to price management alone (Figure 4.5).

5. Make corporate social responsibility and sustainability investments affordable through creative pricing. Yes, your customers will be willing to pay for most of those extra costs.

Our fifth way to be relevant to the board is to position pricing as the solution for one of the most consequential questions of our time.

	Describe	Explain	Predict	Lead to action	Follow up
Purpose	Describe	Explain	Predict	Lead to action	Follow up
Users	Executive level	Business units & regions	Function: sales,marketing	Managerial	Individuals
Coherence	Coherent across the portfolio and intuitive visibility			Reflect different goals and KSF in **specific** segments	
Evolutive	Consistent structure over time			**Evolve** as sources get richer & updates more frequent	
De-averaging	Averages and **composite** indicators			**Variances, root causes, inflections, exceptions**	
Outcomes	Trends, gaps	Traffic lights	Alerts, triggers	Top five exceptions and focus actions	Insights for reflection & issues to investigate
Balanced elements	Financial results **vs. goals,** forecast and history	Price premium and margin **vs. sales goals** and customer risk	Internal/static view **vs. market and competitive** dynamics	Guidance / strategy **vs. sales adherence /** execution	**Efficiency** of quoting process and ease of tool

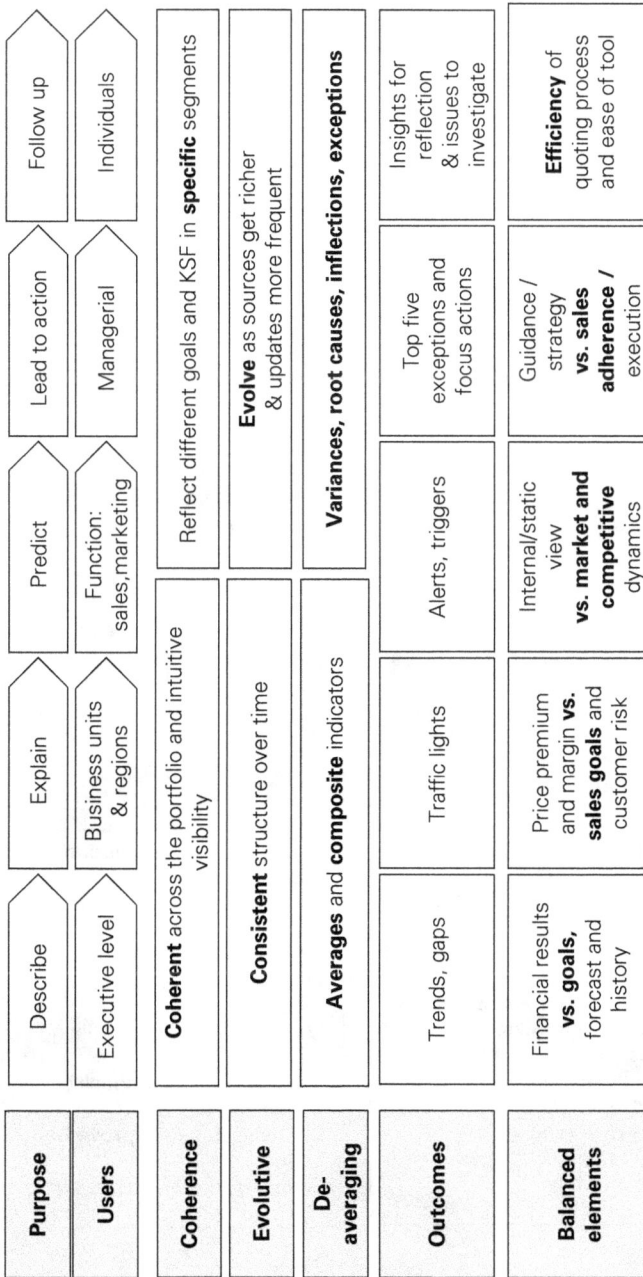

Figure 4.4. The many goals of a pricing balanced scorecard.

Price & margin *Are we achieving targeted price & financial results?*	Sales & customer *Are we preserving sales goals & limiting customer risks?*
❑ **Margin** and **pricing lever** performance ❑ **Price** x **vol.** x **mix** x **cost to serve** analysis ❑ **Price premium** performance ❑ **Price spread and margin spread** ❑ **Quality** mix and **country/region** mix	❑ **Sales vs. price** performance ❑ **Order book %** ❑ Quote **win/loss ratio** ❑ Customer **share of wallet**, average spend ❑ Customer **churn/retention** & acquisition
Adherence & execution *Are salespeople following price guidance?*	Market & competition *Are we agile enough vs. market & comp. trends?*
❑ **% quotes** vs. **floor/target/ stretch** ❑ **Weighed price** achieved vs. targeted ❑ **Lost margin** due to deltas vs. guidance ❑ Top **exceptions to the levers and targets** ❑ Top **reasons** given by sales-people ❑ (% of achievement of sales rep **bonus)**	❑ **Price index vs. market** ❑ **Foreign exchange** impact & currency mix ❑ **Elasticity** derived from quote win/loss % ❑ **Competition and end market** trends ❑ **Supply** trends
Guidance & strategy ***Senior management:*** *Do we have the right price guidance and strategy?*	Effectiveness & actions ***Project management:*** *Are we making the quoting process easier & more efficient?*
❑ Margin **simulation of floor/target/stretch** ❑ Price setting **rules**, thresholds, escalation ❑ **Composite insights & arbitrage situations** ❑ **Cost to serve** performance ❑ T&C and other charges **recovery rate**	❑ **Actions** to influence sales behavior ❑ **Efficiency** of price quoting process ❑ Salespeople **feedback** on process & tool ❑ Data sources **improvement log** ❑ Info **gathered** by sales from customers

Figure 4.5. A pricing balanced scorecard for the board and for the whole company.

Increasingly regulators, citizens, consumers, and shareholders are challenging corporations to respond to the challenges of sustainability, solidarity, and responsibility. However, most such initiatives face a difficulty: while transforming products, supply chains, and business models incurs a higher cost, most companies find that buyers and consumers do not agree to pay a high enough price premium to maintain current levels of profitability. At Manchon & Company, we have experience in breaking the trade-off between doing the right thing and doing the profitable thing. Indeed, a new approach to pricing has not only enabled pricing practitioners to get into board priorities (as an enabler of those new "expensive" policies) but also proved over time to create an entry barrier for competitors.

Which costs and investments can pricing help recover?

Let's begin by dispelling a myth: research shows that even if a typical program that leads to a more sustainable, socially conscious, and environmentally responsible future may eventually reduce the total cost of doing business, it often still increases it in the short term.

We've compiled those overcosts and investments into eight areas (Figure 4.6).

Here are some concrete examples that fall under a mix of the eight categories:

- decarbonating a production line
- promoting short or local supply chains
- relocating offshored jobs
- engaging in the circular economy
- transferring purchases from low-cost suppliers to suppliers respecting higher environmental standards
- providing special discounts in solidarity with segments of the population particularly affected by the crisis.

Environmental quality Compliance with standards throughout product or service life cycle	**Respect for human rights** At all levels and in all places of the supply chain and ecosystem
Safety of consumers and users Respect of regulations, principle of precaution	**Social impact of the economic activity** Territorial anchoring (local production), direct and indirect job creation
Social quality Hygiene & security, fair compensation for labor, protection of union rights	**Economic quality** Transparency and integrity in the distribution of income throughout the value chain
Compliance Audits, certifications, and investments to guarantee the various areas of quality mentioned above	**Governance** The requirements of corporate social responsibility governance: e.g., consistency, traceability

Figure 4.6. The eight costs of sustainability and corporate social responsibility.

What are the challenges that this poses for companies and their managers?

Beyond what governments and regulators (historically in Europe and increasingly in North America) are planning to help alleviate the pressure on corporations (e.g., grants, bonuses, loans, carbon tax reallocation, environmental tariff to import into the EU, international agreements), the companies have to mostly rely on charging a higher price to B2B buyers and B2C consumers. We call this the price premium (vs. less compliant competitor alternatives). The good news is that surveys conducted in the last two years with consumers have shown that a significant portion of them are willing to pay more. The bad news is that outside of some product categories where accepted price premiums may exceed 30 percent (e.g., organic food), companies have found that the actually achieved price premium percentages remain single-digit despite communication campaigns, often deemed (rightly or wrongly) "greenwashing."

The lockdown periods that followed the initial COVID-19 waves generated a heightened interest in public opinions about several of those issues in many countries. Unfortunately, that has failed to materialize (so far) into higher actual price premiums.

The lost corporate muscle of price increase

One explanation for that disappointing translation into price premiums is that the art of increasing prices has been lost in many world economies because the inflationary 1970s and 1980s were followed by decades of low inflation. Further, many technological innovations have been absorbed without significantly translating into corresponding price increases, effectively training customers to expect more for less and salespeople to sell more for roughly the same price.

More and more boards are realizing this strategic capability gap and are mandating the (re)creation of that capability:

- One of our clients (until recently the largest retailer in the world) went as far as to periodically mandate massive small price increases for the sole purpose of pressure-testing what they called their "price increase muscle" independently from the actual pricing strategy!
- The board of another client imposed the creation of a new surcharge against the traditional practice of the industry

("customers would never accept this," "no competitor has done it before"). Interestingly, there was no internal champion for proposing that initiative. It took our credibility with the main shareholder to launch that pilot initiative. A positive factor that the C-suite had failed to internalize was that the market leadership position the company enjoyed in its industry (wholesale business) allowed it to set the tone.

- Switching from a traditional list of product features to the articulation and quantification of their customer benefits (savings in duration, risk reduction, faster certification) needs to be followed by the ability to set up a differentiation of these benefits for each customer segment, and finally by the ability to make the intangible measurable for the customer. This value-based approach applied to sustainability becomes, for example, "what is the dollar value for you of our product's enabling you to get your own sustainability certification faster and allowing you to penetrate new customers?"
- Transparency and customer education means educating the customer about the destination of each part of the cost, and therefore of the price. In B2B, indexation on criteria mutually accepted by all (but not necessarily fully symmetrical in case costs eventually go down) is currently being implemented by one of our clients, not just applied to raw-material price increase but also planned sustainability investments.
- The current wave of accelerated digitalization of some of our clients has allowed them to revisit the price sensitivity of their customer base to environmental issues. On average, they thought lower but more granular testing allowed them to identify the more monetizable portion of their CSR value proposition.

The writing is on the wall: more and more pension funds and shareholders are integrating CSR criteria into their evaluations of the companies they review and invest in. Why wait for board pressure to mount? Why wait for customers to embrace the price consequences of greening the economy? The pricing profession is ready not just to follow but to initiate and innovate. Ultimately, profitability and responsibility are reconcilable. The pricing field has been adept for many years to break trade-offs with insightful analytics.

The author

Augustin Manchon is the founder and CEO of Manchon & Company, the premier pricing consulting firm focused on C-suites and private equity firms. He coaches CEOs in Europe and America, builds self-sustaining pricing capabilities, reinvents business models, monetizes digital platforms, leverages world-class pricing analytics tools and behavioral economics research, and delivers millions of EBITDA with ROIs of 10 times within months.

He is ranked since 2010 among the Top 20 Global Pricing Influencers (Slipstream). Prior to Manchon & Company, he was the founder of the pricing global consulting practice of Deloitte, the global leader of the Pricing & Profitability practice of Accenture and co-managing director of Simon-Kucher & Partners in the Americas. With 25 years of pricing for Microsoft, Walmart, Citibank, United Airlines, Carrefour, Schneider Electric, Renault, Orange, Bain Capital and Bpifrance, he teaches at HEC (Paris), Rotman (University of Toronto), and BPI University (Paris). He holds degrees from HEC, Stern (New York), and ESADE (Barcelona), speaks five languages fluently, and has been featured in over 50 media and conferences worldwide. He can be reached at augustin@manchon.com or www.manchon.com.

SECTION 2

PRICING IMPACT AND PRICING POWER

5

Pricing Impact: A Decade of Documented ROI

Stephan M. Liozu, PhD, Founder, Value Innoruption Advisors LLC

For most pricing professionals, the impact of pricing is real. They live and breathe pricing projects and programs and can see a direct impact on margin and sales. For top leaders, it's less clear. In 2019 I interviewed C-suite executives and CEOs of pricing services and software providers, and the feedback was consistent:

- C-suite executives do not fully understand the effort-to-benefit ratio of pricing initiatives.
- C-suite executives do not completely trust the business cases presented by their pricing leaders. They want to see more

scenario planning, risk analysis, and better integration of execution cost in the ROI calculations.

- C-suite executives complain that pricing business cases are not as comprehensive and crisp as those coming from other functions.

So, clearly, as a profession we must do a better job of justifying and making the case for pricing investments. In 2014 Andreas Hinterhuber and I co-edited the book *The ROI of Pricing* to make a first contribution to the profession. We also published several papers on the topic to help pricing leaders use some of the best techniques and methods to calculate ROI (experiments, big data, Six Sigma, ROI simulators, etc.). That was a good start, but it's not enough.

Based on the series of interviews, I heard the message loud and clear. Therefore, I added the topic to the scope of this book. It's essential that, as a profession, we establish better practices and benchmarks to send clear messages to the C-suite as they rate and prioritize investment proposals from their leadership group. These messages do exist, and each individual provider of consulting services, coaching, or software solutions promotes nuggets and anecdotes of success and impact separately. There is extraordinarily little effort to generate industry benchmarks and average predictive EBIT impact for potential pricing initiatives.

To make it easy for C-suite executives, I collected the most relevant published pricing papers and extracted the nuggets of quantified impact, ROI, and benefits of various types of pricing programs. Some of these papers report impact statistics based on research; others report anecdotes of success from case studies and pilot projects. Having these nuggets can help CFOs and CEOs evaluate and benchmark their own ROI analysis and generate more confidence in the numbers their teams present to them. So, let's get started!

McKinsey & Company—2021—"Digital Pricing Transformations: The Key to Better Margins"

Many companies launch pricing transformations as a way to create value quickly and sustainably. Indeed, pricing excellence in B2B settings—setting the right prices, and ensuring the right price is paid in each transaction—is driven by precision, attention to detail, and agility, all of which digital pricing transformations facilitate. Our experience shows that such transformations, when done well, can enhance pricing to generate **2 to 7 percentage points** of sustained margin improvement with initial benefits in as little as three to six months. (Hudelson, Magnette, Moss, & Prabhu, 2021)

Bain & Company—2020— "It's in the Contract, or Is It?"

Smart contract management thus provides significant benefits throughout the crisis. In addition, it keeps paying dividends once the economy recovers. In our experience, optimizing contracts provides **100 basis points or more of additional revenue and profit.** The benefits can start immediately, using manual efforts to improve the enforcement of contracts that already exist. (Davenport & Murphy, 2020)

Blue Ridge Partners—2020— "Pricing in Turbulent Times"

After taking the steps to deal with immediate challenges, companies need to prepare for the future. Many B2B and B2C firms still have a long way to go in establishing best practice (or good practice) pricing capabilities. In our experience, most companies can realize **EBITDA gains between 300 and 600 basis points** by focusing on improved pricing, so investments in this capability can have significant ROI over the long term. (Regen, Leijon, Bailard, & Sorrow, 2020)

Blue Ridge Partners—2020—"Feeling the Cash Burn? Why Fixing Bad Prices May Help"

The number of bad prices and the margin opportunity from correcting them can be surprisingly high. It's common to uncover instances where customer prices are near or even below cost. We often find companies can generate a **1–2% increase in revenue**—going straight to the bottom line—within one quarter simply by fixing them. (Sorrow & Konkoly, 2020)

KPMG—2020—"How to Maintain Sales and Pricing Discipline in a Downturn"

In a 2019 KPMG survey of 425 companies across six major industries, we found that companies that rank high on pricing maturity have **EBITDA margins of 3 to 8 percentage points** higher than peers. The same survey shows that it takes a dedicated pricing team to reach a high level of pricing maturity. (Crivellaro, 2020)

Oliver Wyman—2020— "Surprising Opportunities in B2B Pricing"

A tremendous gap separates best-in-class and average players in pricing and commercial effectiveness, which means there is ample room for manufacturers to improve margins. While companies in theory know how to set correct prices, most struggle to implement the right governance systems and decision-support tools. The task is all the more difficult as the pace of decision making is likely to increase going forward. Introducing advanced analytics and other tools to support real-time decision making can lead **to margin increases of between 5 and 10 percent**. (Wyman, 2020)

BCG—2020—"Debunking the Myths of B2B Dynamic Pricing"

The transformation at one major automotive manufacturer shows how a company can move from static pricing to a more profitable dynamic pricing approach. The company improved the **cost-efficiency of its incentive program 10%** by shifting it from one based simply on country and vehicle to a more sophisticated program based on criteria such as region, vehicle trim, and the type of incentive.

A petrochemical products wholesaler demonstrated that dynamic pricing can generate significant bottom-line impact in industries that are not generally perceived as rapidly changing. It improved **margins by between 100 and 250 basis points** by shifting from a mostly manual, less disciplined pricing approach to an automated pricing solution based on machine learning.

A B2B distributor in the building material sector increased its **EBIT margin 100 basis points** by using this combined human-machine approach to implement its dynamic pricing program.

A large industrial distributor of maintenance, repair, and operations supplies needed only 12 months to shift its list-price setting to a dynamic pricing engine, augmented by competitive price scraping. The move generated **$40 million in near-term profit improvement** and drove significant volume growth: an increase in the first year of 10% for the entire business and 20% in its most profitable segment. (Brégé et al., 2020)

Bain & Company—2020—
Global Private Equity Report 2020

According to a Bain global survey of more than 1,700 B2B business leaders, 85% of management teams believe their pricing decisions need improvement, and only 15% have effective tools and dashboards to set and monitor prices. When it comes to encouraging pricing integrity, only 13% of companies said they have effective incentives at the front line. The upside from turning these percentages around is significant. Our experience shows that building new pricing capabilities and improving leadership around pricing can add **200 to 600 basis points to a company's bottom line**. (Bain & Company, 2020)

McKinsey & Company—2019—"Pricing:
The Next Frontier of Value Creation in Private Equity"

In our experience, commercial improvements—such as those in a company's pricing, customer and product mix, or sales volume growth—can create tremendous value for both the portfolio company and the PE owner. Specifically, when PE firms tackle pricing in their portfolio companies, we typically see **margin expansion of between 3 and 7 percent within one year.** Factoring in potential pricing improvements can allow PE firms to be more confident in potential upside and differentiate themselves in competitive deals. The direct and rapid margin expansion from pricing transformation creates more value for portfolio companies and investors alike during the holding period. And highlighting a track record of both successful pricing improvements and additional pricing opportunities can result in a higher exit valuation. (Baker, Chopra, Nee, & Sinha, 2019)

McKinsey & Company—2019—"Pricing: Distributors' Most Powerful Value-Creation Lever"

Distributors who embark on end-to-end pricing transformations can **expand earnings by up to 50 percent** with modest or negligible impact on volume. Looking across our database of 130 global and publicly traded distributors, we estimate that a 1 percent price increase would yield a **22 percent increase in EBITDA margins**, and a 25 percent uplift in stock price. Moreover, pricing has a disproportionate impact on a distributor's enterprise value, with an increase of 20 percent for a 1 percent increase in price. (Abdelnour & Baker, 2019)

Simon-Kucher & Partners—2019— "A Practical Guide to Pricing"

A 5% improvement in pricing without volume loss and average margins can **boost profits easily by 30 to 50 percent**. You may already have a cost-cutting strategy in place to boost profits. But no matter how heavily you invest in increasing volumes and cutting costs, this can only take you so far, and intensive efforts have often already exhausted all potential. (Meckes et al., 2019)

Bain & Company—2018—
"Is Pricing Killing Your Profits?"

Further, most companies can raise their game by adopting foundational pricing software tools. For example, based on the performance of historical deals, software solutions can provide frontline reps with real-time pricing feedback on the characteristics of a deal underway. Using dedicated pricing software, whether in-house or from a provider such as Vendavo or Pricefx, is associated with **2.5 times stronger pricing outcomes**, our analysis finds. Yet despite its proven value, pricing software still has only 26% penetration across surveyed companies. (Kermisch & Burns, 2018)

Bain & Company—2018—
"The Formula for Better Pricing in Chemicals"

In an environment like this, protecting margins is necessary, but not sufficient. Instead, companies should be reaching higher, aiming for full potential pricing capabilities that actually expand margins. That won't be easy for chemical producers. A lack of management focus on pricing, combined with misaligned incentives, have left chemical executives far behind their peers in other industries in terms of seizing opportunities to increase profitability through pricing. But the prize is worth pursuing: Our research finds that improving pricing capabilities typically **adds 200 to 400 basis points to the bottom line**—a significant impact in an industry where margins average 10 to 12 percent. (Burns & Schottland, 2018)

McKinsey & Company—2018—
"Advanced Analytics in Software Pricing:
Enabling Sales to Price with Confidence"

Sales leaders can address these challenges head on with new advanced-analytics techniques to gain quantitative deal-structure insights in a B2B setting. It changes the sales conversation fundamentally by moving the focus away from margins and discounts and instead putting it on objective deal scores. Embedding insights deep into the commercial process—including quote configuration, compensation, streamlined approval levels, and a new approach to sales performance management—can create **significant improvements in return on sales: 4 to 10 percent** and sometimes even better is typical in software, higher than in any other industry. (Baker, Kiermaier, Roche, & Vyushina, 2018)

McKinsey & Company—2018—
"Creating Value at Industrial Companies
through Advanced Pricing Techniques"

The increase in raw-material costs could be an unexpected blessing for industrial companies. Faced with lower margins, they're taking a hard look at pricing for the first time in many years and questioning whether their cost-plus approach is truly best for their business. Shifting from cost-plus pricing to value-based pricing may allow companies to **improve return on sales by an average of 5 to 10 percent**. And that means pricing could be the lever that delivers the greatest and most immediate impact in a market where companies face increased competition and soaring costs. (Khanna, Krishnamurthy, Queirolo, & Santhanam, 2018)

Bain & Company—2018—"Dynamic Pricing: Building an Advantage in B2B Sales"

An equipment manufacturer turned to an enterprise pricing software vendor, implementing a cloud-based, configurable quoting solution, accessible to nontechnical sales talent. The program helped **increase operating income by more than 2.5% within the first year**, owing to more dynamic and accurate list prices as well as improved negotiation recommendations. Nearly a thousand frontline sales reps quickly adopted the tool.

One real estate company had implemented a pricing model but failed to reassess it for several years. The pricing team recognized high volatility in the space and had implemented a dynamic model, but higher quality market and property data were changing the paradigm. When the team revisited its dynamic pricing model, it added more accurate supply and demand inputs, detailed floor plan variables and building amenities, **resulting in a 3.5% revenue increase**.

A company selling fuel found that profitability dipped whenever raw-material costs rose. Through a pricing diagnostic and prototype, the company measured potential margin uplift from addressing this issue. They found that price increases didn't reduce sales volumes much, and the difference was offset by better margins. An improved model was rolled out, contributing to a **10% profitability increase**. (Kermisch, Burns, & Davenport, 2019)

BCG—2017—"Building a Strategic Pricing Organization"

Companies can construct strategic pricing organization amid internal differences, but they must focus on four fundamental building blocks: structure, decision rights and influence, skills and capabilities, and size. Companies that create a strategic pricing organization are bound to gain an edge over rivals. In fact, our studies show that **companies' profits are 1 to 2 percent higher** when the pricing organization is regarded as a strategic partner than when it is not. (Hutchinson, Banerjee, Petzke, & Pineda, 2017)

McKinsey & Company—2015—"Understanding Your Options: Proven Pricing Strategies and How They Work"

In our experience, effective pricing strategies and tactics can deliver a **2 to 7% increase in return on sales**. (Chan, Jubas, Kordes, & Sueling, 2015)

BCG Perspectives—2015—"Four Steps to Becoming Fluent in the Language of Pricing"

Pricing fluent companies are significantly more successful than their peers when it comes to enforcing price increases, our research shows. As a result of such wins, they achieve **profits that are 3 to 8 percentage points higher** than those companies that do not speak the language of pricing fluently. (Banerjee, Petzke, Schürmann, Beckett, & Langkamp, 2015)

Concluding thoughts

To extract these pricing impact nuggets, I reviewed over 100 pricing reports published since 2015. I have more of these reports, but they are older. I attach in the appendix a list of additional impact nuggets published in the 2014 *ROI of Pricing* book, which date back to 2001. I want to make sure that the executives reading this book take these numbers seriously. These consulting companies do serious pricing work and have delivered billions of dollars in EBIT gains over thousands of pricing projects. I encourage you to contact these firms to see what the number might be for your organization. As a pricing practitioner and consultant for the past 10 years, I can also share my experience in delivering impact through value and pricing management programs. I confirm the presence of attractive short-term gains through quick wins in 90 days. I also have managed consulting projects with companies like BCG and SKP that delivered between 2 and 5 percentage points of EBIT in just 12 months. Some of these projects have payback periods of several months. This is the power of pricing. This is why most private equity firms today invest heavily in pricing capabilities and systems. Frankly, no other function in any organization can deliver that kind of impact in 12 months. I realize that, as a profession, we need to improve our skills in making stronger business cases and calculating the ROI of pricing investments. I also argue that the C-suite needs to seriously consider pricing as a true level of profit realization. The combination of both can help achieve profitable growth. Post COVID-19, the road to recovery includes robust pricing investments.

Be bold, join the pricing revolution!

References

Abdelnour, A., & Baker, W. (2019). Pricing: Distributors' most powerful value-creation lever. *McKinsey & Company,*

September 16. www.mckinsey.com/business
-functions/marketing-and-sales/our-insights/pricing
-distributors-most-powerful-value-creation-lever

Bain & Company. (2020). *Global private equity report 2020*.

Baker, W., Chopra, M., Nee, A., & Sinha, S. (2019). Pricing: The
next frontier of value creation in private equity. *McKinsey
& Company*, October 23. www.mckinsey.com
/business-functions/marketing-and-sales/our-insights
/pricing-the-next-frontier-of-value-creation-in-private
-equity

Baker, W., Kiermaier, M., Roche, P., & Vyushina, V. (2018).
Advanced analytics in software pricing: Enabling sales
to price with confidence. *McKinsey & Company*, June 14.
www.mckinsey.com/industries/technology-media
-and-telecommunications/our-insights/advanced
-analytics-in-software-pricing-enabling-sales-to-price
-with-confidence

Banerjee, S., Petzke, A., Schürmann, J., Beckett, M., & Langkamp, D. (2015). Four steps to becoming fluent in the
language of pricing. *BCG*, October 30. www.bcg.com
/en-us/publications/2015/pricing-marketing-four-steps
-becoming-fluent-language-pricing

Brégé, C., Bourgouin, L., Langkamp, D., Chu, M., Beckett, M.,
Poirmeur, P., & Niepmann, J. (2020). Debunking the
myths of B2B dynamic pricing. *BCG*, November 20.
www.bcg.com/publications/2020/dynamic-pricing
-b2b-myths

Burns, D., & Schottland, D. (2018). The formula for better pricing
in chemicals. *Bain & Company*, July 25. www.bain.com
/insights/the-formula-for-better-pricing-in-chemicals/

Chan, K., Jubas, J., Kordes, B., & Sueling, M. (2015). Understanding your options: Proven pricing strategies and how they
work. *McKinsey & Company*, March 1. www.mckinsey

.com/business-functions/marketing-and-sales/our
-insights/understanding-your-options-proven-pricing
-strategies-and-how-they-work

Crivellaro, S. (2020). How to maintain sales and pricing discipline in a downturn. *KPMG.* advisory.kpmg.us
/articles/2020/maintain-sales-pricing-discipline.html

Davenport, C., & Murphy, J. (2020). It's in the contract, or is it? *Bain & Company,* May 21. www.bain.com/insights
/its-in-the-contract-or-is-it/

Hudelson, P., Magnette, N., Moss, S., & Prabhu, M. (2021). Digital pricing transformations: The key to better margins. *McKinsey & Company,* January 15. www.mckinsey.com
/business-functions/marketing-and-sales/our-insights
/digital-pricing-transformations-the-key-to-better
-margins

Hutchinson, R., Banerjee, S., Petzke, A., & Pineda, J. (2017). Building a strategic pricing organization. *BCG,* July 31. www.bcg.com/publications/2017/digital-go-to-market
-transformation-building-strategic-pricing-organization

Kermisch, R., & Burns, D. (2018). Is pricing killing your profits? *Bain & Company,* June 13. www.bain.com/insights
/is-pricing-killing-your-profits/

Kermisch, R., Burns, D., & Davenport, C. (2019). Dynamic pricing: Building an advantage in B2B sales. *McKinsey & Company,* February 5. www.bain.com/insights
/dynamic-pricing-building-an-advantage-in-b2b-sales/

Khanna, R., Krishnamurthy, H., Queirolo, A., & Santhanam, N. (2018). Creating value at industrial companies through advanced pricing techniques. *McKinsey & Company,* August 24. www.mckinsey.com/industries
/advanced-electronics/our-insights/creating-value-at
-industrial-companies-through-advanced-pricing
-techniques

Meckes, R., Maessen, A., Bauer, C., Brault, F., Jaeger, L., Schar-wenka, N., Zwirglmaier, K., & Haemer, J. (2019). A prac-tical guide to pricing. *Simon-Kucher & Partners*. www. simon-kucher.com/en-us/resources/books /practical-guide-pricing

Regen, P., Leijon, M., Bailard, B., & Sorrow, C. (2020). Pricing in turbulent times. *Blue Ridge Partners*. www.blueridgepartners.com/wp-content /uploads/2020/03/Pricing-in-Turbulent-Times.pdf

Sorrow, C., & Konkoly, J. (2020). Feeling the cash burn? Why fixing bad prices may help. *Blue Ridge Partners*.

Wyman, O. (2020). Surprising opportunities in B2B pricing. *Oli-verWyman*. www.oliverwyman.com/our-expertise /insights/2017/nov/perspectives-on-manufacturing -industries-vol-12/new-sources-of-value/surprising -opportunities-in-b2b-pricing.html

The author

Stephan M. Liozu is the Founder of Value Innoruption Advisors (www.valueinnoruption.com), a consulting boutique special-izing in value-based pricing, industrial pricing, and digital and subscription-based pricing. He is also an Adjunct Professor & Research Fellow at the Case Western Research University Weath-erhead School of Management. Stephan holds a PhD in Manage-ment from Case Western Reserve University (2013), an MS in Innovation Management from Toulouse School of Management (2005), and an MBA in Marketing from Cleveland State Univer-sity (1991). He is a Certified Pricing Professional (CPP), a Prosci® certified Change Manager, a certified Price-to-Win instructor, and a Strategyzer Business Model Innovation Coach. Stephan authored six books, *B2G Pricing* (2020), *Monetizing Data* (2018), *Value Mindset* (2017), *Dollarizing Differentiation Value* (2016), *The*

Pricing Journey (2015), and *Pricing and Human Capital* (2015). He also co-edited four books, *Innovation in Pricing—Contemporary Theories and Best Practices* (2012), *The ROI of Pricing* (2014), *Pricing and the Salesforce* (2015), and *Pricing Strategy Implementation* (2019). Stephan sits on the advisory boards of LeveragePoint Innovation and the Professional Pricing Society.

Appendix: ROI of Pricing: Reported Impact of Pricing

Source	Impact (%)	Description	Year
Simon-Kucher & Partners	35	Increase in EBITDA for firms with higher pricing power.	2012
Deloitte	3.2	Average operating margin increase of 3.2% for pricing initiatives after 18 to 24 months of implementation.	2012
Deloitte	26	Companies that are pricing leaders are 26% better at managing true profitability.	2012
Gardner	2–4	Pricing optimization software leads to average total revenue improvement of 2 to 4% and a payback of less than 2 years.	2012
Innovation Insights	15	By 2015 best-in-industry enterprises will increase revenue by up to 3% and profits by up to 15% as a result of improvements made using price optimization technologies.	2012
Simon-Kucher & Partners	14	Companies with a dedicated pricing organization are 14% more likely to expect a (strong) increase in EBITDA in the next 3 years.	2012
McKinsey & Company	15–25	A well-executed pricing-improvement program often yields price increases of 2 to 4 percentage points or more; sustaining a long-term price advantage may represent roughly 15 to 25% of a typical company's total profits.	2010
Monitor Group	8	Firms adopting non-value-based strategies earn 8% less in EBITDA than their peers.	2008
Monitor Group	30	Together, the right strategy with an empowered organization can deliver a powerful payoff—operating profits 30% higher than those of low-performing firms.	2008
McKinsey & Company	2–7	Committee leadership on pricing strategy improves a company's operating profit margin by 2 to 7%.	2002
McKinsey & Company	8.7	A one-percentage-point improvement in average price of goods and services leads to an 8.7% increase in operating profits for the typical Global 1200 company.	2001

6

Pricing Power:
The New C-suite Imperative

Manu Carricano, PhD,
Senior Lecturer Innovation,
Operations and Data Sciences, ESADE
& Founder TheTopLineLab

DOES OUR C-SUITE LACK pricing education? There are only very few *pricing* courses in business or engineering schools. Our leaders are trained in finance, leadership, and control, among other things, and yet virtually all curricula omit this key lever of profitability.

Very few of them are able to answer the questions "What would be the impact of a 1 percent price increase on your EBIT?" or

"What volume increase do you need to compensate for the current price erosion?"

With a price war around the corner, these keys to profitability calculation are not just theory but instead allow one to define a clear course of action for organizations in times of crisis.

We believe that *pricing power* goes far beyond that, and that it actually represents the company's ability to monetize its business model. Let us explain.

Operationalizing pricing power

The current crisis has made it even more critical for investors to identify companies having a durable competitive advantage. Why do certain companies outperform their direct competitors? As a growing body of literature suggests, marketing and sales have a significant and important impact on a firm's financial outcomes.

There is a positive relationship between marketing and sales activities and a firm's performance. Activities such as brand building, satisfying consumers, improving customer lifetime value, improving product quality, advertising and marketing expenditure, price and promotions, distribution channels decisions, and new product introductions (Srinivasan & Hanssens, 2009) result in an increased value for the shareholders. Financial outcomes can be measured by stock returns, Tobin's q, and changes to firm valuation.

In recent years, two scholars pushed the approach further by defining an alternative valuation methodology called customer-based corporate valuation (CBCV) that uses customer metrics to assess a firm's underlying value, exploiting basic accounting principles to make revenue projections from the bottom up instead of from the top down (McCarthy & Fader, 2020).

This granular view of how individual customers create value via acquisition, retention, frequency of purchase, and basket amount is a very interesting challenge to traditional methods. However, we also think that it lacks the multiplier effect to optimal pricing and execution, as well as the competitive benchmark dimension, which is very central in understanding how well a firm is performing among its peers.

The pricing power concept is a great candidate for an alternative corporate valuation, too, as it captures not only marketing and sales activities (defense of price premium, price leadership, consistent and efficient price raises, etc.) but also the drivers representing the context in which such activities occur (market conditions, customer dynamics, differentiation position, etc.) as defined by Liozu (2018).

The method we established in 2015 (Carricano & Kanetkar, 2015) aims at providing a parsimonious model of pricing power that's easy to operationalize and measure. We defined pricing power as "the process through which organizations extract a superior value from the market as a result of a higher willingness to pay for their products (and therefore a lower price sensitivity) and/or superior marketing and sales efficiency."

Our model is therefore based on two main metrics (calculations were presented in our 2015 paper and are available upon request):

1 "sensitivity": impact of a price change on demand, a proxy for consumer/customer willingness to pay.
2 "price to profit": impact of a price change (net) on operational profitability, a proxy for the efficiency of the pricing process.

These two items allow us to calculate a pricing power score, which we subsequently applied to large samples of financial statements data. The following illustrations focus on Fortune 500 companies, over the period 2008–2018.

First lesson: Controlling sector dynamics

Our data shed some light on the price dynamics within the different sectors. The vast majority of prices are rigid (economic *stickiness*); in other words, very few are pushing the pricing button. However, many companies from traditional sectors (e.g., automotive, chemicals) are beginning to take a close interest in dynamic pricing (per our frequent conversations with pricing leads).

In this context, most price changes are initiated by a *price leader* (not always the market leader, but rather the player who sends the signal of the rise) and the rest of the players simply follow.

The leader in terms of pricing power is one that is less exposed than its direct competitor to price **sensitivity** (because of its innovation, brand, etc.) and therefore more resilient to market dynamics.

Second lesson: Trajectories of value creation

The relative position on pricing power indicators within each sector is the result of a long process that is both strategic and tactical. Strategic first because it materializes the competitive advantage of the company, its **ability to create value**, through innovation, brand, business approach, and so forth (measured by **sensitivity**: eta). And tactical because the leaders **extract this market value** through an efficient commercial policy, allowing them to translate net prices into profit (measured by the "**price to profit**": phi).

Leaders in pricing power have therefore invested in the process, creating pricing departments (HP, Caterpillar, Stanley Black and

Decker, etc.) or net revenue growth (Coca-Cola, Unilever, AB-Inbev, etc.), relying on state-of-the-art tools (cloud, artificial intelligence) and installing above all solid governance, pricing being by definition cross-functional.

Pricing power is built over time, is consolidated, and adjusts when the competitive environment changes. Figure 6.1 shows the trajectory of one of the leaders (Amazon) we were able to identify over the quarters.

The trajectory that can be observed below oscillates between periods of greater exposure to the market (the eta score) and periods of value extraction thanks to pricing efficiency (the phi score). Overall, over the observation period (2008–18), Amazon generated a huge value, visible in our index as a score of 69 in pricing

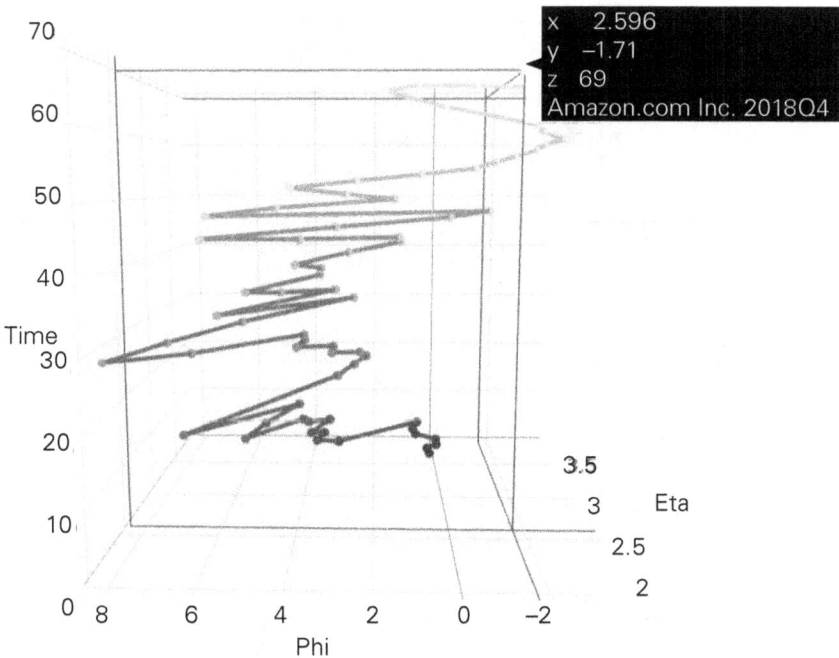

Figure 6.1. Example of pricing power trajectory (Amazon).

power, which puts it in the top quartile overall (vs. direct competitors such as Target or Walmart).

A company such as Amazon is not reducing its exposure to the context (sensitivity is still high) but is excellent at adjusting to it and extracting value through a perfect execution of price changes.

Third lesson: Financial impact

By collecting quarterly data from the US Fortune 500 over 10 years, we were able to measure the evolution of pricing power by sector and its financial impact (EBITDA, stock price, among others). The maturity of pricing in companies is consolidating, reflected by continued growth in the index we measured. Figure 6.2 shows the stock market performance of leaders in pricing power (1st quartile of our measure) against the rest of the sample. Both groups have been impacted by the 2008 financial crisis, but pricing power leaders have recovered much faster and have been creating value consistently ever since.

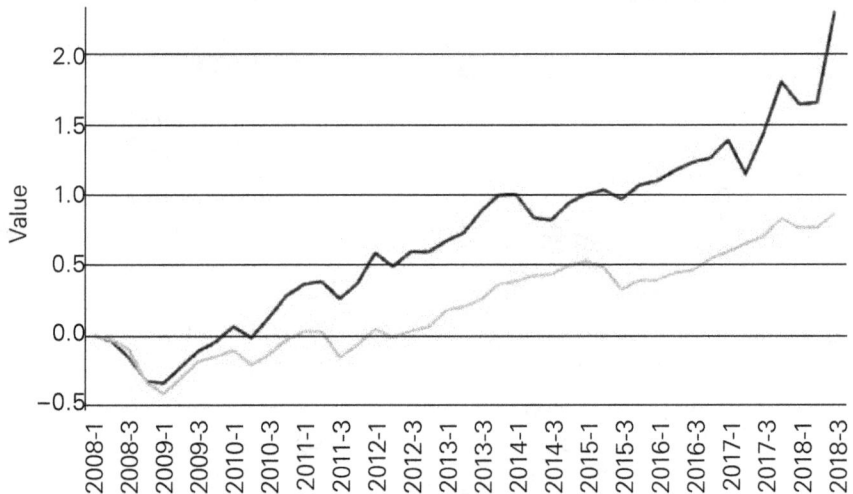

Figure 6.2. Global stock index—top pricing power versus others.

While pricing power gives a rather accurate sense of the alpha generated by all the company's innovation, marketing, and sales processes, it also gives some powerful insights into the growing gap between "top performers" and the rest. Figure 6.3 includes the discrepancies we've seen across the sample between the two groups.

Our sample represents firms with strong brands, efficient processes, and consistent value creation (Fortune 500). Despite these strengths, pricing power leaders have outperformed their peers by 10 points in terms of average yearly stock price increment.

As we discussed, much work is now looking at alternative business value mechanisms, including incorporating the value of client assets (McCarthy & Fader, 2020). Pricing power should be able to account for value creation over the long term while also documenting a key source of shareholder value.

At the same time, such an indicator could allow benchmarking of performance and make executives accountable for the value creation generated through marketing and sales processes.

Learning from top performers

Can we derive best practices from some of the companies that score high in our ranking? Of course. Let's dive deeply into some practical cases to understand better some practical traits of pricing power leaders.

Category	Average Pricing Power	Overall Stock Price Increment	Average Yearly Stock Price Increment
Leaders	2.91	2.41	0.13
The rest	−4.94	0.96	0.03

Figure 6.3. Pricing power leaders versus laggards.

McDonald's: Global value extraction

Value is at the very heart of McDonald's pricing strategy. A very insight-driven company, McDonald's measures value very consistently across its menu board, taking into account product-related value but also other elements such as customer experience. If a restaurant is refurbished, for example, this change in design and inside experience will be measured and included.

Local headquarters can document very accurately changes to be made by franchisees, providing actionable guidelines to execute on their recommendations. But the real strength of the approach lies in the consistency of its application, making value comparable across geographies and measurable against macro indicators fluctuations such as consumer confidence, inflation metrics, and sector indexes. In other words, value as the standard metric system, then adapted to local dynamics.

Coca-Cola: Flexing the pricing muscle

After some years of revenue decline in the mid-2010s, Coca-Cola rolled out a large turnaround plan based on a segmented market pricing approach and the creation of a revenue growth function (that many players then followed).

The segmented market pricing logic aimed at defining the ultimate pricing target based on country maturity. Countries with low market share but very high growth potential, such as emerging markets, would focus primarily on meeting volume targets. In that case the pricing and commercial policies are in the service of volume and market share growth. When growth potential is low, mainly in developed markets, the focus is on price realization, making pricing clearly a priority lever and efficiency of execution a must. Last, in developing markets with high potential and high market share, the goal was to balance volume and price realization.

The creation of the revenue growth function also marked an important step, as it modified the governance of the pricing function. From a tactical, operational mandate, the scope of the function expanded to cover net pricing and growth: in other words, two of the main levers besides volume—price and mix. And the change paid off, as Coca-Cola saw a growth of 3.5 percent in developed markets due to a growth of 4 percent in pricing and product mix. In modern pricing organization, both levers must go together.

Amazon: Speed versus accuracy
It's better to be approximately right than precisely wrong. We could add to this famous quote that you can be wrong as long as you can correct yourself quickly.

The big strength of Amazon is its superb execution capabilities. This is obviously also true for pricing. Whereas Walmart runs 50,000 price changes per month, Amazon executes 2.5 million price changes a day!—a model that is based essentially on speed of reaction, with two main variables that trigger recommended changes (stocks and competition). Amazon seeks to be the fastest follower of the price leader and turns its reactivity into a very powerful asset.

Static prices miss a lot of opportunities, as they don't adjust to context changes (both internal and external). By changing so frequently, Amazon's net prices can be higher on average than a competitor maintaining a flat rate over time. As Jeff Bezos said: "Our success is a function of how many experiments we do per year, per month, per week, per day." This means that in order to truly understand your pricing sweet spot, you need to experiment, try new schemes and pricing points, make mistakes, but then correct them at light speed.

How to get there? Bringing strategy back to pricing

To increase C-level pricing power accountability, it's important to elevate the discipline from tactical to strategic. More importantly, these two domains should be connected into a single flow, with management defining clear strategic orientation and targets while providing clear guidance and tools for execution and control. The topic is vast, but we describe it around two main principles: policies and guidance. Both concepts, as we will see, are the operational translation of our two pricing power indicators (value creation and value extraction).

Designing policies
Policies refer in the mathematical optimization literature to the translation of a model's recommendations to stakeholders. We think that in the data era there is an interesting parallel between model building and strategy formulation, as models represent a simplification of reality in the same way that strategy is increasingly called to translate the complexity of a changing context into guidelines that are simple and flexible enough to execute (Sull et al., 2018).

Therefore, leaders should define clear policies to guide value creation and extraction in a changing environment, among them these:

1 segments as definitions of price discrimination opportunities
2 value as structure of portfolio list-price lineup and pricing tiers
3 competition benchmark to monitor positioning
4 demand response function(s) to simulate impacts of scenarios
5 accurate forecast to control for baseline

These five pillars provide the guideline for defining the rules of execution, allowing also accurate simulations before validating the key strategic choices.

Providing guidance

Guidance refers to the rules of execution and their relative explainability: in other words, the recommendations pushed from the strategic to the operational layer. This is obviously not only about technique but also about steering and transformation.

The logic of rule translates relatively well the expected outcome from the guidelines: "IF customer belongs to segment 1 (country of origin, device, purchase pattern, etc.), THEN his propensity for price increase is…"; "IF product belongs to price tier x, THEN price changes must be bounded between y and z…"

How do we pass this guidance to the tactical agents? In some cases transparency will be central, and changes to be executed will require a specific scrutiny and possibly consensus; in some other cases, optimization and automation will be more important and will advocate for a more "black box" approach.

Whether manual or automated, policies and guidance both aim to facilitate the finding of an optimal response based on defined targets and function of a changing context, as represented by Figure 6.4.

Our thesis, in this short chapter, is that pricing power should be a critical component of the executive's KPIs toolkit. More than that, we think C-levels should be accountable for their capacity to create sustainable value in their markets, easily measurable on this new indicator. The two dimensions of pricing power, as we compute it, can be also operationalized to define simple strategic policies as well as clear guidance for value extraction.

As we saw in our data analysis of Fortune 500 companies over a 10-year period, pricing power differentiates the New World from

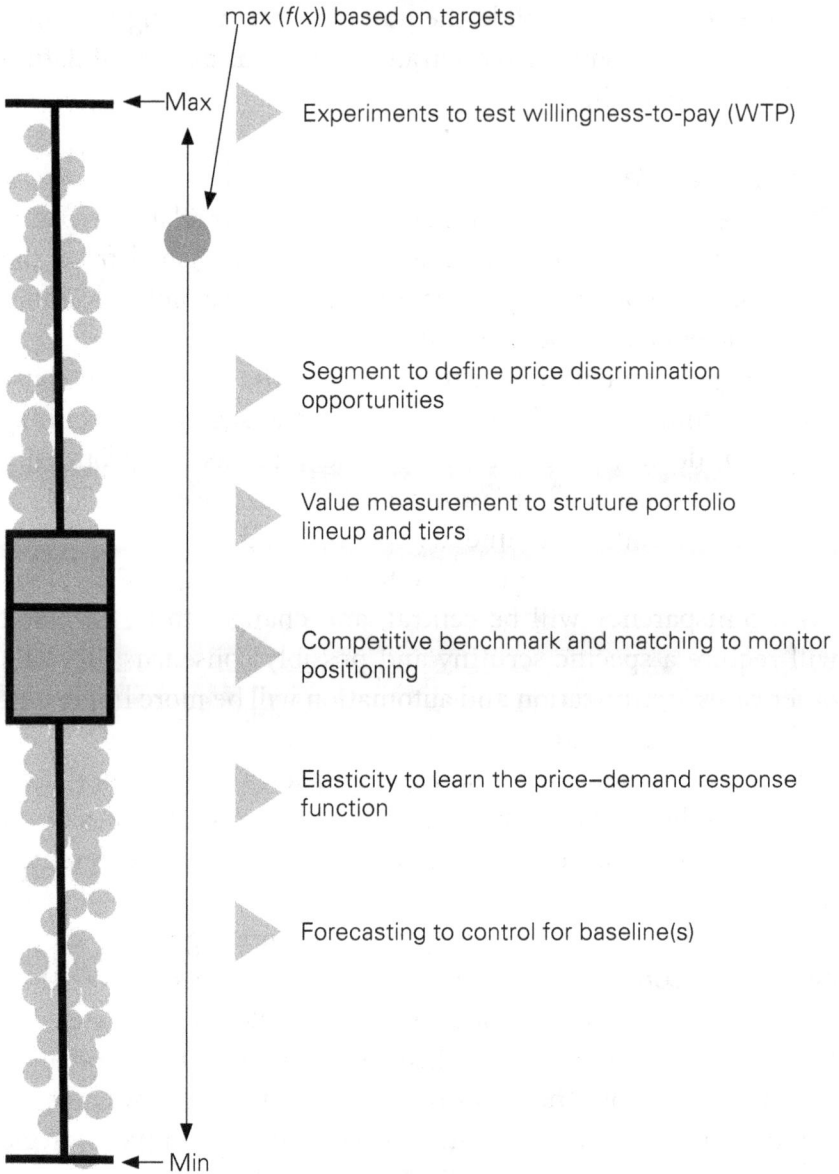

Figure 6.4. Policies and guidance for strategic optimization.

the Old, resilient business models from those exposed to volatility and uncertainty, and value creators from value destroyers.

Implications for the C-suite

There are several immediate implications for the C-suite in the insights we've provided. Below are the actions you should take immediately.

Assess the distance

The real distance is obviously on value creation/destruction. What EBIT level should your pricing deliver? What growth in stock value are you missing because of poor pricing? To make it more actionable, two simple indicators can be implemented: first, *price realization* as the percentage between gross sales and net sales, and second, *net price transfer,* as the percentage of list price increases that are transferred to net prices. These are two very actionable indicators of where your pricing stands.

Change your governance

Impacts come from accountability. A steering committee is the minimum level of governance body to implement with the presence of leadership. But these important events must also be prepared: business cases need to be run by the pricing team with pricing analytics and performance tracking; simulations on main decisions to be made must be executed in a collaborative effort between the main stakeholders (i.e., a price increase prepared by pricing, sales, and control); and an action table must be tied to the simulations and then tracked once decisions are adopted by the governing body, providing clear visibility on the incremental lift of each action decided.

Prepare for scaling

The C-level must aim for the big bucks. Pricing (and the related impact to extract) is a scaling problem. Two main pillars will prepare your organization to scale and extract the same value across multiple territories.

First, solve the data bottleneck. Data are always an issue, and rolling out efforts from the US to France or the UK means that data and process are made comparable and transparent to the multiple stakeholders of the pricing domain. Pricing power leaders have done their homework and have drastically modernized their infrastructure. And last but not least, the key is always people, and human capital must be high on the agenda to connect a brilliant strategy to an impeccable execution.

References

Carricano, M., & Kanetkar, V. (2015). Linking pricing power to financial performance. In *Proceedings of the 44th Conference of the European Marketing Academy (EMAC)*, May 24–27, Leuven, Belgium.

Liozu, S. M. (2018). Make pricing power a strategic priority for your business. *Business Horizons, 62*(1), 117–128.

McCarthy, D., & Fader, P. (2020). How to value a company by analyzing its customers. *Harvard Business Review,* January–February. hbr.org/2020/01/how-to-value-a-company-by-analyzing-its-customers

Srinivasan, S., & Hanssens, D. M. (2009). Marketing and firm value: Metrics, methods, findings, and future directions. *Journal of Marketing Research, 46*(3), 293–312.

Sull, D., Turconi, S., Sull, C., & Yoder, J. (2018, Spring). Turning strategy into results. *MIT Sloan Management Review.* sloanreview.mit.edu/article/turning-strategy-into-results/

The author

Dr. Manu Carricano, Founder of TheTopLineLab, combined top-level academic skills with 20 years' experience in Data Science & Pricing consultancy and was involved in large-scale pricing transformation projects for companies such as GE, Lego, McDonald's, Michelin, BD, Volkswagen, and Decathlon.

He was an executive graduate of the Massachusetts Institute of Technology (MIT) in big data and received his PhD from the University of Bordeaux and MSc from Kedge Business School. His work encompassed a wide range of data science and pricing issues and was published in international academic journals and major industry and academic conferences. He was also a Senior Lecturer in Data Science at the ESADE Business School and was recognized by *CDO Magazine* as one of the top Academic Data Leaders in 2021.

7

By the Numbers: Benchmarking the Impacts of Pricing on Margins

Lindsay Duran,
Chief Marketing Officer, Zilliant

Ideas in brief. Zilliant examines an apparent B2B paradox: how price is simultaneously the leading cause of margin leakage and the most effective lever that companies have to grow profits. Real-world benchmark data and a case study highlight the difference between subjective and optimized pricing.

WHETHER YOU'RE LOOKING AT a boom market or a recession, a demand shock or an undersupply situation, traditional sales or digital commerce, your pricing strategy can make or break your B2B company's overall financial performance. Company leaders often sense that price is the most effective lever they have to grow profits, yet price is also the leading cause of margin leakage in a business. How can you resolve this pricing paradox and establish organizational discipline to use price to your advantage regardless of market conditions? First, as a member of the C-suite, it's important that you be well versed in the basics of the pricing function in order to fully understand and contextualize its impact. This chapter aims to teach those pricing basics and to demonstrate how pricing affects a wide range of financial performance indicators. We examine the current state of margin loss in the B2B world and establish a practical understanding of the various ways that price is expressed in B2B, the common pitfalls within each price mode, and how modern tools can transform losses into gains at scale.

Global B2B benchmark report findings

The average B2B company is losing up to 17.1 percent of margin each year because of subpar pricing practices, according to the latest benchmark data from Zilliant (2020a). This popular annual report is novel in that it quantifies the normalized pain B2B leaders feel but often can't pinpoint. The product of data science-driven analysis of over one billion B2B transactions, the benchmark report brings to light precisely how costly missteps such as misaligned market pricing, inconsistent pricing, and inefficient pricing processes are to the average company.

Misaligned market pricing refers to prices that are broadly asymmetrical with market conditions. This occurs when companies transact business at prices that fail to align rationally with customer size, order size, product value (good-better-best), and other key value dimensions. For example, a small customer may receive a better price than a large customer for the same product, all else being equal. Often, prices are rounded arbitrarily to rule-of-thumb margins or discounts, or deals are transacted below minimum margin thresholds. Misalignment also happens when pricing does not quickly and accurately account for cost changes. Risk exposure to the latter is only increasing as cost changes increase in frequency and unpredictability. Benchmark data show that B2B companies lose up to 6.58 percent annual margin because of misaligned market pricing.

Inconsistent pricing refers to transactions that have too wide a data variance. Typically, these are inconsistent based on market, product, or customer circumstances. In some cases, prices are too high to be competitive or smaller customers receive better prices than bigger strategic accounts.

In other cases, prices fail to reflect customers' true price elasticity, resulting in too many transactions being over- or underpriced. Price grooving is also a common source of margin leakage, creating inconsistent prices where prices are rounded to the nearest dollar or offered at only discrete margins, such as 30 percent, where perhaps a margin of 33.5 percent would have been sufficient to win the deal. Benchmark data show that on a global scale, B2B companies experience an annual margin loss of up to 8.12 percent due to inconsistent pricing.

Inefficient pricing practices occur when pricing and sales teams must rely on heavily manual processes and calculations. Thus, the time it takes to update prices when costs change or to respond to a quote request is far too long and costly. In an environment full of savvy competitors and the increasing pace of e-commerce, "time is money" has never been truer.

Inefficient pricing costs B2B companies up to 2.4 percent annual margin loss.

Why this matters to the C-suite

Although the pains of margin loss are felt most acutely in the boardroom, it's nearly impossible for C-suite members to fix the problem without an understanding of the primary sources of margin erosion. Take advantage of the opportunity to quantify your business's exposure to pricing-related risk as a first step to rectifying profitability issues.

Next up: we explore why these issues are so pervasive and how a better approach informed by data science can typically help companies recoup between 1 and 3 percent of gross margin.

Pricing challenges and opportunities

No one sets out to make these kinds of pricing mistakes. It's widely known in the B2B community that pricing is the most effective lever for increasing margin performance, causing many companies to invest ample resources in the pricing function in recent years. So why do these mistakes continually occur?

Pricing in B2B is difficult because of the acceleration of external pricing triggers in modern business coupled with outmoded internal processes that can't scale to meet the moment. Pricing teams are constantly in a reactive position—trying to pass through increasingly frequent cost changes, setting a pricing strategy that sales reps will honor, making quick decisions based on inventory, or keeping up with the omnichannel demands of customers. In many B2B companies, especially those that are branch-based, pricing is decentralized. They are not set up to learn from mistakes happening in far-flung field offices; nor can they effectively set and govern a true holistic pricing strategy. Without the technology toolset and ability to analyze a massive volume of data and collaborate within a single source of pricing truth, companies find themselves forever behind the market, leaking margin all the while.

In order to diagnose the full extent of margin loss and why it happens at a practical level, it's necessary to understand a typical company's pricing architecture.

Pricing typically takes on similar forms across B2B industries. All of a company's price modes (pricing architectures) have their place, but they tend to drift away from their original intent and are used inconsistently, resulting in margin leakage in many cases. A price mode is a framework for understanding how a company arrives at price for a given customer. Here are the four main price modes and the common problems B2B companies encounter with each:

- **List price**
  - Price lists tend to quickly become stale, as product–value relationships, such as good-better-best and private label, are not reflected and cost changes are not pushed through intelligently or quickly enough.
  - List prices should be a company's North Star, the reference point for discounts. The increasing number of products, relationships, and competitive considerations often render the list price meaningless when managed manually and therefore unusable as a reference price.
  - Companies often further complicate list prices by artificially inflating the price to try to influence pricing decisions made by sales reps—a tactic that rarely works in practice.
- **Matrix/system price.** The grid where groups of similar customers and products are assigned to specific matrices. When assigned correctly, this can be the most profitable price mode. However,

- Often sales reps have the power to reassign customers to more favorable price tiers, causing nearly all customers to get the lowest price. This, combined with stale list-price reference values, causes customers to be misassigned and to receive prices that don't reflect their relationship with the distributor.
- Matrix prices often lack the proper level of granularity, or dimensions, to ensure that the prices are market-aligned and competitive enough to win the deal; thus, they are ignored by sales reps in favor of overrides and special price exceptions. The granularity required to optimize the matrix and to gain market adoption may exceed the resources available in-house.
- As costs change, matrix prices are often cumbersome and difficult to update. Even when this process is relatively efficient, if a small percentage of revenue is transacted on the matrix, companies may recoup only a small portion of a cost increase through price, as other price modes are harder to immediately affect.
- **Customer-specific prices.** There are two types in this category, customer-specific price exceptions and customer contracts, which are reserved for the largest and most valuable customers
  - Companies often see a proliferation of customer-specific price exceptions when matrix prices are not market-aligned. These often lead to margin leakage due to poor price initial setting, poor record creation/management, lack of an approval and ongoing review process, and a fundamental lack of strategy behind the process.
  - It's not uncommon for hundreds of thousands to millions of these pricing records to exist in a business, creating an overwhelming administrative burden and making it

difficult to impossible to execute price changes as costs or other dynamics change.

- Many price exceptions are set with no expiration date, at a net price level or at a generic markup over cost, and fall victim to the "set and forget" conundrum.
- Since customer contracts are reserved for key customers, sales reps are very protective of them. It can be a challenge to enact a price increase, regardless of how outdated a contract is.

- **Override prices.** These are prices that, for any number of legitimate reasons, are deviated from list or matrix prices in a one-off, negotiated capacity.
  - When left without guardrails, these can lead to rampant overdiscounting, based on rule-of-thumb margin targets, inconsistent prices from rep to rep or branch to branch, and misaligned prices.
  - Attempts to institute approval processes can often result in delays and lower win rates if not instituted appropriately.

Why this matters to the C-suite

Without a foundational understanding of the basics of pricing, the appropriate response to margin erosion will remain foreign to any executive. It's one thing to know at a high level where you're leaking margin and why; the next step is applying rational fixes at the level of pricing architecture to ensure that your commercial teams are set up for sustained success. To do that effectively, you must understand how your organization's pricing structure is organized, what percentage of revenue is transacted at each price mode, and how that compares with the intended percentage of revenue at each mode. For example, you may want to have 60 percent of your revenue on matrix, but it may be that only 20 percent is on matrix.

Next up: now that we have identified the price modes and where they often break down, we explain how to fix your pricing architecture.

Fixing the B2B price modes

A combination of data science, data-driven tools, and process improvements can be applied to not only correct these mistakes but also establish a culture of continuous pricing improvement.

- Fixing list prices
  - Use price administration and management software for setting and managing list prices (Zilliant, n.d.). These tools make it easier to add and price new products, handle end-of-life product pricing, manage and adjust product good-better-best relationships, make updates due to cost changes or other competitive and market factors, and cascade list-price changes to other price modes.
- Fixing matrix prices
  - Price management software is well suited to helping you set and manage matrix prices. It should allow pricing teams to segment and assign customers and products into relevant matrices, manage customer and product assignments over time, set order quantity breaks, make updates due to cost changes or other competitive factors, and cascade matrix price changes to other price types.
  - To ensure the values in the matrix are set to achieve the desired P&L objectives, price optimization software is highly recommended and can be used in conjunction with price management software (Zilliant, 2020b).
  - Constraint-based price optimization solves for misaligned matrix pricing. If a pricing model built with constraint-based

optimization could speak, it would say "Tell me all the relationships that I need to respect and I will simultaneously compute all those prices rather than writing a thousand if/then statements." By simultaneously accounting for business rules and price relationship requirements through constraint-based price optimization, you avoid the hazards of conflicting rules.

- Fixing customer-specific prices
  - A combination of price optimization and price management software should be used to generate and update customer-specific prices en masse. The key is to ensure that you have robust deal- or agreement-management software that seamlessly connects to the price management/optimization applications so that sales reps are alerted to customer-specific price changes and can take action quickly.
- Fixing override prices
  - With price management software, companies can create and manage a price segmentation structure and set pricing guardrails for negotiations and overrides.

Why this matters to the C-suite

Any large-scale pricing transformation project will require a heavy dose of disciplined change management. Leadership from the top is an absolute prerequisite to establishing and sustaining successful change. Knowledge of the different challenges and opportunities within each B2B price mode, as well as the best-practice strategies to apply to rectify broken processes, will make all the difference in effectively leading your teams.

Next up: it's clear that two solution approaches—price management and price optimization—are key to overcoming common challenges and transforming price from a problem to an opportunity. First, we take a deeper dive into price management.

Applying price management in B2B

To put price management concepts into practice, let's explore three real-world applications.

Global and country list-price management
Selling thousands of products across many different countries or geographies creates significant price management complexity. The time-intensive process of manually aggregating the right data, sorting through good-better-best product relationships, and adjusting prices based on market dynamics and cost changes creates headaches for corporate price and category managers.

Effective price management is the "easy" button for global and country list prices. It makes arduous tasks repeatable, centralizes essential data sources (e.g., currency exchange rates), applies rule-based strategies for intuitive price updates, and allows users to build KPI cards to understand the calculated impact of price changes across lists.

Cost pass-through
One of the greatest challenges for B2B pricing teams in the last several years has been reconciling tariff costs with their end-customer pricing. As tariffs push costs upward, businesses are often unable to pass them all on to customers. In addition to the financial burden, tariffs become a price administration nightmare. Coupled with increasingly frequent raw-material and supplier cost changes, simply updating prices—across all price modes—to reflect new costs has become an unwieldy process.

With price management tools, teams are able to set up cost pass-through strategies for any price mode at any level of granularity. For example, a pricing team may update matrix prices as a function of supplier cost changes at the customer-group and product-subcategory levels in addition to identifying all the impacted customer price agreement lines and performing a mass agreement update. This allows for prices to be updated quickly in a central location and delivered to sales quoting and agreement tools transparently, so that price changes can be easily calculated, tracked, and communicated.

The right tools eliminate guesswork and help capture more margin and manage cost fluctuations in any environment. When unpredictable tariff actions disrupt the ordinary flow of business and threaten margins, these capabilities are the difference between leaders and laggards.

Real-time market pricing for e-commerce

The fastest-moving sales channel in any B2B business is e-commerce, where competitor prices are constantly changing and customer loyalty is fleeting. If a company's e-commerce prices are misaligned with the market or inconsistent with offline channels, buyers will quickly move to a competitive site. But how does a pricing team keep this channel consistently market-aligned given the increased frequency of external pricing triggers? How can e-commerce pricing be differentiated to honor existing customer relationships?

The answers lie in dynamic pricing, which only becomes possible to attain with modern pricing software (Zilliant, 2020c). Instead of slow and cumbersome spreadsheets and disconnected data sources, price management software allows companies to dynamically set prices using a variety of inputs, including transaction data, cart abandonment data, inventory position, web-scraped competitive prices, and any other reliable data source.

The result is real-time market pricing that reflects the current market price, meets customer expectations for a competitive price, and achieves the desired P&L goals. E-commerce is a fundamental shift in B2B; it must be met with a fundamental shift from reactive to proactive pricing.

A modernized approach to price management is becoming table stakes for B2B companies; to reach the next level of performance, leading companies, with a high need for differentiated pricing, must adopt price optimization.

Why this matters to the C-suite

You must go beyond an understanding of pricing in the abstract and understand how price management can be applied across the price modes. The downstream impact of getting the price right consistently and efficiently is massive in terms of your bottom line and ability to quickly react as a business when market conditions change.

Next up: we take things to the next level with B2B price optimization.

What is price optimization, and how does it work?

Setting prices that make sense for each unique selling circumstance within a B2B company can look like an insurmountable challenge. We covered above how the many ways that a company prices—list, matrices or tiers, customer-specific agreements, spot negotiations and overrides, all of which are interconnected—drive complexity. Distributed pricing decisions, large customer and product counts, and complex product configurations further complicate the pricing process. It can become unmanageable to account for all the factors that influence price, including cost changes, competitive dynamics, product velocity, customer relationships and types, geographies, and order circumstances.

These complexities require a more sophisticated approach to pricing. Price optimization simultaneously accounts for all the factors that drive price, rationally aligns price–customer–order–product relationships simultaneously, and statistically measures what drives price response in the market, all while enforcing necessary guardrails and producing price guidance for all the different ways price is expressed in a B2B business.

The purpose of optimization is to find the set of inputs that lead to the maximum output. In other words, find the prices that result in the desired revenue or margin outcomes for each part of your business. The goal is not just to have different prices; it's to hit certain revenue and margin targets, using price.

The data needed to take this scientific approach to price optimization already exist in most businesses. They're readily available in transaction data—the customer, product, and order data that every company captures in the course of doing business.

From that data, you can segment customers into small groups that have a similar price response and measure the price elasticity on an ongoing basis for each segment. Taking a surgical approach to pricing by measuring price elasticity and setting goal-seeking pricing strategies to maximize revenue or profit can have a dramatic impact on profitability while minimizing risk and improving responsiveness to market dynamics.

Price optimization software allows you to create a statistically and strategically relevant price segmentation structure. The resulting microsegments are typically a function of product, order, and customer attributes. The most effective segmentation structures balance model sophistication with explanatory power. In other words, if you can get to 90 percent explanatory power with eight attributes but to get to 92 percent explanatory power you need to include five more attributes, it may not be worth the trouble or added complexity. Ninety percent will suffice.

Segmentation attributes, such as customer size, geography, order size, product velocity, and product category, are typically arranged in a tree structure. As is common in B2B, there will likely be some nodes in the tree for which there are little to no transaction data available. Advanced statistical techniques can be used to ensure that your optimization model derives clues from nearby nodes in the tree and comes to a determination on the market price. **Importantly, the underlying data science is exposed to the user, empowering them to explore different variations of the segmentation model, add new attributes, or create an entirely new structure as needed.**

Once similar transactions are grouped into the proper segments, price optimization solutions can pinpoint the market price for each segment and begin to use that as the foundation for how to set prices going forward, including factoring in a key, and often overlooked, step: measuring price elasticity to understand how a change in price will impact a change in win rate or volume, segment by segment.

In order to predict the revenue and margin outcome, you have to know how different customers will react to price changes across various circumstances, which requires knowledge of price elasticity. Price elasticity is the single most important factor in setting profitable prices while keeping revenue risk to a minimum. If you don't understand price elasticity for a given price segment, you risk leaving money on the table or losing profitable sales.

Most B2B companies do not use price elasticity to set prices, because they assume they can't. Instead, these companies rely on backward-looking analytics or statistical distributions of prices. It's a long-held belief that price elasticity is impossible to calculate in a B2B selling environment. That's simply not true.

The most effective price optimization solutions use price elasticity to calculate the revenue-maximizing and the profit-maximizing price for each price segment, thus allowing the user to optimize prices for different objectives and detect when segments are priced too low or too high for the market.

True price optimization is not a black box; it's a crystal box. Once a pricing model is built, a pricing analyst or category manager needs a mechanism to interact with it. Given that optimization is a goal-seeking activity, a pricing analyst can set specific revenue and profit goals for different pricing segments at varying levels of granularity, subject those goals to a set of business constraints, and view the predicted revenue, margin, and volume impacts of those price changes before putting prices into market.

Here's an example scenario: I'd like to maximize profitability on product category A in the Southwest region for small customers, but I don't want to raise my prices by more than 5 percent. In a different segment, large customers in the Northeast on product category B, I'd like to take more share and be revenue aggressive but keep a minimum margin of 30 percent and not lower prices by more than 7 percent. And, for all other segments in my business, I'd like to take a more balanced approach to revenue and profitability. Once the optimizer runs the various pricing strategies, the pricing analyst can drill into the recommended price changes across products and customers and view the predicted impact to ensure the strategies will produce the desired P&L results.

The "what-if" scenario capability coupled with the predictive nature of price elasticity is key to using price as a strategic lever to improve profitability.

Why this matters to the C-suite

The many ways in which price is expressed in your business is intertwined with macro factors such as customer behavior, market shifts, cost increases, and competitive threats. Price optimization makes it possible to account for each of these inputs and to take ultimate control of your price response in a goal-seeking fashion.

A world that will only continue to grow more complicated compels business leaders to take a scientific approach to their biggest margin driver: pricing.

Next up: a real-world example of price optimization creating significant margin improvement for a building materials manufacturer.

B2B price optimization case study: Terreal

The building products manufacturing industry is competitive, fragmented, and complex. As countless suppliers battle over the same pool of projects, prices tend to follow a downward trajectory. Often, sales reps face the choice of either losing the bid or slashing the price to a point that decimates profit margin. This is a big problem because material costs fluctuate.

For discrete products manufacturers, who may sell standard products through distributors and have a direct salesforce, it's important to find the right mix of system/matrix and customer-specific pricing while minimizing deviations.

Each of these industry undercurrents rings true for Terreal, a €376 million French manufacturer of clay building materials that employs nearly 2,500 people around the globe. Known for its specialty in terra cotta, Terreal provides solutions for the entire building envelope, most notably roofing, structure, and façade/decoration.

More than 150,000 homes are built or renovated with Terreal tiles each year, and another 20,000 are built with Terreal bricks. The company's rapid growth and expanded global footprint introduced more layers of go-to-market complexity, as customers could buy from regional depots, distributors, e-commerce sites, and retail stores. Aligning prices across sales channels and enforcing rational price guidance among sales reps became a heavy burden.

Terreal revamped its pricing strategy with price optimization to price strategically. Prices that had decreased over time below the floor price have been moved back up to a fair and profitable level. Using price elasticity as a guide, Terreal has been able to run campaigns that surgically change prices in the business to achieve varying P&L objectives. Terreal is now getting fair value for its products, without losing volume or facing customer pushback.

Terreal is now above market performance in terms of volume and price!

Why this matters to the C-suite

Whether you're a B2B manufacturer, distributor, or service company, you'll invariably relate to some of the challenges faced by Terreal from a pricing perspective. The company's story demonstrates that it's possible to measure price elasticity in B2B and use it to create a competitive advantage in your market.

Conclusion

We've set out to underscore the duality of pricing in B2B: it's a margin-cratering problem but also the best margin growth opportunity available. The power of pricing is well known, yet somehow also often overlooked by many in the C-suite. We think this incongruence comes down to sheer complexity. The growth in scale—more customers, more SKUs, more sales channels—continues to outpace the internal capacity to effectively lead a comprehensive pricing strategy. Many think that even if they want to improve pricing, their data aren't clean enough or there are still battle scars and bad memories from a past pricing project that didn't work out.

But failing to address the nagging itch in your business will only lead to more normalized pain. Time is of the essence—you're unnecessarily leaking margin now! As uncomfortable as it might be to take a long, hard look at your current pricing architecture and processes, it's the only way to properly apply the price management and optimization techniques that ultimately bring relief. This approach has worked for companies like Terreal and can work for your business. Here are five actions executives can take today:

1   Quantify the current amount of avoidable margin loss in your business by benchmarking your company against others in your industry (Zilliant, 2020a).
2   Map your pricing architecture and determine the percentage of revenue that falls in each one of the price modes so you can understand what's happening in your business and how the sales team is behaving with respect to price.
3   Lead from the top. This type of change needs to come down from the C-suite in order to be effective instead of emanating solely from a functional area.
4   Collaborate with your internal teams to get a clear view of each price mode, the challenges within each, and the technology toolset currently being used to handle pricing.
5   Find a pricing vendor that can be a true partner from the diagnostic phase to implementation to ongoing investment in your success. Price optimization and management for large B2B companies isn't just a project, it's a paradigm shift. An experienced partner who's "in the boat" is an essential success factor.

References

Zilliant. (2020a). *2020 global B2B industry benchmark report.* resources.zilliant.com/reports /global-b2b-industry-benchmark-report

Zilliant. (2020b). *An introduction to price optimization.* resources
.zilliant.com/blog/an-introduction-to-price-optimization
Zilliant. (2020c). *What is pricing software?*
resources.zilliant.com/blog/a-primer-on-pricing-software
Zilliant. (n.d.). *Pricing administration & management.*
www.zilliant.com/solutions/price-management?

The author

Lindsay Duran is the Chief Marketing Officer at Zilliant. As the leader of Zilliant's marketing organization, Lindsay is responsible for accelerating growth strategies, demand generation, product marketing, corporate communications, sales enablement, and market positioning. Lindsay is also the co-host of the Zilliant podcast *B2B Reimagined* (www.zilliant.com/podcasts/). Before serving as CMO, Lindsay was a top-performing Zilliant sales director for three years, establishing a record of success working with B2B company leaders to identify their unique pricing and sales challenges and remedy the most significant sources of revenue and margin leakage. Before that, she spent three years as Zilliant's director of marketing.

Before joining Zilliant in 2012, Lindsay served as a senior consultant at Deloitte Consulting and held product management and product marketing manager positions at Dun & Bradstreet. Lindsay holds a BS in Public Relations and an MBA from the University of Texas at Austin. She can be reached via email at Lindsay. duran@zilliant.com. The Zilliant Benchmark Assessment is available at benchmark.zilliant.com/.

8

Make Pricing Power a Strategic Priority for Your Business

Stephan M. Liozu, PhD, Founder, Value Innoruption Advisors LLC

Competition is fierce

"Cutting prices or putting things on sale is not sustainable business strategy. The other side of it is that you can't cut enough costs to save your way to prosperity"

—Howard Schultz, CEO of Starbucks
(quoted in Gossage, 2011)

THE BUSINESS WORLD CONTINUES to experience dynamic changes. Change is everywhere, its pace feels exponential, it has tremendously increased competitive pressures, and it has disrupted the world of pricing (Figure 8.1). Faced with tremendous pricing pressures, many executives have succumbed to competitive intensity by entering into price wars, not fully realizing the consequences of such actions (Kramer, Jung, & Burgartz, 2016). A 2016 global pricing study reported that 82 percent of companies complained of pricing pressures, 49 percent were experiencing a price war in their industry, and only 30 percent managed to increased prices successfully in their market (Simon-Kucher & Partners, 2016).

While most firms compete on price, others have realized that, faced with pricing pressure, years of flat demand, and several waves of cost optimization efforts, they must think differently. They cannot cut their way to prosperity. There is no winning in a price war. Firms have no choice but to invest massively in innovation processes to create value for their customers and markets. Call it taking the high road. I call it a courageous journey toward

1. Costs are creeping up: labor, utilities, raw materials, insurance rates, health benefits.
2. Customers are demanding more for less: price concessions, credit terms, service levels, etc.
3. Low-cost competition is putting lots of pressure on price levels.
4. Competitive intensity makes price increases very hard to justify and to capture.
5. Traditional demand/supply and cost/price cycles are no longer valid.
6. Traditional pricing structures for distribution/retail channels are being disrupted.

Figure 8.1. The new pricing reality.

customer value excellence and pricing power (Hinterhuber & Liozu, 2012). There's no other way around it, and Wall Street has begun to pay attention. Financial analysts have begun to assess firms' pricing power (Krishna, Feinberg, & Zhang, 2007). Success stories of pricing power masters have emerged in the financial news (Apple, Starbucks, Google, Lego, Disney, 3M, Grainger, Netflix, Johnson & Johnson, Caterpillar, Sealed Air, and others). On March 26, 2016, Jim Cramer observed, "Sometimes, it just comes down to figuring out who has pricing power: who can raise prices and who can't." He continued, "You can't compete with the lowest-cost producer on price and not expect your stock to get clobbered" (quoted in Stevenson, 2016). There you have it: pricing power is formally on Wall Street's radar.

This trend prompts the following questions: What is pricing power? How can it be calculated? What are the drivers that positively or negatively influence pricing power? What's the relationship between pricing power and profit performance? This paper presents the results of a unique research study on the topic of pricing power with the goal of responding to these critical questions. Since price wars are not an option, and since competing solely on price cannot be the only answer to today's business dynamics, I intend to provide more insights on how a company can generate pricing power, design programs to find it, and deploy tools and systems to capture it in their market. I want to help pricing, marketing, sales, and innovation managers grasp the concept and embed it in the pricing and marketing activities of their firms.

I first explain pricing and discuss how it has recently become more visible in financial circles. I then discuss the drivers and dimensions of pricing power and how firms can generate more of it. Finally, I discuss the impact of pricing power and how to operationalize it in firms. Pricing power, even if you have a lot of it, does not come by itself. It requires attention and intention in organizations, from the CEO down to the front-line facing customers and competitors in the market place.

Pricing power explained

In November 2011 Warren Buffett said, "The single most important decision in evaluating a business is pricing power. If you've got the power to raise prices without losing business to a competitor, you've got a very good business. And if you have to have a prayer session before raising the price by 10 percent, then you've got a terrible business" (quoted in Wachtel, 2011).

This conceptualization of pricing power is not too far from reality. Many people talk about pricing power, but few executives know what exactly it refers to. Warren Buffett's statement put pricing power on the map. However, confusion remains. Practitioners conflate the power of pricing with pricing power. For the past few years, scholars and consultants have published papers claiming the power of pricing and its impact on the bottom line (Jubas, Kiewell, & Winkler, 2015; Liozu, 2017). There is a consensus that pricing is a powerful level of the P&L and that firms that have embarked on pricing transformations show greater profit results than those stuck on cost-based or competition-based pricing strategies (Liozu & Hinterhuber, 2013, 2014).

However, the same cannot be said about the concept of pricing power. The marketing literature is silent about its conceptualization and impact (Carricano & Kanetkar, 2015). Pricing power is traditionally discussed in economics classes, often in conjunction with pricing elasticity or pricing sensitivity in demand/supply models (Bijmolt, Heerde, & Pieters, 2005; Parker, 1992). Although pricing power is close to the concept of inelastic demand, according to which volumes may stay flat or slightly decline (Nagle & Holden, 1987) when prices rise, pricing power refers to continuous increases in demand while prices go up, until firms potentially reach the maximum price they can charge (Huber, 2014). Thanks to Warren Buffett and Jim Cramer, pricing power has recently received more attention from financial analysts and marketing practitioners. Marketing and pricing scholars seem to converge on a definition of pricing power that links price increases and growing demand levels (Carricano & Kanetkar, 2015; Krishna et al., 2007), as shown in Figure 8.2.

Pricing power is demonstrated "when a company can unilaterally define and extract prices without regards to direct competitive pressures. It requires that the firm is able to deliver a product or service to the market that competitors cannot easily replicate. Furthermore, that product or service must be desired, if not preferred, by the market, than its nearest comparable alternative" (Smith, 2016). Simply put, pricing power is the ability to increase prices without losing demand and while maintaining business levels. Other scholars link pricing power to strategy and to the notion of competitive advantage. An example definition is that pricing power is "the process through which organizations extract a superior value from the market as a result of a higher willingness to pay for their products (and therefore a lower price sensitivity) and/or superior marketing and sales efficiency" (Carricano & Kanetkar, 2015).

While the definition is still in development, the materialization of pricing power in practice is not yet fully understood. What does it mean to be able to increase prices or to move pricing levels upward? There are many ways to raise prices or to positively impact the overall price-realization levels of a firm in its markets (Hinterhuber & Liozu, 2012). Through my research of practitioner blogs and short essays, discussions with pricing experts, and experience in pricing strategy, I identified six actions or activities that help achieve that goal (Figure 8.3).

Concept	Definition	References
Price sensitivity	"The extent to which customers vary their purchases of a product as its price changes."	Tellis (1988, p. 331)
Pricing power	Pricing power is the ability to enact price increases.	Krishna, Feinberg, and Zhang (2007)
	Pricing power is related to customer relative preferences for product features and price premium.	Archak, Ghose, and Ipeirotis (2011)
	Pricing power is "the process through which organizations extract a superior value from the market as a result of a higher willing-ness-to-pay for their products (and therefore a lower price sensitivity) and/or superior marketing and sales efficiency."	Carricano and Kanetkar (2015)
	Pricing power is the ability of a company to get the price it deserves for the value it delivers.	Simon-Kucher and Partners (2016)
	Pricing power is demonstrated "when a company can unilaterally define and extract prices without regard to direct competitive pressures. It requires that the firm is able to deliver a product or service to the market that competitors cannot easily replicate. Furthermore, that product or service must be desired, if not preferred, by the market, than its nearest comparable alternative."	Smith (2016)
Price elasticity	The percentage change in sales for a 1% change in price.	Simon (1979), Parker (1992), Tellis (1988), Nagle and Holden (1987), Bijmolt, Heerde, and Pieters (2005)

Figure 8.2. Pricing concepts defined.

- Ability to successfully **defend our price premium** versus competitors
- Ability to **make price moves** first in the marketplace
- Ability to **capture a large share** of the value we deliver to customers
- Ability to **price** and launch innovative and differentiated offerings **at a premium**
- Ability to **raise prices consistently** every year without losing demand
- Ability to **capture** a large share of our intended price increases

Figure 8.3. The materialization of pricing power..

1   Ability to successfully **defend a price premium** versus competitors. Often negotiations with B2B accounts and their buyers become difficult in terms of pricing pressure. A firm's ability to maintain a price premium through value selling is often challenged. Defending a premium against competition and resisting negotiation tactics is a sign of greater pricing power.

2   Ability to **make price moves** first in the marketplace. Pricing leadership means making price moves often and early to establish norms and anchors in the marketplace. When new product categories are created by industry leaders, pricing leaders also establish the value perceptions for these new products or services (Stevenson, 2016).

3   Ability to **capture a large share** of the value delivered to customers. Firms with great pricing power understand the value pool they make available to share with customers and intend to keep a large share of it (Liozu, 2016). And they do not hide the fact that they capture much of that value pool and that they are worth the premium their customers end up paying (Hinterhuber & Snelgrove, 2016).

4   Ability to **price** and launch innovative and differentiated offerings **at a premium**. Pricing power masters introduce superior technologies, products, and services that create true value for customers (Ringen, 2015). With these, they can introduce innovations at a higher price, sometimes cannibalizing previous generations of products, and thus lead their industry technologically (Pino, 2014).

5   Ability to **raise prices consistently** every year without losing demand. Pricing power masters base price increases on delivered value and consistently focus on raising prices to capture value. Some experts distinguish between nominal pricing power and real pricing power whereby a firm's price increase can exceed the industry inflation rate (Huber, 2014). Raising prices also implies being surgical in doing so. One-size-fits-all pricing increases are no longer relevant. Data-supported price increases target pockets of pricing power (Krishna et al., 2007) supported by level of uniqueness and differentiation. Starbucks has demonstrated that such targeted price increases can improve overall price-realization levels.

6   Ability to **capture** a large share of intended price increases. Research by Simon-Kucher & Partners (2012) showed that for every intended dollar in price increase, firms only capture 50 to 53 cents of it on average. Increasing prices and making increases stick is a materialization of superior pricing power.

The drivers of pricing power

My research uncovered six critical drivers that positively or negatively influence pricing power (Figure 8.4). I call them dimensions, as each is composed of several criteria.

```
┌─────────────────────────┐
│ Market conditions       │      ┌─────────┐      ┌──────────────────────────────┐
│ Customer dynamics       │      │         │      │                              │
│ Innovation position     │  ▶   │ Pricing │  ▶   │ Firm performance             │
│ Differentiation position│      │ power   │      │ (EBIT, sales, and EBIT growth)│
│ Competitive pressure    │      │         │      │                              │
│ Supply life cycle       │      └─────────┘      └──────────────────────────────┘
└─────────────────────────┘
```

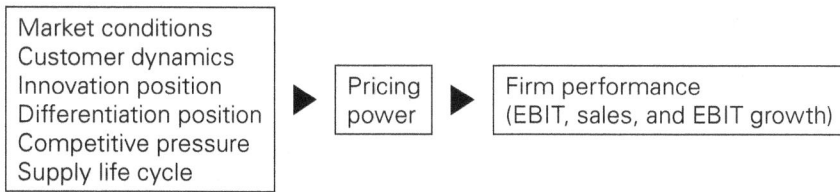

Figure 8.4. The antecedents of pricing power.

During the first steps of my research inquiry, I focused on identifying the relevant drivers of pricing and attempted to group them into six main dimensions. I drew from research publications in the areas of strategy, finance, marketing, pricing, and economics as well as from interviews with clients and peers in the pricing field who had conducted pricing power projects. These dimensions and individual drivers were then tested during pricing capability assessments in several companies, including my current company, Thales. The outcome of this iterative approach is the list of main dimensions displayed on the left side of Figure 8.4.

1. **Market conditions.** This dimension refers to the overall health of markets, including markets that are rich in opportunities, that are growing or at least stable, that are attractive for differentiated offerings, and that present long-term predictability. Market dynamics can positively or negatively influence the ability of firms to deploy pricing strategies, especially those targeted at greater value extraction (Hinterhuber, 2017).

2. **Customer dynamics.** This dimension relates to the behavior of customers with regard to value, perceptions of the price/quality ratio, customer insights, value co-creation, and deeper segmentation opportunities. When customer dynamics are favorable, firms can expand their value-based strategies. They can also

gauge customer preferences and behaviors for products and services and more easily extract pricing power from customer data (Archak, Ghose, & Ipeirotis, 2011).

3. **Innovation position.** Innovation has seldom been linked to pricing power. Innovation position refers to the introduction rate of innovations to market, to the uniqueness and nature of these innovations, to the ability to uncover customers' hidden needs and derive willingness to pay for new things, and to the ability to capture greater value through pricing. The recently reborn Lego company is a good example of the potential link between great innovation position, pricing power, and profit performance (Ringen, 2015).

4. **Differentiation position.** When differentiation exists, companies can formally calculate the differentiation of their offerings and justify the premium to the market (Liozu, 2016). Differentiation can be demonstrated and more easily accepted by customers (Ingenbleek, Frambach, & Verhallen, 2013), leading to superior sales effectiveness (Carricano, 2016). Differentiation position includes elements of price premiums, technical and nontechnical switching costs, and brand equity.

5. **Competitive pressure.** This dimension is the one most recognized and mentioned. Competitive pressure refers to the overall price aggressiveness of suppliers and to the presence of low-cost competitors, inflexible and price-driven request-for-proposal processes, and a general culture of price competition and price war in the ecosystem, including when power retailers are involved (Kadiyali, Chintagunta, & Vilcassim, 2000). Competitive pressures often penetrate the mindset of commercial teams and reduce their confidence in pricing (Forsyth, Gupta, Haldar, & Marn, 2015).

6. **Supply life cycle.** Some industries might be impacted by supply and product life-cycle conditions. This dimension refers

to the rate of product obsolescence in the marketplace, the rate and speed of technological change, and the overall production capacity available for supply. Slow-moving inventory, capacity utilization, and fixed-cost absorption considerations often influence manufacturers' pricing strategies and tactics. They are at the heart of cost-based pricing (Wilkes & Harrison, 1975), especially in capacity-intensive sectors and in industries where price elasticity might vary greatly and quickly in product or brand life cycles (Parker, 1992; Simon, 1979).

Based on these six dimensions, I constructed a pricing power assessment (PPA) instrument composed of 30 individual items, shown in Figure 8.5 (five items per dimension). Each item in the instrument is rated on a scale of 1 to 4. The higher the score out of 120 possible points, the higher the price-power level.

Armed with our PPA instrument and with the support of the Professional Pricing Society (PPS), I collected 128 completed and usable responses from Certified Pricing Professionals around the world. This quantitative inquiry focused on identifying the dimensions having the greatest influence on pricing power as well as the impact of pricing power on firm performance. I also intended to test our PPA instrument for use in predicting levels of pricing power. Figure 8.6 summarizes our research findings.

Pricing power has little to do with pricing; it mostly has to do with innovation and differentiation. While the relationships between innovation position and differentiation position with pricing power make sense, my study is the first formal research study to statistically validate them. More interesting is the lack of significance in the relationship between competitive intensity and pricing power. Often, leaders succumb to competitive pressures and wave the "white flag" when faced with competitive pricing pressures (Liozu, 2015). This might also explain why so many leaders declare that they feel they're in a price war (Simon-Kucher

Market conditions	1	2	3	4	Score
Our markets are rich in profitable opportunities	1. No	2. Rarely	3. Sometimes	4. Yes	
Growth in market demand is healthy and sustained	1. No	2. Rarely	3. Sometimes	4. Yes	
Market demand is stable and steady (no steep demand-and-supply cycles)	1. No	2. Rarely	3. Sometimes	4. Yes	
Markets are attractive for innovative and differentiated offerings	1. No	2. Rarely	3. Sometimes	4. Yes	
We have a healthy pipeline of opportunities and existing orders	1. No	2. Rarely	3. Sometimes	4. Yes	

Customer dynamics	1	2	3	4	Score
We have the opportunity to sell value to various customer stakeholders besides procurement/sourcing	1. No	2. Rarely	3. Sometimes	4. Yes	
Most customers understand the concept of quality/price relationship and value	1. No	2. Rarely	3. Sometimes	4. Yes	
Customers engage actively in innovation co-development and value co-creation	1. No	2. Rarely	3. Sometimes	4. Yes	
We are able to segment our customer base into distinctive clusters offering growth avenues	1. No	2. Rarely	3. Sometimes	4. Yes	
Customers are sensitive to and interested in recurring revenue models and multiyear contracts	1. No	2. Rarely	3. Sometimes	4. Yes	

Innovation position	1	2	3	4	Score
We bring lots of unique innovations to markets	1. No	2. Rarely	3. Sometimes	4. Yes	
We are able to introduce regular radical or disruptive innovations to markets	1. No	2. Rarely	3. Sometimes	4. Yes	
Our innovation teams are able to uncover customers' hidden and unmet needs	1. No	2. Rarely	3. Sometimes	4. Yes	

Figure 8.5. Pricing power assessment instrument. (*Figure continues on next page.*)

Innovation position (continued)	1	2	3	4	Score
Most customers value the introduction of differentiated product and service innovations	1. No	2. Rarely	3. Sometimes	4. Yes	
We are successful in capturing a price premium for our innovations	1. No	2. Rarely	3. Sometimes	4. Yes	
Differentiation position	**1**	**2**	**3**	**4**	**Score**
Premium suppliers can maintain a certain price premium in the market	1. No	2. Rarely	3. Sometimes	4. Yes	
We are able to extract true differentiation that is acknowledged and perceived by the market	1. No	2. Rarely	3. Sometimes	4. Yes	
There are technical switching costs that somewhat protect our business	1. No	2. Rarely	3. Sometimes	4. Yes	
There are "nontechnical" switching barriers, which protect our business (brand, reputation, loyalty, etc.)	1. No	2. Rarely	3. Sometimes	4. Yes	
Only a few competitors can reach the required level of product and service quality	1. No	2. Rarely	3. Sometimes	4. Yes	
Competitive pressure	**1**	**2**	**3**	**4**	**Score**
We have aggressive price competitors in the market	1. Yes	2. Sometimes	3. Rarely	4. No	
We have too many competitors in our markets	1. Yes	2. Sometimes	3. Rarely	4. No	
Our markets suffer from a culture of price war and price competition	1. Yes	2. Sometimes	3. Rarely	4. No	
Our channel partners are tremendously price driven	1. Yes	2. Sometimes	3. Rarely	4. No	
We have large customers with a very strict RFP process (including government)	1. Yes	2. Sometimes	3. Rarely	4. No	

Figure 8.5. Pricing power assessment instrument. (*Figure continues on next page.*)

Supply life cycle	1	2	3	4	Score
Products/services quickly become obsolete in our industry	1. Yes	2. Sometimes	3. Rarely	4. No	
Our business must frequently change its products and practices to keep up with competitors	1. Yes	2. Sometimes	3. Rarely	4. No	
Technology changes more quickly in our industry than in other industries	1. Yes	2. Sometimes	3. Rarely	4. No	
The industry overall supply capacity utilization is….	1. Low	2. Average	3. High	4. Full	
New capacity in our industry can be built up in….	1. <1 year	2. 1–1.5 years	3. 1.5–2 years	4. >2 years	

Total Pricing Power Score (out of 120 possible points)

Figure 8.5. Pricing power assessment instrument.

1 **Innovation position** is the most significant positive driver of pricing power (regression coefficient of 0.385 at 100% confidence level).

2 **Differentiation position** is the second most significant positive driver of pricing power (regression coefficient of 0.347 at 100% confidence level).

3 **Competitive intensity** has no significant impact on pricing power (no significance).

4 **Pricing power** is significantly and positively related to relative firm performance (regression coefficient of 0.209 at 99% confidence level).

5 **The aggregation** of all 30 drivers of pricing power into one construct is positively and significantly related to pricing power (regression coefficient of 0.288 at 99% confidence level).

Figure 8.6. Research findings (sample size of 128 distinct organizations).

& Partners, 2016). My research indicates that the response to competitive pressures might not be more price competition or price wars but more innovation to significantly improve the level of true differentiation. This study also demonstrates a positive and significant link between pricing power and firm performance as defined EBIT, sales growth, and EBIT growth, also a first. Finally, I tested the validity of our PPA instrument. The aggregation of the 30 items into one index score significantly and positively explained the level of pricing power. By taking this PPA, managers can therefore predict the level of pricing power potential in an organization for a specific market. Taking this assessment as part of a price capability and maturity assessment is a first positive step in the pricing power journey.

The impact of pricing power is real

Wall Street is paying more and more attention. Over the past few years, financial analysts have made stock recommendations based on pricing power (Forbes, 2013; Kulikowski, 2016; Petro, 2014; Rasmussen, 2013). Best-in-class companies with superior pricing power are often mentioned in financial news. Recent examples include Lego's rebirth (Ringen, 2015), Netflix's fast global growth (Wang, 2016), Verizon's results when faced with intense competition (Levy, 2016), Disney's unstoppable price increases (Holodny, 2015), and Starbucks' continuous but targeted pricing increases (Taylor, 2016). These firms all face tremendous price competition in their relevant markets. They have responded by continuing to innovate and to focus on their differentiation power while managing pricing with discipline. Pricing power is the ability to introduce a new iPhone 8 at a price over $1,000 and to sell 50 million of them. It is also about having brand loyalists lining up at 3:00 a.m. to be the first customers to buy this new and expensive phone (Team Trefis, 2017). Does Apple face price competition? You bet they do!

Pricing power is not just a B2C thing. Many companies in the B2B world enjoy high levels of EBIT or EBITDA in the midst of flat demand, modest inflation, and price competition. 3M is one such example (Pino, 2014). Others are shown in Figure 8.7. These are companies traded on stock markets and very visible to the world. For each of these large companies, there are thousands of small and medium business who also manage innovation, differentiation, and pricing religiously. My research provides another confirmation that pricing power increases profit power. A similar study conducted in 2011 showed that superior pricing power leads to superior financial results when comparing the stock value of the top performers in pricing power with the S&P 500 index over a 10-year period (Carricano, 2016).

Having pricing power is not enough

The intentional management of pricing power as one of the drivers of firm performance provides the necessary evidence for more

Company	2016 operating income
Lego	35%
Disney	30%
Cisco	26%
3M	24%
BASF	24%
Bayer	24%
Johnson & Johnson	23%
Honeywell	21%
Apple	21%
Monsanto	20%
Starbucks Coffee	20%
PepsiCo	16%
Eastman Chemicals	15%

Figure 8.7. Examples of pricing power champions.

firms to get started. I can finally further confirm the power of pricing as well as the importance of managing pricing power as a priority.

But pricing power does not come on its own. You might have it or might think you have it, but you will have to go get it; it will not magically appear in your bottom line. So, the key word in the first sentence above is the word *intentional*. A firm might have the necessary position in the marketplace to capture pricing power through innovation, differentiation, and customer management, but its leaders might not understand where their pricing power resides and how to capture it fully. For that, they must invest in the right tools and systems to properly identify the pocket of pricing power, as shown in Figure 8.8.

Essential to this process is the deployment of advanced pricing tools and systems that allow business leaders to conduct these critical activities: scientific segmentation, pricing and

Pricing tools, systems, and methods	What is it?	How does it enable pricing power?
Scientific segmentation	Methodology using qualitative and quantitative data to classify customers into homogenous segments based on preferences, purchasing behaviors, customer needs, and pricing historical data	Defines pricing strategy by segment / develops good-better-best approach / uncovers segment value drivers / defines segment-specific pricing and revenue models
Pricing analytics platform	Pricing software focused on critical pricing analysis: pricing cloud, pricing waterfall, margin bridges, price sensitivity, price elasticity	Uncovers pricing opportunities / identifies price outliers / discovers profit leakages / extracts pure price effect / reports discount effectiveness
Pricing optimization software	Pricing software using data, algorithms, and mathematical analysis to determine how customers will respond to different prices for its products and services through different channels and for different customer segments	Identifies areas of pricing power / defines targeted price increases / models outcome of pricing choices / models pricing level of product versions
Value-based pricing software	Cloud-based software to manage the process of value-based pricing and publish dollarized customer value propositions for the sales team	Systematizes the quantification of customer value / calculates the customer value pool / assists in price premium justification / models value in the new product development process
Pricing research	Primary pricing research techniques such as conjoint analysis, A/B price testing, online pricing intelligence, willingness-to-pay research, price perception and satisfaction	Derives willingness-to-pay for new products / estimates the value of functionalities and product attributes / dynamically tests acceptance of price level / collects competition pricing levels

Figure 8.8. Pricing tools and system to enable pricing power.

customer analytics (Healy, 2014), pricing optimization, and pricing research. These tools and systems enable pricing power. They inform a firm's pricing strategies and tactics. Each of these tools offers tremendous documented benefits to firms who deploy them (Hinterhuber & Liozu, 2015). They also empower go-to-market teams with the right information to make intelligent decisions when faced with pricing opportunities. I often call this being in control of one's pricing destiny. There are other tools and systems available to identify and extract pricing power, including CRM systems, business intelligence platforms, or simply a spreadsheet software analyzing the right data.

So how do you operationalize PRICING POWER?

Over the past 24 months, I have conducted dozens of PPAs and have had the privilege to enter into deep strategic discussions with go-to-market experts on the drivers of pricing power and what its impact is. The first reaction once the PPA is taken is generally: "Now that I know that I have a 56 percent pricing power score, what do I do with this information?" This is the trigger I look for, as it helps get into action mode. I propose the following actions and activities to begin paying attention to pricing power and to operationalize it in an organization.

1   **Understand where you are starting from by conducting a formal PPA as part of a comprehensive pricing capability or pricing maturity assessment.** "What gets measured, gets managed," Peter Drucker said (quoted in Prusak, 2010). Before getting to the pricing power zone, you need to understand where you are starting from. Figure 8.9 shows the type of pricing assessments that are generally conducted by firms willing to embark on a pricing transformational journey (Liozu, 2015). Adding my 30-item

PPA to the overall assessment process can highlight the areas that managers need to prioritize to boost their pricing power, keeping in mind that these areas will be outside of the pricing realm.

The interesting part of the debrief and synthesis from the pricing capability assessment—but specifically from the PPA—is to look at the overall pricing power score across divisions, functions, and regions. So it's less about paying attention to the 56 percent pricing power score and more about exploring why sales might think the score is 43 percent while innovation teams stand at 67 percent. Differences in perceptions might allow teams to openly discuss their pricing power and might encourage them to bring real structural issues to the surface (Liozu, 2013). Results from the PPA can also be included in the overall summary and long-term change roadmap.

2 **Pay attention to and mobilize intention toward pricing power over time.** "Where focus goes, energy flows," said Tony Robbins (Team Tony, n.d.). Pricing might become an organizational strategic priority for a firm and not just a pricing project. That implies mobilizing much more than the

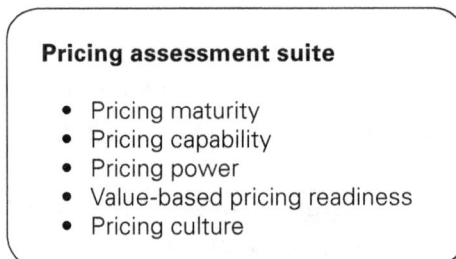

Pricing assessment suite

- Pricing maturity
- Pricing capability
- Pricing power
- Value-based pricing readiness
- Pricing culture

Figure 8.9. Types of pricing assessments.

pricing team! Pricing power touches critical aspects of the firm's go-to-market strategy. That requires some form of alignment between the marketing, sales, innovation, and pricing teams in the form of language, objectives, compensation systems, and performance indicators. I posit that tracking pricing power over time is essential for creating this required level of alignment. Imagine the recent comeback of Lego with EBIT levels surpassing the 30 percent mark (Ringen, 2015). One can imagine Lego managers following their pricing power score year after year and integrating that score into their group performance dashboard.

3 **Take action with the drivers of pricing power that you can control. This is the heart of the discussion.** Often managers will engage in the pricing power discussion by saying that they cannot control most of the items or drivers in the PPA. This reaction reflects a potential lack of courage and mindfulness to look at what really drives their pricing performance. And this is where we start pushing back, by discussing what is controllable and what is not, as shown in Figure 8.10, and by telling them that pricing is not going to solve their structural problems related to strategy, innovation, and differentiation.

There is much that managers can control in the areas of innovation and differentiation, two of the biggest drivers of pricing power. I list some examples in Figure 8.10, but there are many more. In general, the discussion pivots away from pricing toward deep discussions of differentiation strategy and investments in value-based innovation. So I move away from the long and unproductive discussions on price concessions, pricing pressure, and price wars to discussions of competitive advantage, willingness to pay, and customer delight.

Dimension	Controllable	Uncontrollable
Market conditions	Industry innovation leadership / corporate communication campaigns on value / leveraging business development efforts	Economic crisis / deep commoditization mindset / shrinking industry profit pool
Customer dynamics	Investing in customer intimacy / investing in scientific segmentation / reinforcing customer insights process	Industry consolidation / customer strategic size / professionalization of procurement
Innovation position	Tracking innovation rate / investing in innovation / thinking about self-disruption	Corporate cost-cutting program / shareholder pressure for more dividends / more innovative competitors
Differentiation position	Strengthening customer experience /reinforcing switching costs / investing in brand power	Disruption by new entrants / dilution of differentiation during recessions / radical shift in value perceptions
Competitive pressure	Anticipating competitors' behaviors / managing coordinated & controlled responses / communicating a clear strategic positioning	Number of competitors / industry price wars / behavior of low-cost players
Supply life cycle	Technology roadmap / creative self-destruction / developing integrated solutions	Accelerating of obsolescence / government regulation / industry overcapacity

Figure 8.10. Using the dimensions of pricing power in the strategic planning process.

So, what is your priority?

Pricing power has gained popularity since 2011, thanks to Warren Buffett and Jim Cramer. Financial analysts on Wall Street are choosing stocks partly for firms' ability to raise prices and not lose volume and market share, especially during times of economic uncertainty. This paper aimed to help managers with the definition of pricing power, give them an assessment instrument to begin measuring it, and offer practical recommendations for operationalizing it. I hope to see more anecdotes and research studies supporting efforts to make pricing power an area of focus for profitability improvement. Pricing power can be an extremely powerful tool to improve profit power when placed at the top of the agenda, when it is managed with attention and intention, and when proper investments in tools, systems, and methods are made to capture it. Are you paying enough attention to your pricing power? Would you rather enter into price wars or focus on boosting your pricing power? It's time for your organization to invest in the proper tools and systems so that you can better control your pricing destiny.

About the research

In 2015 I designed and executed a research project with support from the Professional Pricing Society (PPS), the world's largest professional pricing association. The research consisted of four steps:

1   I began with a literature review on the topic of pricing power to lay the foundation for the inquiry.
2   I conducted qualitative interviews with six pricing professionals and consultants to complete our conceptualization of pricing power and to validate a newly developed pricing power assessment (PPA) instrument. These professionals shared their existing assessment methods and provided in-depth feedback on the instrument and its theoretical dimensions.

3 I tested the PPA instrument in various organizations and at various conferences between 2013 and 2015 by adding the instrument in pricing workshops.

4 4. I distributed an electronic survey to the 750 Certified Pricing Professionals of the PPS. These are pricing professionals in organizations that manage pricing strategically and who underwent an intense certification process. I obtained 128 completed and usable surveys (a 17% response rate). These firms ranged in size from fewer than 250 employees to more than 10,000: 66 (51.6%) with up to 10,000 employees, and 62 (48.4%) with 10,000 or more. Over half the firms (67.2%) were located in the Americas, 23.4 percent were in Europe/Africa, and 9.4 percent were in Asia and the Pacific. About half (53.9%) the firms engaged in manufacturing, 30.5 percent in services, and the remainder (15.6%) in retail. Most (79.7%) identified as primarily B2B.

Based on these 128 responses, I conducted several statistical analyses (ANOVA, correlation analysis, and multiple regression with model fit analysis) to test the causal relationship between the six antecedents of pricing power, pricing power itself, and profit performance. Finally, I successfully constructed a pricing power index using the 30 variables distributed among the six dimensions of pricing power.

References

Archak, N., Ghose, A., & Ipeirotis, P. G. (2011). Deriving the pricing power of product features by mining consumer reviews. *Management Science, 57*(8), 1485–1509.

Bijmolt, T. H., Heerde, H. J., & Pieters, R. J. (2005). New empirical generalizations on the determinants of price elasticity. *Journal of Marketing Research, 42*(2), 141–156.

Carricano, M. (2016). Who are the pricing power leaders? Pricing power as a sustainable competitive advantage. *AEE: Aalto University Executive Education,* June 6. www.aaltoee .com/blog/who-are-pricing-power-leaders-pricing -power-sustainable-competitive-advantage

Carricano, M., & Kanetkar, V. (2015). *Linking pricing power to financial performance.* Paper presented at the European Marketing Conference.

Forbes, W. (2013). Small caps with pricing power in niche markets. *Forbes,* June 5. www.forbes.com/sites /wallaceforbes/2013/06/05/small-caps-with-pricing -power-in-niche-markets/#63d961a2d601

Forsyth, J. E., Gupta, A., Haldar, S., & Marn, M. V. (2015). Shedding the commodity mindset. In A. Hinterhuber & S. Liozu (Eds.), *Pricing and the sales force* (pp. 30–37). New York, NY: Routlledge.

Gossage, B. (2011). Howard Schultz on how to lead a turnaround. *Inc. Magazine,* April. www.inc.com/magazine/20110401 /howard-schultz-on-how-to-lead-a-turnaround.html

Healy, P. (2014). Ticket pricing puts "Lion King" atop Broadway's circle of life. *New York Times,* March 17. www.nytimes.com/2014/03/17/theater/ticket-pricing -puts-lion-king-atop-broadways-circle-of-life.html

Hinterhuber, A. (2017). Value quantification capabilities in industrial markets. *Journal of Business Research, 76,* 163–178.

Hinterhuber, A., & Liozu, S. (2012). Is it time to rethink your pricing strategy? *MIT Sloan Management Review, 53,* 69–77.

Hinterhuber, A., & Liozu, S. M. (2015). Pricing ROI, pricing capabilities and firm performance. *Journal of Revenue & Pricing Management, 14,* 211–228.

Hinterhuber, A., & Snelgrove, T. C. (2016). *Value first then price: Quantifying value in business to business markets from the perspective of both buyers and sellers.* Abingdon, UK: Routledge.

Holodny, E. (2015). Disney is demonstrating what "pricing power" is all about at its Magic Kingdom. *Business Insider,* November 27. www.businessinsider.com /disney-demonstrates-definition-pricing-power-2015–11

Huber, J. (2014). The importance of pricing power. *Base Hit Investing,* March 14. basehitinvesting.com/the-importance-of-pricing-power/

Ingenbleek, P., Frambach, R. T., & Verhallen, T. M. (2013). Best practices for new product pricing: Impact on market performance and price level under different conditions. *Journal of Product Innovation Management, 30,* 560–573.

Jubas, J., Kiewell, D., & Winkler, G. (2015). Turning pricing power into profit. *The McKinsey Quarterly,* March. www .mckinsey.com/business-functions/marketing-and-sales /our-insights/turning-pricing-power-into-profit

Kadiyali, V., Chintagunta, P., & Vilcassim, N. (2000). Manufacturer-retailer channel interactions and implications for channel power: An empirical investigation of pricing in a local market. *Marketing Science, 19*(2), 127–148.

Kramer, A., Jung, M., & Burgartz, T. (2016). A small step from price competition to price war: Understanding causes, effects and possible countermeasures. *International Business Review, 9*(3), 1–13.

Krishna, A., Feinberg, F. M., & Zhang, Z. J. (2007). Should price increases be targeted? Pricing power and selective vs. across-the-board price increases. *Management Science, 53,* 1407–1422.

Kulikowski, L. (2016). Morgan Stanley's 18 stocks with big pricing power opportunities in low inflation. *The Street,* February 28. www.thestreet.com/slideshow/13471010/1 /morgan-stanley-s-18-stocks-with-big-pricing-power -opportunities-in-low-inflation.html

Levy, A. (2016). Verizon is starting to show off its pricing power. *Business Insider,* July 8. www.businessinsider.com /verizon-is-starting-to-show-off-its-pricing-power -2016-7

Liozu, S. M. (2013). Do you have a pricing problem? *Pricing Advisor,* March, pp. 5–6.

Liozu, S. M. (2015). *The pricing journey: The organizational transformation toward pricing excellence.* Stanford, CA: Stanford University Press.

Liozu, S. M. (2016). *Dollarizing differentiation value.* Sewickley, PA: VIA.

Liozu, S. M. (2017). State of value-based-pricing survey: Perceptions, challenges, and impact. *Journal of Revenue and Pricing Management, 16,* 18–29.

Liozu, S. M., & Hinterhuber, A. (2013). Pricing orientation, pricing capabilities, and firm performance. *Management Decision, 51,* 594–614.

Liozu, S. M., & Hinterhuber, A. (2014). *The ROI of pricing: Measuring the impact and making the business case.* Abingdon, UK: Routledge.

Nagle, T., & Holden, R. (1987). *The strategy and tactics of pricing: A guide to profitable decision making.* Englewood Cliffs, NJ: Prentice-Hall.

Parker, P. M. (1992). Price elasticity dynamics over the adoption life cycle. *Journal of Marketing Research, 29,* 358–367.

Petro, G. (2014). Why pricing power is the real secret to value investing. *Forbes,* August 6. www.forbes.com/sites

/gregpetro/2014/08/06/why-pricing-power-is-the
-real-secret-to-value-investing/#37f898625658

Pino, I. (2014). 1 industrial company with incredible pricing
power. *The Motley Fool,* April 21. www.fool.com
/investing/general/2014/04/21/1-industrial-compa-
ny-with-incredible-pricing-power.aspx

Prusak, L. (2010). What can't be measured. *Harvard Business
Review,* October 7.
hbr.org/2010/10/what-cant-be-measured

Rasmussen, A. (2013). Picking stocks by their pricing power.
Globe and Mail, July 18. www.theglobeandmail.com
/globe-investor/investment-ideas/number-cruncher
/picking-stocks-by-their-pricing-power/article13308254/

Ringen, J. (2015). How Lego became the Apple of toys. *Fast Company,* January 8.
www.fastcompany.com/3040223/when-it-clicks-it-clicks

Simon, H. (1979). Dynamics of price elasticity and brand
life cycles: An empirical study. *Journal of Marketing
Research, 4,* 439–452.

Simon-Kucher & Partners. (2012). *Global pricing study 2012.*
Bonn, Germany: Author.

Simon-Kucher & Partners. (2016). *Global pricing study 2016.*
Bonn, Germany: Author. www2.simon-kucher.com/sites
/default/files/simon-kucher_gps_insights_2016
_web_en.pdf

Smith, T. J. (2016). What really is pricing power? *LinkedIn,* January 27. www.linkedin.com/pulse/what-really-pricing
-power-tim-j-smith

Stevenson, A. (2016). Cramer: Apple pricing power stronger than
ever. *CNBC,* March 23. www.cnbc.com/2016/03/23
/cramer-apple-pricing-power-stronger-than-ever.html

Taylor, K. (2016). Starbucks is quietly raising prices. *Business Insider,* November 21. www.businessinsider.com /starbucks-is-quietly-raising-prices-2016-11

Team Tony. (n.d.). Where focus goes, energy flows. www.tonyrobbins.com/career-business /where-focus-goes-energy-flows/

Team Trefis. (2017). Apple may have unprecedented pricing power for the iPhone 8. *Forbes,* May 16. www.forbes.com/sites/greatspeculations/2017/05/16 /apple-may-have-unprecedented-pricing-power-for -the-iphone-8/#43eaac6a3ac6

Tellis, G. J. (1988). The price elasticity of selective demand: A meta-analysis of econometric models of sales. *Journal of Marketing Research, 25,* 331–341.

Wachtel, K. (2011). Warren Buffett: There's only one thing that matters to me when I'm investing in a company. *Business Insider,* February 18. www.businessinsider.com /warren-buffett-pricing-power-beats-good -management-berkshire-hathaway-2011-2

Wang, C. (2016). Bull says Netflix's subscriber miss was actually proof it has pricing power. *CNBC,* August 29. www.cnbc .com/2016/08/29/bull-says-netflixs-subscriber-miss -was-actually-proof-it-has-pricing-power.html

Wilkes, F. M., & Harrison, R. (1975). Classical pricing rules, cost-plus pricing and the capacity constrained firm. *Journal of Business Finance & Accounting, 2,* 19–37.

9

The ROI of Pricing Projects: More Than a Billion Dollars Generated for Customers

Frederico Zornig, President, Quantiz Pricing Solutions

Journey to $1 billion of impact

MY FIRST EXPERIENCE WITH a pricing project was in 2002, while working for Johnson & Johnson. After a global initiative by the company to form Six Sigma Black Belts with a focus on pricing during 2001 in the US, I took responsibility for leading a comprehensive price management project involving several processes such as the implementation of a new commercial policy, a new price list (based on a new pricing methodology and no more markups), a new order capture system by the sales team, and a simulation and negotiation tool with customers, alongside an ERP change in company (the new ERP was being implemented almost concurrently with the pricing project).

The result obtained for Johnson & Johnson was remarkable. We brought, after a year of implementation, top-line growth of more than 20 percent in a mature business unit, which came from several years of very modest growth, if any. Much of this growth occurred through an improvement in prices practiced in the market, since volumes were practically stable. The impact on gross margin was over 10 percentage points in that year alone.

I received an award from the company the following year for the project's results and a promotion to sales and marketing director in Brazil. I stayed at Johnson & Johnson for another four years, but I soon imagined that it would be possible to replicate the way we developed the project at J & J with any other company in the market. It was enough for me to take the knowledge and experience acquired so that with a team of professionals from the client company we could join forces to structure solutions that could impact the business in the same way that I experienced as an executive.

So, for the market, Quantiz Pricing Solutions was born in 2006. Ever since, I've been able to follow my path as a CEO, consultant, MBA course professor at FGV/SP (a leading business school in São Paulo, Brazil), speaker at pricing events, and author, with several articles and a book published on pricing.

The importance of price in a company's results
Many studies have demonstrated the importance of prices in a company's results. One of the best known was conducted by the

consulting firm McKinsey in the early 2000s using published balance sheets of the 1,200 largest global companies at that time. In a simple but interesting way, the authors estimated the impact on net profit of each of these companies and on their overall average considering variations (improvements) of 1 percent in each of the main levers of business results: sales volume, direct variable costs, fixed costs, and prices.

The study consisted of varying positively by 1 percent one of the four lines of the balance sheet above while keeping the others unchanged. The results were revealing. While an increase in sales volume, reduction of variable costs, and reduction of fixed costs showed single-digit gains in profit, the capture of 1 percent higher prices brought an average gain of more than 10 percent in net profit. The percentage values themselves don't matter too much, as they vary by company, but the order of magnitude shows that the price lever is much more powerful than any other variable for the impact on the bottom line.

I reinforce, then, that the main lever to improve a company's results is the price it practices. However, in the market, what I hear most is that we have to gain volume or market share or reduce costs. When I ask about prices, the answer is often that the market sets the price.

I participated in a round table organized by a business magazine a few years ago with some of the country's top finance executives, one of whose panelists had an interesting discussion with me, claiming that the price is wherever the market sets it. This thought came from a business leader representing a company that had more than a 40 percent market share at the time. Given this level of representativeness, my question for him was, "Who is the market?" Even with smaller stakes than this, many companies need to set prices in the market and influence competitors instead of being held hostage to unthinking reactions or acting as simple followers of competitive actions.

Further, every company should assess how a 1 percent price improvement could bring additional results to shareholders. It's evident when performing this exercise that companies working with tighter margins, such as wholesalers, manufacturers of commoditized products,[1] and sectors that are highly dispersed with several competitors would benefit much more percentage-wise than companies already operating with very healthy margins. Regardless, captures of 1 percent or more, from my experience in more than 10 years of consulting projects, are highly feasible and are available to almost any company that has the desire and conviction to implement more price management strategies.

Projects generating value

After 14 years and more than 140 projects, I can share some of the results and benefits of pricing projects based on these experiences.

To assess the impact that Quantiz had on the market, we surveyed all the projects conducted. I present the average impacts generated to give you an order of magnitude of what pricing is capable of accomplishing for a business.

Of course, factors such as sector level of competitiveness, product or brand differentials, preproject pricing stage, project team quality, and execution capacity, among many other variables, can affect results. Sometimes competitors make our lives a little more difficult as well. In other cases, we realize that they're doing nothing, which helps us achieve better numbers.

To begin evaluating the projects' results, we took the average annual revenue of those clients for whom we monitored the results

---

1   *Commoditized product* is a term I use to define something very common but not necessarily a commodity itself. A commodity is soy or oil, for example, for which prices are set by an exchange in Chicago or London. A commoditized product, on the other hand, has several similar forms or substitutes, but they can still be differentiated in some way, such as by brand or by quality.

at the time of the project, without any monetary correction, which totaled R$ 3.5 billion. Bear in mind that these are values that have been available since 2007; currently, on average, they should be much larger than that in nominal terms given Brazilian inflation over this period.

The average result obtained in terms of increased contribution margin generated by the projects, measuring total contribution margin generated in reais (or dollars) in the current year versus the previous year for the same stores (or the same items) and/or measuring the impact on the total contribution margin in reais comparing a pilot area with a mirror area, was between 0.5 percent (the lowest result we consider successful for companies with commodity products) and 14 percent (the best result obtained, so far).

Translating this to profits, these results generated, on average, an increase of 2.79 percent in the company's revenue linked with a high degree of confidence in pricing initiatives. That is, for each R$ 1 billion in revenue, we were able to generate a gain of R$ 27.9 million in gross BRL (Brazilian reais). Multiplied by the average annual revenue of the customers for which we measure these gains, we have an annual impact of practically R$ 98 million in total (R$ 3.5 billion × 2.79%)!

Multiplying by the number of years we've been in the market (nearly 15 years), it would be something like R$ 1.4 billion generated by our projects. Besides, almost another half of the projects we did were implemented without our participation or results from monitoring, and we know that our clients approved them because they either hired us again or referred us to other clients. Therefore, we can imagine that they must have obtained similar results, which would lead us to another amount close to R$ 1.4 billion generated over these years of work—therefore, almost R$ 3 billion in additional profit generated in total!

As of this writing, the dollar is worth just over R$ 5.00. But during the years for which we evaluated our projects, it varied between R$ 1.50 and R$ 4.00 (end of 2019); these higher dollar values are occurring only now, in 2020. The average dollar for the period of analysis is a little below R$ 3.00. So, converting the almost R$ 3 billion reais generated in our projects, we can assume that we generated just over $1 billion in additional profit for our clients during these years.

Some might think that the total looks like a good value but that dividing by the number of years and number of customers renders it less interesting. Some initiatives can have a much greater impact. And they're probably right to think that way. The difficulties of being able to capture value in pricing projects are numerous. First, we don't control the whole process. An important part of our prices ends up being interconnected with the prices of our main competitors. If they start a price war during the project, or at any other time, what we can capture is difficult.

Another relevant aspect is that products that are heavily influenced by the cost of raw materials end up being held hostage by market fluctuations related to supply and demand that override much of what pricing can or cannot do. Finally, in some companies, overcoming barriers to change is difficult, and in some cases, their teams end up boycotting the initiatives.

Even so, most of the time, as shown above, we achieved results and relevant impacts for a business. Wouldn't it be interesting for your company to be able to count on a 2.79 percent higher revenue directly impacting this amount on your absolute contribution margin in reais (or dollars)? Most of the CEOs I talk to think so.

It's also important to note that the focus must be on the absolute contribution margin in reais (or dollars). I experienced a negotiation where the CEO wanted to increase his percentage contribution margin from 27 percent to 30 percent. I said that this would be easy to do because simply by raising prices, the percentage margin would reach 30 percent. He quickly understood and replied about volume. And then I answered that he was correct, and that that is why we need to measure the absolute margin and not the percentages. Interestingly, the project at that company resulted in a loss of percentage margin, reaching 27 percent, but with an absolute margin gain of just over 7 percent. In other words, some prices fell in favor of greater volume in some lines, compensated by other products becoming more premium, resulting in busier factories and better total results. After all, pricing can help any company increase market share and profit margins at the same time.

My experience working with the C-suite

Key learnings and why C-suite involvement is essential to the success of pricing projects

During my career leading Quantiz, I have met well over 500 CEOs from the most important firms in Brazil. CEOs come from very different backgrounds, from traditional graduates of the best universities with an MBA in the US to businessmen who left school without even completing high school and managed to build empires. Personalities are also different. Some are more expansive and engaging; others are quiet and prefer to listen more than talk.

Given this diversity, it's impossible to generalize about behaviors as common to all. For this reason, we have to develop strategies to ensure the involvement and support of CEOs in projects.

The importance of CEO involvement can be presented in three main pillars: point north, ensure commitment, and embrace change.

Beginning with the right strategy, it's imperative that we be clear about where we're going or want to go, that is, what the company is trying to reach, so that the pricing area or project can structure the correct pricing strategy to achieve the result.

In a simplistic way, if a company needs to differentiate itself and wants to seek technological leadership in the sector, for example, it isn't low prices that will bring the expected results; instead, it's R&D investment, product performance, great services—all of which require money. Hence, a premium price strategy might be more suitable for the long-term goals of such a firm.

Likewise, if another company seeks market share growth and needs to compete on low prices to achieve this goal, the entire structure must be efficient; we need economies of scale, access to suppliers or raw materials under favorable conditions, among other things. A lack of alignment between corporate strategy and pricing strategy risks undermining the success of the initiative.

Any project needs to be implemented before it can bring results. Pricing projects have an impact on commercial, marketing, and sometimes even finance processes. In addition, it's common to see changes in mix, volume, and distribution that affect production, logistics, and supply chain.

In other words, given this chain of impacts within the organization, the entire company must be committed to supporting the project. One way to ensure commitment is a good communication plan from the CEO, supporting an understanding of the importance of the project and its impacts.

In addition, by aligning incentives, you can keep the different areas involved more united around a successful project.

Finally, companies that do not change will eventually die. CEOs must lead and embrace change and prepare the organization to move forward, breaking with old habits and trying new ones. For our most successful projects in Brazil, CEOs were key in leading change in their organizations. Many were hiring our firm to help them move ahead with their pricing and revenue management initiatives.

On the other hand, CEOs who won't get involved or who don't believe in what's being developed will most likely be responsible for the failure of any initiative. Fortunately, they're the exception, not the rule. But I've experienced situations in which CEOs spoke of seeking profitability and margin growth but refused to lose a single point of market share; others diverged on the objectives for each area, asking marketing/pricing to focus on margins but the commercial team to say that the goals for volume were what mattered. And I also had a skeptic CEO who simply said that he didn't believe in rules and processes for the commercial area, which should have complete flexibility in conducting its negotiations.

Evidently, in such environments, pricing projects can't easily thrive.

The biggest lesson I learned from some frustrating experiences was, before beginning any project, to always align expectations with the CEO of the hiring company. Having clarity of direction, purpose, and willingness to lead the change are the necessary requirements so that initiatives like these can generate the expected results.

The top 10 benefits of adopting strategic pricing

Pricing projects don't just affect financial results. Pricing brings not only quantitative but also qualitative results. Several aspects can be improved in a company through price management processes. Below I list and briefly describe each one so that you can evaluate your own company and see which could be applied to obtain qualitative gains in management. The list is not exhaustive. There are many other qualitative benefits one can think about when a company has a clear focus on implementing strategic pricing management, but I believe introducing just a few will be good enough to start thinking about all the possibilities.

1. Positioning yourself in the market

Positioning your products in the market is a constant challenge, as consumer preferences change, competitors' prices fluctuate, inflation forces price adjustments, margins of sales channels can vary significantly, and, in the case of Brazil, our tax model leaves the situation even more complex.

So, given all the variables we have to control, what seemed easy before ends up complicated. Many companies try to simplify by assuming an X percent standard above or below the competition, but this system eliminates their strategy, and their products end up being held hostage by the prices of competing brands, which in most cases is harmful to their business and only favors the competitors. That's, of course, when they know what they're doing. Because if they're also lost or following you, the situation won't be good for any of the players.

In this sense, a pricing project can offer clear methodologies for how to set prices, including adequate margins in the chain, positioning based on price ranges by channel or region, or even national prices if we follow a single price strategy. In this process, we can include surveys of customer perception of value, if the product, brand, or service has differentials, of course. We can also use mathematical modeling to find optimal prices or exponential positions for product lines with good-better-best variants, among other possibilities.

Price positioning also reinforces the brand's pricing power. Knowing how to position yourself in the market and execute your pricing strategy well allows your company to avoid unnecessary price wars and educates the consumer about the value of what you have to offer. Therefore, knowing how to position your prices in the market can be a qualitative gain that ends up yielding financial results.

2. Making your commercial policy reflect your business strategy

I still remember one of our first projects when the CEO of a beverage company, explaining his strategy, told me that his company needed to stop being a brewery in order to become a real beverage company. My response was quick because the company's entire discount policy was still attached to beer volume: that is, "if you want to do good business with us, buy a lot of beer and we'll have the lowest price."

In this scenario, your strategy would never be implemented in the market. Distributors and customers, in general, continued to buy more and more beer instead of other items in the portfolio in order to earn more and more discounts, rebates, and bonuses.

By aligning our commercial policy through granting discounts mainly for the product mix (quantity of items) ordered and reducing the importance of discounts in the volume of beer, we began to achieve the sale of soft drinks, energy drinks, water, fruit juices, and other items produced and bottled by the company.

This is just an example. Our business strategy may have different needs. For example, I need to spread my sales, so it doesn't make sense to differentiate the price much between large and small customers. The regularity of purchases is something strategic for our logistics, so I have to create some incentive for our customers to buy regularly and frequently to optimize my operation. I may have a strategy for reducing cash flow, so I can offer a good discount for payment in cash or through other forms of payment where the fees are lower. And so on.

At Quantiz we have a list of more than 20 incentives we've used in several projects over time. Each company needs to define its strategy and then choose which incentives to offer to the market so that it can be executed. Think of trade policy as the link between strategy and execution!

3. Being transparent with your commercial policy

Since we're talking about commercial policy, an important pillar for it to survive in the market is its credibility. It's useless for a company to define a commercial policy if the sales area negotiates everything as an exception or outside the established rules. Such behavior will lead customers to bluff all the time, and, within a few months after defining a commercial policy, your company will end up negotiating case by case, without an underlying strategy, and remaining in the hands of what each salesperson thinks is the best strategy.

Therefore, giving the commercial policy full transparency is fundamental for it to begin gaining credibility in the market. It may seem strange to many sales managers that it opens all avenues for the customer to know how to make a good deal with the company, but studies show that when negotiation limits are made clear, buyers accept the rules and tend to do business more easily.

Also, if the incentives are well structured, for each discount offered there will be an interesting counterpart for the company and something valued by the customer. It's a typical win-win negotiation. It's excellent when we achieve this in the market. We gain credibility and trust from our customers, and that has value.

4. Reducing conflict between sales channels

When implementing a transparent commercial policy in the market, in addition to the benefits mentioned above, another important component that can be defined is the role of each channel and their respective prices within ranges that do not make them compete with each other.

Evidently, in the much more volatile, agile, troubled, and uncertain world we are currently experiencing, sales channels often end up mixing. Some companies, as a result, begin looking for an omnichannel price guaranteeing consumers prices, if not equal, within a very close range regardless of the channel. This is also possible only with clear and well-executed policies.

But in most situations in Brazil, companies have different channel strategies by region. One of our clients, for example, had a direct salesforce in the State of São Paulo with excellent coverage. If they left low prices for wholesalers in this state, their direct sales would certainly be affected, and they would end up migrating the volume to the wholesaler, who generally paid lower prices than the final customer in a direct sale.

On the other hand, this same company depended heavily on distributors and wholesalers to get its products to more distant regions of the country, in states like Acre, Rondônia, and others. In these states, it made sense to offer aggressive prices so that wholesalers could take the products to more retailers in those regions where their own salesforce was unable to adequately cover the market.

To increase complexity, we are currently faced with marketplaces and companies selling over the internet at prices often much lower than traditional retail channels. If the company that manufactures these products does not want to see a price war between its business partners, it needs, through a clear commercial policy, to define appropriate margins for each channel and thereby establish its sell prices. In other words, the price management of the entire chain should be organized by the industry so that the value it offers its end consumers isn't lost in the sales channels.

5. Segmenting your customers

We just talked about how differentiating prices by sales channel is one way to segment the market. However, this is often not enough, because even within a specific channel, we may have very different shopping behaviors among the channel's participants.

In general, in addition to quantitative segmentation, we should think about customer purchasing behavior. It's common to have at least four purchase profiles: the loyal customer, who values your company and doesn't press too hard for price; the price customer, who's just the opposite, who presses hard for price and isn't very concerned about which company they will buy from; and the convenience customer, who doesn't press for the price, because they have some urgent need but little value for what they offer. Finally, the customer profile that grows the most in almost all markets is the one who seeks the best cost-benefit ratio. In other words, they value differentials and quality but negotiate or seek lower prices.

Therefore, knowing how to segment customers not only by their quantitative and objective profile but also by purchasing behavior is necessary to adapt the offers and prices for each of these segments. Each profile responds to different incentives, so the suggestion we leave is that the company needs to define a variety of solutions to reach the greatest possible number of customers in a structured and organized way, maintaining control over which customer receives which offer.

Another way of thinking is to let customers self-segment. For this, the company needs to build a menu of offers and let each customer choose the one that makes the most sense.

A client in the medical equipment field worked in this direction. Customers had the option of purchasing an imaging machine at the lowest possible price, but without any additional services. At the other extreme of supply, in addition to the machine being able to be purchased for financing, customers could purchase preventive maintenance plans, warranties, and consumables, and even outsource the operation of the machines themselves, and there were many combinations of options between these two extremes.

That is, each customer could choose the best way to be served: from the customer who just wanted a price to the customer seeking a complete solution to their needs for imaging operations in a hospital.

6. Defining your prices by perceived value, not just by markup

A company can choose from several methods to form prices. The most traditional and most frequently used, based on our experience and on research from major consultants, is what we call a markup. In this method, the starting point is the cost of the product, and the manager defines the objective margin they would like to obtain for the product, estimates a certain volume of sales, and thereby defines the markup, which is nothing more than a factor that applies to the purchase or purchase cost.

It's an easy method to use. It has additional advantages, such as the near certainty that the margin obtained will be close to the adopted markup and a guarantee that its costs will be covered. However, its greatest weakness is precisely to be directed toward financial objectives or goals within the company, ignoring competitors' prices or perceived value by the customer (B2B) or consumer (B2C).

In this perception of value, it's precisely the great opportunity to capture greater margins for the products and services that we offer to the market. Whenever a company has a competitive advantage that's relevant to any segment in which it operates, there's an opportunity to price by understanding the quantitative value that customers perceive and how much they're willing to pay for these advantages.

To assess these perceived values, some kind of research with your customers is necessary. There are several research techniques available to help a company define this differential value, and it's not the purpose of this chapter to explain them. The idea here is just to reinforce that the result of a pricing project can be a change in the way companies price their products, adding more sophisticated methods and allowing greater capture of value for what's offered.

7. Increasing your profitability (sustainably)

Price increases have limits. A common mistake is to believe that after a few rounds of price increases, even for differentiated products with low elasticity, volumes will remain stable or experience minimal drops, guaranteeing a permanent increase in profitability.

The problem is that the market is dynamic, and there are acceptable price ranges for any product. In other words, as we begin to approach the upper limit of this price range, we begin to put this strategy of consecutive price increases at risk.

For price increases, I speak of those real price increases and not just a replacement for inflation. Nominal price increases are almost expected annually for an inflation reset or some other adjustment in the tables, but real increases are those that go beyond just an inflation pass-through. Some involve a whole product repositioning, with new benefits or marketing campaigns. Others, however, merely reflect a new positioning found by some product-line equation technique that finds positioning exponentially, for example.

In these cases, in the absence of research to support the new positions, many companies end up adopting a practice of trial and error, which is also valid. Dynamic pricing algorithms test consumer limits and responses all the time. The big mistake here is to ignore these limits and to increase prices, believing that the product, once inelastic, will always be inelastic.

All products have limits. A good example of this was the launch of the Apple X at prices of around US $1,500. Even with all the strength of the brand, pricing power, and loyal customers, Apple experienced a lower demand than expected precisely because they probably exceeded what many would accept. Of course, the price ranges might vary from customer to customer, but it's clear that many customers might have similar price ranges.

Whenever a previously inelastic product begins to suffer from greater elasticity, it's a reason for concern. The entire pricing project needs to be sensitive to these limits to ensure that the results are sustainable. There's no point in eagerly attempting to capture value without respecting how much a product, service, or brand can handle.

Good price projects focus on absolute margins, as we've already said, and this absolute dollar margin must always be increasing. A sudden drop in this indicator is a strong sign that something's wrong!

8. Aligning the commercial team's compensation with the company's objectives

A relevant aspect for the success of any pricing initiative is the alignment of the organization's objectives with its employees, especially those on the commercial team.

We've tried many times to implement pricing projects, seeking to increase margins or improve profitability, where the entire sales team was commissioned. That is, it received a percentage of sales revenue regardless of the margin obtained in a transaction. Any lost sale was one fewer commission and soon something to be avoided at all costs. Even if the cost of this was for the company to sell at a loss!

This is not a simple problem to solve. We often need to involve the human resources or legal departments to review employment contracts, remuneration rules, and so forth.

However, although it's difficult to change and can even lead to the loss of some good sales staff, I recommend that any company seeking to embark on a pricing journey ensure the alignment of incentives and remuneration of its commercial team with the objectives of the company.

Going further, the objectives should be common to the entire organization. Sales, logistics, finance, marketing…When we enter companies that already remunerate their teams with objectives associated with profit or margin, their implementation ends up being much easier.

I remember a commodities company that we operated long ago where we were received by the commercial area as saviors. They'd adopted a remuneration model based on profitability a year earlier but were having difficulty bringing this increase, which impacted the team's bonuses and awards.

When, at the kickoff, the president announced to his employees that our goal was to help them find opportunities to improve profitability, which would lead to more bonuses for the salespeople, we received a standing ovation! This happened only once, and it was one of the projects where the implementation went smoothly, with virtually no inconveniences, and the results exceeded everyone's expectations!

9. Optimizing your prices systematically

From my first projects as a consultant in 2006 and 2007 to the time of this writing (2020), I've seen the biggest transformation in solutions happen in technology. Large databases, more information, business intelligence systems, open-source analytical tools, pricing algorithms, among other transformations, have opened up a range of opportunities for increasingly robust, responsive, dynamic, and systematized solutions.

The use of Excel, the tool I used to develop price simulators, analyses, and graphs, among other things, no longer serves. It has important limitations relative to larger databases, automation, and so forth. And the speed at which this tool stopped serving was amazing.

Currently, projects need to be developed using Microsoft PowerBI with adaptations programmed in 6\3 Python using statistical functions brought from R (statistical software). Others, even more robust, require systematic pricing algorithms using AI in the cloud with machine learning. At Quantiz we use Azure, from Microsoft, but one could use any other company that offers this type of platform.

In other words, price optimization was always something very distant in the mid-2000s when I began doing projects; today, it's trivial for many companies that have the data, culture, and investments necessary to reach this level of sophistication.

From the point of view of consumers, it's increasingly clear that they accept dynamic prices as a way for retailers and companies to offer their products and services. Otherwise, Amazon wouldn't be what it is today!

Another advantage of this type of systematization is the elimination of human error. We cannot manage thousands of items with all their possible combinations using a spreadsheet. We need to use the currently available alternatives.

Finally, the costs involved in this type of solution have been dropping for 10 years. In the past, we could say that a high investment requirement was justification for not doing a systematization project. However, given the fees offered today by several suppliers, even this excuse is no longer valid.

10. Managing your price strategically

If you've reached this point in the chapter, it's because you like what you've read, and this topic sums up everything said so far.

For any company to reach the stage where it will be doing strategic price management, it will need to accomplish most (if not all) of the aspects we've covered.

Having robust processes for defining strategies, business policies, customer segmentation, value surveys, systems, and compensation aligned with objectives, among other activities, are not easy or simple tasks. Unfortunately, many organizational leaders still see prices as tactical or trivial, something that doesn't deserve all the attention of the C-suite.

As I mentioned at the beginning, I've been working with pricing for over 20 years. I've participated in business transformations based on strategic price management that allowed companies to change their level in terms of brand recognition, market share, profitability, price positioning in the market, and pricing power, among many other benefits.

Finally, I invite everyone to rethink the strategic importance they're giving to price management in their companies. There's probably no area in the company that has greater potential to unlock quick and consistent gains for the business. Think strategically. Think pricing!

The author

Frederico Zornig is a founding partner of Quantiz Pricing Solutions. With over 25 years of professional experience, he has worked on more than 150 major pricing projects in Brazil and Latin America with some of the most important companies in the market in various sectors of the economy. He has been a member of the Professional Pricing Society and a presenter at its Annual Pricing Conferences for over 15 years, both in Brazil and abroad. He taught Pricing at FGV/SP for over 10 years in MBA and other graduate-level courses. He is the author of two books and several articles on pricing published in Brazil and abroad. A graduate in Chemical Engineering from UNICAMP, he holds an MBA from the University of Illinois. He can be reached via email at fzornig@ quantiz.com.br or through his company website, www.quantiz .com.br/.

SECTION 3

PRICING TESTIMONIALS

10

The Thales Way:
Seven Surprising Insights
from a Pricing Journey

*Camille Brégé, Managing Director
and Partner in the Paris office
of the Boston Consulting Group;
Karen Lellouche Tordjman,
Managing Director and Partner in
the Mexico City office of the Boston
Consulting Group;
and Pierre Schaeffer, SVP, CMO,
Thales Group*

WHEN A LARGE COMPANY undertakes a pricing improvement program for its business lines, the overarching objectives and expectations are usually easy to express: find some basic improvement areas for pricing, identify substantial upside, and then achieve it quickly with a combination of tools and training.

But those simple statements often face considerable skepticism and resistance, not only from senior executives but from team members involved in marketing and sales. No matter how compelling the upside promises are, there's a risk that the C-level team thinks that a solution requires too much time and effort, especially in a decentralized organization. It will be complicated, disruptive, and expensive, with limited impact. Likewise, there's a risk that team members will see "pricing initiative" as code words for something that will be time-consuming, distracting, boring, or intimidating.

The French industrial conglomerate Thales, however, showed that this skepticism and resistance are either exaggerated or misplaced. The group has seen its gross margins improve from 25 percent to 31 percent after a series of pricing initiatives undertaken since 2013 as part of its 10-year transformation effort (called DIX). The Thales CFO recently reported that the group's revenue is growing by around 5 percent per year, with half that growth from acquisition and the other half organic. They attribute the organic growth to improved product competitiveness, increased management focus, and a fundamental shift from cost-plus pricing to value-based pricing.

Boston Consulting Group (BCG) worked closely with the Thales teams on some of these pricing initiatives, at the group and business-line level. Together, we uncovered several insights that will help both C-level executives and team members overcome their initial skepticism and engage actively in initiatives that yield real, lasting benefits.

We summarize the seven most important and surprising insights below.

Insight 1: You can't always grow your own pricing talent

Finding skilled people to manage and perform pricing at a high level is challenging. Pricing touches so many functions (marketing, sales, sometimes product development) and is both qualitative and quantitative. People who are equally comfortable as storytellers and data scientists are in short supply.

This raises a critical question that Thales also faced: should a company promote from within, creating new attractive career paths, or bring in talent from outside the organization?

There's no watertight answer to that question. It depends on how well the necessary skill sets match the existing pool of talent. You need people who are quantitatively strong but who also understand business implications and can appreciate the difference between pricing theory and an actionable business lever. In addition, pricing is a "soft" topic, especially in businesses that depend heavily on price negotiations. The pricing leader may set the guidelines but is usually not present when the salespeople negotiate the final prices. The ability to communicate with the salespeople is a vitally important skill, from the standpoint of training, tools, and general advice.

It didn't make sense to transfer team members from one business line to another. Thales needed a deeper and stronger bench, so the group recruited from the outside for the pricing roles at some business lines. At the same time, a new central team assumed responsibility for pricing training and implementation, under leadership from a pricing expert recruited externally. This team, under the leadership of Stephan Liozu, served as a catalyst for top management involvement and for the ongoing momentum. Liozu and his team also established training and certification programs to enhance internal capabilities.

Insight 2: Disrupting within the existing structure is better than changing the structure

As the 2020s dawn, ideas for business model innovation abound. From the subscription economy to "anything as a service" to outcome-based pricing, companies in almost every sector are thinking about how they can transform their business models in order to achieve faster growth and greater differentiation.

While BCG would always encourage firms to think big and aim high, sometimes the fastest and most enduring improvements occur when a company focuses on finding better ways to improve what they already do. As CMO Schaeffer points out, Thales did not change the structure right away.

"We started by creating a network of pricers, and then animating this network," he said. "Now that the organization is mature, we are making some changes, such as the creation of the role of bid-pricing manager."

The successes Thales has experienced confirm that sometimes it's better to disrupt within an existing structure than to change the structure. This "walk before you can run" thinking fits well with the initiatives the Thales Group undertook.

The business lines within Thales have very different products and customer bases. One unit sells parts to aircraft manufacturers; a sister unit sells parts maintenance services to the airlines that buy or operate those aircraft. Others business lines specialize in specific types of aircraft (e.g., helicopters) or certain customer groups (e.g., military). The selling processes of the businesses also vary. Some are purely transactional; others have longer selling cycles due to bidding processes and negotiations. Some of the units already use subscription models.

Rather than consider ways to blow up or redirect those markets and models, Thales focused instead on customized ways to help each business line get more out of its existing market and its current business model. The work began with defining each business on its own terms: How many customers do they have? How much of the business is transactional versus recurring? How loyal are the customers? What is the mix between small- and big-ticket items? How have these data trended in recent years?

Analyses of these trends quickly revealed improvement potential. One business unit discovered that it had underpriced its products and services when it either had a captive customer (no competition) or had "invisible" offerings, which are those that the customer considers a lower-effort purchase decision. Whenever the product was visible and faced competition, the unit could tighten the logic it used to set prices. These efforts within the existing system yielded revenue improvement of between 0.9 percent and 4.6 percent and much larger margin impacts, depending on the product or service.

Insight 3: "KISS" still matters in the 2020s

Amid all the buzz about unprecedented technological advancements over the last decade, it's refreshing to experience that the old acronym KISS ("Keep It Simple, Stupid") remains relevant so deep into the 21st century.

The "tools" part of the solution for the pricing initiatives at Thales could have involved sophisticated, state-of-the-art black boxes that would generate precision prices with the push of a button. Instead, they relied on conventional spreadsheet software.

Why use Excel-based tools when you can take a powerful black box off the shelf? The Excel option is good news for executives and team members in many ways. First, building customized tools on an Excel platform is a huge advantage in terms of cost and simplicity. The organization doesn't need a huge IT implementation that requires ongoing specialized training, above and beyond the actual pricing training. Excel is already installed, and users are familiar with and conversant in it.

There are many reasons we normally do not see spreadsheet-based solutions as a best practice. Files can get corrupted, users can change cells, and the user interface is not ideal. At the same time, when team members are improving their pricing skills, it helps for them to "feel" where the prices come from. In general, the lower the pricing maturity of a team is, the wiser it is to skip the black boxes—at least at first—and teach people how to build the price number from the ground up, so that they understand the mechanics and see what's involved.

"Our organization is full of Doubting Thomases," Schaeffer said. "We need to see things work before we believe in them." That has inspired a culture of pilot-testing instead of grander "big bang" rollouts, another argument for starting with Excel-based tools instead of black boxes.

Sophisticated tools can play a role after a team's maturity level has developed. If you overshoot and go with a black box too early, you can kill a team's enthusiasm and end up reinforcing the skepticism you wanted to eliminate. It's better to build an accessible bridge so that a team can be comfortable taking the next level.

Insight 4: Mobilizing top management is essential in many ways

The size of the opportunity from pricing improvement—combined with the fact that pricing directly or indirectly impacts so many functions—should make pricing not only a topic top managers should monitor but also something they should actively engage in and guide.

Nonetheless, many B2B organizations have historically treated pricing as a lower-level tactical matter rather than a strategic challenge. As a result, efforts to improve or optimize it would generally take place "bottom up" rather than "top down," with senior managers and C-level executives only tangentially involved. Top managers, as we mentioned at the outset, are often skeptical about the time and effort involved in a complex and potentially disruptive initiative.

The program at Thales took an entirely different approach by mobilizing top managers as active participants in the various pricing initiatives. Thales viewed both bottom-up and top-down support and engagement as essential success factors. Senior managers and C-level executives took part in both word and deed.

One reason for the heavy involvement of business unit leaders is that Thales is a large, diversified, and decentralized B2B group comprising several business lines, each with autonomous, independent decision-making power. A fully integrated, one-size-fits-all program on any business issue—but especially pricing—makes no sense for a business group of that kind, even if some superficial similarities exist across units. Approaching the project in such a manner would be worse than trying to fit the proverbial round peg in a square hole. It would mean trying to cram triangular, rectangular, and oval pegs into that same square hole as well, with little or no chance of short-term or long-term success.

Insight 5: Getting sales onboard is a mindset challenge, not a monetary one

In line with the second insight above, each of the pricing initiatives at Thales endeavored to work within existing systems rather than impose new ones. The same thinking applied to sales incentives. Incentive systems are common targets for pricing initiatives at B2B companies because they often create conflicts between volume or revenue targets and profit or margin targets. The idea behind changing incentives is that a company can improve its pricing performance—and thus its profitability—by bringing objectives and incentives into better alignment and rewarding the "right" behaviors.

Thales left the incentive systems and the key performance indicators (KPIs) for sales teams unchanged. Instead, the group focused on trainings that helped salespeople understand how sensitive certain KPIs—such as customer satisfaction—are to their actions. Salespeople tend to like their clients and want to preserve good customer satisfaction scores. Refusing to give discounts, or asking explicitly for higher prices, could not only jeopardize those scores but perhaps put the relationship at risk.

The counterargument is that customers will naturally always have some level of dissatisfaction with pricing, unless a firm's prices are egregiously low to begin with. That level of dissatisfaction is manageable, however, as long as any price changes have a strong underlying story built on quality and value arguments. In other words, it's fine to have higher prices as long as the reasons are sound.

One important approach at Thales was to ensure that the salespeople heard that message clearly and loudly from their colleagues, not only from an outside party or a central pricing team. Few things are more convincing than the stories and insights from someone who has had relevant firsthand experience with implementing price changes. These exchanges, supported by internal benchmarks, encouraged salespeople to emulate the techniques and performance of their colleagues rather than rely solely on their own interpretation of the training materials.

This simple but powerful approach helped salespeople overcome their mental barrier to seeking higher prices. Changing mindset and behaviors was more effective and less risky than experimenting with different monetary incentives.

Insight 6: The answer to the question "decentralized or centralized?" is "both"

It's easy to say "don't reinvent the wheel," but how do you ensure that an organization avoids that trap? It comes down to finding the right way to exchange knowledge and train staff.

There's a misperception that training is synonymous with lectures, Q&A sessions, and homework. The alternative idea is that people will naturally train themselves if you give them the right platform. Thales took the latter approach to knowledge exchange by facilitating the sharing of ideas among team members. Rather than take a strictly centralized or decentralized approach, the group tapped into the strengths of both approaches. A central team identified and classified problems and drafted the playbooks with solutions. But instead of forcing ideas on other teams, the central pricing group publicized the results, created awareness, and encouraged interteam exchanges.

Centralization creates efficiencies because a business unit can find and adapt a solution from a sister business rather than coming up with their own solution from scratch. But decentralization improves effectiveness because it respects the specific circumstances of each business line. The playbooks give them a head start toward a solution rather than a strict top-down mandate.

Insight 7: The first six insights lead to speed and inspiration

The process of implementing pricing changes and achieving upside can move very quickly. After only three months for the specific initiatives we participated in, each of the Thales business lines learned what its strongest pricing levers are and had the guidance and tools to take advantage of them.

When an organization keeps in mind the insights we described above, its pricing initiatives can move faster than senior leaders and team members might think, be simpler and leaner than they think, and deliver real impact sooner. The success with pricing initiatives can also inspire an organization to undertake more far-reaching sales and commercial transformations, as Thales has done.

•

C-level executives are sometimes skeptical of pricing improvement initiatives, which inevitably require tools and training. They view the initiatives as potentially complicated, disruptive, and expensive, and worry that their marketing and sales teams will find the efforts to be time-consuming, distracting, boring, and intimidating.

The work we completed together with Thales showed that a large and diverse industrial conglomerate can achieve quick margin improvement without shocking the system or breaking the bank. The surprising insights above demonstrate that a company can find and implement simple but effective solutions that team members can embrace.

The authors

Pierre Schaeffer is SVP and Chief Marketing Officer of the Thales Group, located in Paris, France. Throughout his international career, serving brands like Apple, Kodak, or Michelin, Pierre has successfully defined and executed growth strategies in a variety of B2C and B2B high-technology markets. Since joining Thales six years ago as Chief Marketing Officer, Pierre has installed and orchestrated the global marketing function with a special focus on enhancing customer-value-based innovation and practices at the service of customer satisfaction and the group's profitable growth ambitions. Pierre holds a degree in chemical engineering and a DEA in artificial intelligence. He can be reached at www.linkedin.com/in/pierreschaeffer/.

Camille Brégé is a Managing Director and Partner in the Paris office of the Boston Consulting Group. She leads the B2B Pricing topic for BCG, and she is a core member of BCG Gamma, the data science team of BCG. Over the last 14 years, she has worked for major industrial goods companies, focusing on holistic top-line strategy development, implementation of new pricing models, and optimization of pricing performance leveraging advanced analytics and artificial intelligence. You can reach her by email at brege.camille@bcg.com.

Karen Lellouche Tordjman is a Managing Director and Partner in the Mexico City office of the Boston Consulting Group. She leads the Customer Experience topic globally for BCG and is a BCG Henderson Institute fellow, researching the future of customer interactions. Over the last 17 years, she has worked for many companies across the world, in Europe, in the US, and in Latin America, helping them design and implement customer-centric transformations, leveraging digital and data. You can reach her by email at lellouche.karen@bcg.com.

Leaders Set the Tone for Strategic Pricing: An Interview with Sonya Roberts, President, Cargill Salt

11

Valerie Howard   Sonya, it's such a pleasure to have this opportunity to interview you for Stephan's book. You've had an incredible career. Those of us who have the good fortune to have been in your presence know how you glow with leadership capability and expertise, but for those readers who haven't yet had the pleasure to meet you or see you speak—can you help our audience with a brief perspective on your background and career?

Sonya   Thank you, Valerie. Today I'm the president and group leader at Cargill Salt, a division of Cargill,

233

Incorporated, one of the largest privately held corporations in the US. I began my career in finance at Conoco [ConocoPhillips] and moved through various positions of increasing responsibility in strategy, planning and leadership over 19 years. I came to Cargill in 2008 and assumed leadership roles in sales and marketing and general management.

Valerie Thanks so much for that background, Sonya. Now, given that this is a book about pricing, some may be surprised to see a leader from commodities businesses providing perspective on pricing. Isn't pricing in commodities typically predetermined?

Sonya You're right that the products themselves—lubricants at ConocoPhillips and salt here at Cargill—are likely to be considered commodities by our customers. Salt is simply NaCl—a pure and simple chemical makeup. But it's everything around that commodity—whether it be our service, our technical expertise, our people, our product quality, our geographic location, or the credibility we've built around our brand—that makes us unique and drives our customers to choose Cargill. Cargill wants to deliver products and services to help stakeholders thrive, ultimately to be more successful with us than anyone else. Success will always mean something different to different stakeholders, so it's our job to find out how a customer defines success. Once you understand what your customer wants, strategic pricing is simply about understanding your value proposition, communicating your value proposition, and capturing/measuring your value proposition tied to your customer's wants. That happens in just about every industry.

In salt, some customers will be very concerned that their shipments are reliably delivered within a very narrow time window. Some customers want to have access to technical expertise. Some customers just want the cheapest price every time. You need to understand what your customers value. These elements of reliability, responsiveness, and relationship help to build trust that isn't easily replaced by a substitute vendor. As you truly understand and deliver on your customer's needs better than competition, enabling them to thrive, you in turn can economically benefit.

Valerie For many businesses, they may not be tracking all these variables consistently. Most order statements contain a limited set of information: products, order date, expected delivery. How would you recommend that business leaders approach uncovering the variables that drive differing perceptions in value?

Sonya You've got to push the bounds. As Nelson Mandela said, "I never lose. I either win or learn."

Every interaction with a customer is an opportunity to learn what drives real value and then engage in sensible risk-taking to capture that value. You must move beyond only talking to buyers or you'll seldom move beyond price negotiations. Customers' buyers will almost always tell your sales team that a price increase is going to push them to walk away. If they didn't say that, they wouldn't be doing their job. But unless you test it, you'll never know where you sit relative to your customer's next-best available option. If you've never lost business in a particular market segment, I'd argue that you're leaving money on the table.

Valerie That makes a lot of sense. Each buyer is going to have different needs and a different willingness to pay based on the constraints of their own business. But it wouldn't scale well to drive these extensive conversations in every negotiation. How can you scale uncovering the value perceptions of your buyers?

Sonya This is where understanding your market segments comes into play. Among your customers, there are similarities in buying behavior that may reveal how the buyers in certain segments perceive you—what makes your business preferable to the competition and perhaps which aspects of your offering they don't value.

What's key is that these commonalities in buying behavior don't necessarily coincide with generic market segmentations. What I mean by that is that simple revenue size, industry, and geography segmentations may not get you to the right answer. Often you must go much deeper to understand the real market segmentation.

What we did at Cargill Salt is work with a software pricing company to make sense of our buying communities. By leveraging the power of statistical science to comb through our historical sales data, they were able to identify the variables of each transaction that would drive significant variation in purchase price. Once we had this understanding, we could coalesce the "price segments" and predict what the actual willingness to pay of our customers was. We could also identify where we had been underpricing and had significant revenue recovery opportunity and where we were overpricing and could capture additional market share.

Valerie   Can you share why—amid all the potential areas of strategic investment—pricing was a prioritized initiative for your team at Cargill Salt?

Sonya   At Cargill Salt, we were updating our strategy. In that strategy work, we highlighted inorganic (e.g., acquisitions, joint ventures, venture capital) opportunities and organic opportunities for growth. In those discussions, strategic pricing was identified as an organic growth opportunity. While there were many organic opportunities identified in this process, strategic pricing was one of the most immediate and impactful levers.

Valerie   Even though there's typically so much upside in improving pricing, we see a lot of skepticism when we present the opportunity. How was it that your teams were so convinced of the priority at Cargill Salt?

Sonya   Admittedly, there was significant skepticism in seeing that initial opportunity assessment. Your ego tells you "there's no way I'm leaving that much money on the table." But we realized that even if we were just leaving some of that money on the table—there was enough upside to get after it. Why not?

After the initial consulting work, we had to figure out how to turn our opportunity into realized dollars— and we recognized that implementing a pricing system would be one step toward capturing this value. With that in mind, we brought in three pricing system vendors who reviewed our transactional data and really validated for us that there was significant revenue to recover—and began to paint the picture of the tactical steps that would secure and protect that revenue recovery. What I'll tell you now, in retrospect, is that whatever they tell you your opportunity assessment is—*it's conservative!* Your real potential is probably double what they've evaluated.

Now, in contrast to this experience at Cargill Salt, earlier in my career I had once evaluated running a pricing initiative when I worked in the lubricants business at ConocoPhillips. I wasn't ready and our leadership wasn't ready. We were very focused on volumes, and, because we were running our plants really hard to achieve the desired efficiencies, opening ourselves up to the potential risk of losing business was not a mindset with which we were comfortable.

In fact, PROS (the strategic pricing software we selected) had reached out to me in my role at ConocoPhillips, and it became clear to them that I wasn't ready, and that my teams weren't ready for this kind of initiative. I talked about maintaining volume and how important it was to maintain economies of scale with our product. I stated that we would *not* be willing to lose customers because of pricing. Coincidentally, years later, this same PROS salesperson reached out to me at Cargill Salt, and he recalled our conversation from ConocoPhillips. After this conversation, he said to me, "You weren't ready for strategic pricing then, but you're ready now."

Valerie Wow. It really helps to hear the contrasting perspectives on what it takes to "be ready" for a pricing initiative.

Sonya Yes, there's significant contrast between the two situations. When I consider how I presented the pricing initiative to my boss at ConocoPhillips, I went to him and said, "I think we're going to do this pricing thing and it's going to be an investment." I wavered and was unsure about it. I recognized that there were strong headwinds: I couldn't lose volume, my customers already thought we priced too high, we weren't keen on initiatives requiring a lot of training, and we didn't have good data. In the end, we determined that we didn't have a strategy and that the culture was not conducive to making this change.

Now at Cargill Salt, the corporate strategy team came in and helped us build our strategy—of which strategic pricing was one component. Each of the leadership team members was assigned different levers to implement from the strategy work with tangible goals. I was assigned strategic pricing and given a target that I thought was aggressive. Nevertheless, the pricing manager and I put our heads together and we decided to make "something" happen. With the help of many, it took off before we knew it.

People got very engaged. My boss was incredibly supportive. What was so key in the way he supported me was that he allowed me to take "sensible risks." He never made me feel as though a failure would lead to being walked out the door. His encouragement actually allowed me to get really bold in the risks I was willing to take. We began by piloting our hypothesis—taking some small risks in specific areas and with specific customers. When I reviewed the success of our price tests, I started getting really energized. I went to him to share our proposed next steps, and he gave me a look suggesting that I might be crazy. I was confident in the results we saw in the pilot to extrapolate this to a wider swath of customers. I told him, "I'm telling you this will work." To this, he responded, "I'm trusting you to do this." That's what I needed to hear.

Leadership culture drives the success of your efforts. That trust that my boss gave me and my team was transformative. He gave us the support, essentially the air cover, that allowed our organization to take "sensible risks." He spoke highly of the initiative whenever possible to the organization, so it was clear that we were aligned.

Valerie That's incredibly inspiring. It's so invigorating to hear how one leader can have such a powerful impact on culture and mindset. Can you share how this support enabled and encouraged you to inspire others within Cargill Salt?

Sonya Absolutely. You've heard the phrase "culture eats strategy for breakfast"? It was so evident in this change. If we didn't have leadership support and alignment, this would have been impossible. I would say that the most tenuous area for any pricing initiative is the sales organization. Salespeople respond to clear measurements. Also, salespeople, like all of us, want people to like them, and they want their customers to be happy. It's human nature. They have little interest in delivering the news of a price increase that has the potential to cause conflict.

Because our pricing team was supported by my boss, I felt confident that I could give air cover to my sales team. There was opportunity in pricing precisely because we hadn't been supporting sales in the right ways historically. Our historical pricing process was run on a spreadsheet and wasn't very sophisticated. With the advanced procurement systems of our buyers, we had essentially been sending our salespeople into the gun fight of pricing negotiations with a switchblade.

Now, we had real, market-driven, scientifically validated price guidance based on our value proposition in different market segments. We could now support our sales team to hold our own ground in those negotiations with buyers.

And there was no better evidence for how this price guidance could transform the sales negotiation than with one of our most experienced sales representatives, David. Now, with the market evidence we had at hand, we were able to determine that some of David's customers were being priced so far below the floor recommendation and that he was going to need to consider doubling their prices to course-correct. Of course, David was resistant. But I was able to say to him, "I'll take responsibility if you lose those customers." I paid forward the air cover my boss was giving me and allowed David to take "sensible risk."

And you know what? David got every one of those deals. He became the pricing evangelist within our sales organization. He helped us win credibility among the naysayers and show evidence that the price guidance could be trusted.

In addition, we provided more training, we added pricing into their goals and objectives, and we began reporting pricing results by department. The change wasn't simply implementing a pricing technology; it involved changes in process and tools, staffing, organizational structure, and culture.

Ultimately, not every salesperson could get comfortable with this kind of change, and some chose to leave as a result. But the culture was transformed into one where we could encourage and support one another in taking the risks that would be necessary to grow and improve the business.

Valerie   Can you tell me more about how your tactical approaches to pricing changed? What was different between the before and after of this pricing initiative?

Sonya   Well, as I mentioned before, salt is certainly a commodity product, but it's a very large industry. The market uses about 265 million tons globally, of which 50 million tons are sold in the US alone each year. At Cargill Salt alone, we have over 4,000 customers, 12,000 ship-tos with over 200,000 shipments per year. And the pricing for this complexity was all being managed in *spreadsheets*. It's no wonder David had prices that needed significant revisiting.

With a technology in place, we were able to systematically deliver price guidance precisely tailored to the unique conditions of each engagement. As my director of strategic pricing said, *"Before PROS, we had price bands and averages and it was very subjective. After PROS, we have guidance that is very segmented and sophisticated, and based on a particular customer and market."*

Valerie   The transformation efforts you led at Cargill Salt were impressive. What advice would you give to other leaders seeking to embark on a similar transformation?

Sonya   Well, I would say that there are four key elements to change: (1) process and tools, (2) staffing, (3) organizational structure, and (4) culture.

Processes and tools are essential to drive adoption, ensure adherence to governance, and capture and measure results. The *processes* needed to be transparent to provide trust in what we were asking the sales team to do. One of the ways we approached this is that we would provide our sales teams a price envelope (floor, target, expert pricing levels) that allowed them some autonomy in the price negotiation—but we would also show them the evidence of similar customers who had been willing to pay the higher prices. The processes could not be so cumbersome that people fought them. For example, if they were at or above the target pricing levels in the envelope, they needed no approval. To price below the floor level, they needed vice president approval. The *tools* had to make the change administratively easy. The technology could not be a barrier to adoption, and it was essential to consistent measurement and data tracking. It's your source of truth to not only determine what the price guidance should be but also to continuously measure and improve your pricing strategy. For us, it was key that the technology enabled comprehensive visibility into pricing analytics while simultaneously enabling speed and agility in pricing management.

Second, when it comes to staffing, you've got to consider whether you have the right people in the right jobs to move your transformation forward. Does your staff have the necessary skill set to make this change? What development or training will be needed? What about your sales leaders? They're integral to this process. The processes around staffing must support this strategic direction. We reevaluated the measures used in our incentive program. We revised our job descriptions and our performance review discussions to include strategic pricing skills. The team to implement and maintain this discipline is essential. As I noted earlier, if it's truly a transformation, expect that some people will opt out and leave the business.

Third, is your organization's structure aligned for success? Your pricing leader needs to have an equal seat at the table with your sales and marketing leaders. If they're buried in the organization, or worse yet, if they report to the sales leader, they will have limited authority in the organization and will struggle to influence the outcomes.

Last, you've got to consider your culture. As I've mentioned a few times, my leadership's air cover allowed me—even *encouraged* me—to take "sensible risks." You have to encourage taking sensible risks with authenticity. As leaders, what you say, do, and reinforce (SDR) will make the difference to the success of this work (e.g., appropriately celebrating wins and losses that fit your pricing strategy).

The journey is not a straightforward, upward climb and requires continuous and disciplined focus. This last point on culture and continued reinforcement is key. As people change, process adherence becomes lax, and/or priorities change, it's easy to backslide and see performance wane. It's not a "set it and forget it" process. You need to recommit to it periodically.

I'll share an example to highlight what I mean about what it takes for leadership to drive forward the right culture. A sales leader I was working with sent out an email celebrating his team's recent win. I read through the email and noticed that there was no mention of value captured, only volumes. When I went to my pricing team to inquire about the deal, the pricing analyst said they felt like "we gave it away." Now, I'm not against celebrating wins, and this could still be considered a win, but we needed to reposition *how we discussed that win* if we want to move the needle on strategic pricing. This email from the sales leader should have celebrated the win with the caveat that we priced below our floor and then clearly explained the rationale for doing so. In this case, we were entering a new market with a customer that had never seemed receptive to changing suppliers. We were lowering their cost of switching while we piloted this business with them. You can still drive forward a profitable business with occasional trade-offs like this—you just need to maintain transparency and alignment within the organization about why a pricing trade-off was made and how it will be recovered or why it was a necessary sacrifice. Cheering on winning volume alone will send the organization the wrong message. Further, you should celebrate losses as well. There are times that it's healthy to encourage a customer to buy from their next-best alternative. Making a deliberate decision to shed business because value propositions are not aligned should also be celebrated. What you say, do, reinforce (SDR) as a leader will ultimately determine your organization's success in strategic pricing.

Valerie   Sonya, thank you so much for sharing these important perspectives on driving forward transformative change in pricing. It's clear that your leadership has been instrumental to the positive results that Cargill Salt was able to achieve.

Sonya   Thank you, Valerie.

The authors

Sonya Roberts leads Cargill's salt business, which produces and sells deicing, water softening, food, industrial, and agricultural salt products in North America and Europe. She brings three decades of experience to her role overseeing strategy, execution, and financials across 2,000 employees and 25 production facilities in North America and the Dutch Caribbean. Most recently, Sonya established and led growth ventures and strategic pricing for Cargill's North America protein business, where she developed and implemented business strategies, entered emerging businesses (alternative proteins and seafood), led the pet treats business, evaluated and executed business development opportunities, and implemented strategic pricing.

Since joining Cargill in 2008, Sonya has served as the managing director of Cargill's value-added protein business, where she led the egg and Canadian chicken businesses and helped generate hundreds of millions in revenue with a team of 1,600 employees. She was also the vice president of sales and marketing for Cargill Salt, where she was responsible for all aspects of the customer experience.

Sonya began her career with Cargill in the power and natural gas business, where she developed and oversaw the customer trading strategy. Prior to joining Cargill, Sonya was a leader with oil and gas company ConocoPhillips for 19 years. During her time with the company, she led US and global teams and held positions in strategy, marketing, business operations, and finance. Sonya holds a bachelor's degree in finance from the University of North Texas in Denton, Texas. She and her husband live in Minnesota and have two teenage daughters. Sonya is currently a board member of MBOLD, Redwood City Saltworks, Catallia Mexican Foods, and SPX Flow. She is also a member of the Executive Leadership Council.

Valerie Howard, Solution Strategy Director at PROS, manages the go-to-market strategy for the PROS pricing, industry, and partner solutions. Prior to PROS, Valerie held leadership roles in pricing and revenue management, where she experienced first-hand the transformative benefits and competitive advantages that can be realized through AI and technology. Valerie earned an MBA from the McCombs School of Business at the University of Texas and a BS in Electrical Engineering from the Cooper Union for the Advancement of Science and Art. She is a frequent speaker at pricing conferences and has written for *Digital Commerce 360, Top Business Tech,* and others.

12

Voices from Pricing Practitioners

The Impact of Pricing Is Real

Dr. Gernot T. Dambacher

PLEASE ALLOW ME TO begin by sounding a note of warning, addressing a misconception I've faced on various occasions: pricing is Sisyphean labor; please don't think it can be considered "done" at any point.

Here is our pricing story: the focus on pricing in Evonik began in 2006 with the establishment of what today would probably be called the commercial excellence team; then, it was known as a marketing, sales, and innovation academy, driven by external [McKinsey and Prof. Homburg & Partner] support. From the beginning, pricing was positioned as a global "module," and after I joined the MSI Academy in 2007, I was running pricing projects with several business lines. I began as a senior pricing consultant and in early 2008 became the head of module and later cluster pricing.

In executing pricing projects, it soon became obvious that we were experiencing serious issues with data quality, quantity, and availability at the customer-product level. We considered investing in external pricing software (e.g., PROS, Vendavo) but ultimately built our own. After excessive data cleansing and optimization and a few years, our software was up and running smoothly; as of this writing, it hosts a four-digit number of active users. We ran dozens of pricing projects for many years, developed several tools to meet our pricing needs, and invested heavily in trainings for colleagues in operational roles, fulfilling our "academy" aspiration. As a parallel step, we built teams of dedicated pricing professionals in the operational units to ensure long-term anchoring in execution.

As a corporate function, we had to justify our existence to the businesses, and so early on we began systematically tracking the monetary benefits generated through our activities—not by us but by our internal customers. Upon completion of each project, high-ranking representatives of the business lines were asked to assess the amount of sustainable annual gains created, and I can report that the benefits exceeded the investment in the organization by a *very* substantial factor. In price hygiene activities using price-volume scatterplots alone, millions of euros were gained as additional EBIT, by just "price cleaning" *one* single BL (out of more than 20). Once everyone in the company understood that every single cent gained in price directly ends up in the EBIT, pricing gained momentum.

In the early days, our activities were strongly supported by our CEO, who is known to be very marketing- and sales-minded. By allowing us to invest in pricing and by helping us overcome numerous obstacles, this support was essential for the success of Evonik's pricing transformation. And so today the company has more than 60 dedicated pricing professionals in place, supported by suitable and widely accepted tools, processes, concepts, and methods for pricing—all of the above based on dependable data.

Pricing is a journey along a bumpy road, and it will take longer than expected—but we can clearly see the monetary benefits today, and we're convinced that they'll be retained and expanded. The journey continues…

The author

Dr. Gernot T. Dambacher has spent 12 years, almost half his industry career, in pricing, and spearheaded the pricing transformation of Evonik Industries AG, a $15 billion global specialty chemicals company. In the first half of his professional career, he worked in various operational roles in Germany, China, and the US, including as Business Line Head at Asia Pacific, before entering the pricing world. He recently left Evonik with the sale of its methacrylate business—today known as Röhm, the inventors of Plexiglas®—to Advent International.

The Power of One Percent

Jens Pfennig

In an internal analysis on the impact of pricing back in 2009, we discovered that by giving fewer discounts and realizing a 1 percent higher deal price in a specific business segment, Software AG's operating profit segment contribution would increase by an average of 2.5 percent at constant cost.

Such opportunities to significantly increase revenue and profitability are rare and drew everyone's attention. To successfully leverage the potential, it was imperative that everyone in sales and the sales support functions understood and felt accountable that their effectiveness in selling and defending the value that Software AG is bringing to our customers has a major impact on our company's profitability.

Not understanding and/or considering the financial net effect, colleagues sometimes made concessions in different ways, such as granting high discounts, long payment terms, diversion from contract standards, deliverables—ultimately giving away that 1 percent revenue and 2.5 percent operating profit.

To put this into perspective:

- Based on the above, it's obvious that a 1 percent price reduction (due to a higher discount) will reduce the company's segment operating profits by 2.5 percent at constant cost.
- A 5 percent general lower deal price does require 12.5 percent additional segment revenue from more than 100 other incremental deals to compensate for the loss in profitability.
- 100 percent of the price reduction hits the bottom-line profit.
- If any salesperson believes that in order to secure a €500,000 deal, they need to drop the price by 1 percent—which is "just €5 thousand"—it might not seem unreasonable. But if every salesperson does this and you are a €500 million revenue company, your operating profit could decrease by €5 million.
- Our salespeople are the last line of defense in protecting and optimizing the company's revenue and margin, so they should be supported in the best way possible by the entire organization and recognized for their professionality (low discounts and fewer concessions) when selling and defending the value to our customers.

The most critical success criteria have been clearly the attention of the board, their active communication and guidance on this initiative, and the active involvement of the chief revenue officer and chief finance officer in any relevant deal not conforming to given guidance and standards.

Over time, this focused practice, together with a more customer-value-driven selling approach, has contributed significantly to the past decades' positive EBIT development of nearly +100 percent.

Especially during and post COVID-19, management focus and discipline on price and discounting will even become more important to ensure companies' profitability.

The author

Jens Pfennig is the Senior Vice President for Global Pricing, Business Operations, and Chairman of the International Pricing Committee, Software AG, with 30+ years of pricing experience

The Benefits of Executives Paying Attention to Pricing

Ole Iacob Prebensen

A year and a half ago, our former CEO said, "We are operating in dynamic markets with many opportunities. Creating value for customers means making what the customer needs, and we must do it now and we must do it right." This statement didn't make headlines internally, but from a pricing perspective it was powerful. Why? Over the last decade our company had successfully implemented the Lean program at our plants worldwide. Because we are a raw materials manufacturing company, cost-effective production has been instrumental. Some of the company's segments have managed to survive because of this program. But little focus has been given to pricing. Cost-based pricing has been the mantra—decentralized to the management of each segment and divisions, and no center-led or centralized approach done to facilitate a broader or common pricing understanding.

One of roughly 30 segments in the company began a value-based pricing journey with the support of division top management. Two years later, the specialty product line was merely sold out after an increase of 300 percent of sold volume and 12.5 percent price increase for one specific product. The global customer base understood and appreciated the value these products provided their operations—all based on transfer of experience through case studies and history.

Simultaneously, the rest of the company was still in a cost-based scenario world. And even before the COVID-19 pandemic hit, several segments were struggling to meet their financial targets.

A few weeks after our new CEO arrived in 2020, he asked, "How are we on pricing?" This raised eyebrows in the C-suite and shifted some of the internal focus of optimizing production to how we could become customer-centric and dollarize our portfolio. Our company had already decided to move forward with implementing a new CRM system throughout the entire company. But customer value management (CVM) was not in focus. During the process of setting up a CRM system, several pricing strategies were discussed, including dynamic pricing through the introduction of pricing software, but this is still in the thinking stage.

During the last couple of years, an informal group of upper-management leaders have met regularly to assess the company's marketing approach. After a thorough discussion of how to proceed with the question raised by the CEO, these members decided to include pricing in their meetings. Soon after, members of the segment who successfully implemented the specialty product line through a value-based approach were invited. As a result, focus is currently shifting to customer segmentation, value-based pricing, and a mindset where pricing excellence is key to continued success. Today the company is slowly heading in a direction where the ultimate goal is to uncover and capture the value created for each customer.

The author

Ole Iacob Prebensen has extensive leadership experience in public service and in the oil and gas industry. Prior to working in global marketing for a Norwegian industrial company, he spent almost two decades in large international oil-service companies. He has a visionary approach to business whereby customer-centricity is at the heart of his leadership execution. From sales to global technical support, R&D, marketing, and global responsibility for introduction and sales of new technology, his strategic approach of solving customer challenges through value-pricing methodology creates win-win situations for all. Ole Iacob Prebensen holds a BSc in Business and Management.

Winning the Leaders for Pricing Is Winning Pricing with the Leaders

Frank Rautenberg, PhD

For a leading player in the animal health industry, pricing did not receive a high level of attention outside of annual budget discussions. This changed with the setup of a pricing excellence function. The pricing function began by identifying significant price increase potentials for a key revenue driver based on a price–value analysis versus competition in several countries. First insights from internal discussions were enhanced by a willingness-to-pay study. The price strategy for this revenue driver was reviewed, and floor prices were introduced. Within months this action paid off through partly significant net price increases without triggering volume pushback.

This development drew further attention from top management, which asked the pricing function to expand their activities to other brands and to address further pricing opportunities. Further price action was taken, and their impact was made transparent to top management.

In parallel, a new price-governance framework was set up: strategic pricing decisions could not be made without the sign-off of leaders from marketing, sales, and finance. Through this approach, the pricing function became more and more involved in cross-functional price decision-making processes and sharpened its profile as trusted advisor in collaborative cross-functional pricing activities.

We learned from this experience that mutual empowerment between a pricing function and C-level executives is a key success factor for pricing: the freshly created pricing function focused its initial action on areas already receiving high attention from C-level executives. Initial price action was targeted, for example, at one specific product line, one brand, or selected geographies.

Once the first pricing change was implemented (e.g., a floor price introduced for a product line, a price strategy developed for a major innovation), the impact of this action was made transparent. The pricing function received the mandate to clearly show

how KPIs have changed, for example, net sales, profitability, or market share, and how this is related to pricing action.

These insights had a strong potential to convince C-level management of the benefits of professional price management. It created their buy-in for the extension of the pricing function's activities, including their willingness to fund the next steps in the company's pricing journey.

In summary, we see several key success factors in establishing a close connection between a pricing function and C-level executives:

- Keep pricing narrowly focused in the beginning (e.g., focus on one brand, one geography, or one channel).
- Track the impact of the pricing changes and make the financial impact transparent to C-level management.
- Involve functional leaders in the initial pricing decisions and extend their involvement to standard operating procedures (e.g., launch price decisions, price reviews, strategic price increases).
- Gradually expand the involvement of key decision-makers in the organization: for example, if pricing is attached to marketing, it should also involve early sales leaders and reach out to finance leaders.
- Don't stop at the involvement of management at the C-level; work simultaneously with different layers in the organization: country managers, regional leads, brand managers, sales controllers, and so forth.
- Continuously expand the scope of pricing activities to further brands, geographies, new pricing topics, and so on, in close collaboration with the respective functions while always seeking endorsement from the C-level suite and making them a change partner in your pricing journey.

The author

Frank Rautenberg, PhD, is a highly experienced, passionate pricing professional. During nearly one decade with a leading pricing consultancy, he has led multiple projects for leading companies in the health care industry. Since 2015 he has been working in the animal health industry in leading positions in pricing. Frank is a graduate in industrial engineering and management from the Karlsruhe Institute of Technology in Germany and holds a PhD in management science.

Pricing Team Using Software to Solve Business Problems

Cavan Reinsborough

Problem. Do you have complexity in your B2B business? Is this complexity hiding blind spots? In our company, complexity was something we continued to live with, as we "trusted" our sales team to do the right thing even when they didn't know what the right thing was. For example, our B2B firm sells over 400,000 products, from over 100 vendors, to over 20,000 customers. To add to this, our customers would negotiate special pricing on items that were "important" to them, called contracts, so we have almost two times more contracts than actual customers—complex? Despite these challenges, salespeople were responsible for managing the overall customer agreements, which meant that they were able to change pricing as they deemed necessary.

Solution. My role reported to the president, and their position was that the sales team needed to be the decision-makers on the overall customer relationship, with the support of pricing. Based on this I was able to lobby for an investment to work with a SaaS provider to develop a program that could capture the skill set of the pricing team in our decisions related to customer-level pricing. As a result, we built a business tool outlining, by customer legal pricing terms and conditions, profitability, real-time current product price and usage, target pricing (recommended), and the positive or negative impact of changes.

Positive impact

QUANTITATIVE
- Prior to the tool, reps could make changes without understanding their impacts—we created a process to get approvals based on impact number and profitability.

  Year 1 saw $1.2M in rejected price reductions (potential margin leakage).

QUALITATIVE
- Improved confidence from leadership team in the pricing function.
- Sales teams were being held accountable to measures that lead to improved decision-making for the company.
- Sales team were paid based on margin dollars, so they liked the information to support the pricing objections allowing them to make more money.
- We introduced target pricing to teams.
- We removed pricing interference by leveraging skill sets into tools.

The author

Cavan Reinsborough has nearly 25 years of pricing experience, more than five years as a pricing executive, and close to 20 years of pricing management experience, with five different companies.

Profit-Optimizing the Salesforce

Bob Vezeau

There's nothing mystical about the concept of B2B pricing excellence. It's merely a cohesive set of policies and practices that allow a firm to understand the value it brings to specific segments of customers relative to competitive offerings and to achieve a fair split of the difference. When well executed, pricing excellence can bring as much as a 10 percent overall price improvement, virtually all of which accrues to the bottom line.

The real challenge is practical execution. Senior management appreciation of the challenges and reinforced commitment to the goal are prerequisites to the extended focus needed to achieve pricing excellence. Many daunting obstacles must be overcome. Consistent and accurate transactional data is the most familiar hurdle. Another is that customer procurement departments work tirelessly to commoditize even your most unique innovation.

I would contend, however, that human nature is the minefield most responsible for failed pricing initiatives. Sales managers cling to past practices of applying standard markups to their costs, giving away productivity advantages or unique value creation, and missing sales opportunities because of cost disadvantages. Perhaps the biggest impediment to achieving pricing excellence is a misaligned sales incentive.

A few years ago, I was tasked with creating a pricing excellence structure for our business. After two years of intense work, we had created the infrastructure, training, and reporting needed to support our goal. In this endeavor we had the unwavering support of our senior management. We had achieved about 150 basis points of margin improvement from pricing. But I knew that this was only the tip of the iceberg.

You see, we employ a commissioned salesforce. At the time, those commissions were a flat percentage of gross sales. Reps were effectively disincentivized to put business at risk in order to achieve a reasonable level of profitability, let alone pricing excellence. In effect, their incentive was set to optimize revenue rather than profitability. After highlighting this issue for our leadership, I was charged with designing a new commission plan that would align with our business strategy and pricing excellence.

A cross-functional steering team and a sales council composed of high-profile reps and sales managers were assembled. Our senior leaders explained "the why." We conducted workshops and achieved consensus on design parameters to promote not only sales growth but also profitability and to emphasize the sale of strategic products. Our final design included a progressive commission rate structure tied to contribution margin.

We created a new sales commission dashboard, sharing more information than ever before with our reps. Individual sales rep impacts were calculated. Considerable attention was devoted to our communication and training plans. The transition included a three-month preview, followed by a six-month "guardrail" period. After that, we were fully on the new plan. Through it all, our senior leadership stood strong, resisting the many calls for exceptions. Six months later, our margins had improved by 400 basis points! Most important, however, the change created a fundamental shift in the culture of our commercial teams.

The author

Bob Vezeau is the Vice President of Strategic Pricing at WestRock. He can be contacted at www.linkedin.com/in/robert-a-bob-vezeau-3659674/.

13

Voices from Pricing Experts

"Blocking and Tackling"

By Vernon E. Lennon III
and Jered W. Haedt (US)

W HEN WE LAUNCHED, OUR team saw an opportunity to focus on what we saw as an underserved market for pricing excellence, mid-market companies. Over the last 10 or more years, we've learned much about the numerous mid-market industries in which we've provided our expertise—the simplest insight being that mid-market companies want to grow to become a billion-dollar company quickly.

Although that doesn't come as a shock, it does provide some insight into the business frameworks resulting from this aggressive growth. While innovation can play a large role in aggressive growth, mature companies (or even product categories within them) tend to grow through acquisition, and this impacts who, how, and why they utilize external expertise.

The C-suite in the mid-market, often beholden to private equity ownership, would prefer quick fixes to business process improvement, and thus the consideration of software is front and center. Software considerations for these organizations, however, can become problematic because of disparate technology stacks, taxonomies, data structures, and more; thus, the simple application of software becomes complex. As a result, either the price tag increases or the scope decreases to mitigate the complications.

Although we are an asset-based consultancy and enjoy leaving tools behind, a large majority of our engagements begin with a focus on the people–process–technology (P-P-T) continuum. We begin by ensuring that clients have the right people with the right skills in the right go-to-market roles. Then we dissect and streamline the supporting processes, such that standard transactions flow smoothly, quickly, and profitably, while delineating remediation processes for the smaller percentage of nonstandard transactions. Focusing on these two areas first helps normalize the production and processing in aggregated organizations and creates a more homogenized approach to the marketplace. With the understanding and consistency in application of the human resource structure (including KPIs) and clear tollgates built into go-to-market business processes, the focus can now turn to technology.

Although the desire for a quick software fix is often there in our initial discussions, the application of this P-P-T approach coupled with sprint (quarter-length project plans) protocols becomes very attractive. These short, highly defined plans provide immediate ROI through quick wins, along with KPIs to track longer-term improvements. These sprints can then be layered to absorb increasing complexities or to focus on new acquisitions. An additional benefit of these sprint protocols is the ability for them to be done 100 percent virtually if needed, and obviously we have taken advantage of this during the pandemic.

The virtual application, though, does require steadfast leadership within client organizations; so while the time requirement doesn't increase, the need for project presence is paramount to "stick to the plan" and maintain scope.

In an interesting example of the above, we had been working with a northeastern data technology company before the pandemic, applying our P-P-T approach, including a complete redesign of their internal pricing tools. By building the basic blocking and tackling pieces of the business, we were able to pivot with the onset of COVID-19. Early in 2020 they came to us asking whether we could accelerate the internal gains and embolden the analytical bench through dashboards and pricing ladders and create a custom software environment for their pricing tools to reside in. As of the writing of this brief, we will be working through those new tasks along with commensurate maintenance throughout the year, thus making them completely self-reliant by 2022.

The authors

Vernon E. Lennon III is the CEO of Pricing Cloud LLC, with over 20 years in pricing.

Jered W. Haedt is the Chief Science Officer of Pricing Cloud LLC, with over 12 years in pricing.

Lead Your Team by Asking Better Questions

Janene Liston (Switzerland)

One of the things we faced repeatedly in implementing pricing projects was concern or fear from managers (usually sales) that "my team won't make the changes." One case in particular I remember quite vividly. It was the end of a highly successful project kickoff week. We were going through the checkout with the management team. We got to the director of sales, who said, "This has been excellent. I really believe that this project can bring great things, but…"

Silence. You could hear the collective inhale from everyone in the room as we braced for what came after the "but."

"But…," he said, "I don't think my sales team will do it, and I can't make them." Bomb dropped.

He was being honest; he believed in the project and felt that it would fail. I canceled my return trip so that I could meet with him the following Monday morning.

As we spoke, I realized that he believed he would need to force his team to make the changes and that it wouldn't work. He was probably right that it would not be super successful. There was a better path forward.

"Have you ever heard of those *Nanny 911* TV shows where a family has a professional nanny come in to *fix their children*?" I asked. Skeptically, he said, "Yes?"

"What's the first thing the nanny does?" He laughed and said, "Fix the parents' behavior."

"Yes" I said. "Because the children's behavior is a reflection of the parents' behavior. Similarly, your sales team's behavior is related to your behavior."

There was a better way to get the team onboard. It wouldn't require forcing anything on anyone. It would involve him changing the questions he's asking his team.

Through the kickoff week we had identified that they had an issue with project discounting. Considering that, I challenged him for the next month to change what he did when his team asked for a discount approval. To date, the escalation process had been only a margin review exercise. We were about to change that.

"Just ask your sales reps three questions," was my request.

"First, who's the customer and what's the context (strategic, nice to have, etc.)?"; "Second, what's the competitive situation?"; "Third, what price do you think we need to offer to get the order?"

A month later I returned. He shared that his team now showed up with the answers to those questions prepared as well. They were granting fewer discounts and were more strategic about it.

For a leader, the most powerful way to influence behavior is to begin by asking different questions. When implementing pricing transformation, buy-in is not enough. Behaviors must change at all levels, led from the top. In the case above, the shift in the sales reps' behavior led to better price quality. This leader saw a clear path ahead of him. He felt more empowered to help his team make the required changes needed for a successful pricing transformation project.

The author

Janene Liston, the Pricing Lady, is Europe's most trusted pricing strategist for small businesses. She is a Certified Pricing Professional, an entrepreneur, and a European Public Speaking Champion with more than 20 years of experience in product management and pricing. Having done pricing transformation projects in companies such as Siemens and Syngenta, she now helps small and medium enterprises build the right pricing strategies for their businesses, working with them to create, communicate, and charge for the value they deliver and to build more sustainably profitable businesses.

How to Accelerate the ROI on Pricing in Less Than 90 Days

Joanna Wells (Australia)

The financial benefits of a world-class pricing team are incredible: based on our consulting experience and capability research, a world-class pricing team generates an additional margin of 3.0 to 7.0 percent each year. No matter what!

Here's how.

From 2016 to the time of this writing, a major Australian fuel business engaged Taylor Wells Advisory to support them with their pricing optimization and analytics project. The business was experiencing considerable margin pressure. Demand for fuel was dropping each year, and production and operations were too costly to maintain in Australia.

At this point, the business's pricing system was fixed, ultimately cost-plus, and reliant on multiple systems. Their pricing department was mostly accountants who implemented standard, finance-led pricing. The C-suite recognized that pricing was capping their revenue potential and leaking substantial margin. Their aim was to move from cost-plus to dynamic pricing using best-in-class strategy, people, and systems. A key element, therefore, was to improve existing pricing team capability and performance. Using our transformation solution, we undertook a detailed assessment of the business, pricing, teams, and culture. We helped the business build a new pricing department using the latest organization design and pricing strategy. When required, we brought in specialist talent to accelerate the ROI on pricing and assist with technical issues.

In 12 months, the new teams delivered an additional 1 to 2 percent margin through basic price management. After three years, over 85 percent of pricing department staff stayed on the team, and 63 percent were promoted internally based on individual ability and potential. In financial terms, the results were as follows:

1 72 percent reduction in total cost of employment
2 $8 million savings in total project costs
3 average EBIT growth of 10 to 15 percent each year

The organizational impact of this approach to pricing achieved multiple outcomes, as depicted in Figure 13.1.

Here are the top five things we've learned about pricing, people, and systems:

- A pricing-team-led transformation model is more sustainable and effective than a consultant-led transformation.
- People and culture can make or break strategy.
- Organizational design (i.e., team setup) is a leading indicator of short-term pricing success.
- Who you recruit as pricing leader will determine margin expansion success in the first two years of team establishment.

1 **Clarity gains** from well-dimensioned team structures, clear roles, and accountability.
2 **Composition gains** via cross-functional collaboration, reducing headcount by 15%.
3 **Shape gains** in operational speed, efficiency, and cost reductions via right size and process centralization.
4 **Location-scaling** decision-making through team accountability and task automation.
5 **Capability gains** in pricing performance, superior execution, and problem-solving speed.

Figure 13.1. Outcomes of a world-class pricing approach.

- The people mix on your pricing team largely determines the speed and effectiveness of problem-solving, systems integrations, price trials, and implementations.

In 2020, pricing is more important than ever because of the COVID-19 disruption. The old way of setting and managing prices is a serious profit risk. Businesses can't afford to overcharge customers or to undersell offers when customers are more risk-averse than ever and reluctant to spend.

The author

Joanna Wells is Director of Taylor Wells, an advisor in a global pricing and organizational advisory firm. She works with clients to internalize pricing expertise and to drive strategy transformation. Our business is building world-class pricing teams using pricing strategy and organizational design. Taylor Wells helps clients hire the right people and advises on how to remunerate, build capability, and motivate pricing and commercial functions. More information can be found at www.taylorwells.com.au/.

Founders Need to Consider Pricing More and Earlier

Sho Shinohara (Japan)

Founders need to pay more attention to pricing from the early phases of starting a new business. Based on my experiences through seminars or mentoring for over 500 founders in Japan, there are many cases where pricing isn't well thought out or where the discussion of pricing is postponed for too long.

I emphasize for founders that adequate consideration of pricing from an earlier phase accelerates identifying critical value for each customer and differentiators of your products to focus on. It facilitates more effective developments and proposals with greater confidence. As a consequence, founders can realize more profitable and sustainable business much faster.

Here are five considerations for founders when thinking about pricing from earlier stages to improve their business and better realize monetization.

- Develop a customer understanding of pricing, too: "whether customers have problems" is not enough for customer understanding. It's important to investigate "who has the greatest willingness to pay for solving their problems," "how much customers will pay for that," and "why they can say so." Considering these points well beginning with the early phase accelerates the finding of appropriate customers and prices. Consequently, it increases the feasibility and sustainability of the business.
- Focus on more valuable factors to pursue: resources are limited at founding, and perceived value, willingness to pay, and the factors that customers appreciate vary. Through deep-dive consideration of which factors customers perceive as more valuable and worth paying for, founders can prioritize their development and think about how to improve those factors more directly.
- Find and propose unnoticed value from broader views: not all customers can show clearly what they highly value or what they really need today. Therefore, it's important for founders to seek and propose not only perceived value to customers but also "not yet perceived" value from a broader view. It will help founders find new markets and opportunities to have fewer competitors and more pricing power.
- Sharpen value propositions for turbulent times: the COVID-19 crisis affects customers' behavior and decisions. In such times, founders need to sharpen their value proposition and pricing

for a more limited budget and for changes in selling situations like online or shorter time proposals. It requires a more simple and impactful message with appealing value and price.

• Update and resonate pricing methods with the current environment: environments are changing with the times. In particular, for founders aiming to provide a new value in a new market with digital technologies, existing, simple cost-based or competitor-based pricing may not fit well today. In considering leveraging and monetizing data or new business models such as SaaS or XaaS, founders need to continue updating and resonating their pricing methods and tools with new circumstances.

It's often said that "pricing is a long journey"; however, it shouldn't be the last thing founders discuss. The sooner, the better. It would be great if founders were to begin their pricing journey and realize more valuable and sustainable business sooner.

The author

Sho Shinohara is President and Chief Value Officer at Alivespit Co. Ltd., Certified Public Accountants, in Washington, US. He can be reached at www.linkedin.com/in/shoshinohara.

Case Study of Pricing Impact

Gregor Buchwald (Germany)

Introduction

Shocking news about cost-cutting as well as head-count reductions are in the media almost every day—yet the revenue side is rarely addressed. However, we at Prof. Roll & Pastuch Management Consultants believe that a diligent optimization of price management can increase profits by at least 3 percent. To underline our claim, I outline one of our most successful pricing projects.

Initial situation

In this project we worked for TTS Marine, a large international ship supplier. Over the years, as a result of the large extension of the firm, price-setting had become an unstructured process. A major challenge for TTS Marine was to set adequate prices for their 30,000 spare parts. The spare part pricing was merely based on a cost-plus approach, neglecting any specificity of the individual spare part. As a result, we could observe large inconsistencies within the price architecture. For example, interchangeable spare parts that the consumer could receive from multiple sources were priced too high, whereas the prices for TTS exclusive parts were too low. Clearly, TTS Marine was in need of a new pricing system.

Procedure and methodology

Our goal was to evaluate the value of each individual spare part and to identify for which spare parts higher margins could be achieved. We did this by applying the concept of value-based pricing. Value-based pricing identifies the product's value to the consumer and thus the costumer's willingness to pay. The prices are then set accordingly. Given the vast number of spare parts at TTS Marine, each individual spare part could not be analyzed for itself. Thus, in a first step, we categorized the spare parts based on the technical product hierarchy into distinct product groups. In a next step, we identified and selected several so-called value drivers that influence the customer's willingness to pay. A value driver can be anything from the competitive intensity to the criticality of a spare part for the functioning of a machine. The product groups

Value score pricing

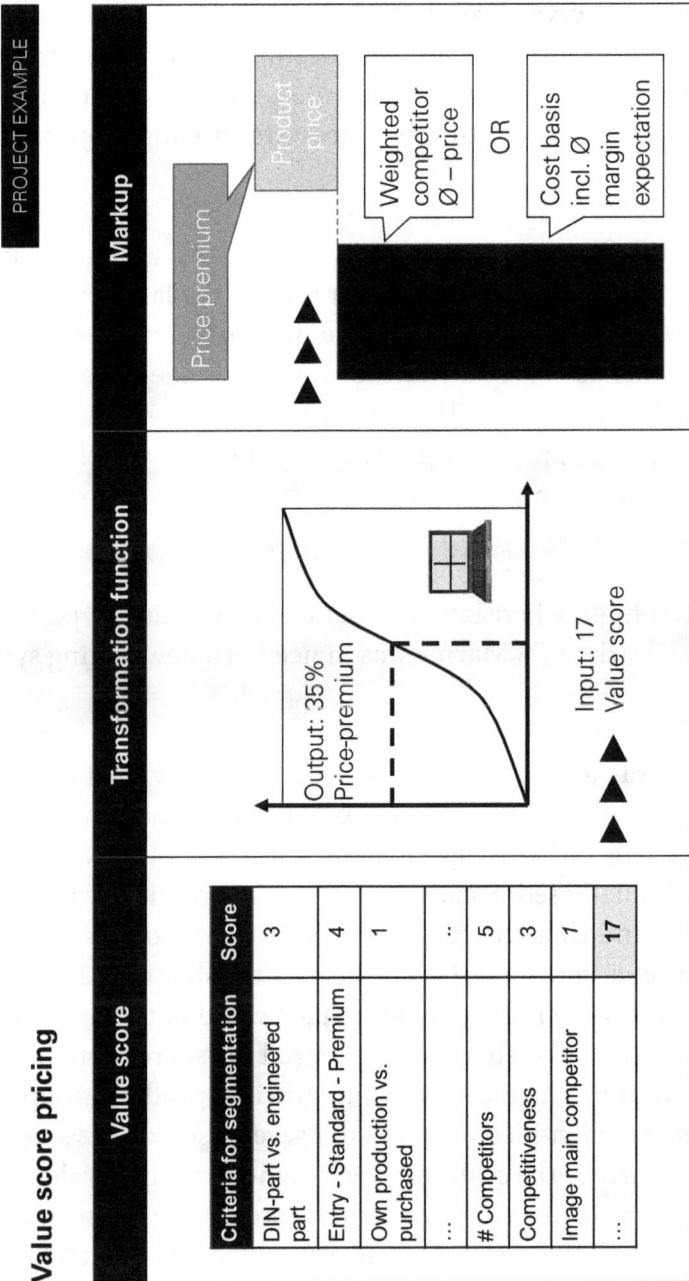

PROJECT EXAMPLE

| Value score | Transformation function | Markup |

Value score

Criteria for segmentation	Score
DIN-part vs. engineered part	3
Entry - Standard - Premium	4
Own production vs. purchased	1
...	...
# Competitors	5
Competitiveness	3
Image main competitor	1
...	**17**

Transformation function

Output: 35% Price-premium

Input: 17 Value score

▲ ▲ ▲ Value score

Markup

Price premium

Product price

Weighted competitor Ø – price

OR

Cost basis incl. Ø margin expectation

Figure 13.2. All relevant price drivers can be aggregated in a common scoring model for differentiation of markups.

were individually assessed and given a score for each value driver. The individual scores per value driver were then summarized into one value score per product group. In a final step, we translated the value score into a markup factor to be applied on the cost basis. The procedure we applied is schematically outlined in Figure 13.2.

Results
Our project resulted in a highly differentiated and strongly value-oriented pricing logic for the entire spare-parts portfolio. TTS Marine now has a system in place that allows it to set prices based on meaningful dimensions and that is understood by every TTS Marine employee. When implementing our new logic, we reduced the prices for more than 1,000 parts. The sales in spare parts increased by 15 percent. Furthermore, the new price structure has led to a major improvement in TTS Marine's customer perception, and our consulting fee was amortized after only four months.

The author

Gregor Buchwald is Managing Partner at Prof. Roll & Pastuch Management Consultants and has 20 years of pricing experience. More information can be found at www.roll-pastuch.de/en/.

Developing a Go-to-Market Pricing Strategy for a Digital Attacker

By Maciej Wilczyński (Poland)

Introduction
Software-as-a-service companies grow mostly through the power of the market, right trend waves, and substantial premium multipliers generated by heavy capital investments. We don't know

what the future holds, but we do know what the past held. Whenever a crisis hits, we see that average profitability drops. One of the things we know about SaaS is that you need to achieve the "rule of 40%" to ensure reasonable valuation. This rule combines profitability and growth. If these two things combined exceed 40 percent, it's a good performance indicator. In 2020 the ratio of private SaaS companies achieving it dropped from 13 percent to 7 percent. What was mostly affected? Profitability. The previous growth fuel was depleted. Companies applied heavy discounting for customers and had a reduced salesforce, and those panic price cuts caused the loss of a lot of value. That's why we believe that in the next postpandemic years, SaaS pricing becomes more important than ever.

Initial situation

Company X is a VC-funded SaaS platform from Berlin, aiming to challenge the financial accounting market for small and medium-sized business owners. In general, the platform allows users to collect all their accounts into one system, manage invoices, reimburse expenses, and ensure complete tax-related financial control. Just before the launch, the Valueships team was asked to prepare a go-to-market pricing strategy. Usually we recommend doing the pricing research before product development to ensure that we are building only these features for which there is high client willingness to pay. However, in this case, the team was not yet familiar with this approach.

Procedure and methodology

Our goal was to identify the right pricing strategy for Germany's initial entry market. We typically divide our projects into two work streams: desk research and primary research.

Desk research allows us to understand the current price perception and establish the right baseline. We know how much the competitors charge and the market consensus on packaging and billing models with these benchmarks. It's also possible to better understand the overall pricing strategy sophistication.

Primary research is performed after the initial market scan. In this approach, we talk to the customers and run the quantitative survey. This effort allows us to understand price sensitivity, revenue-maximizing price, elasticities, buyer personas, packaging, billing models, overall attitudes, and customer pain points (this survey also helps with UX/UI research). You don't need to have a robust sample to have 80 percent accuracy. Considering the German market, 166 survey responses were sufficient to drive meaningful results.

One of the things we discovered was that willingness to pay is substantially higher than what the market already charges. In other words, we saw that it's possible to price the main pricing plan at €89, while medians for the competitors (from different fintech categories) were between €25 and €35. To determine this, we used the Van Westendorp price sensitivity meter. As Figure 13.3 shows, the price elasticity is steep till ~€55 and then flattens until €89. This means that you would leave a lot of value on the table if you were to employ competitor-based pricing.

Results

Our project resulted in three main achievements.

First, we ensured that our client's pricing reflects the premium value the product provides and captures a maximum willingness to pay. In this case, the significant impact was to set the price 40 percent higher than the market median. It also ensured that the customer acquisition payback period is reduced to only three months, whereas the average payback of the customer acquisition cost on the market is five to seven months.

Second, revenue and billing models now align with customer preferences. For instance, we knew that almost half the potential

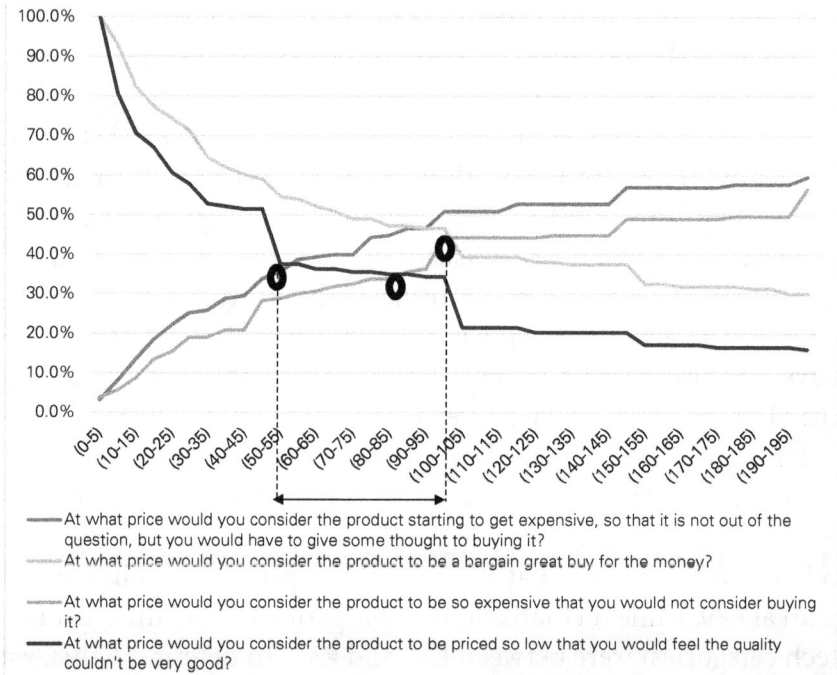

Figure 13.3. Van Westendorp price sensitivity meter.

SMB owners would not buy the product anyway because of strong reluctance to using digital tools. Of the remaining half, around 20 percent use tools they're not satisfied with, and the rest are open to trying something digital. This streamlined the client's overall knowledge and the user experience and sales process function; for example, it changed the promotion activities to a greater focus on value for the various buyer personas.

Third, our client increased their pricing and research capabilities, and they have the whole roadmap created for the following features development efforts. Their product team begins from the price and then builds the product around it. For instance, they now begin with creating add-ons, then move toward bundling them in pricing plans, and once the features commoditize, the team enforces them to the base or freemium packages.

The author

Maciej Wilczyński is a co-founder and CEO of Valueships, a consulting boutique for subscription businesses, serving mostly SaaS/D2C Valueships that solve acquisition, retention, and monetization problems of their clients through data analytics and research. He is an ex-McKinsey & Company marketing and sales consultant and has worked with top Fortune 500 companies in industries including software, banking, telco, insurance, and retail/e-commerce. He is finishing his PhD in strategic management with a focus on the pricing capabilities of SaaS companies. He is the author of multiple publications, an MBA/postgraduate lecturer, and a guest speaker. He is also a co-founder of Stanversity, a university lecturers platform connecting the best scientists with the universities in need of new study courses, primarily on the postgraduate and MBA levels. He is excited about tech, B2B pricing, monetization, digital marketing, customer insights, and quantitative and qualitative research. He can be reached on Facebook at fb.com/wilczynski24, on Twitter @wilczynski24, via LinkedIn at www.linkedin.com/in/wilczynskim/, and via email at maciej@valueships.com.

The Strategic Imperative for Smarter Pricing in the Digital World

Craig Zawada (US)

As the global economy continues to emerge from the worst pandemic in more than a century, one overriding fact is inarguably true for virtually every business and industry sector: *the old rules no longer apply*—and this is especially true for pricing. Gone are the days of standard fixed prices, face-to-face interactions, endless rounds of negotiations, and other process friction. While managing pricing is and should be a top issue for CEOs, it needs to shift from being something to be *managed* to a function that *delivers market-relevant prices with speed, and through channels in which customers want to buy.*

Problems with current pricing practices
- **Reliance on high-touch.** Buyers today want an efficient transaction that they believe is fair and equitable. The outdated high-touch sales cycle is dramatically out of step with buyers who have increasingly grown up in the Amazon world of e-commerce. *Instead of high-touch, they want low-touch or no-touch.* McKinsey & Company found a 42 percent decrease in the number of buyers who prefer to order from a sales rep in person.
- **Lack of market-driven prices.** Companies need the agility to quickly reset market pricing based on current conditions and to deliver the right price at the right time through digital channels. Our research found that 64 percent of buyers would switch to suppliers that offer personalized, dynamically adjusted market prices.
- **Complex buying processes.** Gartner found that 77 percent of B2B buyers report that their latest purchase was very complex or difficult. In many companies, prices and policies are created to solve managerial problems, such as variations in pricing or overnegotiation. That leads to processes ostensibly designed to protect the company, rather than facilitating a purchase.

Recommendations to light up digital channels with smart pricing
- **Tie pricing into digital transformation.** Too often, pricing is an afterthought of digital transformation. Make

pricing a central component of digital transformation initiatives because it's an irreplaceable element of sales experience. For example, a glass manufacturer's e-commerce sales grew from 10 percent to 80 percent of total sales in two months during the pandemic because it was able to deliver a frictionless price to customers. Pricing was central to its digital transformation.

- **Transition to self-serve pricing.** In certain B2B markets, high-tough pricing will endure for large, complex sales cycles. However, companies can improve pricing performance simply through faster pricing cycles (think hours, not days) and begin to transition their businesses from 80 percent high-touch to just 15 to 20 percent high-touch and push pricing out to self-serve channels and dealer portals. With a flexible quoting system and the capabilities for real-time price adjustments, an oil field services company fared much better than competitors who were hindered by manual price updates.

- **Build trust in pricing science.** Pricing technology has made huge advancements to recommend market-relevant prices. Algorithms can make pricing adjustments to reflect margin goals, buying history, region, market history, economic forecasts, inventory levels, seasonality, and more. This is an essential requirement for creating the no-touch self-serve pricing described above. Facing the significant downturn of travel demand, one hospitality supplies distributor needed to quickly accommodate an increase in sanitary services products and a reduction in the more typical purchases of towels and toiletries. Although the company faced furloughs, the investment in pricing science and technology allowed it to ensure that its pricing adjusted to reflect market conditions and protected profitability.

The author

Craig Zawada is the Chief Visionary Officer at PROS. A widely published author, Zawada is perhaps best known for co-authoring *The Price Advantage,* recognized as one of the most pragmatic books available on pricing strategy. Prior to joining PROS, he was a partner and leader in the Marketing and Sales Practice at McKinsey & Company.

SECTION 4

PRICING MATURITY AND CAPABILITIES

14

Pricing Success: Get It Right Today, Tomorrow, and as an Ongoing Competency— A Complete-Solution Approach Drives Optimum Impact

Terry Oblander, Chief Growth Officer, INSIGHT2PROFIT

A S A BUSINESS LEADER, you must prioritize a myriad of opportunities for your organization from internal to market-facing initiatives. Each year and quarter have themes that roll up to a strategic vision and plan. You've probably heard by now or know that pricing is the most powerful lever of success, and while other initiatives may help the bottom line, pricing drives both the top and bottom line to a greater degree than any other opportunity. Perhaps you previously implemented a pricing approach or did a study but did not get the desired results. Avoid fretting and don't give up, because pricing is not a one-time project or an event-based tactic. Many organizations shy away from pricing initiatives because of a fear of losing customers and/or sales volume, lack of dedicated resources (e.g., whose responsibility is pricing) and tools, or navigating the change management pitfalls. Additionally, pricing results can be fickle from the standpoint that they may be perceived to provide an initial "pop" in results that deteriorates over time.

Pricing is complex and needs to incorporate both science and art, especially when dealing in business-to-business-related negotiated transactions. It is for these reasons that implementing a complete, ongoing solution allows you to get the most from the most powerful lever in your C-suite toolkit, pricing.

Pricing does not need to be a greenfield expedition into the territory of the unknown. While the journey is not always smooth, these roads have been traveled, and expertise is more abundant today to help you navigate. By dedicating focus on pricing, organizations unlock their organic potential and create organizational alignment based on data-driven decision-making resulting in long-term profitability. This chapter describes how the fusion of pricing consulting and technology—which incorporates people, model, process, and technology—eliminates failure and drives the most profitable, sustained impact.

All organizations desire sustained, incremental profit improvements. The least used, though most impactful, way to achieve this goal is through **price optimization**—not the headline price paid by a customer but the net margin earned by the organization for the transaction. While price optimization comes in different forms, the definition we use in this chapter is *net pocket margin*—the amount of money made after all costs are accounted for. To achieve the most optimal net pocket margin within your business, you must get granular with your data down to the customer and product levels, and you must fully understand the cost to serve each of your customers. Figure 14.1 illustrates what we mean by net pocket margin.

Once an organization understands how pricing has historically impacted their bottom line and why, they can make the requisite changes to realize ongoing profit gains. The choice of whether to go it alone or whether to partner with vendors to improve profit is typically based on an organization's beliefs across a few dimensions (see Figure 14.2).

As illustrated below, the goal of price optimization is not to revert to the historical average or to merely realize sustained gains but rather to achieve a gain that is both sustainable and incremental going forward. This, in essence, is **continuous improvement**. Our research and experience with over 500 client engagements have shown that the fusion of people, process, and technology working in tandem with an objective and data-driven model offers the most sustainable yet improvable basis on which to transform organizations. Figure 14.3 illustrates the value proposition of continuous improvement.

Strategic insights codified into business processes produce strong, lasting results. Specialization has typically divided these capabilities into two camps—strategy consulting firms and pricing software companies—because of their disparate strategies

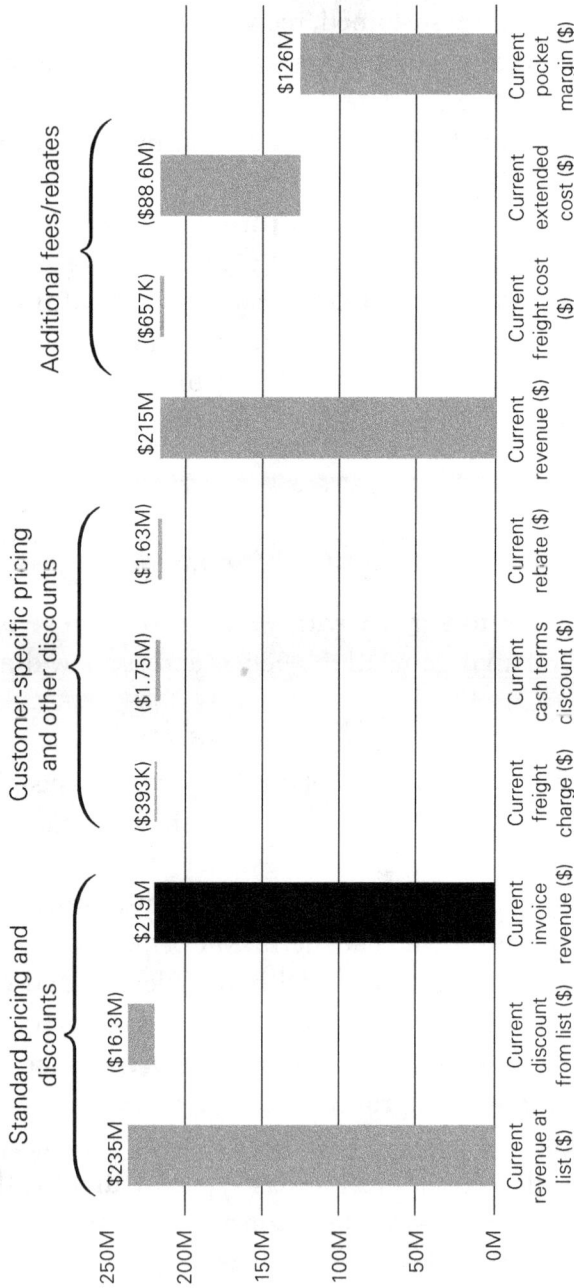

Figure 14.1. Net pocket margin illustration.

Most organizations are unable to aggregate, cleanse, and interpret internal data and, consequently, have limited visibility into actual pricing outcomes and fully burdened customer-level margins.

Typical client challenges

Disparate and disorganized data from internal and external sources
- Limited visibility and insights from data

Lack of tools and technology
- Outdated data analysis tools (e.g., Excel) and lack of specific profit optimization technology

Lack of internal domain expertise
- Typically, no single individual responsible for overall price strategy

Inability or fear of driving change
- Inadequate training, limited resources, and lack of internal catalysts limit "do-it-yourself" approach

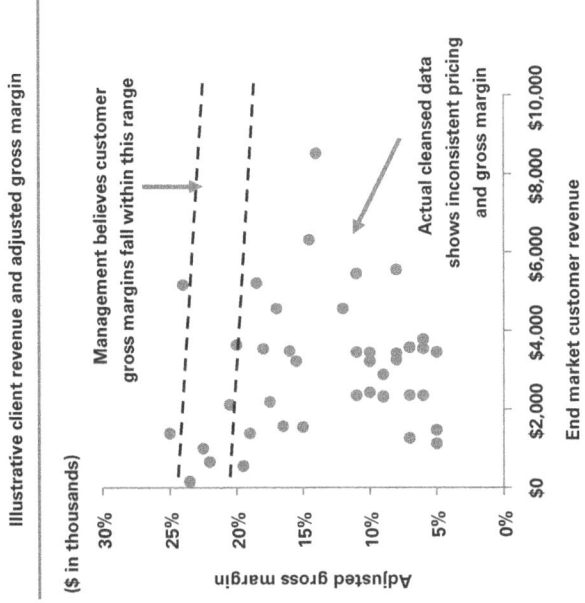

Illustrative client revenue and adjusted gross margin

($ in thousands)

Adjusted gross margin

Management believes customer gross margins fall within this range

Actual cleansed data shows inconsistent pricing and gross margin

End market customer revenue

30% 25% 20% 15% 10% 5% 0%

$0 $2,000 $4,000 $6,000 $8,000 $10,000

Figure 14.2. Typical client challenges.

Insight:
Strategy + implementation + technology

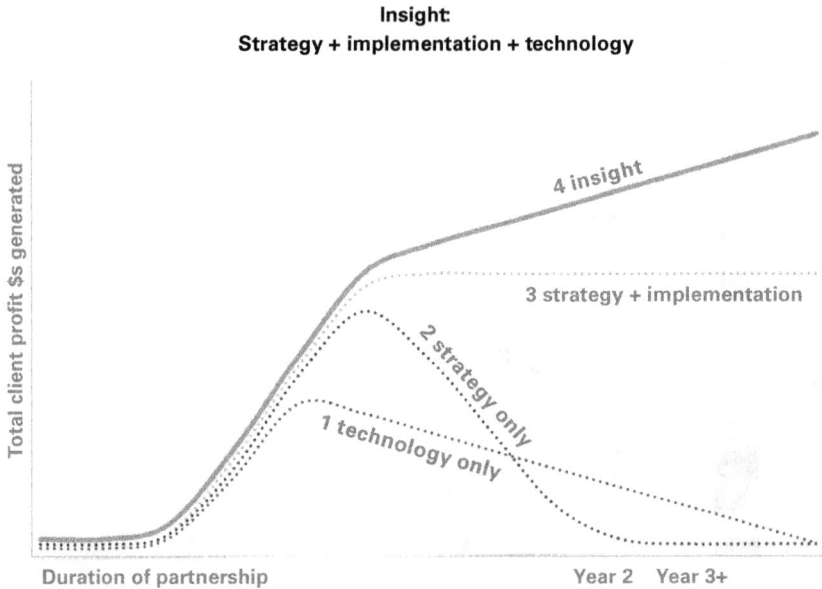

Figure 14.3. Continuous improvement illustration.

and approaches. A vendor that combines both elements can be hard to get right because of the differences in business models (one-time/monthly consulting fees vs. monthly/annual subscription fees), investment decisions (adding people vs. adding R&D development), and related enterprise valuations. However, it's this convergence of people and technology that organizations need in order to accelerate their capabilities around commercial excellence, thus ensuring differentiation of their own products and services within the market.

As organizations look to partner with vendors, they're typically presented with a consulting firm that can produce a comprehensive report and pricing strategy analysis or a "black box" software algorithm that tries to predict target prices. While both elements (i.e., strategy and software) are needed, they are incomplete when engaged separately and won't achieve continuous improvement without the requisite change management and ongoing process enhancement discipline. Profits realized from the initiative may only register as a short-term blip in performance if the organizational behaviors don't become embedded in the company culture. As a result, the effort will not yield the expected return on investment, and the valuation of the organization will suffer over time because of sizable investments yielding decaying returns.

From its inception, INSIGHT2PROFIT ("INSIGHT") sought to fill the greenfield space between consulting and technology by designing a complete solution that fuses knowledge and expertise with software consistency and predictability. INSIGHT brings people, process, and technology together around an objective, data-driven decision-support model to ensure the optimal value capture of every transaction. Optimal pricing teases out customer nuances, cost-to-serve factors, proper segmentation, and demand drivers, allowing the organization to win on best-fit transactions, thus gaining market share and optimizing profitability. One can drive transformation in pricing and profitability by following the INSIGHT IMPACT process (see Figure 14.4) and creating foundational improvements that grow into centers of excellence.

To illustrate, let's review an example with a company in the food distribution space; the client engaged in both qualitative and quantitative discovery to help determine and measure the profit opportunities. Leveraging technology and dedicated data engineering professionals to compile disparate data across multiple data sources yielded insights within a few weeks. The outcome of this phase was a detailed profitability opportunity roadmap through which the initial area of focus, to achieve near-term profit impact, was determined. Trust and confidence along with collaboration ensued among the client and vendor teams as the information was synthesized and the size of each opportunity was understood (see Figure 14.5a and Figure 14.5b).

Quality of Pricing® sell-side diligence

Exit planning

Continuous improvement

People

Technology

Process

Customer

Target

Order

Product

Model

Duration: 2+ years

Implementation

- Dynamic model
- Training and change management
- Tech and systems integration
- Measurement

Duration: 3–5 months
Average: 3 months

Strategy

Data engineering
- Transactional data
- Third-party data
Qualitative discovery
- Process documentation
- Interviews
Opportunity roadmap

Duration: 4–12 weeks
Average: 6 weeks

Acquisition

Quality of Pricing® buy-side diligence

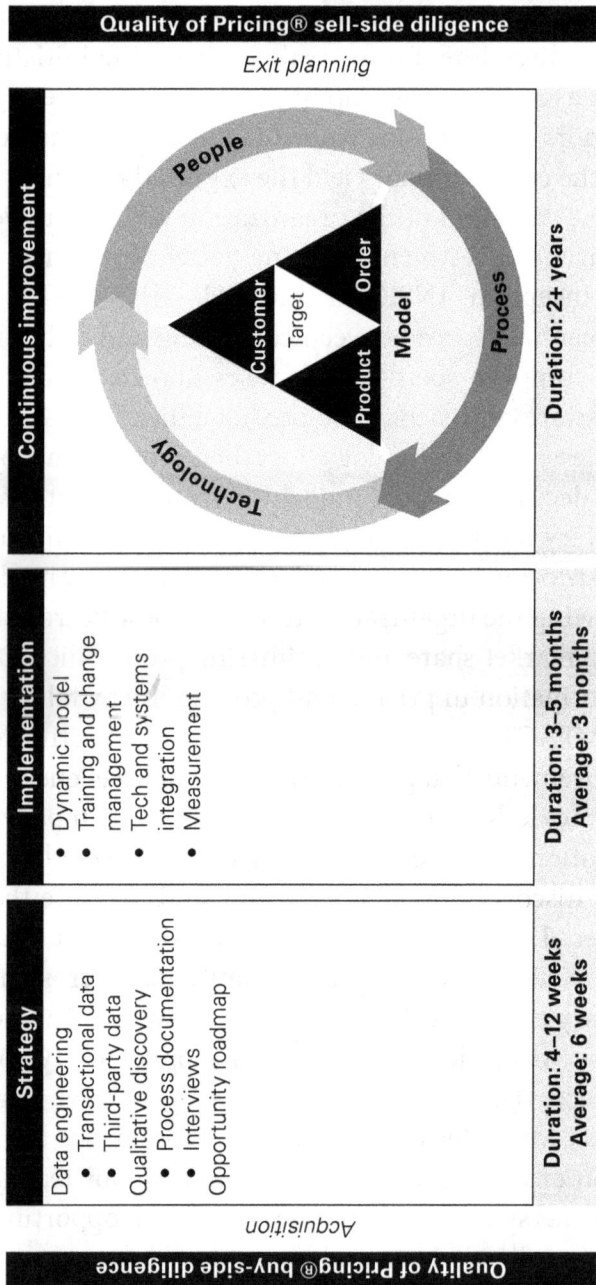

Figure 14.4. Impact process illustration.

The design of a future solution begins to materialize near the end of the strategy period and takes fuller shape as the opportunity is selected. A data science group then begins to create the custom model that will be the center of future pricing recommendations. Through analysis of historical data and client interviews to help identify and understand competitive value drivers, the data sources (or model inputs) become clear. Development of the order of and logic for how the model comes together (i.e., rules and parameters to manage risk) are incorporated and reviewed with the client team for feedback.

In this specific client example, the **strategy** phase demonstrated a concern with the client's ability to win new business because of delays in turnaround times and tracking of quotes. Through analysis, calculating the extent to which decreasing quote times and increased tracking would improve the client's win rate was determined. While this analysis may seem to solve the problem, the real work begins with designing and implementing a strategy and winning the hearts and minds of the organization to do business differently. This moves us into the next phase of the IMPACT process, which is implementation.

During **implementation,** all the necessary data factors and criteria that are material for the client to win deals in the market are incorporated. These inputs differ greatly from organization to organization. Even where two entities are within the same industry, there can be different models designed based on each organization's unique set of competitive differentiators. It's this differentiation that allows for profit optimization and makes every model unique to the client. Figure 14.6 reflects unique model input options developed for this food distributor.

As the model is constructed during implementation, real historical data and current test cases are run through it, producing target prices by customer/product. These recommended targets

Qualitative analysis: Despite having resources in place and strong internal knowledge, the company lacked structure and controls to sustainably execute price management systems

Area	Low ◄————— Maturity ————► High			Opportunity areas
Price structure	Cost-plus	Cost-plus with segmented bands	Market-based approach	Market-based approach, continuously optimized	Market-based pricing model
Processes and controls	Ineffective or missing price guidelines, no price controls	Limited price guidelines, no price controls	Structured price guidelines, controls in place	Comprehensive price guidelines, continuously optimized, controls continuously enhanced	Defined margin and freight optimization strategies
Systems and tools	No price performance training, no price management system	Limited price performance tracking, no price management system	Accurate price performance tracking, price management system in place	Best-in-class price performance tracking, price management system heavily utilized	Establishment of RFQ/RFP tools and processes
Resources	Pricing part of an existing role	Limited pricing resources	Dedicated pricing resources	Well-trained, sufficient pricing resources to meet business needs	Eliminate administrative work for pricing team
Change management	No counter-sourcing training, negotiations based on price	Price recognized as strategic initiative, team leadership engaged	Robust price training, execute price strategy, sales leadership engaged	Robust price training, sell on value and achieve price goals, sales reps engaged	Value-based sales training and workshops

Quantitative analysis: Built transactional price waterfall to understand profitability and where leaks may be occurring

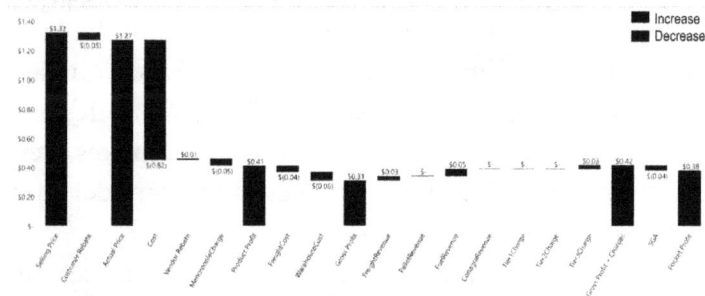

Figure 14.5a. Profitability opportunity roadmap illustration.

Opportunity	Details	Impact potential
1 Differentiated price increase	• Implement quick-win initiative via a base model for select customers • Communicate new pricing to customers	
2 Transform the quoting experience—RFQ	• Accelerate time to quote—from days or weeks to on-demand • Systematize tribal knowledge into algorithm • Automate with technology • Process to support immediate pricing for all customer and item combinations	**$500–750K**
3 Systematize the price review	• Develop a refreshable pricing model that learns over time to drive margin $ • Integrate value drivers to identify risk profile of a customer/product • Identify and correct margin outliers vs. their peers	**$1M**
4 Transform the quoting experience—RFP	• Accelerate RFP process • Build model that addresses a more price-sensitive group • Automate with technology and integrate into current processes and systems • Leverage analytics and product positioning to enhance account margins	**$800K**
5 Optimize inventory management	• Develop model driven off demand, inventory, and replenishment planning factors • Robust change management to enhance cross-functional processes	**TBD**
6 Turn freight into a profit lever	• Develop freight pricing model to support optimal delivered price • Ensure speed to accurate decision to enhance process	**~$1M+**
7 Improve wallet share and customer/ product mix	• Identity gaps within current customer's product portfolio to further penetrate accounts • Establish processes for empowering the sales team to react to targeted opportunities • Use advanced analytics including predictive volumes trending to track customer behavior changes	**TBD**

Figure 14.5b. Profitability opportunity roadmap illustration.

1 **Inputs and cost**
- Item
- Order quantity
- Customer
- Customer region
- Customer industry
- Source warehouse
- Costs
  - Landed cost (warehousing, vendor costs, market costs, purchase agreements, etc.)
  - Outbound freight

2 **Identify peer group**
- Item
- Pricing peer group

3 **Identify Identify optimal base margin according to peer-group factors**

Example	Target margin		
Pricing peer	Competitive	Moderate	Stretch
High-cost items	11%	13%	15%
Low-cost items	15%	18%	21%

- Factors
  - Market perspective from category management
  - Historical margin data
  - Cost curve alignment

4 **Adjust margin target according to factors associated with . . .**
- Customer
  - Region competitiveness
  - Customer win/loss rate (on past quotes)
  - New vs. existing customer
  - If new customer: sales rep input opportunity score or base on sales rep team (strategic vs. transactional)
- Product
  - Win/loss rate
  - Price sensitivity score
  - Temperature control requirement
  - Safety requirement
  - Quote volume trend (proxy for demand)
  - Futures trend
- Order
  - Order size
  - Shelf-life requirement
  - Special packaging requirements

Figure 14.6. Model input illustration.

are reviewed with sales professionals and management to begin to align on the price impact on a net basis. Because of the granularity of the inputs within the model, the model will reflect and be sensitive to those cost-to-serve elements that drive profitability by customer and product combination. As part of the change management process, getting early buy-in from the sales team—whose familiarity and involvement with accounts have an impact on customer relationships—on the logic and purpose of the model is critical to its ultimate success. The goal is to empower the sales team so that they own the process, the content, and the outcome, which will ultimately drive greater profit realization.

Once the model is nearing finalization—typically within 45 days—the development, implementation, and sales training of the tools and analytics are created. Often, piloting the tools and model can be an important step toward ensuring a successful launch. Data visibility is also an important implementation success factor. In our food distributor example, providing the sales representatives the data input of the recommended price gave them the confidence they needed in the quoting tool (Figure 14.7). This resulted in very little variance or very few overrides of the recommended price. When it comes to implementation and buy-in, transparency equals confidence.

Implementation should also include written scripts, in-person role playing (e.g., simulating price negotiations to bolster their bargaining and communication skills), step-by-step user guides, communication letters, guidelines, and frequently asked questions to ensure a successful launch. It's important to be hands-on to support the commercial team through this implementation phase.

Once the tools have gone live and the model is being used throughout the organization, the measurement component of the implementation phase determines whether the client's results are tracking toward their forecasted goals. Measurement provides immediate feedback about what tactics have proved successful

CLIENT RFQ

User:

New Quote	Quote Status

Customer Search	
Customer Name	ABC Ingredients Co.
Customer Number	123-456789
Customer Parent Name	
Opportunity Name	
Region	Northeast
Default Warehouse	
Payment Terms	Net 10
Delivery Address	
Customer Freight Terms	Prepaid
Comments	

Total Sales Dollars	$0.00
Total Margin Dollars	$0.00
Total Margin %	0.0%
Total Quantity	0.00
At or Above Target	1
Price Deviation	0
Requires Approval?	No

Quote ID	987654
Order or Annual?	Annual
Created By	jdoe@jdoe.com
Created Date	2020-05-11
Quote Status	Draft

Product Name	Item Code	Annual Volume	On Allocation	Weight	Package Type	Special Order Item	Min Order Quantity	Delivery Charge	Target Price	Quoted Price	Quoted Delivered Price
		0.00		50.00	Box	No	50	$0.1030	$1.4630	$1.4630	$1.5660

Figure 14.7. Quoting tool example.

and what challenges remain. Within five months, you've studied the data, built a model, and implemented a process that will boost profitability. To see real results flow through the P&L statement in a short period bolsters confidence that the level of effort is worth it and helps the commercial teams stay focused to continue to achieve and exceed their targets. Relative to a consulting project that may not yet have the finished report handed to the client before six months, the time-to-value equation is unparalleled. Further, the integration of the pricing model and tools into workflow systems and reporting provides real-time, granular data regarding win rates, quoting turnaround time, and usage levels, allowing necessary adjustments from an informed position.

Many organizations do not have baselines for quoting, but implementing the approach in this example allowed transparency into the actual performance. Note that new tools and processes were developed and helped drive improvements in quote turnaround time from anecdotally being within a one- to five-day turnaround to 78 percent of quotes turned around within 24 hours and 85 percent within 48 hours.

With the model and tools now being used for all the client's customer transactions, and the reporting and analysis demonstrating areas of success, optimization isn't over. Models and approaches to increased profitability aren't static. Internal and external factors affect the organization and/or the market at large and its imperative to incorporate these new data points and adjust the client's strategy and tactics accordingly. People, process, and technology can get better. The efficacy of a model can be improved. These inputs become immensely powerful levers to create the ongoing, incremental profit improvement that achieves the value proposition (Figure 14.8).

During **continuous improvement**, optimization of all facets of people, process, technology, and the pricing model, leading

People

Established a culture where the sales reps share best practices and challenges during dedicated sessions on an ongoing basis to ensure stabilization and growth of usage, adoption, and impact.

Sales rep RFQ tool usage

Process

Upon finding changes in mix trends, this led to the implementation of a new **churn reporting process** to manage scenarios where customers may have churned because of price.

Customer count churn bridge

Technology

Built **mobile capabilities** for reps to have remote access to the quoting tool, including approvals.

Model

Moved from a dynamic to a **learning model**
- Intraday data updates for faster refresh times
- Model parameters tuned based on win-rate data
- Third-party data incorporated into the model data

Win-rate data by region

Sales Region	Won Quote Lines	Win-Rate Denominator	Win-Rate
Region 1	21	73	28.8%
Region 2	20	99	20.2%
Region 3	11	59	18.6%
Region 4	3	11	27.3%
Region 5	4	9	44.4%
Other	0	2	0.0%
Total	59	253	23.3%

Figure 14.8. Continuous improvement areas example.

to incremental value creation, continues. In this client example, note that the opportunities to improve were found across all these facets and translated into detailed execution plans to capture additional value. For example, through the measurement phase, it became clear that one region was facing unprecedented competitive price pressure, resulting in lower-than-expected win rate (Figure 14.9). While this region accounted for only 5 percent of the total revenue, it still needed to be addressed. The pricing model was adjusted to incorporate this regional price driver, and the subsequent win rate increased from 16 percent to 24 percent, a 50 percent improvement. Based on the size of the business in this region, that win rate extrapolated over the course of a year would mean an additional $100k in revenue and $20k in profit to the business. On the technology side, the quoting tool was linked in real time to the client CRM, enabling seamless creation of quotes, thus improving quote turnaround time and ease of use (Figure 14.10).

INSIGHT worked with the client to identify the opportunities and make the necessary adjustments to create sustained, incremental profit improvement. Through hundreds of engagements, it's clear and evident that the best outcomes result from the fusion of pricing consulting and technology. When organizations do not follow the process from beginning to end, a wide variety of results occurs. For example, taking a software approach typically creates an initial pricing model that feels relevant at the beginning; however, as the internal and external environment changes, the ability to do the proper change management and transparency of the recommended target price becomes less clear to the commercial team. This variance in the pricing increases greatly, in some cases resulting in the recommended price being ignored. Because of the level of investment and focus that pricing transformation requires, it shouldn't be treated as an event or flavor-of-the-month exercise.

Win rate by sales region
- Recently tuned parameter for region 3 to produce more competitive pricing
- Region 3 has lower win-rate % than other regions
- Compliance in region 3 is 200 BPS higher and generated additional revenue vs. prior months
- Win rate on quotes with data is 23%
- 73% of quote lines qualified for win rate are within 5% of the target price
- Will continue to monitor wins by region moving forward

Sales region	Won quote lines	Win-rate denominator	Win rate
Region 1	21	73	28.8%
Region 2	20	99	20.2%
Region 3	11	59	18.6%
Region 4	3	11	27.3%
Region 5	4	9	44.4%
Other	0	2	0.0%
Total	**59**	**253**	**23.3%**

Quote loss reasons by category

Item category	Total quote lines
Competitive pressures—price	42
R&D	29
Minimum order quantity	12
Competitive pressures—delivery times	3
Vendor not approved	1
Competitive pressures—T&C	1

Region	Total quote lines
Region 2	17
Region 3	13
Region 1	10

Figure 14.9. Continuous improvement opportunity (region) example.

Changes in order volume—customer case count

Purchases occurred, but with potentially leaking margin

Total cases	Purchased since last update	Extraordinary change	Item class purchase	Any SKU purchase	No purchases
157	9	20	48	42	38
		Do we know why price has decreased?	*Are they switching to an in item of lower profit per pound?*	*Have they gone to a competitor for this specific item class?*	*The 38 unique line items represent non-repeat margin dollars; 16 of the 38 cases are segment A customers*

Root Cause
- Moved to competitor
- Item no longer needed
- Shift in ongoing buying pattern

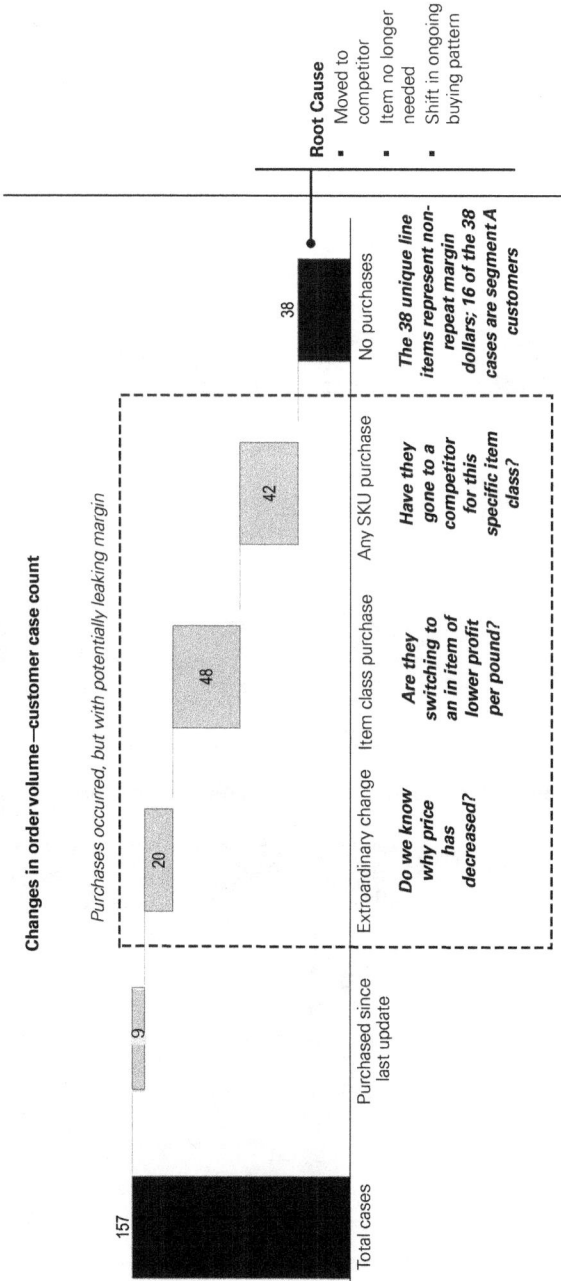

Figure 14.10. Continuous improvement opportunity (process) example.

Pricing is not something to "set and forget." Building a pricing center of excellence is a journey, and it's important to understand both where you are and where you want to go (Figure 14.11). Once ready to begin the journey, you can turn this critical commercial area into a competitive advantage that will unlock and catapult your growth potential in ways no other investment can fulfill.

Win rate by item category, single region

Product category	Won quote lines	Win-rate denominator	Win-rate
Category 1	1	20	5.0%
Category 2	7	32	21.9%
Category 3	8	19	42.1%
Category 4	4	18	22.2%
Category 5	6	16	37.5%
Category 6	1	15	6.7%
Category 7	2	11	18.2%
Category 8	10	16	62.5%
Category 9	3	11	27.3%

Target quote recommendation compliance by sales rep, single region

Created by	Within 5% of target	Average change from target
Sales rep 1	69.2%	4.9%
Sales rep 2	47.4%	5.7%
Sales rep 3	81.0%	3.1%
Sales rep 4	93.3%	0.9%
Sales rep 5	72.7%	4.6%
Sales rep 6	64.7%	6.9%
Sales rep 7	83.3%	3.6%
Sales rep 8	66.7%	5.7%

Figure 14.11. Continuous improvement actions example.

In summary, pricing is a journey through every organizational life cycle. It's not an area to ignore or avoid, but one to dig into, embrace, and reap the rewards from. That said, how you approach this journey is just as important as beginning the journey and staying dedicated to it. Most important, there are no shortcuts or skipping steps along the way if you want consistent and sustainable results. If you decide to endeavor down this path, then understand that organizational change and follow-through must

1 Model enhancements
Improve pricing accuracy over time
- **Finding:** Categories 1 and 6 have a significantly lower win rate than other product categories
- **Action:** Adjust model parameters for these categories to be more price sensitive and drive better price recommendations; review competitive situation, market trends, regional data (*quarterly*)

2 Pricing optimization
Capture incremental margin; track and iterate
- **Finding:** Category 8 has high price compliance
- **Action:** Dig in to see whether compliance is driven by pricing that is too low and potential need for price increases; do we have a competitive advantage in this region? (*quarterly*)

3 Change management
Drive behavior change where necessary
- **Finding:** Certain sales reps have notably lower compliance with target recommendations
- **Action:** Identify root cause (demand-driven, price confidence, lack of incentives) and implement training, individual coaching, tool changes, or new incentives to improve underperforming sales reps (*quarterly*)

become a competency of your organization just like any other function or competency you possess. The reason so many organizations don't unlock the full value that pricing affords is that they direct less focus once the initiative is off the ground. The dynamism of business requires ongoing analysis of the data, engaging customers in their concerns and opportunities, and reevaluating the changing market landscape. As illustrated in Figure 14.12 and Figure 14.13, the change an organization can realize is transformational. Optimizing this process takes time, but it's important to get started quickly so that early successes can be sustained and improved upon.

When you're ready to make sustained, incremental profits a reality in your business rather than a hope, reach out to a complete-solution partner like INSIGHT2PROFIT. Selecting a partner that understands the journey and brings a complete solution of people, process, technology, and sophisticated models will yield rapid results and ongoing opportunities to optimize your pricing and, ultimately, your profitability and business value. INSIGHT will help you understand your starting point and set reasonable goals of progress that will help you drive quick wins today and the sustainable, ongoing profit gains for tomorrow and beyond.

The author

Terry Oblander is Chief Growth Officer at INSIGHT2PROFIT. As Chief Growth Officer, Terry is responsible for developing and executing INSIGHT's long-term growth strategy. Over the past 10 years, Terry has led pricing and profit improvement engagements across hundreds of companies and helped to develop INSIGHT's approach to continuous value creation for its clients.

Prior to joining INSIGHT2PROFIT, Terry spent 12 years working for a Fortune 500 building materials business, where he had

INSIGHT's Solutions Enable Data-Driven Decisions to Realize More Consistent, Higher Margins

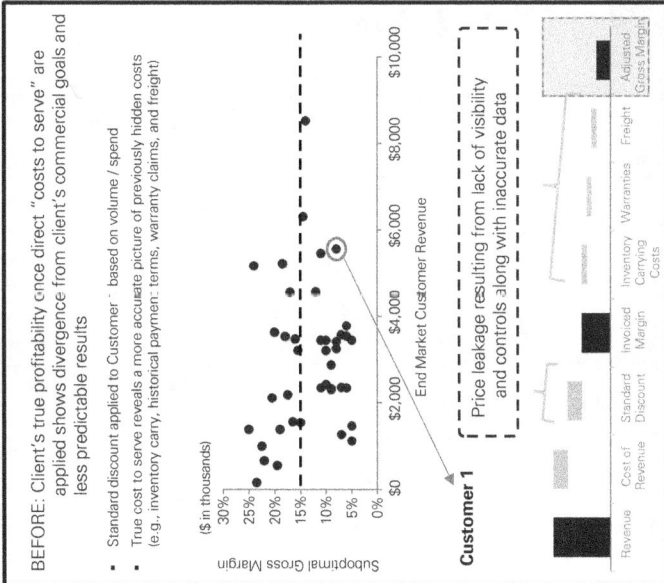

BEFORE: Client's true profitability once direct "costs to serve" are applied shows divergence from client's commercial goals and less predictable results

- Standard discount applied to Customer 1 based on volume / spend
- True cost to serve reveals a more accurate picture of previously hidden costs (e.g., inventory carry, historical payment: terms, warranty claims, and freight)

Price leakage resulting from lack of visibility and controls along with inaccurate data

AFTER: Net price improvements through differentiated, value-driven approach realize margin optimization, consistency, and clarity

- Dynamic model factors in relevant costs (e.g., inventory carry, historical payment terms, warranty claims, and freight costs) to new customer transactions to ensure net margin targets and differentiation by customer
- Price discount customized based on actual margin opportunity

Price leakage minimized through data science, expertise, change management, and technology

After Full Solution

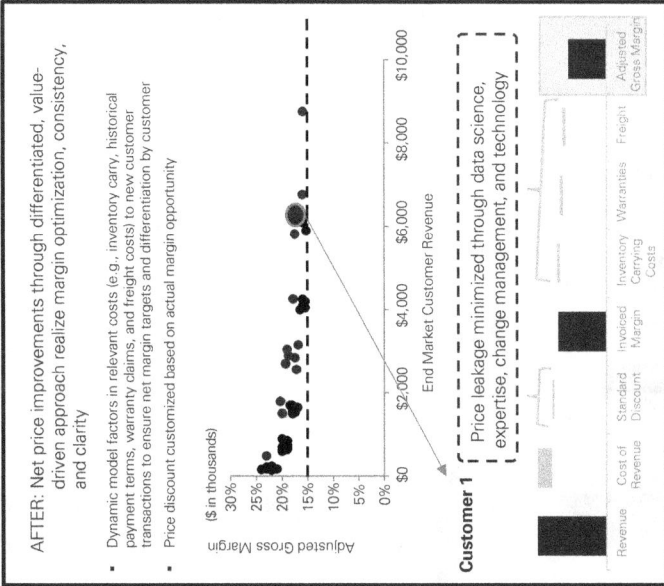

Figure 14.12. Transformational solution.

Area	Goal	Center of excellence maturity		
		Good – – – →	Better – – – →	Best
People	**Clarity** Do you have clarity of the strategy and execution for probability/profit optimization?	Underdeveloped strategy with limited buy-in	General alignment on strategy and engagement, limited clarity of execution	Pricing is part of the culture: full organizational alignment and buy-in on the strategy and execution
Process	**Speed** Do your processes enable rapid execution against plan?	Limited clarity to guidelines and accountability, gaps in process	Partial accountability for existing guidelines and controls, cumbersome process	Comprehensive, dynamic processes integrated across the organization that enable quick and smart action
Technology	**Adoption** Is your technology easy to use and driving adoption of business strategies and processes?	Restricted tools and integration across systems, processes, and people	Existing tools aren't always used or reliable and require manual work	Best-in-class, streamlined technology across all systems, tools, processes, and people enable ease of use
Model	**Impact** Does your model consistently drive desired impact?	Model exists with limited or unknown results	Model is used and produces some desired impact	Learning model provides optimized recommendation for every scenario, delivering consistent impact

- Upon start of partnership
- After profit realization
- → Continuous improvement objectives

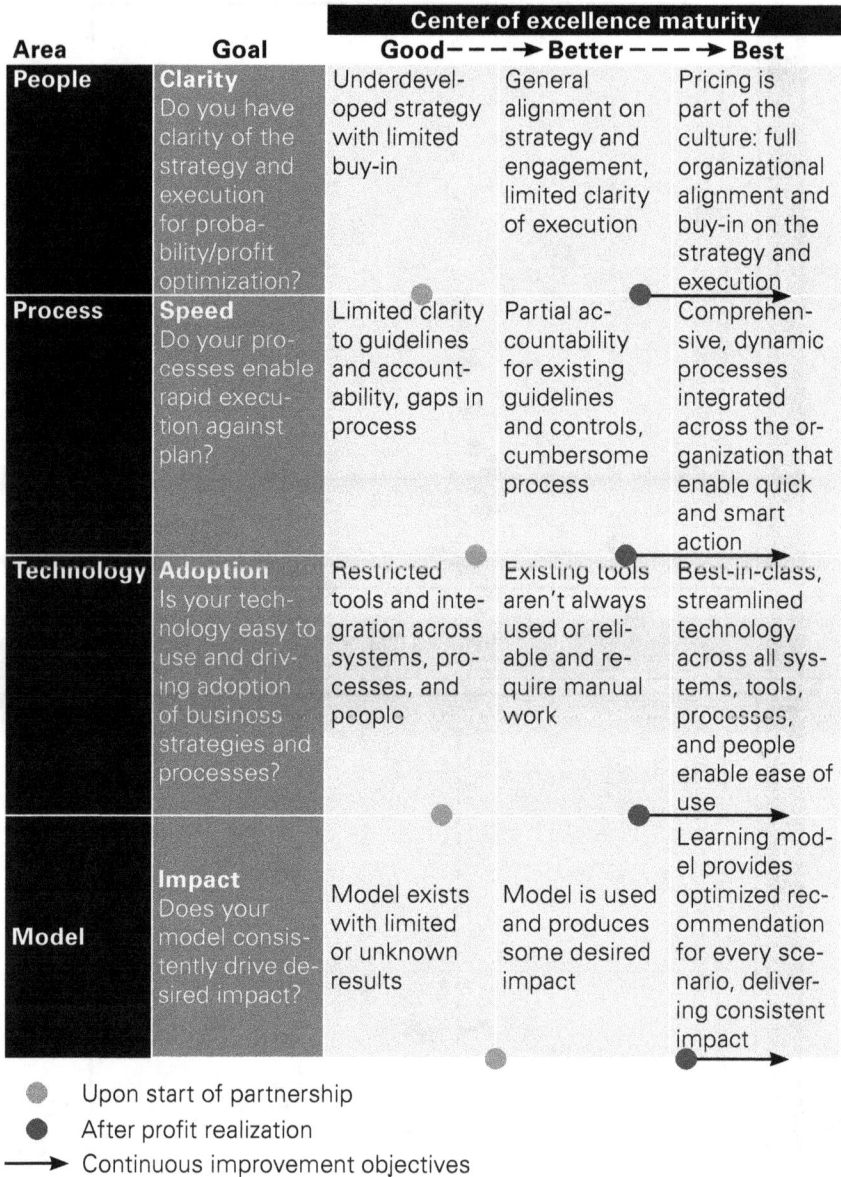

Figure 14.13. Pricing journey example.

a record of driving profitability improvements working with cross-functional teams. Terry holds degrees in business from the Ohio State University (Fisher College of Business) and an MBA from Cleveland State University. He can be reached via email at toblander@insight2profit.com and at LinkedIn: www.linkedin .com/in/terryoblander/.

About INSIGHT2PROFIT

INSIGHT2PROFIT is one of the largest, fastest-growing companies in the pricing and profitability solutions space. INSIGHT helps companies grow and sustain enterprise value through decades of experience in pricing expertise, data science, and change management. INSIGHT's unique combination of people, process, and technology results in real change and exceptional ROI and delivers continuous profit growth for its clients beyond a one-time lift. INSIGHT predominantly serves private-equity-backed businesses, delivering to date over $1 billion in enterprise value for our partners in manufacturing, distribution, business services, consumer services, consumer products, and technology.

15

The Value Capture Gap and How Executives Can Shrink It

Mark Stiving, PhD, Chief Education Officer, Impact Pricing

Leaving money on the table

B2B EXECUTIVES: TAKE A moment and think about how much value your customers get from using your product or service. How much do you reduce their costs of operations through efficiency or effectiveness? How much do you increase their revenue with capabilities they can sell to their customers? Whether it's cost savings or revenue growth, they bought and used your product to help them increase profit. Let's call this realized value, the additional profit they earn because of your company's product.

Now, think about how much your customers pay for your product. Are you capturing your fair share of the value you deliver? Most executives and companies I talk with answer "no" to that question. The difference between what you think your fair share should be and the price you get paid is a gap. It's your value capture gap.

Said differently, your value capture gap (VCG) is the value you think you should be able to capture (expected captured value; ECV) minus the value you do capture with price (actual captured value; ACV). Think of this as money you left on the table. It's money you think you should have made but didn't.

VCG = ECV – ACV

To shrink your VCG, you have two choices: increase the value you capture (ACV) or lower the value you expect to capture (ECV). Let's start with raising ACV.

ACV: Actual captured value

Raising ACV is the essence of pricing. The prices you win deals at are the amount of value you capture. To increase ACV, you must focus on pricing. More importantly, you must focus on value.

Put yourself in the shoes of a buyer. They have to make a purchase decision based on their perceptions of the value they believe they will receive and the resources it will cost them.

The more value buyers believe they will receive, the more they are willing to pay. If you want to raise the actual captured value, you must help buyers increase the amount of value to expect before their purchase. This likely means sales and marketing must improve how they communicate and capture value. The two most powerful and fundamental tools I've seen help with this are value conversations and Stiving value tables.

Value conversations

A value conversation means talking with your buyers so you and they can both estimate how much value they will receive from your product.

Here are two facts.

- Your buyers do not know your product well enough to know the value it will deliver.
- Your salespeople do not know the buyer's company well enough to know the value you'll be able to deliver.

In other words, nobody knows the value that a buyer will receive by using your product. A value conversation is a way for your salesperson and your buyer to work together to estimate that expected value.

You may already have an ROI calculator, thinking that it fulfills this role. Your buyers fill in the inputs, and the calculations show a phenomenal return. But your buyers don't believe it. What did you think the last time a salesperson showed you a complex spreadsheet demonstrating that they'll make or save you a ton of money? You didn't believe it. You thought there might be tricks. You're not sure of the results. That's exactly what your buyers believe about your ROI calculator.

Yet, a value conversation is essentially a fluid ROI calculator. Instead of having predetermined fields to fill out, your salesperson asks open-ended questions like "What problems do you hope to resolve?"; "What measurable result do you expect to achieve?"; "What will that result be worth to you in terms of profit dollars?"

Imagine that your salespeople (and your marketing team) are able to learn from a buyer what's most important to them and then have the business acumen to guide that buyer as they calculate for themselves the dollar value of achieving those most critical results. When a buyer calculates their own ROI, they're much more likely to believe it.

Learning to conduct value conversations isn't trivial, but there's a formula. They require logic, math, and business acumen. They require practice to be effective. However, they are magical. You're helping your potential customers understand their own value while you learn it as well.

Stiving value tables

The second powerful tool is a Stiving value table. One massive impediment to capturing more value is that your team probably doesn't know what *value* means. Very few people do. I think of value as what a buyer is willing to pay. The key to value is knowing how buyers determine their own willingness to pay.

Here's a quick thought experiment. Think about a recent buyer of one of your products. How much were they willing to pay? Now the hard question: how did they determine that?

Of course, it's impossible to know precisely, but you should be able to make some pretty good estimates. Most salespeople and marketing people are clueless. If they don't understand value the way a buyer thinks about it, they can't effectively communicate and capture value. Instead, what they do is talk about your products and features, hoping buyers hear a feature that resonates with them. Products and features aren't valuable. Solutions to problems and results are valuable.

Here are some things you can do to check the veracity of my claim that your team probably doesn't understand value.

- Ask them what value means to a specific customer. See how easily they respond.
- Ask them the five most important reasons your buyers buy from you. Then ask several buyers. See how similar these are.
- Carefully study your website and marketing materials. If they talk a lot about features and products, it's an indicator that they don't understand value.

On the other hand, indicators that your team understands value include their talking a lot about the problems you solve for the buyers. They may talk about the results a buyer could expect. Problems and results resonate with your market.

Your buyers have a problem. They buy a solution. They achieve a result. Value is the dollar value of that result. These are the four columns of a Stiving value table: problem, solution, result, and value.

The solution is your product and its features. Companies often find it most comfortable to build a Stiving value table by starting with the solution column because they know their product so well. Start by listing what you think are the most critical features in your product.

You built every product and feature because you believed it solved a problem for your market. What was the problem? Put it in first-person language and make sure it contains some pain. Don't write "I need a <feature>." Instead of "I need an easy way to find people to hire," say "I can't easily find a list of qualified people for job openings, so I spend a ton of time trying to build one." Any single feature may solve multiple different problems.

When your product solves a problem, your customers should derive a result. Try very hard to make this result quantitative. The result of solving the problem in the previous example could be saving five hours per job opening just by creating a list of qualified candidates.

Finally, the value is the dollar value of the result. Suppose a customer saves five hours per job opening and has 10 openings per month. That saves 50 hours per month. Multiply that times a fully burdened hourly rate of $60 to yield a value of $3,000 per month.

Each buyer is different. The result and value columns will be different for each buyer, but knowing what might be typical is the key. Once your team has created the first one, talk to several customers and buyers. Learn from them. The information in these Stiving value tables feeds your salespeople's ability to conduct effective value conversations.

ECV: Expected captured value

To shrink your value capture gap, you could just lower your expectations, but that's silly. Instead of lowering expectations, make sure they're reasonable. The act of setting expectations logically will help your team capture more value (increase ACV).

The most value you can capture from a buyer is the amount that buyer is willing to pay. My recommendation is to set your ECV equal to your buyer's willingness to pay (WTP). It's impossible to achieve that entirely, but it's a great goal, and it's more tangible than your "fair share." It's more tangible, but not definitive. It's impossible to know precisely how much anyone is willing to pay. Instead, you'll learn a couple of rules of thumb in determining WTP for your buyers.

A buyer's WTP depends on the decision being made just before the purchase. They are deciding either *will I?* or *which one?*

Usually, buyers make which-one decisions just before buying. They choose between alternatives. For example, imagine you decide to buy a new car. You've just made a will-I decision. Then you go shopping, comparing a Mercedes with a BMW. Now you're making a which-one decision. Your willingness to pay for a Mercedes depends on the BMW's price and the differentiation you perceive between the two vehicles. In a which-one decision, the value of a product depends on the price and features of the competition. This is called *value in choice* because value is relative to a competitive alternative.

Sometimes buyers make only a will-I decision and never go on to make a which-one decision. A competitive alternative may not be available or just wasn't considered. Popcorn at the movie theater and gasoline in the middle of nowhere are two great examples of will-I decisions. The value of one of these products is the value of solving the problem. This is called *value in use.*

An interesting example is the value of air. Having air to breathe is worth a lot. The value in use is close to infinite. However, you don't pay for it, because you have free air all around you. The value in choice is zero. Air is either worth everything or nothing, depending on whether you're making a will-I or a which-one decision.

WTP for will-I decisions

A rule of thumb that I've seen work in many industries is that a buyer is willing to pay about 10 percent of their value in use if there's no competitive alternative. The 10 percent number might seem low, but it's because of risk. The buyer isn't confident that they'll get the return. They aren't sure what unforeseen expenses might crop up. If you can increase the certainty in the buyer's mind, you can also increase your percentage.

If you revisit the Stiving value table from earlier, the values we entered in the table were the value of solving the problem, the value of the result. These are all value in use. If there's no competitive alternative, then add all of these up to get the total value. Remember, each customer receives a different value. One caution, though: be careful not to double count. Go through the list of results, and if the value calculations are based on the same result, you only get to count it once.

WTP for which-one decisions

If your buyers choose between your and a competitor's product, you need to think slightly differently. The Stiving value table can still be used but needs to be modified somewhat.

For will-I decisions, the table was based on the value of solving the problems. For which-one decisions, you need to think of the value of your differentiation based on the incremental problems you solve.

The process is the same. In the solutions column, list your differentiated capabilities. In the problems column, list the problems your differentiation solves. In the results column, you need to articulate the result they'll obtain with your product relative to the result they would obtain from your competitor's product. If you get the results column right, the value column is calculated the same as before, using logic and business acumen. To be more accurate, you'll also want to include negative value for the capabilities where the competitor is better than you.

You'll likely need one or more different value tables for each competitor. After all, your differentiation is relative to who you are being compared with.

Here's a rule of thumb for calculating a buyer's WTP when making a which-one decision. Add up the value of the differentiators. Don't double count. Your buyer's WTP for your product is approximately the price of your competitor's product plus half the differentiation value.

You may be wondering why half here and only 10 percent for a will-I decision. The reason is that the buyer has already said yes to *will I?* Now they're making a choice. You're essentially saying to them, "Our product is better and will make you more money. All we want to do is split that incremental profit with you."

The goal of this section is to estimate your expected capture value, ECV, more accurately. This requires knowing whether your buyer is making a will-I or a which-one decision and then estimating WTP. One remarkable result is that the process of more accurately estimating the prices at which you should be winning will help build the tools to increase the prices at which you do win, ACV.

Wrap up

We began by asking whether you're capturing your fair share of the value you deliver to your customers. Most companies don't. But is it because your team doesn't understand what your fair share means, or is it because they aren't able to communicate and capture the value?

Throughout this chapter, we talked about value, but what does this have to do with pricing? Everything!

Value-based pricing means charging what your customers are willing to pay. The more they value your product, the more they're willing to pay. Even if your salespeople and marketing people do a great job of communicating value, you can only capture it if you price for it. All these concepts are tightly interrelated.

Here are some actions executives can take. I recommend performing them in this order.

1   Test your company's understanding of value. You'll likely learn that there's much room for improvement.

2 Have your product teams create several Stiving value tables. This will open their eyes to see value the way your buyers see it. It also creates documentation to help sales learn to sell value.

3 Teach your sales and marketing people how to have value conversations. It's the most effective technique to discover and communicate value.

The value capture gap is a curious concept. Executives resonate with the fact that they aren't capturing their fair share of value. But once they decide to dig in, they learn that it's about how to win more at higher prices. This only happens when companies learn to communicate and capture more value. That sounds a lot like pricing to me.

The author

Mark Stiving is a pricing educator and advisor with a PhD in marketing (pricing) from UC Berkeley and more than 25 years of experience helping companies implement value-based pricing strategies to increase profits. A pricing educator and advisor, Stiving has helped esteemed companies like ADP, Cisco, Fiserv, Sabre, Splunk, and Thermo Fisher as well as hundreds of small businesses and entrepreneurial ventures. He's the author of the highly rated and readable book *Impact Pricing: Your Blueprint for Driving Profits* as well as weekly blogs since 2010. Stiving hosts the popular podcast *Impact Pricing*. See more content from him at www .impactpricing.com/. Mark lives in Reno, Nevada, with his wife, Carol, and dog, Jake.

16

The Value of Commercial Excellence— Through an Economic Downturn and Beyond

Mitchell D. Lee, Profit Evangelist, Vendavo

Introduction

THE C-SUITE HAS NEVER experienced more pressure to deliver success, to unlock the growth and profitability of the business. Commercial excellence is the how. And the idea is simple: it's getting the right price, for the right product, to the right customer, at the right time.

While we were all asked to slow down and stay home in 2020, business launched into a rapid-fire transformation. The global pandemic greatly accelerated the need for change across most industries, in every geographic location. In response, companies either began or sped up their push to digital business, all in the spirit of heightened productivity, increased efficiencies, and, of course, improved customer experience.

In the throes of World War II, Winston Churchill called it out: "Never waste a good crisis." Some organizations have taken this statement to heart and shifted their focus to commercial excellence activities—the digitalizing of their sales and business processes that connect their front-office CRM with their back-office ERP systems. Their goal was to thrive amid the turbulence, not simply survive it. That meant powering remote work and digital commerce. Meeting customers where they were—online—and aligning business strategy with agile and dynamic tactical execution. Think of what that would mean for your business: your offering, for your customer, without delay, at the price the customer is willing to pay. Every day.

In this chapter, we look not only at what constitutes commercial excellence processes and what some companies have done to transform with digital technology but also how that shift has advanced their business model and boosted profitability. Because it's never about technology for the sake of cool, new tech—rather, it's about evolving your people, processes, and technologies to align with your organization's growth goals.

The right time is right now to take the next steps toward commercial excellence.

What is commercial excellence?

Let's go a little deeper into the concept of commercial excellence. It encompasses the set of business processes that reside between your back-office ERP system and your front-office CRM. Commercial excellence is the articulation of what should occur between a sale and order fulfillment and digitalizing that process for optimal efficiency, accuracy, and profitability.

A critical link between your back office and front office
Most large enterprises wouldn't be able to function efficiently and profitably today without their ERP backbone. ERP systems have proved to be more than capable of handling sales-related back-office requirements related to order fulfillment. On the customer-facing, front-office side of the business, most large enterprises have rolled out some sort of CRM solution—if for no other reason than to address contact/account management and the "this looked really cool in the 1990s" user experience of ERP that just doesn't cut it (Figure 16.1).

Here we are almost a quarter of the way into the 21st century, and the use of ERP, CRM, and other enterprise systems has played significant roles in the ongoing gains in productivity and efficiency that large companies have enjoyed over the last 25 or more years. ERP systems can "handle" quoting and pricing. CRM

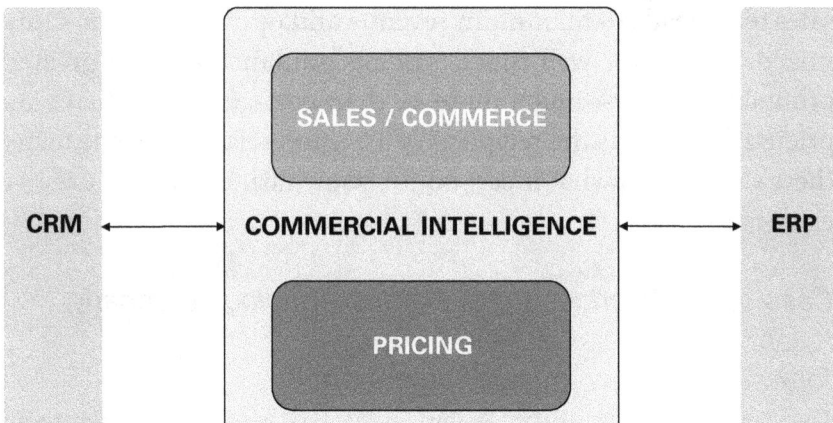

Figure 16.1. Capabilities for commercial excellence.

systems can provide a wonderful experience tailored to the user who has to face a customer. But when it comes to making sure the right product at the right price at the right time is presented during the quoting process, most ERP and CRM solutions come up short.

To address such challenges, you need digital middle-office capabilities to link your front office with your back office. To address them well, you must focus on commercial excellence.

Commercial excellence should cover these business process capabilities:

- Customer accounts
- Product/service
- Pricing
- Sales/channel
- Analytics capabilities and insights
- Process integration

One of the more critical components of your middle office is pricing. The right price, in real time, placed in the hands of your sales team leads to maximum revenue and optimal margin. Optimized price with well-timed pricing guidance is your greatest profitability lever—much more so than cost-cutting. When your pricing function is the recipient of a commercial excellence focus, there's no end to what it can do for your business. Below are two examples.

Case study: World-leading water technology company, Xylem, enables value-based pricing for one million product configurations
To improve profitability, Xylem, a global leader in water technology, knew they needed to move away from a simple cost-plus

approach and price their products by the value perceived. With more than one million product configurations across more than 150 countries, however, that seemed a stretch goal.

To price products that range from generally available, common components to specialties available only from the company based on customer perceived value across all markets, this leading innovator implemented a pricing solution that enabled value-based pricing but also global alignment across regions, product lines, and business units as well as timely, accurate generation of quote pricing for new configurations.

The company chose to launch the project within their spare-parts business. They began by dividing their spare parts into three segments:

- key parts designed by the company
- general parts designed by the company but less specialized
- standard parts

Key parts are the most important components to price correctly for profitability. To ensure accuracy, market surveys were conducted with customers and internal employees to develop perceived value for key parts across eight countries. Three levels of key price drivers were identified and used to develop using AI/ML pricing techniques.

Customer perceived value was considered along with product attributes such as weight, diameter, and power. The repair threshold for each piece of equipment was also included for pricing evaluation. Products that are economical to repair instead of being replaced are reflected in the customer's options in pricing.

These and other insights were used to build a framework to support new parts pricing, with easy price maintenance and revisions—all tied to the company's value-based and market-driven pricing strategies.

"I receive a lot of questions about why pricing is the way it is and now I can quickly look up the product and explain the logic of the pricing. Sales now agrees and can defend that price," says Niklas Lindstrom, pricing manager at Xylem.

Based on the value Xylem was able to generate within spare-parts pricing, the company has chosen to support pricing for the company's portfolio of 300 base products, which in turn has millions of possible product configurations.

The challenge was to price a configuration for quoting, without having to create an identity/part number for each variation—especially if it wasn't actually sold. This would have generated millions of unused records—unnecessarily burdening the resource planning systems.

Pricing methodology was built by pricing the components (see Figure 16.2).

These calculations can now be quickly calculated to enable the sales team to quickly build bespoke quotes for each of their customers' requests (Figure 16.3). This delivers impact across three categories.

- Pricing quality
  - Market instead of cost-based pricing
  - Logical, aligned pricing throughout the portfolio
  - Elimination of manual quoting and pricing errors

| Configured price | Base unit price | Complexity factor | Added components |

Figure 16.2. Pricing methodology based on pricing components.

> Xylem began their commercial excellence journey in their aftermarket business unit—an area historically viewed as necessary but unexciting.
>
> Value generation and bottom-line improvement has been so great that the original equipment manufacturing BUs are learning the ropes and implementing their next steps in commercial excellence.

Figure 16.3. Xylem's commercial excellence journey.

- Pricing efficiency
  - Value as the pricing driver, instead of one-off, uncoordinated product pricing
  - Prices that are easy to explain with appropriate context
- Single source
  - ERP, configuration, and quotation tools all use pricing from one source

Case study: Smarter pricing lights the way to improved margins for optical fiber giant Corning

Corning Optical Communications is the world leader in passive optical fiber, with more than $3.5 billion in annual sales of products and solutions for optical-based infrastructure. Corning invents, makes, and sells some of the most important innovations in the world, including highly engineered glass, optical fiber, and ceramic substrates that are core technologies in LCD televisions, telecommunications networks, and emissions control systems.

When older database technology proved lacking and limited, the 167-year-old engineering and manufacturing leader with more than $10.5 billion in total annual sales looked to identify price, margin, and profit opportunities. By shifting focus to replacing older, on-premise pricing data warehouses for approximately 200,000 SKUs and implementing a hosted solution that was easy to use and scalable, Corning experienced over $10 million in positive financial impact in the first year alone.

"Our internally developed analytics system had limited capability and could only be used by trained specialists that had licenses to the software," says Ken Foret, manager, pricing enablement, Corning Optical Communications. "Each time a business user wanted to see a different slice of the data, they had to engage with one of our specialists, which was time-consuming and prone to many iterations. Our new platform can be accessed directly by the user where they can easily manipulate the data to drill down on the attributes and measures that are helpful for them to make quick business decisions."

In addition to lightening the IT workload, enhancing security, and reducing expenses, the cloud-hosted option offered IT professional services, ensuring that value was delivered.

"The biggest benefit we experienced with professional services was in go-live preparation and planning," says Foret. "The pricing consultants worked with us to outline metrics for success, set goals, and then measure those goals precisely and consistently. Those resources have made a huge difference in helping us prove value and progress throughout the organization."

Pricing consultants supported solution design and configuration, change management, and value measurement. Specific value cases created for Corning included identifying negative-margin and low-margin transactions, creating a process for monitoring and managing costs-to-serve on a granular and actionable basis, and establishing business routines for optimizing pricing in general and creating value-based pricing for key products.

"Professional services helped us climb the learning curve faster, implement more smoothly, and deliver on the value of this investment which we've calculated in the first year at approximately $10 million in positive financial impact," says Foret. "Their professional services have been crucial to our success."

Corning augmented their commercial excellence journey by leveraging partners, freeing up focus for strategy and execution.

Deciding up front the metrics for success and planning for consistent measurement made it easy to prove value and progress.

Figure 16.4. Corning's commercial excellence journey.

Outsourcing the hosting and upgrades of their pricing system has allowed Corning's pricing and sales teams to focus on strategy and execution, rather than technology.

"Our 225 active users on our product-line management teams are the primary users, and they've seen the biggest gains," says Foret. "Visibility into pricing and margin patterns through our dashboards gives them better information to make smarter, faster decisions. As marketplace conditions or inputs change, we can adjust more quickly" (Figure 16.4).

Assess your commercial excellence maturity

To move ahead on your commercial excellence journey, begin by seeing where you are today. Assessing your current state will help you prioritize and guide your next steps. The commercial excellence maturity model (see Figure 16.5) identifies four stages of progressing maturity: unstructured, disciplined, adaptive, and optimized.

Maturity can be considered across each of the six key business process capabilities that make up your middle office.

- Customer accounts
- Product/service
- Pricing
- Sales/channel

STAGE

1

Unstructured

"One size fits all"

Value propositions of products/services and prices are uniform across all customers and delivered through an ad hoc and chaotic experience.

STAGE

2

Disciplined

Simple rules

Simplistic and basic rules are used to organize actions for routine offers. Approval processes for nonstandard situations are established but time consuming.

STAGE

3

Adaptive

Basic segmentation

Sophisticated rules are used to organize actions for most offers. Approval processes for nonstandard situations are established and straightforward.

STAGE

4

Optimized

Customer-centric commercial excellence

A detailed and nuanced understanding of each customer enables offerings that are tailored for value and that are priced accordingly—through an easy, digital experience.

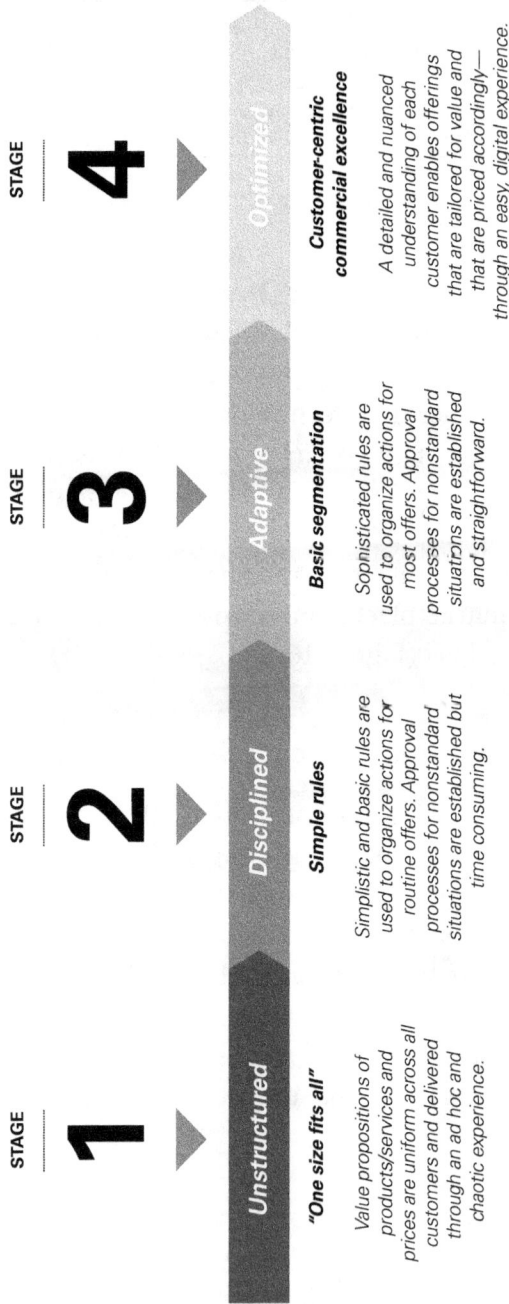

Figure 16.5. Commercial excellence maturity stages.

- Analytics capabilities and insights
- Process integration.

By considering your status for each of the business capabilities, you can quickly determine your maturity in that area as well as your maturity in overall commercial excellence. With your organization's maturity status in hand, you can then compare your overall status with that of other B2B organizations to frame your next steps for improvement.

To take action, though, you need to understand specific differences. Breaking down commercial excellence into its components makes the task of setting the relative importance of taking action for improvement much easier. By forming a basis of comparison, the next steps of quantifying the effort versus benefit and calculating the initiative's ROI can become much more granular for proper investment prioritization.

Let's look at a simple description of the maturity stages across each of the business process categories.

Customer accounts

In the **unstructured** stage, customer accounts are somewhat disorganized, with parent–child relationships unclear and problems with aliases, account ownership, and so forth.

In the **disciplined** stage, account management is clear and consistent, with customer categorization based on basic external (e.g., industry) and internal (e.g., size) attributes.

The **adaptive** stage is characterized by customers who are classified/segmented into detailed groups across multiple attributes such as their industries, costs-to-serve, revenue and margin metrics, and commercial behavior.

In the **optimized** stage, you'll have customers who are segmented into microsegments beyond customer-level, based on additional attributes and classifications.

Product/service

In the **unstructured** stage, your product offering is general; the same portfolio is used for most or all sales opportunities. There is basic knowledge of the products and their value propositions within sales.

The **disciplined** stage means that product offerings are organized into catalogs by region or industry (market). Sales is trained on the market-specific product strategy, but execution is variable.

In the **adaptive** stage, products are suggested as part of an intelligent, guided selling process. Rules engines generate recommended products based on customer needs and strategy.

In the **optimized** stage, products are dynamically suggested (e.g., cross-sell, upsell) for specific situations using data-driven artificial intelligence that supports the selling process.

Pricing

In the **unstructured** stage, there are no formal pricing strategies or processes in place. Price-setting is rudimentary, and the deal desk is nonexistent or irrelevant. Customer pricing is ad hoc.

In the **disciplined** stage, you have basic price-setting practices in place (cost-plus or competitive-based pricing). The deal desk is functional but focused mainly on low-margin deals, and customer pricing is market-based.

In the **adaptive** stage, price-setting is dynamic, based on multiple market signals. The deal desk is also now focused on peer-deal analysis and deal-scoring and customer pricing is peer- or segment-based.

In the **optimized** stage, price-setting and the deal desk are predictive and allow for proactive setting of deal guidance before sales sends in their requests. Customer pricing is based on a full, segment-specific optimized price envelope, incorporating several dimensions.

Sales/channel

The **unstructured** stage is characterized by ad-hoc, chaotic sales execution and a poorly defined (or executed) sales process and a patchwork of systems or tools for managing the sales process. Channel management is ad hoc.

The **disciplined** stage reflects an existing sales process supported by a CRM or maybe CPQ system but is not consistent in execution. Channel management becomes tactical and reactive.

In the **adaptive** stage, sales processes are largely followed, supported heavily by a few key selling tools like CRM, CPQ, and so forth. Selling tactics are supported by rules and policies. Channel management is more strategic.

In the **optimized** stage, sales processes are dynamic and completely digital. Content for sales is dynamically generated through data-driven artificial intelligence. Sales can focus on selling customer value.

Analytics capabilities and insights

In the **unstructured** stage, basic financial reporting and metrics such as revenue, gross margin, and so on are rolled up at dimensions such as region, channel, or industry.

The **disciplined** stage indicates the use of granular price and margin diagnostics through tools like the pocket price waterfall. Analytics are descriptive and get to the root cause (what happened and why).

The **adaptive** stage includes transactional data, and market data are used to forecast and predict potential outcomes and scenarios. Human decision-making uses descriptive and predictive analytics.

In the **optimized** stage, you have internal and external data signals, combined with business rules, and strategies are used for prescriptive analytics—guiding decisions in the commercial/sales process.

Process integration

In the **unstructured** stage, product, pricing, and sales processes and teams are not aligned at all and may have different—even conflicting—goals or objectives and metrics.

The **disciplined** stage is when product, pricing, and sales processes and teams are aligned in some cases, but not all, and may have different, conflicting objectives and metrics.

In the **adaptive** stage, product, pricing, and sales processes and teams are aligned in most cases and have some shared goals and objectives that align with common metrics.

In the **optimized** stage, your product, pricing, and sales processes and teams are aligned in almost all cases, and you have comprehensive and aligned goals and objectives that also align with common metrics as well as with incentive compensation plans.

Note that the process integration can act as a limitation on your overall effectiveness: even if your other scores are relatively high, the lack of integration can severely impact your ability to reap full value.

A commercial excellence maturity assessment will provide you an overall score for which stage your organization falls into, based on your input. It will also provide you stage scores for each process capability and, most importantly, practical steps you can take to advance your maturity.

How do you compare with your peers?

In addition to knowing your own maturity ranking, it's helpful to know how you stack up against other B2B organizations. As you can see from the averages of scores collected over the past few years across B2B industries in Figure 16.6, scores cluster in stage 2, or the disciplined stage. This makes it plain: most organizations have ample opportunity for growth as the surrounding market landscape continues to evolve and as competitive forces increasingly drive change for improvement.

If you'd like to assess your maturity and see how it compares with other B2B organizations, take 10 minutes to respond to the questions here: www.vendavo.com/ce-maturity-assessment/.

Upon completion, you'll receive a report outlining your status for each of the commercial capabilities. The report will also provide considerations and practical suggestions for how you can move to the next level of maturity and what you should expect at the next level of performance.

Technology requires a combination of people and process

The fundamental challenge of the C-suite is to assign investment of effort and resources, working within today's constraints to balance the "now" with the "future." For commercial excellence, it means embracing change and orienting your organization for agility. In many cases, commercial agility is equated with automation of business processes. Yes, commercial excellence means application of the appropriate software for your business processes, but success requires combining deep experience with best practices to bridge the commercial gap between your CRM and your ERP.

My colleague Robert Irwin, head of business consulting for Vendavo's EMEA operations, considered the combination of people, process, and technology in his 2021 article "7 Key Truths about RFPs & Picking the Right Partner." In it, he outlined key

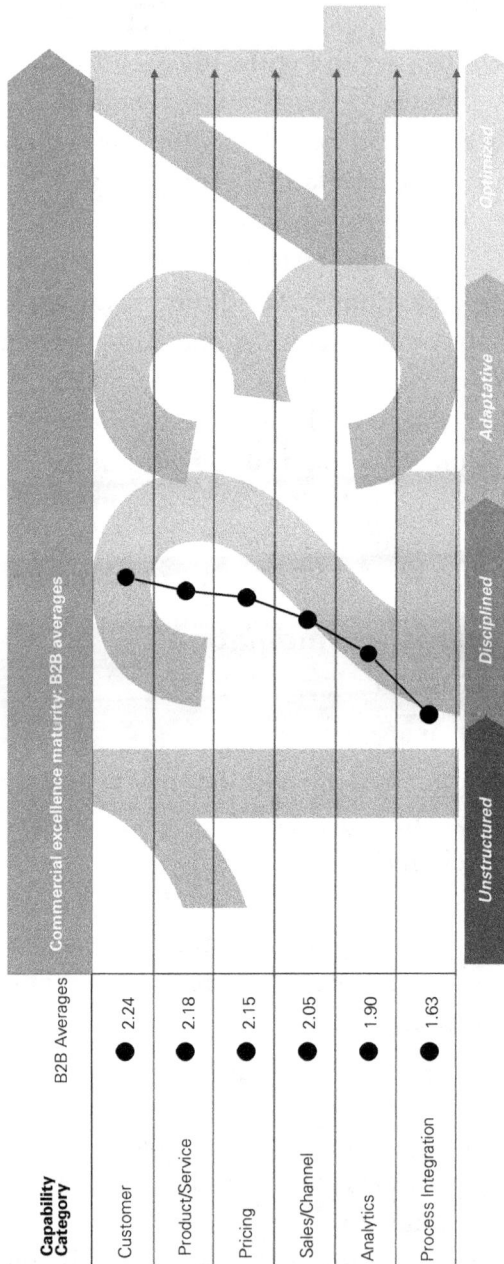

Capability Category	B2B Averages	Commercial excellence maturity: B2B averages
Customer	2.24	
Product/Service	2.18	
Pricing	2.15	
Sales/Channel	2.05	
Analytics	1.90	
Process Integration	1.63	

Unstructured   Disciplined   Adaptative   Optimized

Caution: your level of process integration, if low, can often act as a limit on value realization even if you have strong capabilities in other business process categories.

Figure 16.6. Commercial excellence maturity: B2B averages.

objectives to consider when beginning your commercial excellence journey and, most importantly, selecting a partner to ensure ongoing success.

He notes that the process of using RFPs as the means to select a software vendor, especially for business or commercial process management, simply doesn't deliver good results. It's fundamentally flawed.

That's because the process is inherently divisive. If your goal is to reduce risk by building a true, long-term partnership with a company that will support you on the journey to addressing significant major strategic change (e.g., optimization of your commercial excellence processes), then an RFP is almost always a poor way to proceed.

He notes as one of the seven truths that projects don't tend to fail because of the technology chosen. More often than not, they fail to succeed because of other reasons: people and process.

A recent study by NewVantage found that cultural challenges remain the biggest obstacle to business adoption. Executives cite multiple factors, including organizational alignment, agility, and resistance, with **92.5 percent** stemming from cultural challenges (people and process) and **only 7.5 percent** related to technology (Figure 16.7).

So, we have RFP processes that consume a huge effort and inordinate time, that don't work well, and that are designed to select

People	62.5%	Cultural
Process	30.0%	challenges: 92.5%
Technology	7.5%	

Figure 16.7. Principal obstacle to business adoption. Source: NewVantage, Big Data Executive Survey.

technology rather than evaluate partner fit. In the end, the technology assessment **addresses only 7.5 percent of the total project risk**.

The C-suite needs to change the conversation. The first step is to understand that **you are not selecting a "vendor"** or someone who simply makes a sale. The journey to commercial excellence obviously includes the acquisition of commercial excellence software, but that's just the beginning. It's much better to select and work with a **long-term strategic partner** for that journey rather than a vendor motivated by a one-time transaction.

"Fit" comes in many forms: definitely functional (the technology does need evaluating—don't ignore it), but also related to culture, competence, and value position. This assessment cannot be completed as a theoretical exercise, with a question-and-answer-based response, and it will take more interaction than just a three-hour presentation and demo session.

A good partner will work with you not only to build a joint business case but also to ensure that the solution is set up to measure success on a continuous basis.

Irwin's observations are backed by facts and real-world results. When the right combination of people, process, and technology is applied in a practical, pragmatic manner, the outcomes are impressive and undeniable.

PVM/variance analysis: What's working in your business

Particularly meaningful are the situations where business metrics are easily understood and calculated and compared consistently. An especially useful methodology is variance analysis, or price-volume-mix (PVM) analysis (Figure 16.8). This process is also often called a revenue walk and is typically applied for easy

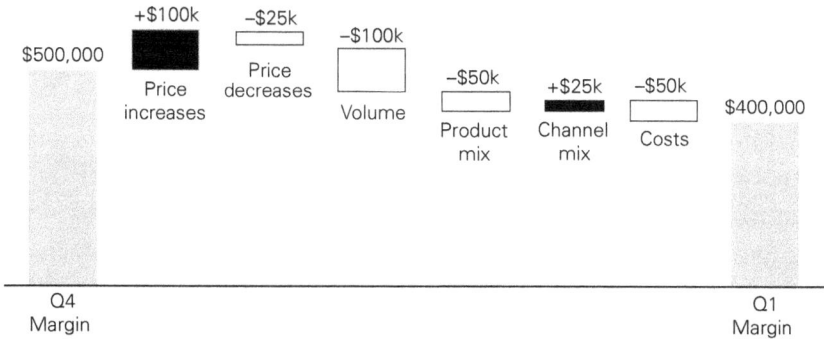

Figure 16.8. Price/volume/mix: Variance analysis—simple in theory, complex in practice.

comparison from one period to another, to determine high-level drivers and to assign accountability for the categories.

By including costs, and even the granularity of COGS and costs-to-serve or exchange rates, it becomes a margin walk, and with these views, corporate-wide comparisons can be made to plug margin holes and find best practices. Although a relatively simple exercise at a high, corporate-side level, in practice, the nuances required by the finance team often make this difficult to reliably repeat over the long haul—the effort is useful, but because it's viewed as a project and the analysis lives in an Excel spread-sheet, and it is conducted by one or two people in the central finance function.

It's not a process designed for easy repetition. And when multiple business units are asked to routinely report on a well-understood comparable basis, the valuable insights are strangled by a project-based tool, and the project is put on the shelf.

On the other hand, when flexible, purpose-built solutions are available—meaning that the nuances can be standardized and easily repeated across time periods or used to compare business units, customers, or products—the value of combining people and process with technology truly emerges.

Let's review four real-life examples.

First, a leading global agricultural company was struggling with their pricing journey, seeing limited financial benefit. The organizational focus had been limited to minor transformational changes. By engaging their best people with experts in pricing and change management and employing purpose-built PVM tools, they were able to achieve bottom-line improvements in one business unit equal to 1.3 percent of top-line sales ($26.4M) and identify another 2.8 percent in actionable opportunity. A key stakeholder said, "This has been the most productive exercise we have been through with any external consultancy." They're rapidly turning their attention to deploying their commercial excellence learnings to other BUs in the organization.

Next, in Europe, a global industrial manufacturer was facing reduced scope of business opportunities, as most of their ongoing business was tied to a small number of large OEMs and constrictive distributor contracts. Again, by combining repeatable, reliably consistent PVM analyses with pricing and business management experts, they were able to identify an additional €60 million over a five-year period by identifying data-driven segmentation based on key value attributes. Their list-price management success prompted their global pricing manager to say that they had "identified significant opportunities to improve margin without compromising on our growth strategy." The company is continuing the partnership to combine people, process, and technology for further value capture as they roll out to additional business units.

Then, turning to the process industry, a leading global chemicals company was experiencing continued margin leakage due to a lack of intelligent yet timely pricing guidance. The use of PVM and other advanced analytics drove insights and learnings that were then applied with structured change management. Their global pricing manager said that the initiative "brings a huge amount of experience to the table and...to our success." Their bottom line improved by €72 million, or 3 percent of revenue. Further, they have targeted an additional €30 million in margin by acting on the data-driven insights.

Finally, a leading international distribution company was facing resistance in making pricing and commercial excellence a strategic priority, due to a lack of executive buy-in. By combining deep expertise in pricing and change management, best practices and quick wins led to rapid overall adoption and committed executive alignment. Straightforward adherence to base and target price guidance yielded $1.6 million almost immediately, with another $6.1 million uplift in benefits in one year. For distributors operating on very thin margins, application of PVM analyses can yield a massive improvement in the margin percentage for the business unit, and, in this case, equivalent to 5.3 percent of net invoice. The global strategic manager was thankful, speaking of the initiative, "We really appreciate the effort and support."

Pricing as your most influential growth lever: A look at the [value] numbers

The above are specific examples—the totals and the averages tell a story as well. Even in times of turmoil, companies can reexamine their priorities and ensure that the actions they're taking improve the top line and the bottom line and strike that balance of delivering benefits for all stakeholders now *and* in the future.

Irwin (2021) notes a particularly bizarre observation: even though all projects require a business case with a compelling ROI, many companies will fail to set themselves up to measure that ROI over time.

Assessing the current performance of an investment's value delivery is a basic concept in business unit management. This same ongoing performance measurement must also be applied to the commercial excellence journey. Journeys usually involve bumps in the road, generating questions around the value being delivered. Without routine measurement processes, explanations become projects—but they deliver insights that are too late to drive action. Commercial processes, especially around pricing, vary significantly from company to company. A good partner will augment your expertise and help you establish processes and KPIs that drive long-term success.

In 2020, during the height of the turbulence, Vendavo engaged with 31 of our clients, combining their intimate knowledge of their business platforms with our expertise in business processes, pricing strategy, and change management to perform 91 individual data-driven analyses. As a result, these clients achieved bottom-line, measured performance improvements of $667 million for an average $21.5 million improvement per client (Figure 16.9).

Looking at these averages, the "average person on the street" would say that to ignore these clear benefits—to have some priority other than improving the commercial processes that capture the value of your offering—would be some variation on misfeasance, malfeasance, or nonfeasance. This is especially true in

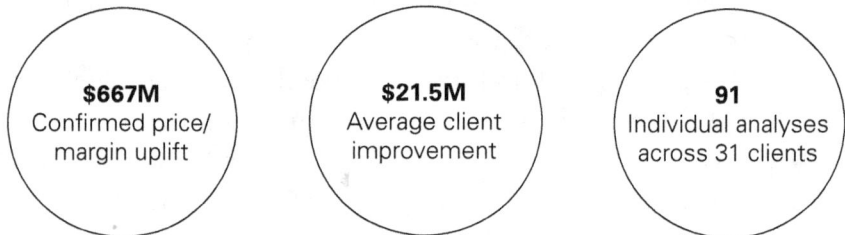

$667M
Confirmed price/
margin uplift

$21.5M
Average client
improvement

91
Individual analyses
across 31 clients

Figure 16.9. Performance improvements: 2020.

tough times, when achieving stability and success paradoxically requires great dynamic agility.

With a focus on the proper combination of people, process, and technology solutions, it's truly possible to unlock more of the value inherent in our business models—at any point of the business cycle.

Implications for the C-suite— and anyone else with P&L responsibility

Commercial agility is no longer a competitive differentiation. At today's rate of change, it's a fundamental requirement for survival. Investments have long been made in manufacturing and logistics capabilities to be responsive to market variations, but the same companies that spend hundreds of millions of dollars annually on manufacturing planning software, or integrated financial reporting systems, still try to bridge the commercial excellence gap with spreadsheets.

So, as a business leader, here's your call to action (see Figure 16.10).

1 Assess your commercial process capabilities, both qualitatively and quantitively.
2 Compare your commercial process capabilities with that of your immediate competitors as well as your suppliers and customers.
3 Prioritize your next steps for commercial excellence based on relative gaps, required effort and investment, and the projected benefits.
4 Augment your capabilities with a partner that can provide the requisite technology, combined with relevant experience and business process expertise.

Figure 16.10. Call to action.

The steps to improve commercial excellence are straightforward, just as the concept is actually very simple: the right price, for the right product, to the right customer, at the right time. But commercial transformation isn't easy. You need a good partner who'll be honest with you and who's committed to the long term. It takes hard work, collaboration, and a vision based on shared experience. And if you don't think the effort is worth it, don't worry. Someone else will do it for you, very soon.

References

Irwin, R. (2021). 7 key truths about RFPs & picking the right partner. *Vendavo,* January 19. www.vendavo.com/pricing/7-key-truths-about-rfps-picking-the-right-partner/

The author

Mitchell D. Lee is the Profit Evangelist at Vendavo, applying decades of experience in the technical, operational, marketing, and commercial arenas of the chemical industry to unlock business value. Prior to Vendavo, Mitch was with BASF and Orica in product marketing and business management, driving operational optimization, pricing excellence, and margin improvement as well as personal engagement in high-value sales negotiations. Mitch also has deep experience with raw materials supplier portfolio management, having negotiated large-scale and long-term supply agreements with leading global manufacturers.

17

Best Practices in Pricing and Offer Design for B2B Digital Solutions— Executive Edition

Scott Miller, CPA, CMA, Founder, Miller Advisors, Inc.

Scenario 1: Video capture technology

DOUG HAD ALL THE qualities of a typical successful entrepreneur: highly motivated and passionate about his business, extremely creative in his thought process, with a visionary product solution mindset. He built a successful business in school bus video capture technology, a company that was ultimately purchased by an up-and-coming larger firm that sold similar solutions more broadly to the law enforcement, transportation, and waste management fleet industries. He remained onboard as SVP with the goal of taking his business unit to its next stage of growth.

Historically, the new company applied a cost-plus target margin pricing approach on hardware alongside installation service fees. But the industry was undergoing a major disruption. It was no longer about hardware sales—a key competitor was providing subscription offers alongside high-value solution bundles: receive a video camera, unlimited cloud video storage, video management software, and replacement of hardware every 2.5 years. The offer was so compelling that it propelled that competitor to the number-one market position within a few years. Doug knew that their business models needed a new direction and initiated development and investments in both video management software and cloud services. But he also identified a key gap within their company's core capabilities: they lacked expertise around best practices in value-based pricing and offer design. And with multiple industry segments and bundle potentials to consider, this would most definitely be a complex undertaking. Enter a need to accelerate his own, his team's, and his company's pricing capabilities and expertise.

Scenario 2: Global IT tech services

Company XYZ was a large $10 billion global IT services organization that provided leading-edge IT services to major sectors including banking and state governments. Over time, their services developed a need to integrate high-value innovative digital solutions for their client base: these *digital enabler* solutions were developed to improve how their own consultants managed and delivered IT projects and included customized software solutions for their clients. Some business units at the time identified opportunities to further commercialize these in-house digital solutions, but "we're a services organization, not a software company" was the executive mantra at the time.

But that mindset began to change. After a few M&As with other service firms, it quickly became apparent that those firms adopted a successful recipe for creating highly profitable recurring revenue from software in addition to their standard services revenue. Some of their acquired companies were earning as much as 80 percent margins on their commercial enterprise software—incredible for a company that typically operated under the industry's cost-plus 30 percent service margin standard. They also came to realize that many of their software-related solutions were underpriced at the expense of an overfocus on the service revenue component.

In addition, the pressure began to mount from their investor community: "What percentage of your sales is recurring revenue? What's the company's SaaS strategy?" Subscriptions and recurring revenue were now viewed as the Holy Grail for driving higher company valuation compared with one-time service engagements, and digital solutions were the cornerstone to achieving their next phase of growth.

With higher investments and a strategic shift toward digital solutions, it became quickly apparent that the product teams lacked the skillsets and expertise to properly monetize these newer solutions. Guesswork and cost-plus continued to drive a suboptimal pricing approach. Enter the need for best practices in pricing and offer design in the digital era.

The executive role in driving company-wide pricing excellence

Doug and Company XYZ's opportunities and challenges are common scenarios in the digital era. *Digital transformation* has truly become a reality (i.e., no longer just a buzzword), and executive teams are being challenged to ensure not only that they deliver new innovation and digital solutions as part their growth strategy but also that their teams maximize both the revenue and monetization potential for these new offerings.

However, all too often there is a lack of understanding around how to productize, price, and sell these new solutions, resulting in a failure to achieve the desired growth strategy or to recoup major digital investments.

As in Doug's case, executives don't need to *be* the expert in pricing, but they should have enough awareness around best-practice concepts to provide enough guidance to their teams in order to strive for maximizing revenue, profitability, and growth potential. In some cases, migrating to new pricing and revenue models will be a fundamental shift in how that company conducts business—all aspects of the organization can be impacted—from people to processes to systems. The implications of changes to pricing strategies can never be overestimated, and executives that are well tuned to the concept of *value-based pricing* will have a sound understanding around both benefits and implications to their organization.

Pricing excellence is a journey. Achieving best practices in B2B digital solution pricing can be a journey for one's organization. Global product teams, as in the case of Company XYZ, will need to be realistic about what can be achieved in the short, medium, and long term. Much larger pricing transformation initiatives, such as migrating the portfolio from on-premise to SaaS, requires company-wide coordination and major changes across systems, cross-department processes, training, policies, and client contractualization. But there are always quick-win pricing opportunities that can impact more immediate gains. Key to a successful pricing-improvement journey is to plan, prioritize, and establish realistic expectations across the organization.

Consider investing in a pricing center of excellence (CoE) and/or pricing experts. In many cases, especially for national and global organizations, it will be beneficial to have pricing champions, or even a skilled pricing team, in place to navigate the organization along its journey to higher levels of pricing maturity: Company XYZ, the IT tech firm from our scenario example, invested in building an in-house corporate team with pricing and go-to-market commercialization expertise who engaged with well over 80 different global business units (BUs)—each BU having growth and recurring revenue objectives for their digital solutions. This team would help identify some quick wins while supporting longer-term pricing initiatives around major pricing transformation initiatives (e.g., migration from on-premise to SaaS) and/or future roadmap products (e.g., major version upgrades, new innovation AI modules). The company became more value-focused from a pricing and product development perspective and improved their pricing capabilities and maturity over the course of the next two to three years.

The Software Pricing Framework: A company toolkit for value-based pricing

Everyone has an opinion about pricing, and, at times, it can be the loudest person at the table who ultimately wins the pricing decision (and, in many cases, this is the C-suite!). But guesswork and "crystal balls" are far from an effective process that, 99 percent of the time, results in suboptimal pricing outcomes. Alternatively, best pricing practices and higher pricing maturity help establish a value-based approach, alongside consistency, and improved end-to-end pricing delivery across an organization that surpasses, from a growth and financial perspective, outcomes that would otherwise be achieved under more ad-hoc pricing approaches.

Successfully developing a value-based pricing approach for digital solutions involves using the right offer-design approach, the right company-wide price–value training, and the right approaches to executing pricing for profitable B2B deal wins. This continuous pricing-improvement cycle and company-wide process is captured within the Software Pricing Framework™ (Figure 17.1).

Figure 17.1. The Software Pricing Framework.

Offer design. From strategy to value analysis to price structure development (packaging, metrics, tiers) to financial analysis—the offer-design phase ensures that product and pricing teams bring in the right inputs and analysis to drive the most favorable value-based segmented pricing and offer structures. Financial analysis and price stress-testing is the final output of this phase to ensure that both sales and product teams are driving profitable go-to-market solutions.

Enablement. Whether it's internal sales teams, channel partners, customer success representatives, or even technical support staff—enablement is a critical activity for understanding how one's software is packaged, priced, and linked to one's *value story*. New pricing strategies and business models are accompanied by "all-on-board" organizational alignment programs and effective communications that bring transparency to new pricing structures and deliver new monetization opportunities as well as awareness and compliance with respect to new pricing guidelines and policies.

Execution. Applying an effective bid-evaluation process, assigning pricing negotiation policies, and applying pricing approval matrices avoids a "race to the bottom" price approach when submitting best-and-final-offer (BAFO) for deals. As well, consistently monitoring win/loss outcomes, new subscription-based key performance indicators (KPIs), and insights from post-bid-award reports are critical to acting as an early warning system for ongoing readjustment to pricing and offer structures.

Pricing ecosystem (PECO). At the center of the framework is the PECO; this includes all other people, processes, systems, and policies within an organization that are impacted by changes to pricing strategies, structures, compliance, policies, and cross-functional teams impacted by pricing. Just think about all the department touchpoints within an organization that are impacted with changes to pricing: sales, accounting, legal, sales operations, contracting, reporting, IT, and customer service, among others. These teams must be informed and consulted during the pricing review process, and executives will need to challenge product and pricing teams to ensure that they've adequately socialized and vetted PECO implications and risks for any new pricing strategies with other departments.

An executive crash course in value-based offer design

As previously mentioned, executives do not need to *be* the pricing expert, but understanding various pricing concepts and implementation considerations (e.g., PECO) helps establish a larger vision for developing a successful value-based company-wide pricing strategy.

Offer design can be broken down into four main subprocesses: strategy, price–value analysis, pricing structure (packaging, metrics, and tiers), and financial analysis. In many ways, these four offer-design subprocesses can be considered analogs to skydiving (Figure 17.2).

Following these four subprocesses within the offer-design phase will ensure that your organization has conducted a rigorous and well-thought-out assessment of pricing strategies and tactics that sets the stage for your final go-to-market commercial offers.

Strategy (the 10,000-foot view)

All too often, teams are quick to jump into developing pricing structures without understanding the high-level product, sales, and pricing strategy. These are all key considerations that should be top of mind with executives when evaluating pricing options from their product teams.

Strategy is a first step to gathering the right inputs that determine the go-forward short- and long-term offer-design approach.

Data for segmentation

Strategy (10,000-foot pricing view) begins with gathering key inputs and strategic analysis that determine pricing guidance principles, product, and customer segmentation strategies.

Price–value analysis (2,000-foot pricing view) seeks to determine approximate price positioning based on perceived value, requirements, use cases, and price sensitivity across key segments.

Package, metrics, and tiers (500-foot pricing view) seeks to create a price list based on segmented price structures (packages, price metrics, and tiers) as well as discounting guidelines and approval matrices.

Financial analysis (ground-level pricing view) is the final phase, which involves conducting price stress testing as well as a profitability and cash flow analysis that contributes to the final decision around commercial offers and pricing policies.

Figure 17.2. The four offer–design subprocesses within the Software Pricing Framework.

Not only does a strategic assessment help guide offer design; it also helps drive product strategy decisions, including product positioning, new product introductions, product marketing, and value selling as well as value innovation and portfolio investments (Gale & Swire, 2012). The product strategy review process involves integrating and interpreting the implications of a variety of inputs from the strategy-related categories shown in Figure 17.3.

Product management teams will need to spend adequate time to gather, discuss, and interpret strategic insights and determine how these impact the short-, medium-, and long-term go-to-market pricing, customer, and product strategies. From a pricing and offer-design perspective, this strategic analysis should be documented as a set of guiding principles for designing and selecting optimal offer structures.

Objectives	Segmentation analysis
Customer perceptions (voice-of-the-client)	Roadmap strategy
Value proposition (differentiation, SWOT analysis)	Innovation strategy
Market industry analysis	Third-party partnerships
Competitive analysis	Channel and channel-partner strategy

Figure 17.3. Strategic analysis components: Setting the stage for pricing strategies.

The importance of strategic analysis can never be overestimated: it's the precursor to building sound pricing strategies, structures, and tactics. Ensure that your team reviews these each quarter to identify new opportunities and changes within a fast-moving market. A more in-depth strategic assessment should be kicked off two or three months prior to annual strategic planning reviews to ensure that adequate time is spent to assess and extract major insights that will influence future product and pricing initiatives.

Price–value analysis (the 2,000-foot view)
Value-based pricing is defined as setting prices according primarily to reflect the perceived or estimated value of a product or service to the customer (rather than according to the cost of the product or historical prices)—a concept that should be championed by

every executive at every opportunity. The challenge for product and sales teams, however, is that this is easier said than done. But with the right tools, one's teams will be able to articulate a solution's value and successfully link the offer and pricing conversation to that value story.

There are two pricing tools that executives should be aware of: economic value analysis and price–value trade-off analysis. These tools are a starting point for any product team seeking to establish the 2,000-foot price positioning views that will serve as the price targets for the underlying roll-up of the price structure (packaging, metrics, and tiers).

Tool 1: Economic value. From our original scenario, Doug and his video capture company were exploring pricing in those cases where city-installed cameras could identify vehicle infractions (e.g., capture license plates for those vehicles driving in bus-only lanes) that allowed municipal agencies to issue tickets, thereby generating new revenue. Historically, they could price their cameras based on standard installation fees and cost-plus pricing for the camera and storage hardware (say, a one-time fee of $600 per camera system). But this innovation was delivering *significant* financial benefits to the municipality in terms of new ticket revenue generation: each transit-installed infraction camera system could generate upwards of $4,800 per month in tickets (or $57,600 per year). With over 200 transit-bus-wide camera installations, that translated to well over $11 million per year in new ticket revenues. "We're going to be generating massive revenues for the cities," mentioned Doug, "so we need to evaluate new pricing models."

The solution for Doug and team was to price their new bundle based on *economic value,* thereby adopting a value-based pricing approach for their new innovative solutions. In their case, the economic value was the generation of new ticket revenues (with the added benefit of improving road safety). With each camera system generating $4,800 in tickets per month, it could be possible to develop a high-value cloud-enabled camera system for a $1,499 per month subscription with no upfront installation fees or upfront hardware purchase—an extremely lucrative and high-margin offering with payments tied to cash inflow from ticket revenue.

Similar to Doug's scenario, other companies adopting new innovative solutions can adopt economic value analysis as a starting point to articulate value that's music to your client's ears—what client doesn't want to hear how your solution improves their own revenue growth, cost savings, cash flow improvement, and/or mitigation of financial risk?

As a rule of thumb, pricing for new innovation is about 10 to 15 percent of the financial benefits provided to clients. This can increase with increasing confidence around achieving the financial results (to as high as 50–60% in those cases where outcomes are guaranteed). Be sure that your teams apply realistic expectations around these financial benefits and link to relevant key performance indicators (KPIs) on the client side where possible. Financial benefits backed by case studies, pilot programs, industry reports, and customer referrals help build confidence in potential financial outcomes and ultimately increase your client's confidence in your pricing strategy.

Tool 2: Price–value trade-off. "We keep investing in product improvements, but all we do is continue to match competitive pricing. I know we should be monetizing our investments better, but we're unsure how these enhancements translate into pricing." Company XYZ's challenge isn't uncommon. Where product and sales teams struggle to articulate value, they'll also struggle to price and monetize that value. One approach is to better understand the relationship between price and value using the *price-value trade-off* tool.

This tool is particularly useful not only to better linking the price and value relationship but to *understanding the client's buying decision drivers* and how your solution compares with the next-best alternatives. Ultimately, this analysis seeks to *quantify* both price and value using a decision scoring approach, factoring the trade-off that a client segment makes between price and perceived value. One major advantage of using this tool for larger B2B client opportunities is that it also mirrors the commonly used scoring approach used by procurement arms as part of their vendor selection process.

Using our example from Company XYZ, their digital solution had significant value compared with the competitive mix. Their product and sales team, however, would often just match pricing to a main competitor (Figure 17.4). Despite being considered outstanding in perceived value, they weren't capturing that value as a premium price. The center of excellence pricing team applied the decision scoring mechanisms provided in a recent deal to help the product and sales team game-play how much more they could price as a premium while still confidently winning deals. It was determined that the team could price upwards of $720,000 above the next-best competitor price and still be favorably positioned to win deals (with highest 6.5 total score) based on their value advantage positioning.

Typically for B2B digital solutions, decisions are based 30 percent on price and 70 percent on value. Higher price-sensitive segments above this 30:70 ratio will begin to see purchase decisions going to lower-priced competitive offerings; in such cases, Company XYZ's product teams would need to lower their price premium potential or even seek an alternative lower-value (and lower-priced) product offering that's more suitable for that price-sensitive segment.

Executive teams must ultimately be the loudest champion for *value-based pricing* across their organization, and the economic

Scenario 1: Company XYZ prices based on market (matches Compeon)

Company	Price	Value	Decision weighting 30% Price score	70% Value score	100% Total score[1]
A	$1,530,000	Good	6.2	6.4	6.3
B	$1,210,000	Acceptable	6.7	5.0	5.5
C	$943,000	Marginal	7.5	4.8	5.6
XYZ	$1,530,000	Outstanding	6.2	6.9	6.7

1 Calculated as price score × 0.30 + value score × 0.70

Scenario 2: Company XYZ prices based on value (Premium)

Company	Price	Value	Decision weighting 30% Price score	70% Value score	100% Total score[2]
A	$1,530,000	Good	6.2	6.4	6.3
B	$1,210,000	Acceptable	6.7	5.0	5.5
C	$943,000	Marginal	7.5	4.8	5.6
XYZ	$2,250,000	Outstanding	5.4	6.9	6.5

2 Revenue gain for XYZ = $2,250,000 − $1,530,000 = $720,000 gain

Figure 17.4. Using price–value trade-off analysis for price setting.

value and the price–value trade-off analysis tools are but a starting point for their product and sales teams to quantify value and successfully link their pricing strategies to the value story.

Pricing structures—Packaging, metrics, and tiers (the 500-foot pricing view)

This next subprocess within offer design focuses on creating well-defined commercial pricing and offer structures that integrate the 2,000-foot view price positioning findings from our previous price–value analysis. During this subprocess, teams will need to assess (a) optimal packaging formats that support pricing and monetization objectives, (b) ideal metrics that address differing use cases and requirements across client segments, and (c) tiering that considers volume discounting and price levels. The goal of this phase is to develop an indicative commercial price list alongside guidelines and policies that manage allowable negotiation and price floors. These commercial price lists also standardize your sales approach, improve sales quote turnaround times, and embed your team's price–value analysis in your client offers.

Packaging your solution

Similar to restaurant menus, digital solutions can be sold either à la carte or bundled—these bundles can be used to target different segments with differing needs (value) and differing price sensitivities. It will be important to assess which package best aligns with your objectives. Functional packages, for example, may be preferred where clients integrate a mixture of different vendors into a larger system—a common occurrence with large ERPs with differing functions including finance, payroll, HR, and cash management. In this case, applying a modular approach where a client must first purchase a baseline core system before purchasing the ERP module could put a software firm at a disadvantage over a firm that sells a software component as a functional standalone. Alternatively, modular packages may prove more beneficial during a mature life-cycle phase that enables monetizing a legacy client base with new innovations and feature sets. Types of software packaging include those shown in Figure 17.5.

Be sure that your teams have adequately assessed package types *before* embarking on new product roadmap developments to ensure that your organization's product teams maximize how they monetize their solution with both new and current clients.

One size fits all

Good-better-best

Functional

Modular

Customized

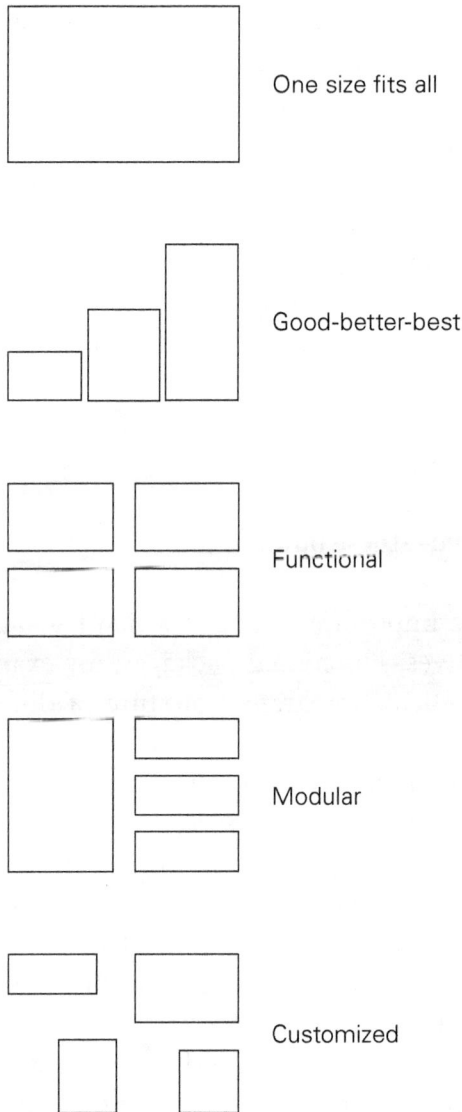

Figure 17.5. Digital solution packaging types. Note that packaging can also be a hybrid mixture of the above (e.g., good-better-best can be applied within functional and modular package offers).

License and Subscription Metrics

A solution metric is a standard unit of measure that links a fee structure to six possible software dimensions: access-based (who is accessing), architecture-based (resources being accessed), content-based (what's being accessed), usage-based (how much and how often it's being accessed), and outcome- and revenue-based metrics (Figure 17.6). In a more simplistic software pricing environment such as B2C, one metric can serve as the basis for determining the pricing strategy—and typically that metric is a per-named-user subscription fee. However, where B2B offerings are concerned, a greater degree of solution complexity and client use cases often calls for the use of multiple underlying metrics that roll up to determine the overall license or subscription fee.

"Which metrics are ideal for our solution?" There's no silver bullet answer—but there's a process for evaluating the options. Each solution is unique from one company to the next and requires an assessment to evaluate potential packaging and metric options while weighing the respective pros and cons. A few rules of thumb during this assessment phase to consider: ensure that your metrics are link to value delivered, are scalable ("you grow as your client grows"), address and monetize differing use cases for your solution, can be measured and billed, are sellable, and ultimately support your desired strategic objectives.

Financial analysis (ground-level pricing view)

The last subprocess within the offer-design phase involves conducting financial analysis and price stress-testing to determine price structure breaking points, potential for pricing and offer structure rework, and even the possibility of reevaluating the larger product and segmentation strategies. For many executives, this is where the pricing and offer structures become

Access-based	Architecture-based	Content-based	Usage-based
Platform fees	**Environment fees**	**Actual content**	**Per usage**
• Platform access fee	• Number of interfaces	• Content library 1	• Per transaction fee
• Platform (non-production/test)	• Server license	• Content library 2 …	• Per reports accessed
	• Hosting license	• Third-party content	• Per message/call (APIs)
	• Per instance		• Per batch job vs. on-demand
Location-based fees	• Per connection/node	**Insights**	
• Country/region fees	• Storage (per GB or TB)	• By dataset type	**Usage ranges** (such as between X and Y volumes)
• Localization fee		• By report type	• Transaction ranges
	Customization	• By model type	• Reports accessed ranges
User/device fees	• Per custom report or per page		
• Named user	• Per custom dashboard	**Advanced features**	**Proxy for usage**
• Named user (by profile)	• Per thousand lines of code	• Advanced reports	• Company size (revenue)
• Named user (limited)		• Advanced models	• Number of FTEs
• Daily active user (DAU)	**Workflows**	• Enhanced data	• Budget size
• Concurrent user	• Workflow type 1		• Number of customers
• Per connected device …	• Workflow type 2 …		• Number of accounts
			• Number of branches

Outcome-based	Revenue share
• % of cost savings	• % of transaction fee
• Per closed/won loan	• % of customer revenue

Figure 17.6. Examples of B2B licensing and subscription metric types.

inputs into a final business case view: "Are we profitable in the short and/or long term? What are the expected cash flow views? What is our expected payback period under subscription models? How does profitability change across product offers and client segments?"

For price stress-testing, model inputs and financial views will need to be tested across a variety of different possible scenarios to determine where a price model may have some unforeseen nuances, improvement areas, or even high-risk areas that will require rework. These risks can ultimately influence adjustments to one's pricing structure and offer design, identify which profitable client segments to target (and unprofitable segments to avoid), prioritize internal activities to mitigate certain costs, or even highlight a need to change the product strategy itself.

Conclusion and implications for the C-suite

Both Doug's video capture firm and Company XYZ came to realize that their companies could greatly benefit by investing in improved pricing practices. Your company, too, could realize significant financial gains and growth factoring the following considerations.

- **Become your company's top champion for value-based pricing in the digital era.** Employees will quickly take to your "value" commentary cues in company meetings and adopt a value-driven culture that's strongly linked to monetizable and profitable growth.
- **Invest in improving your pricing maturity and capabilities.** Acknowledge where your company could benefit from frameworks, expertise, and pricing tools in the short and long term. A diagnostic of your current capabilities can help

set the stage for short- and long-term pricing-improvement plans.

- **Treat pricing as a process.** From value-based segmented offer design, to enablement of sales teams with the price–value story, to laser-focused execution of deals that drive the desired pricing outcome, treat pricing as an end-to-end company process and continuous improvement cycle while avoiding suboptimal, ad-hoc guesswork.
- **Be innovative! The B2B digital solution era is all about recurring value to client.** As in Doug's and Company XYZ's cases, be sure to explore innovative bundling solutions around hardware, software, and services that migrate your company toward more lucrative recurring revenue client engagements.

Ultimately, pricing is a journey and a process. With a solid foundational understanding of B2B industry pricing practices and by adopting processes and tools defined within the Software Pricing Framework, your organization can embark on their journey toward developing and implementing optimal value-based and segmented offer structures that not only compete in the market place but also deliver material improvements to your organization's recurring revenue and market performance.

References

Gale, B. T., & Swire, D. J. (2012). Implementing strategic B2B pricing: Constructing value benchmarks. *Journal of Revenue and Pricing Management, 11,* 40–53.

The author

Scott Miller is a leading expert in enterprise B2B software pricing, offer design, and deal-win tactics. With over 20 years of pricing experience that includes over 50 major pricing transformation initiatives as well as hands-on global pricing director roles with $10 billion technology firms, Scott understands the nuances and complexities of B2B and B2G pricing in the digital era. He is also a CPA, a CMA, a published author, and a speaker on best-in-class pricing practices. Scott is based in Toronto, Canada, and can be reached at scott@miller-advisors.com.

SECTION 5

PRICING AS A FORCE OF TRANSFORMATION

18

Bionic Pricing: Augmenting Human Intelligence

Camille Brégé, Managing Director and Partner in the Paris office of the Boston Consulting Group, and Amadeus Petzke, Partner and Associate Director in the Berlin office of the Boston Consulting Group

I F CASH IS THE lifeblood of a business, as many entrepreneurs and business leaders argue, then pricing is the heartbeat. Regardless of the strategies and tactics companies use to either stimulate or to calm it, it remains one of the most vital organic parts of the business.

But despite the fundamental role of pricing, most companies to this day relegate it to middle management. C-level executives tend to remain hands-off, even though the evidence that better pricing means better profits has been clear and compelling for decades.

But the days of second-rate status for pricing are ending rapidly. This is not only because companies are recognizing that artificial intelligence (AI) has the potential to create step-change improvements in a company's ability to tap into customers' willingness to pay and thus earn higher profits. They are also realizing that the frontier is wide open for companies that can shake up their industries with AI-based pricing initiatives and create competitive advantages that may be difficult, if not impossible, for existing competitors to erode. Conquering this frontier requires commitment and focus from senior leadership. First movers can enjoy a huge advantage because the global business world is much closer to the infancy of AI-based business practices than to their maturity or sophistication.

A recent report by the Bruce Henderson Institute (BHI) and the Massachusetts Institute of Technology (MIT) showed how wide open that pricing frontier is, and how lucrative it can be for first movers. BHI and MIT surveyed more than 3,000 managers around the world and interviewed executives and scholars. They found that a majority of companies are developing AI capabilities but that so far a mere 10 percent are obtaining significant financial benefits with AI (Ransbotham, Khodabandeh, Kiron, Candelon, Chu, & LaFountain, 2020, p. 1). Digging deeper into the findings, however, reveals the hidden opportunity that pricing offers. As an example, in the tech sector, only 12 percent of tech companies use AI for pricing. But they're twice as likely to succeed in their AI transformation!

We interpret those findings to mean that pricing is one of the fastest ways for an organization to achieve meaningful financial improvement while gaining a comfort level with AI. If we boil the challenges of AI-based initiatives down to two things—mindset and more money—AI-based pricing is a fast and reliable way to achieve both.

Our own engagements at Boston Consulting Group (BCG) confirm that several companies are using AI-based pricing to achieve significant financial benefits. A B2B distributor in the building materials sector increased its EBIT margin by 100 basis points when it used a combined "human-machine" approach to implement its dynamic pricing program (Brégé et al., 2020). That approach describes the secret to implementing AI-based pricing and reaping the upside: the right combination of human intelligence and AI, or what BCG calls the bionic company (Hutchinson, Aré, Rose, & Bailey, 2019).

Figure 18.1 shows that a bionic organization needs to focus on strengthening the human side, building up the technical side, and defining the right outcomes. All are equally important. Rather than yield to the relentless progress of AI and the breakthrough technologies that support it, the bionic company harnesses and integrates the best of what both humans and machines have to offer.

Top-down leadership is important to accelerating a company's transition to any bionic approach. But top-down leadership is indispensable for successful bionic pricing: it's easy to view pricing in the 21st century as a technical, tactical exercise, but the opposite is true. Pricing has become a strategic exercise that integrates humans and machines together in ways that require new competencies, new organizational models, and new forms of interaction, all sustained by a new form of leadership. Once leaders overcome that misconception about pricing, it's easier for them to envision

Outcomes

Strategy and Purpose

Commercial data and digital platform

People and ways of working

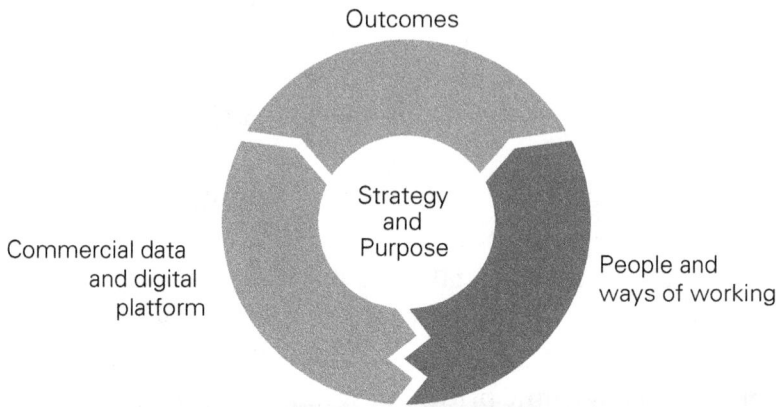

Figure 18.1. The "bionic" organization unites technology, people, and outcomes.

their company's strategic entry into the frontier of AI-based pricing and to prepare their teams to conquer that frontier.

In the rest of this chapter, we dive into the four prerequisites to successful bionic pricing on the human side, the side that CEOs need to take a strong active role in.

Introducing the idea of bionic pricing

At a high level, the idea of a bionic company seems intuitive in today's environment. But the implementation of that bold idea raises several important questions that are especially urgent for pricing:

- What do traditional tasks and functions look like when a company becomes bionic?
- What are the challenges of making the transformation to a company that lives up to the definition of bionic?

- What's at stake for companies that wait too long and move too slowly?

To understand the future role and nature of pricing in the bionic company, we can find clues in the evolution of pricing over the last three decades, in parallel with advancements in technology.

Pricing is obviously quantitative and analytical, but over the years most of the hard math involved finding the right markup to costs. The advent of technologies we take for granted today—price scanners and advanced market research methods using personal computers—ignited an explosion of data that helped companies test even more hypotheses about what drives customers, costs, and complexity and to set their prices accordingly. The most advanced companies began to further differentiate prices, applying a refined understanding of how customer needs and value creation translated into willingness to pay.

The next evolutionary step was dynamic pricing, which in its most extreme form allows companies to charge personalized prices in real time. As we noted in a recent publication, dynamic pricing has "transformed into a way for any company to deploy artificial intelligence (AI) to process the myriad financial and commercial inputs in order to achieve pricing's Holy Grail: the right price decision at the right time for a specific customer" (Brégé et al., 2020). Data became ubiquitous, and hordes of savvy data scientists began to use AI to process it.

That's an impressive trajectory, so let's trace it further into the future. A completely human path without the support of technology is obviously unrealistic. But growing fears about technology and automation demonstrate that a completely technological path—with less and less human intervention—is at least feasible. Companies will therefore have a choice between two sharply different paths to follow:

- **The technology path.** It's reasonable to expect that algorithms will get smarter and smarter and marginalize humans. One probable path would lead to a complete triumph of AI because it offers so many advantages in speed, processing power, and reliability. Under that scenario, AI would alleviate the need for human intervention and monitoring and eventually render humans irrelevant. The good old "art" in setting prices will turn into a "science only" process, as decision-makers "outsource" this costly activity to engines running 24/7 and delivering constant value surpluses.
- **The bionic path.** Remember that *bionic* means combining the best that humans and technology offer. Rather than impede or halt the technical progress, decision-makers should accompany it and manage it. This means "insourcing" pricing and integrating it more deeply in the organization, from the C-suite down to the front-line moments when customers make their purchase decisions. Pricing evolves into a high art, backed by the best science.

We emphatically do not believe that pricing will continue to accelerate down the technical path alone, which is a one-way street to full automation. In fact, our expectation for the future is exactly the opposite! Bionic pricing is the best choice, but success is not guaranteed.

The four prerequisites of bionic pricing

Companies will face numerous challenges in terms of talent, organization, interaction, and leadership style. They need to continue their commitment to customer-centricity, but they also need to go deeper into technology, data processes, and advanced analytics, and to interpret the insights generated by the science.

Outcomes

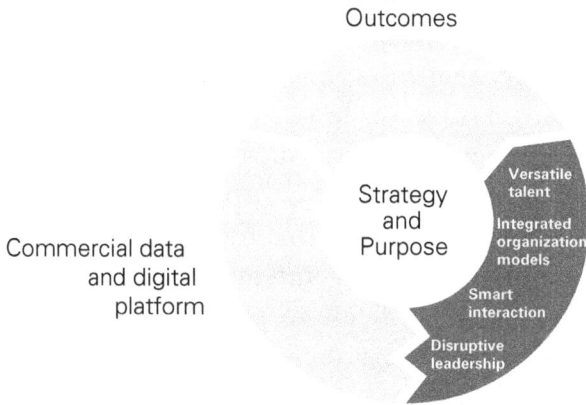

Figure 18.2. The four prerequisites of bionic pricing, emphasizing the human side.

This translates into four key prerequisites for bionic pricing (Figure 18.2).

Versatile talent. The C-level executives set the tone and the direction, and the data scientists manage the technology. But who will be the bridge between the two? This is where the role of the pricing manager evolves. The traditional pricing manager provided guidance, administration, and, in some cases, specific price recommendations. It was a tactical, back-office role, but it transforms into a much more significant role in a bionic organization. The manager of bionic pricing has an active and accountable stake in the company's go-to-market strategy. This new breed of manager needs not only to think strategically but also to be technically savvy, flexible, adaptable—someone who lives and breathes the customer experience. Instead of setting day-to-day prices or programming the algorithms, they "own" the process. They steer all aspects of the pricing process by setting the right (strategic) guardrails, and then controlling and optimizing the results.

Integrated organization models. The bionic organization thrives on integration rather than separation. That makes it an ideal fit for pricing, which is inherently cross-functional but hampered by the fact that sales, finance, and marketing often work on it in their own silos. The bionic pricing organization dissolves the boundaries between those silos by establishing a common language, a common basis for collaboration, and shared objectives and KPIs. One could say that these new organization models improve "human–human" interaction as well. This not only applies internally but extends to partnerships and outsourcing decisions. When knowledge, data, and competencies are available on the open market, should a company tap into those resources or invest in developing its own intellectual property? Those decisions are easier to make when they reflect cooperation across functions rather than narrow views within functions. Having a siloed organization is riskier than ever, as the exchanges and collaboration with outside partners becomes vital.

Smart interaction. The bionic company has numerous new interfaces that contribute to optimal pricing. In a world where humans and machines must establish a partnership, the company must rethink each of these relationships:

- **Human to machine.** What strategic guardrails and guidance do managers provide the AI systems and the algorithms to ensure that their outputs are current, relevant, and impactful?
- **Machine to human.** What outputs does the machine need to produce to provide decision-makers the best possible guidance?

The BHI/MIT study found that organizations that enable humans and machines to continuously learn from each other in this manner are five times more likely to realize significant financial benefits than organizations that learn with a single method, such as a pure machine-to-machine tech solution (Ransbotham et al., 2020, p. 2).

Disruptive leadership. Bionic pricing thrives on action and adaptation. Running that organization requires leaders who know how to enable and empower their teams within a clear set of key principles. These leaders know when to engage resources from a broader range of inputs, when to keep the focus narrow, and when to step back to let the organization move faster.

In that spirit, this form of leadership is disruptive because it encourages constant change. Leaders exert less control over daily tasks and spend less time defining and defending functional territories. Instead, they allow individuals to grow and to tear down those boundaries. They provide inspiration for continuous and creative disruption.

The important difference is that this is purposeful disruption as opposed to wild, chaotic disruption or change for the sake of change. It fulfills an overarching principle that we'd call "constant progress at the right pace." Such an organization does not mistake a plateau for a peak. The speed of progress may change, but there are no ends and no optima to pursue.

What's the key leadership challenge in an organization that's constantly improving and evolving? It lies in holding people accountable for results. Using a system of performance measurement and constant feedback, such organizations live up to the name "test and learn" rather than merely aspire to it.

The CEO's decisive role in successful bionic pricing

Regardless of what we see and hear in scary forecasts and science fiction stories, the term *AI* itself implies an intimate, ongoing link to humans. The word *artificial* literally means man-made, and the implication is that humans must continue to remake and redirect AI to ensure that it still serves the company's short- and long-term goals.

The future of pricing therefore needs humans and machines. While the IT professionals lead the technological side by augmenting *human* intelligence with technology, data science, and especially the right design to unleash these powers, the C-suite—and especially the CEO—must take a more active role in pricing. The C-level executives orchestrate the application of augmented human intelligence by upgrading talent, streamlining organizational models, fostering new collaborative ways of working, and holding leaders more accountable.

Taking humans out of the pricing process would be tantamount to taking marketing and strategy out of the pricing process. Technological evolution will not alter the fact that pricing is not only one of the four P's of marketing but also the single biggest contributor to the top line. More than ever, companies need to think like marketers and keep their focus on customers. Understanding how customers interact with prices and respond to them is essential. Otherwise, the customer relationship becomes transactional, negating the investments companies have made in innovation and in establishing a unique selling proposition.

Leaving the algorithms on their own can lead to one of the countless epic fails that have received media attention. One of Amazon's algorithms rounded niche DVD sales from 0.2 items per month up to one full item per month, leading to massive ordering that swamped the distribution centers. Algorithms designed for competitive price matching can trigger negative price spirals without proper additional guidance.

But even without these outrageous glitches, letting the relationship become transactional would also reduce prices to tactical weapons, ignoring the fact that pricing begins with strategy. It's imperative that companies keep their eyes on the bigger picture and remain one step ahead of competitors who challenge their market position. The algorithms may provide answers for the next step, but companies can use other forms of AI and augmented human intelligence to think several steps in advance, using scenario planning and war-gaming to anticipate the responses to potential actions.

Humans are also better equipped to understand and resolve issues of price fairness and price stability. Fairness seems to be a simple concept at first glance, but its dimensions are neither easy to define nor constant. Egregious examples of gouging, for example, have given us our own cultural and even strategic sense of a "fair price"—but how does one translate that into the hard-and-fast rules that make pricing AI so efficient?

Price stability is also an aspect that companies could turn into a KPI because dynamic price changes can irritate customers and harm the purchase experience. Price is part of the customer experience, and too much dynamism can train customers to forgo a purchase if they think prices will fall in the near future. Concepts such as everyday low prices (EDLP) go to the other extreme because they have few price changes and foster trust between a company and its customers.

In short, the implementation of state-of-the-art pricing is not a technical challenge as much as it is also a strategic human challenge that requires top-down leadership. It's about strategy, marketing, and customer-centricity. These aspects are no less important in B2B markets, where value creation and value sharing between seller and customer often mean looking beyond the pure price. Different approaches to pricing and monetization are increasingly becoming sources of competitive advantage, and the more the CEO leads the transformation to a bionic organization, the greater the chances a company has to lead its industry by making AI a true source of competitive advantage.

References

Brégé, C., Bourgouin, L., Langkamp, D., Chu, M., Beckett, M., Poirmeur, P., & Niepmann, J. (2020). Debunking the myths of B2B dynamic pricing. *BCG*, November 20. www.bcg.com/publications/2020 /dynamic-pricing-b2b-myths

Hutchinson, R., Aré, L., Rose, J., & Bailey, A. (2019, November 7). The bionic company: Winning the '20s. *BCG*, November 7. www.bcg.com/publications/2019/bionic-company

Ransbotham, S., Khodabandeh, S., Kiron, D., Candelon, F., Chu, M., & LaFountain, B. (2020, October 19). Expanding AI's impact with organizational learning. MIT Sloan Management Review and Boston Consulting Group.

The authors

Camille Brégé is a Managing Director and Partner in the Paris office of the Boston Consulting Group. See page 231 for full bio.

Amadeus Petzke is a Partner and Associate Director in the Berlin office of the Boston Consulting Group. He leads the firm's Pricing Enablement Center in Europe and is a member of the group's global pricing leadership team. Over the last 15 years, he has worked with more than 100 major and multinational companies, focusing on holistic topline strategy development; implementation of new pricing models, policies, and solutions; and the enablement of pricing capabilities. He is a regular speaker at conferences and leading industry events in Europe and has published extensively on pricing over the last decade. You can reach him at www.linkedin.com/in/amadeuspetzke or by email at petzke.amadeus@bcg.com.

19

Pricing and Commercial Agility to Survive the Resurgent COVID-19 Crisis

Mark Billige, CEO of Simon-Kucher & Partners, and Dr. Andreas von der Gathen, CEO of Simon-Kucher & Partners

Commercial agility—a rare combination of capabilities—is what will separate the winners from the rest as the pandemic persists

THINKING RIGHT NOW ABOUT an "after corona" world— what we would normally call a recovery—will only divert resources from your company's true existential challenge: surviving the wild roller coaster of the "with corona" period that will endure for the next 18 to 24 months until a vaccine becomes widely available.

Many companies are understandably eager for a quick return to normalcy when governments relax their stay-at-home restrictions. But this recurring pandemic promises to take a very different course, likely confronting companies with rounds of devastating economic impacts that will force them to manage unprecedented complexity and volatility.

What "vaccine" can a company take to steel itself against these impacts?

In short, the ultimate key to surviving this crisis is commercial agility: the ability to make resilient design, sales, cost management, and pricing decisions with unprecedented speed and flexibility—over and over again—until some form of equilibrium returns to your market.

Companies that already have superior commercial agility— reflected in how flexibly their go-to-market models respond under extreme stress—will need to capitalize on that rare and valuable asset. Many that lack it at least know what it takes. It means implementing those exciting aspirational ideas that highlight their transformation plans but that are usually postponed because the consequences would be too disruptive and far-reaching.

Right now, disruption is occurring on an unimagined scale, with no end in sight. There are no more excuses for waiting.

Companies without sufficient commercial agility will need to either build it or buy it immediately, or face the withering effects of never finding a new equilibrium in any episode of the crisis.

What makes commercial agility the key to survival

For most companies in most industries in the "with corona" period, three things will hold true:

- **You can forget what you know about demand patterns.** Most companies recover from a "singular" economic crisis—such as a deep recession—when customer demand reignites. But in a resurgent crisis, volatile demand shape-changes before a company's eyes. In some cases, a combination of fear and confusion drives customers to find new ways to buy a product or service, or alternative ways to solve their problems. Their urgent searches create opportunities for other companies to tap into new segments. The longer a resurgent crisis endures—and the more stops and restarts it experiences—the more customers will adjust their willingness to pay as they become accustomed to new behaviors, new buying patterns, more relaxed quality standards, and product scarcities. Some customers will revert to their old ways as fear and confusion subsides, but many won't.
- **You can forget about one "alphabet recovery."** The answer to the question of whether the recovery from the COVID-19 crisis will have a U, V, or L shape is "all of the above." No one knows how often COVID-19 will force economies—and thus companies—to hit the reset button between now and the beginning of 2022. But we anticipate multiple episodes of government intervention with sudden stops and uneven restarts. Future stops may trigger downturns and

slowdowns that eat back into or even wipe out all the gains from the previous restart.

- **You can forget about time periods.** A resurgent crisis renders months, quarters, and year-on-year comparisons irrelevant. The only period that matters now is the one you're in, likely measured in weeks. The only fixed future date that matters is when a vaccine is available in mass quantities, but even then, there's no certainty about how long it will take for some form of economic stability to emerge.

In a resurgent crisis, demand fluctuations in some industries are already an order of magnitude greater than what any company or manager has ever experienced, with underlying causes that are likely to make lasting and fundamental changes to demand patterns. The corresponding stress on the go-to-market models will likewise be far greater than in any previous crisis, primarily because of severe restrictions on how companies can conduct business. In an era defined by social distancing and other constraints on human-to-human interaction, it's much harder for many businesses to sell their products and services, deliver them, and, even more importantly, maintain control over customer safety and the customer experience.

In all probability, these stresses on the go-to-market model will surge and recede several times as demand remains volatile and the pandemic lingers. The greater a company's commercial agility, the greater its ability will be to minimize or defuse that stress and turn it to its advantage. Agility in offer design, sales, cost management, and pricing—combined with the economic resilience to endure several resets—will greatly increase its chances of surviving the multiple stop-starts and emerging stronger when a resurgent crisis ends.

Commercial agility allows a company to maintain control over its pricing, its value proposition, and its sales channels while—in the interest of speed and efficiency—devolving as much decision-making responsibility as possible to the people closest to the customers. Doing that is not part of most companies' DNA. In our experience, most companies swing toward an extreme response in a time of crisis: either they exert excessive control or they delegate vast responsibilities without adequate structure or tracking.

Navigating the crisis map

A classic economic crisis has one standard "linear" scenario: demand declines, putting temporary stress on the economic model but little or no stress on the go-to-market model. When renewed confidence eventually releases pent-up demand, the recovery's overall gains more than offset the losses in the downturn. But the overall constraints on a business don't change. Nothing stops the business from running normally in the period of weaker demand.

Instead of one basic scenario, the COVID-19 resurgent crisis has four scenarios or spaces, as shown in Figure 19.1. The crisis is giving customers a crash course in what they don't need and what they can live without, and companies are quickly confronted with what they can (or can't) do well in response. Both their economic models and their go-to-market models have come under duress, creating a double-barreled nightmare that has no precedent for a playbook. We expect most companies to experience the demand extremes and the stresses of at least two of these scenarios in the next 18 to 24 months, perhaps even simultaneously, depending on how the pandemic progresses in different markets around the world.

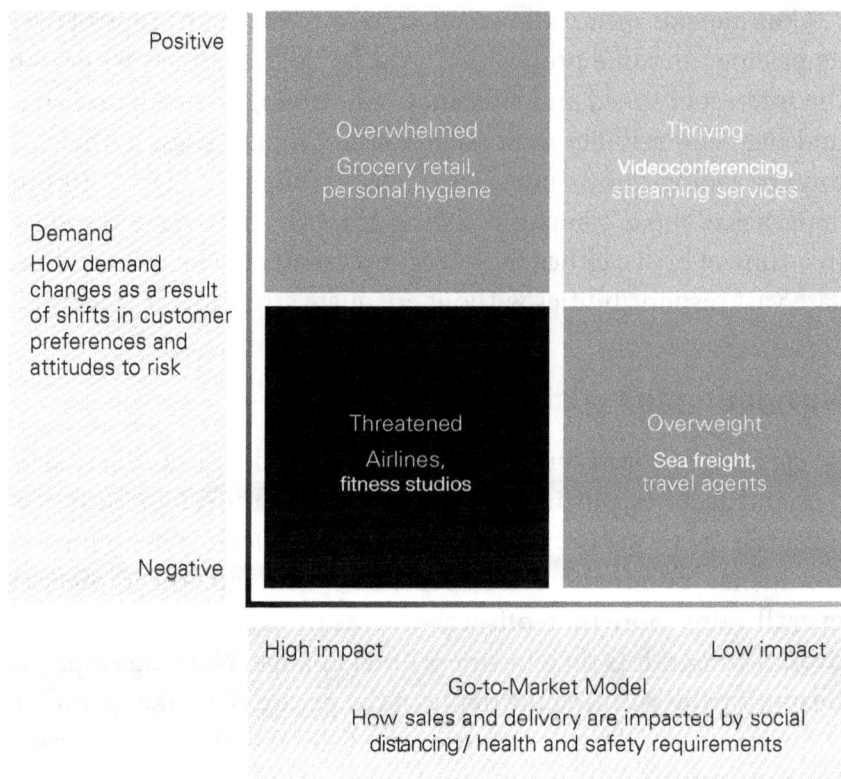

Figure 19.1. COVID-19 crisis map.

The demand effects represented on the vertical axis are multi-dimensional, not simply a "higher or lower" calculus easily measured in straightforward changes in volume or revenue. The axis also indicates the extent to which shifts in the market—defined in terms of customer needs, occasions, product alternatives, and channel choices—are working to your advantage or working against you.

The go-to-market effects on the horizontal axis indicate the extent to which lockdowns, social distancing, and other requirements are impeding your ability to sell and deliver a product or service and manage your customers' safety, experience, and engagement.

In normal situations, the decline in demand is usually not sufficient to warrant a rethinking of either the economic or the go-to-market model. But this crisis poses a challenge to customers' ingrained habits. The hard truth is that many businesses continue—even through a conventional recession or crisis—primarily because their customers cling to their established ways and see neither a desire nor a need to change. A resurgent crisis gives them enough impulse to overcome their inertia, and many old habits will never return to the old "normal."

Right now, every industry—and every player in those industries—lies within one of the four spaces that we elaborate on below. Whether they can move to a better position, or defend a desirable one, will come down to their commercial agility.

Thriving

Situation. The crisis map has no safe spaces, but this is the most desirable one. Demand shifts are working in a company's favor, and the effects of social distancing and other measures don't inhibit the company from absorbing greater demand, addressing new segments, and responding with different price-product combinations. Profitability and cash flow are essential in this crisis, and this space creates the most lucrative opportunities. That's why competitors will strive to reach this space as well, if they aren't already there. Competition will intensify, and success through multiple crisis episodes will come down to commercial agility.

Survival moves. The biggest challenge of this space is staying there: How do you protect share, and how do you retain (new) customers throughout the crisis and beyond it? How do you rethink your offers and enhance your sales processes to preserve or increase your advantages? Companies here need to divert resources to capitalize on surging demand and adopt pricing models (e.g., free-to-paid or subscriptions) that will help them monetize and hold the demand. They'll also need to review and perhaps expand their range of channels.

Examples. Videoconferencing, streaming services, remote IT support.

Overwhelmed

Situation. Demand shifts have worked in your favor but are straining your operations. For example, grocery retailers and companies that offer nondiscretionary goods (especially in health and safety) are seeing huge, sustained spikes in demand. The downside of this favorable demand profile is that the capacity of your business may not be able to absorb it while maintaining quality and service standards. Prolonged negative customer experiences—such as longer queues, extended waiting periods, lower levels of support, and stockouts—degrade the normal customer experience and can compel customers to renew their search for adequate alternatives or simply revert to their old habits.

Survival moves. If ever there was a time to make mass improvements to your revenue and operating models and invest in digital capabilities, this is it. Companies in this space need to urgently examine their operating model: what can you change to improve customer experience and economics? The mission here is to beat your competitors into the *thriving* space and avoid sliding down into *threatened*.

Examples. Grocery retail, personal hygiene, cleaning products, home exercise equipment, domestic parcel services.

Overweight

Situation. This space corresponds most closely to what companies witness during a conventional downturn, recession, or crisis. Demand shifts have worked against you because of out-right declines or changes in the nature of demand. But the stress on your go-to-market model is low, warranting few if any changes.

Survival moves. Companies here can fall back on proven crisis responses that help them maintain customers and volume without sacrificing margins. They should reduce capacity and provide discounts in kind rather than lowering their prices. They should also invest in reducing barriers to purchase.

Examples. Sea freight, travel agents.

Threatened

Situation. This is the most dangerous space on the map. The crisis is exposing the major weaknesses in a company's go-to-market model. Companies here tend to sell discretionary products and services in a largely physical setting to customers who have many other alternatives. The ones that require human-to-human contact and that have no obvious digital mirror (e.g., transportation services, dentists, and beauty salons) face complete collapse unless they literally invent additional ways to deliver their products or services.

Survival moves. Companies here have little hope of reaching another space on the map unless they reinvent the whole business. They need to organize teams to redesign the customer journey and find new revenue models and value propositions that will work in a "with corona" world. At the same time, they need to shut down business models that have no obvious future for the next two years and determine what assets have potential value in another space. Failing that, the final option is to shutter the business completely, wait, and try to reduce costs massively. Some companies might be able to survive a few months in that suspended state, but it is doubtful whether they could last a year or two.

Examples. Airlines, fitness studios, mass transit lines, sports leagues, trade fairs.

The joker in all four spaces is government intervention. First, the extent and the frequency of governments' tightening and loosening of restrictions have vast first- and second-order effects on customer demand and on how companies go to market. Second, some governments are trying to prop up consumers, either through direct payments or by providing payroll protection to businesses to offset revenue losses and to keep unemployment down. Some are also subsidizing certain businesses or industries directly.

The crisis also shows how overarching labels for an industry—logistics, for example—can mask the true effects of the crisis on an individual firm. Domestic parcel delivery firms around the world are overwhelmed, as they can hardly keep up with surging demand. But the companies that operate oceangoing freight vessels have seen much of their demand evaporate, leaving them with persistent excess capacity.

The five pillars of commercial agility

Within a resurgent crisis, we have defined commercial agility as the ability to make resilient design, sales, cost management, and pricing decisions with unprecedented speed and flexibility—over and over again—until some form of equilibrium returns to your market (Figure 19.2).

Agile design
The shifts in demand also include changes in customer needs, occasions, product alternatives, and channel choices. The more pronounced and persistent these shifts are, the more they'll make rigid product and service designs—and in many cases the

1 Agile
design

2 Agile
sales

Manage volatility...

3 Agile cost
management

4 Agile
pricing

5 Economic Resilience
Profit orientation ⊕ Resilient revenue model

Lengthen
runway...

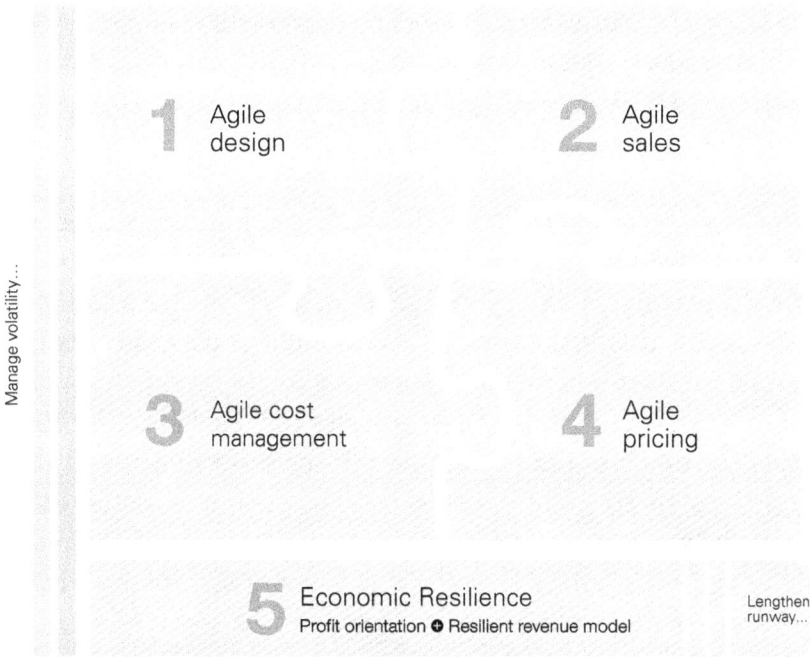

Figure 19.2. The five pillars of commercial agility.

processes that created them—vulnerable to competitors who can better meet customers' needs, without jeopardizing customer safety, experience, and engagement.

Agile design begins with rethinking your minimum viable product (MVP). For airlines, cinema chains, and sports teams, what's the MVP that accounts for social distancing and the resulting lower density or load factors? Retailers, restaurants, and personal services firms obviously face the same challenge that may confront companies in most industries at some point: how do you design a product or service that succeeds on customer experience, customer safety, and economic feasibility in a world defined by social distancing? Answering that question in a B2B environment is more nuanced because many services will still work, but not as well. They'll be clumsier and costlier, and they'll raise the bars for the quality levels that buyers will demand and tolerate. The more customized a B2B service is, the lower the margins tend to be. B2B companies need to understand that the MVP really is an MVP, and not merely the same thing at a lower price.

The basic recommendations that transcend industries include converting services and in some cases products to digital forms while decreasing capacity and fixed costs. If you have a digital basis already, this is the time to accelerate it and exhaust its full potential.

But two particular types of businesses may be harder hit than others. The first is premium suppliers. If the shifts in demand alter perceptions so strongly that customers become accustomed to accepting "less for less," what adjustments do premium suppliers need to make to their MVP without sacrificing their brand advantages and pricing power?

The second group comprises the young companies commonly known as unicorns: firms with high valuations but low profitability. Their model depends on having enough time for their exponential growth—often propelled by low prices, excellent service, and a strong brand—to translate to the bottom line. A resurgent crisis compresses those timelines massively while also greatly increasing the risk of these business models. While some are thriving thanks to the commercial agility they built into their DNA from the outset, the compressed timelines may force many of them to alter or abandon their original plans.

Agile sales

Digital selling and e-commerce channels now need to move from the long-term "wish list" to the top of the sales department's priority list. This is especially true for remote sales: the ability to replicate face-to-face or field sales interactions as closely as possible using communication tools such as videoconferencing.

In short, firms now need to become experts at remote selling, and they need to move quickly. Many firms already have a mix of traditional field and remote sales, with key accounts usually receiving close personal attention through the traditional field channel. Sustaining that level of attention is now impossible, meaning that the mix must change radically in favor of remote sales. Even if travel restrictions loosen, conducting "normal" field sales will be very inefficient for at least the next two years. The expense will drive up cost of sales, never mind the general burdens of traveling in a social-distancing world.

This transition will require specialist training on two fronts. First, there is the "hard" side of implementing the new tools, understanding the technical aspects of conducting product demonstrations remotely, and demonstrating the ROI in this environment. Then there is the "soft" side, as salespeople learn how to understand customer needs, build trust, and work their way around the decision-makers without the advantages of a personal presence. This will be particularly challenging for large-ticket items.

The small silver lining is that many firms have an immediate opportunity for improvement. We estimate that 23 percent of a typical field sales representative's time is spent traveling. Firms can now redirect that time to far more productive uses.

Agile cost management

Commercial agility does not come cheap. The cost of doing business will increase, especially in capacity-driven businesses. Some companies may also repatriate their supply chains because the lower risk of disruption offsets the comparative cost advantage of foreign sourcing.

At some point, the companies making these investments will need to pass along at least some of those costs through the value chain. This is another point where agile pricing comes into play: how can a company increase its prices at a hypersensitive time when any such moves risk being viewed as profiteering or as price-gouging?

Answering this question requires companies to find the right timing, the right levels, and the right level of differentiation, all backed by a communications plan that minimizes the risks of misunderstandings. Companies can benefit from adopting concepts from revenue management. These include demand forecasting as well as the intense monitoring of key indicators.

In a B2B environment, efforts to pass through costs and raise prices will probably meet stiff resistance from buyers, who will be taking whatever steps possible to reduce their own costs. But a combination of advance planning and flexibility can mitigate this resistance. Such a plan should be developed at the customer-product level because contract terms and price lists may preclude price changes at some customers.

The sales organization should be prepared with target prices and fallback plans for every account. Salespeople should be able to respond quickly with preauthorized concessions, sweeteners, or other alternatives. Detailed scripts and FAQs will enable salespeople to explain and defend their actions with one confident voice.

The critical step is real-time tracking. Execution will not improve if you follow a traditional calendar to make assessments. The combination of real-time tracking and a flexible incentive model will help keep salespeople focused.

Agile pricing

The longer demand remains volatile—in both form and extent—the more it will expose the risks and flaws of rigid pricing models, especially ones highly optimized for a market that essentially no longer exists.

We recommend several ways for companies to add agility to their pricing processes and price models. First, companies will need to move to differentiated pricing as quickly as possible, ideally at the microsegment or even the individual level. Differentiated pricing is no longer a distant goal as you wait for technology and customers to catch up. It needs to happen right now.

Doing this will require changes to governance and tools. The need for efficiency, flexibility, and speed dictates that companies decentralize their decision-making so that business units, teams, and individual salespeople can make price decisions with the right combination of authority and guidance. This in turn will require an infrastructure for delivering pricing guidance and monitoring selling prices in a structured, real-time way.

B2B companies will need to provide significantly more guidance on what a "good" price is and tighten their discounting guardrails and their escalation procedures. B2C companies need to seize opportunities to tighten the accountability around their discounting and promotional policies. In both situations, the need for greater analytical power, deeper and more reliable data sets, and human intervention raises the stakes. Some companies will seize these opportunities to stake out a position in the *thriving* space, then shift their focus to securing their gains.

Economic resilience

The final pillar of commercial agility is an economic model that can cope with the further shocks that we feel this crisis will inevitably cause. "Resilience" is used in many business contexts, but in terms of a resurgent crisis, it has two very specific meanings. First, companies need to emphasize profit and cash flow over market share. The time for razor-thin margins is over, as is the time of preserving "strategic customers" through cross-subsidization. High volatility may limit access to outside capital, which places even greater priority on a company's ability to self-finance any necessary investments and preserve enough money to weather multiple downturns.

Second, this is the ideal time to implement—and even force—shifts to recurring revenue models such as subscriptions. For many companies, this idea resides on that list of "down the road" transformations that usually seemed too difficult, expensive, or disruptive in a stable or growing market. But right now, the advantages of shifting to a subscription model can be a matter of survival, even if the initial transition is not yet optimal in terms of execution.

Five urgent questions about your company's commercial agility

For most companies, whether and when to reinvent their commercial models is no longer their decision. The answers are "yes" and "now." The "with corona" period will last for so long that they will not see the "after corona" world unless they fundamentally change how they do business.

The COVID-19 crisis is exposing the inertia and old customer habits that have propped up many business models. Shifts in demand are leaving some companies overwhelmed and struggling to keep up; others face record-high levels of idle capacity. Only a handful of companies have found a way to thrive. But this crisis is resurgent, meaning that companies will most likely need to weather multiple stops and restarts. The only way to reach the "after corona" world is through greater resilience and commercial agility.

Surviving the crisis will depend on how managers answer these five questions:

- How do we need to redesign our offer to deliver a safe and engaging customer experience *and* still make money?
- How well can our sales model adapt to a remote world?
- What are our playbooks and processes for managing inevitable cost-base inflation in our pricing?
- How prepared is our pricing model and decision framework to respond quickly enough to volatile demand?
- How can we ensure that our revenue and profitability models are resilient enough to endure multiple episodes of the crisis?

The authors

Mark Billige is CEO of Simon-Kucher & Partners, elected to lead the consultancy with Andreas von der Gathen in 2019. During his 15-year career with the company, he grew the UK business as Managing Partner and served on the company's global board. Mark joined Simon-Kucher in 2006 in the firm's London office. In 2010 he was elected into the partnership and was appointed UK Managing Partner one year later. Mark has gone on to become one of the world's leading experts in pricing and monetization strategy, advising the CEOs and boards of UK businesses as well as the value creation teams of leading private equity firms. He is a regular commentator in the press and broadcast media on these topics as well as a guest lecturer for MBA programs at the world's top business schools. Mark began his career in the Telecoms, Media and Technology practice at PwC Consulting while qualifying as a chartered management accountant (ACMA). He subsequently moved into the telecoms industry, joining the corporate finance team at FLAG Telecom / Reliance Communications and eventually taking over as pricing manager.

Dr. Andreas von der Gathen is CEO of Simon-Kucher & Partners. Before becoming CEO on January 1, 2020, he had already been working for Simon-Kucher for more than 20 years as a Partner. He founded and led the global Consumer Goods & Retail practice, specializing in sales organization, product pricing, and brand strategy for national and international clients in all stages of the consumer goods value chain. Andreas has conducted many projects with a variety of customers, ranging from international and national ingredient suppliers to fast-moving consumer goods companies and retailers. In many of these projects he has helped companies improve their pricing with the ultimate goal of finding ways to increase profits. He has written two books on marketing and brand valuation and co-wrote the book *Instruments for Strategic Analysis* with Hermann Simon, Simon-Kucher's founder. He has published numerous articles on pricing, sales, and branding and is a frequent speaker on these issues at conferences and seminars. Andreas studied business administration and economics at the University of Bochum and received his PhD for his work on brand management, valuation, and controlling.

20

Pricing Is the Key to Digital Selling Maturity

*John Bruno, Vice President
of Commerce Strategy, PROS,
and Valerie Howard,
Solutions Director, PROS*

THERE'S NO QUESTION THAT we're now firmly in the era of digital selling. B2B buyers have moved online, driving a sea change in expectations. Customers want more control in the buying experience, particularly in more options to engage where, when, and how they want. Yet, even with many advancements in technology, most B2B enterprises have been slow to take advantage of the significant opportunity in digital selling.

Many B2B businesses have historically approached the needs of their customers with high-touch service levels and limitless customization options. The complexities required to handle the unique needs of each buyer have historically required a hands-on approach to pricing and selling. But more and more B2B buyers are choosing a fast, easy (maybe even self-service) transaction over the white-glove services of a salesperson. Unfortunately, a reliance on manual processes and disconnected systems for the configuration, pricing, and quoting processes behind every sale will hinder even the simplest deals and create inconsistent experiences that open the door to more agile competitors.

For this reason, the ability of these organizations to drive forward improved digital purchase experiences for their customers will mark the difference between businesses that will thrive and those that will struggle for survival. Thankfully, there's an achievable *and profitable* path to driving forward the digital purchase experiences that customers desire.

The key that is often overlooked is that beginning with a focus on improving pricing processes can drive compound benefits that will accelerate sales and fuel the business's digital transformation. By beginning with a focus on pricing, many businesses can achieve a return on investment sizable enough to fund the entirety of their digital sales transformation journey.

2020 rewarded the ready and punished the laggards

At the time of this book's publication, the global economy is emerging from the worst pandemic in more than a century. The coronavirus crisis of 2020 had unforeseen impacts on every business and industry sector and drove home the inarguable fact that the old rules no longer apply. Given mandatory shutdowns on a global scale, many businesses had to reinvent themselves seemingly overnight—they had to find alternative options for face-to-face interactions and quickly scale up their digital capabilities.

Most traditional businesses were already feeling the competitive pressure from startups and digital natives to deliver on better self-serve experiences for their clients. But trying to steer an established B2B enterprise into successfully leveraging digital channels and overhauling longstanding internal processes is no small feat. In a 2017 Innosight study, 70 percent of executives surveyed acknowledged that they needed to transform their business (Anthony, Viguerie, Schwartz, & Van Landeghem, 2017). More specifically, these 70 percent agreed with the statement that "[we] need to change our core offerings or business model in response to rapidly changing markets and disruption." (And this was before the pandemic!) A 2018 Hanover Research[2] survey of over 700 B2B leaders shows that most businesses had already begun to take action; 99 percent reported that they had a digital transformation initiative planned, of which 58 percent were already underway.

However, while digital transformation efforts continue to underpin the strategic initiatives of nearly every enterprise, many digital initiative undertakings lack clarity in the objective of their digital transformation. Hazy goals alongside ever-widening scope contribute to the notoriously low success rates of digital transformation projects: consistently less than 30 percent according to four McKinsey studies from 2012 to 2018 (Martin, 2018).

While 68 percent focus their efforts on digitizing the businesses' operating model to drive efficiencies and reduce costs (the most popular investment area for digital initiatives), these efforts overlook the significant opportunity and criticality in expanding value delivery to clients and partners through better online, self-serve experiences. Author Greg Verdino (2015) offers a clear, concise, and alternate purpose for digital transformation saying

---

2   In 2018 Hanover Research conducted a survey of 703 B2B executives on their perspectives of AI, digital transformation, and eCommerce. This survey was commissioned by PROS.

that, "Digital transformation closes the gap between what digital customers already expect and what analog businesses actually deliver."

Before 2020 many digital transformation initiatives plodded along without a sense of urgency. But the overnight shift from face-to-face to virtual interactions made it clear which businesses were ahead of the game and ready to accommodate a digital buying experience. According to a June 2020 Hanover Research global study of 210 purchasing professionals,[3] 70 percent of buyers claimed that they were shifting their wallet share during the COVID-19 crisis to alternate vendors for competitive pricing (40%), supply availability (39%), and better digital purchasing experiences (35%).

It's clear that businesses that had previously prioritized delivering on coordinated pricing and personalized, self-serve purchasing options were able to turn 2020's coronavirus pandemic into market-share gains.

B2B buyers and sellers agree: Pricing is the problem

While buyers have been ready and willing to transact significantly more through digital channels, Greg Verdino (2015) is precise in his pronouncement that there has been a gap between what analog businesses can currently deliver and what the digital customer expects. When attempting to purchase through digital channels, purchasing professionals commonly struggle with a lack of product information, unrealistic or irrational pricing, and inefficient responses to their online inquiries (Figure 20.1).

The challenges buyers face in purchasing online are consistent with the concerns B2B suppliers have with selling online: struggling to quickly find the products they desire at the price

---

3   Hanover Research Study commissioned by PROS.

Products not readily available ████████████████████████ 32%

Realistic prices not available ███████████████████████ 30%

Incomplete / not enough product information ████████████████████ 28%

Slow/inefficient responses to inquiries ████████████████████ 28%

Unable to find product specifications ███████████████████ 27%

Slow quote turnaround times ██████████████████ 26%

Slow internal approval/review processes █████████████████ 25%

Uncertainty regarding delivery date █████████████████ 25%

Out-of-date product catalogs █████████████████ 25%

Inefficient search capabilities ███████████████ 22%

No challenges ████ 7%

0%   10%   20%   30%   40%

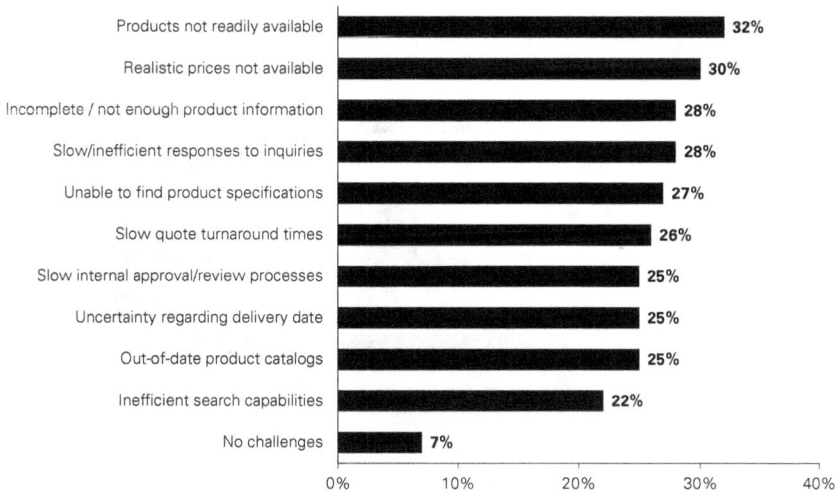

Q: What are the greatest challenges that your organization faces when making business purchases online? Select up to three options. (N=1,031)

Source: 2019 Hanover Research Survey of Purchasing Professionals commissioned by PROS.

Figure 20.1. Buyer challenges in purchasing online.

points they expect. When selling through digital channels, vendors struggle to maintain competitive pricing, protect their price attainment, and direct customers to the products that would interest them.

Many e-commerce delivery teams fail to see that delivering dynamic, personalized pricing is a key component of an online channel's success. Because the technological requirements for dynamic pricing are often overlooked, many businesses leverage static price lists that are only periodically updated and, as a result, usually lagging in their market relevancy and certainly not personalized for customers who may have contracted discounts. Unfortunately, these practices will discourage buyers who perceive the presented prices to be unrealistic and may even drive these buyers to a competitor who can offer realistic or personalized pricing through the ease of a digital channel (Figure 20.2).

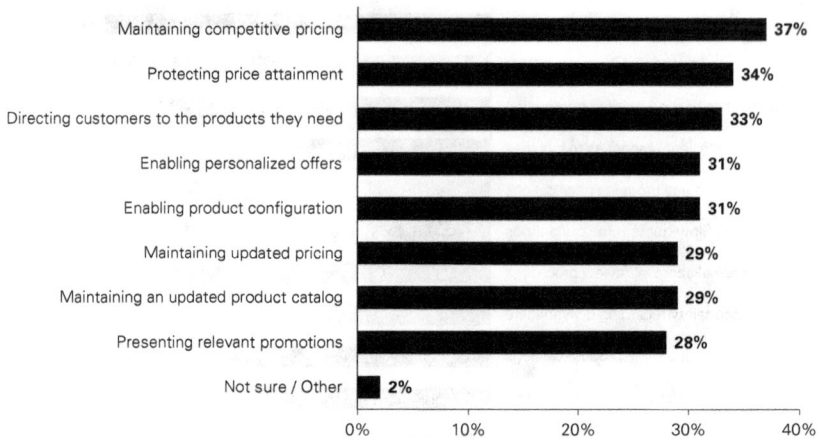

Q: What are your top concerns with your e-commerce channels? Select up to three options. (N=703)

Source: 2018 Hanover Research Survey of B2B Leaders commissioned by PROS.

Figure 20.2. B2B seller concerns with selling online.

Even before the pandemic, research showed that online pricing was a top concern for business buyers *and* sellers. Prioritizing pricing coordination is key. Pricing is the number-one reason buyers leave their current supplier, and getting the price right is the number-one concern of vendors in digital selling.

Key trends of businesses successfully leveraging digital channels

As of 2018 merely 20 percent of B2B businesses were transacting most (>50%) of their sales through digital channels.[4] What separates these businesses in their success in these channels is their focus on purposeful coordination across sales channels.

---

4   In 2018 Hanover Research surveyed 703 B2B executives on their perspectives of AI, digital transformation, and e-commerce. This survey was commissioned by PROS.

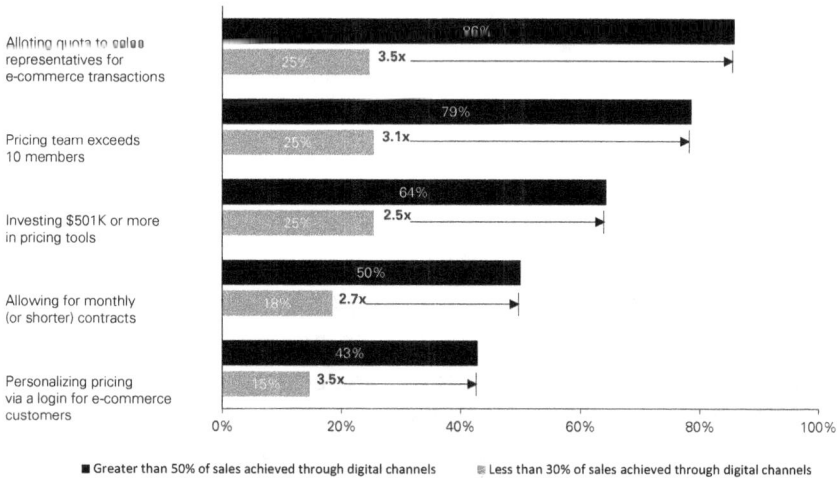

Figure 20.3. Key trends of suppliers selling primarily through digital channels vs. sellers lagging in digital selling.

A survey of 164 finance and pricing professionals made clear that there were key trends that separated those businesses able to drive transformative volumes through digital channels from those that achieved mediocre results. Those key trends include incentivizing salespeople to leverage e-commerce channels, investing in pricing personnel and technology, enabling greater agility in contract length, and personalizing prices for e-commerce customers (Figure 20.3).[5]

This analysis validates that B2B buyers desire the fast and easy experiences of online purchasing and prefer the vendors that are personalizing digital channels with consistency and transparency. They want to move easily between channels when and how they need, and they want to feel that they can trust the business they

---

5   In 2018 Hanover Research surveyed 164 pricing professionals on their price strategy perspectives. This survey was commissioned by PROS.

are buying from to deliver a fair price regardless of where and how they buy.

While Figure 20.3 shows a clear distinction between those achieving success in digital selling and those lagging behind, most of these organizations are currently in the middle of their digital sales transformation. They are likely in the midst of technology implementations and process overhauls. Many will attempt to tackle their transformation from multiple disconnected angles, often prioritizing the attraction of new customers over the transition of existing customers to digital experiences.

Although it may seem simpler to focus the digital experience on new customers, the key to success is to empower existing, traditional customers to use digital options. The roadmap to digital selling success in this next section shows how businesses can incrementally improve on the existing buying experience to drive forward advancement in their digital selling maturity in an achievable and profitable way. Key to this journey is laying the foundation for scalable, agile pricing management and improving on price optimization capabilities through each subsequent stage.

The six stages to digital selling success

There are six key stages in the journey to achieving strategic success in digital selling (Figure 20.4). While the advancement from one stage to the next will drive significant and measurable gains, together the best practices within these stages provide a tested roadmap for enterprises seeking to advance their digital selling capabilities:

- Stage 1: Traditional selling
- Stage 2: Initial price management
- Stage 3: Sales process acceleration

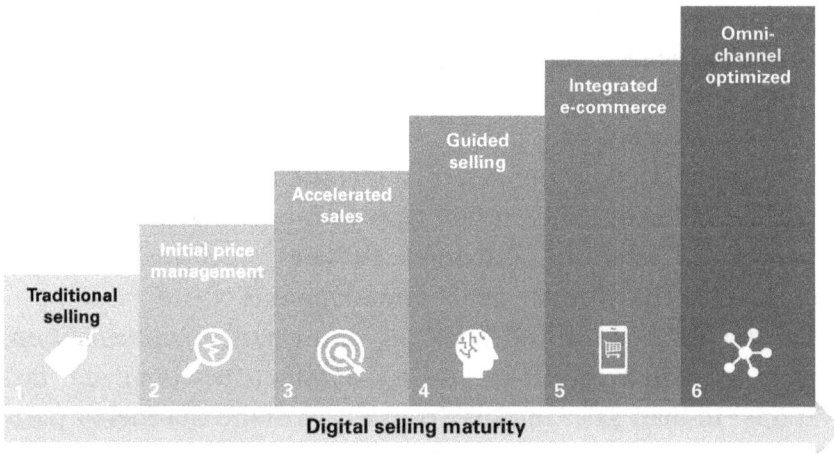

Figure 20.4. The digital selling maturity model.

- Stage 4: Guided selling
- Stage 5: E-commerce integration
- Stage 6: Omnichannel optimized commerce

The objective within each maturity stage is to build on the results of earlier stages. Like compound interest, advancing through the six core stages to digital selling success provides compound benefit, so that a business that follows this path to digital selling not only will continue to stay ahead of their competitors but will accelerate away from them in market reach, revenue growth, and customer loyalty. For example, prioritizing basic price management capabilities in Stage 1 of your digital selling transformation establishes the basic price coordination systems that are key to delivering increasingly improved price personalization and optimization in subsequent stages.

The digital selling maturity model shared here will help you assess the current standing of your business and evaluate which gaps you should prioritize to best accelerate your business's maturation into the next stage of digital selling.

With this model, your business will improve on your abilities to deliver a responsive, personalized, and consistent experience across channels. Continuous, incremental improvement in these key areas of buyer concern will help your business move beyond reliance on traditional, disconnected sales processes and drive you closer to the ultimate goal of omnichannel optimization.

In the most advanced stage of omnichannel optimization, buyers trust that they'll receive a consistent, personalized, fast response to their sales inquiry irrespective of the channel or partner they choose to transact through. Such high levels of trust accelerate purchases, expand market share, and maximize the potential of your sales reach.

The path to digital selling

Each stage on the path to digital selling is a critical step toward achieving digital selling maturity. Although businesses may have some pieces of each stage already in place, it's important to understand how businesses build on each key capability from one stage to the next in order to advance in their capacity to deliver on digital selling.

For each stage, we describe the behaviors that define businesses within that stage of maturity and the prescriptive actions that each organization can take to advance into the next stage of digital selling maturity.

Stage 1: Traditional selling

Many businesses will find themselves in Stage 1 (Figure 20.5), where a path to digital selling may seem unattainable or even irrelevant. Businesses here should take heart that the greatest and

Stage 1 concerns:
- Lack of analytical insight
- Revenue leakage
- Gut-feel pricing
- Slow pricing updates
- Slow sales responses

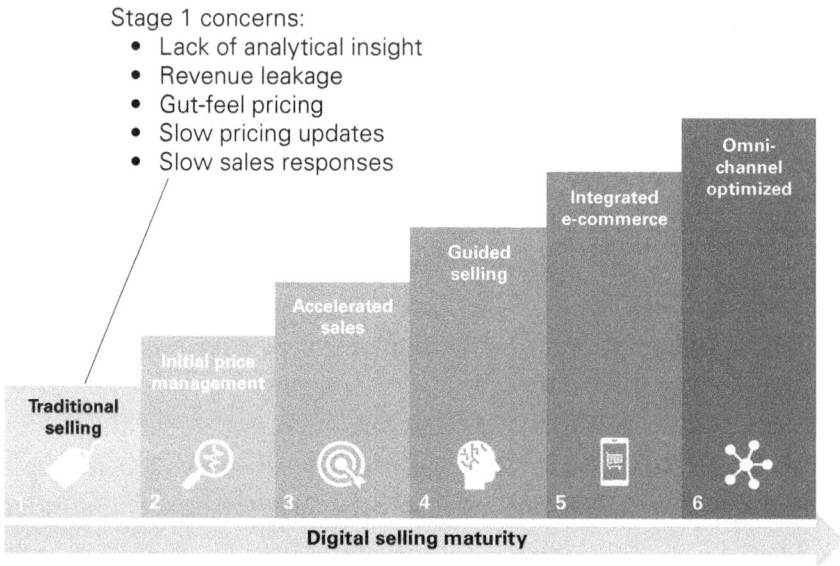

Figure 20.5. Stage 1: Traditional selling.

most foundational opportunities for improvement lie within this stage. Focused attention to the implementation of basic pricing analytics and price management capabilities will provide the pricing infrastructure necessary throughout the digital sales transformation journey. Moving forward with even relatively small, incremental steps can quickly deliver a differentiated and preferred buying experience for clients.

BEHAVIORS

Businesses in Stage 1 are experiencing one or more of the following:

- **Lack of analytical pricing insight.** As a result of price lists and quotes managed through disparate systems, there's typically a heavy reliance on spreadsheets for analysis in this stage. Businesses in this stage struggle to measure price attainment and profitability at aggregate and granular levels. Because it may often take days or weeks to effectively evaluate the potential profitability of each customer deal, slow responses often lead to missed opportunities or the revenue leakage of overdiscounting.

- **A reliance on "gut-feel" pricing.** The absence of readily available deal-level, market-level, and customer-level price and profit analytics often leads to reactive pricing requests from sales executives under pressure for a fast, competitive response from their buyers. This inconsistent approach to quoting often drives high variance in pricing across customers. Although sales may win the deal, often they'll have traded off potential profits that could have been protected through a more strategic, analytical approach to pricing.
- **Slow and cumbersome pricing updates.** A reliance on disconnected or manual systems for price management may mean that it takes days to weeks just to gather the required data to evaluate a potential price update. If there's a reliance on multiple levels of authority for price reviews and approvals, price updates may take weeks to months and hamper the business's ability to respond to more agile competitors or dynamic market conditions.
- **Customers complain of slow responses to quote inquiries.** When sales teams are burdened with administrative, manual tasks and cannot easily self-serve the information they need to provide a requested quote, customers will become frustrated with their slow response times. These slow response times often lead to losses to competitors who are better equipped to respond quickly with a competitive, market-relevant offer.

KEY STEPS TO DIGITAL SELLING ADVANCEMENT

To advance to Stage 2, businesses in this stage should prioritize the following initiatives:

- **Employ pricing analytics.** To advance in digital selling maturity, businesses in Stage 1 need to gain visibility into price and profitability attainment across the business. Leveraging pricing-focused analytics is key to seeing the breakdown of profitability at both granular and aggregate levels and will typically require the integration of multiple data sources (ERPs, CRMs, data warehouses, etc). This foundation of analytics is key to supporting consistency in measurement, driving cross-functional alignment, and accelerating decision-making within the business.

- **Identify and address revenue leakage.** Once pricing analytics are in place, price outliers can be easily identified. With recognition of the most severe sources of revenue leakage, organizations can begin to build a plan for price recovery across the most egregious clients, products, and sales reps.

- **Guardrails for quotes and discounts.** With an assessment of current pricing behavior, pricing teams can begin to define recommended pricing guardrails for sales. These price guardrails may consider regional or market segment behavior in order to support sales in more quickly determining the market-relevant price for each client engagement.

- **Automate pricing calculations and updates.** To advance to the next stage, businesses in Stage 1 need to employ price management capabilities that allow for automated price updates. Connected data sources and price analytics will enable the business to be more agile in determining how they want to respond to changing market conditions with their pricing.

Stage 2: Initial price management

Businesses in Stage 2 are beginning to take the key initial steps to centralizing and operationalizing pricing management (Figure 20.6). This critical first step is foundational to assessing the current customer and market trends necessary to establishing basic pricing and selling strategies.

BEHAVIORS

Businesses in Stage 2 are experiencing one or more of the following:

- **Initial capabilities for revenue analytics.** With basic insights into price, sales, and profitability analytics, the business is better able to lay the groundwork necessary for a

Stage 2 concerns:
- Limited pricing analytics
- Slow, manual quote processes
- Lagging adoption of pricing strategy
- Heavy reliance on price exception process
- Significant variation in pricing across customers

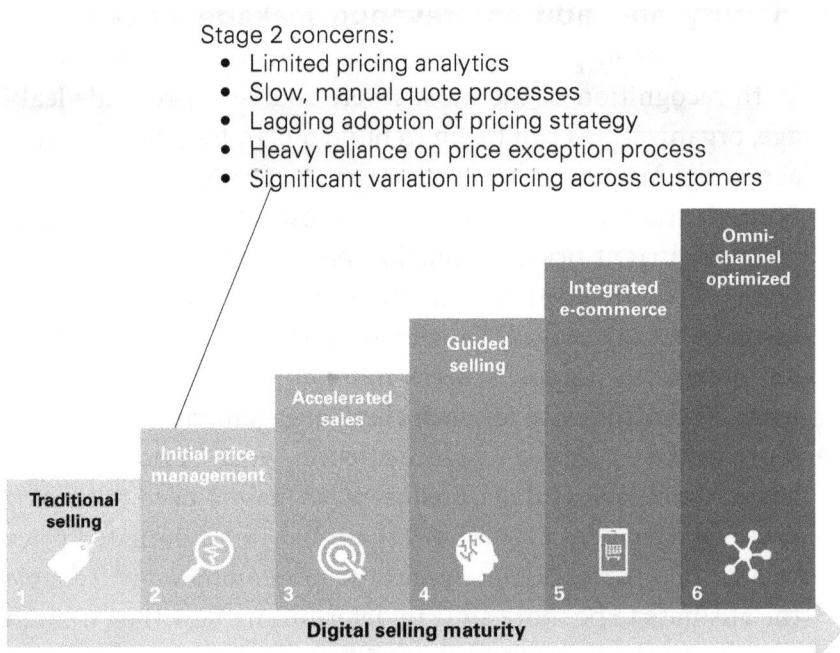

Figure 20.6. Stage 2: Initial price management.

proactive price strategy. A consistent approach to measuring deal-level, product-level, customer-level analytics supports trade-off analysis that is key to protecting profitability and improving price decisions.

- **Sales teams still struggle to deliver fast customer responses.** Sales teams continue to be burdened by manual processes and spend significant time pulling together information to meet customer requests. Disparate systems and out-of-date pricing lead to a great deal of effort spent chasing down escalations.

- **Lagging adoption of pricing strategy.** While businesses in Stage 2 may have defined their pricing strategy, disconnected systems and processes mean that it remains a challenge to get that price strategy into the hands of sales teams and partners. Adding to this challenge, sales teams typically express resistance to price recommendations declaring that they know their markets better than anyone.

- **Heavy reliance on the deal desk for price exceptions and special discounts.** While a price strategy may have been defined for businesses in this stage, most deals continue to require routing to the deal desk for "special discounts" to appease buyers who invest heavily in price pressure tactics and seek to commoditize their vendors' offerings.

- **Significant variation in pricing across customers.** While there's greater perspective on the market-relevant price in Stage 2 than in Stage 1, challenges in operationalizing the intended price strategy mean that there will continue to be high levels of variance in pricing across the customer base.

KEY STEPS TO DIGITAL SELLING ADVANCEMENT

To advance to Stage 3, businesses in this stage should prioritize the following initiatives:

- **Empower the sales team with effective quoting tools.** Deploy a quoting system that can support the sales team in quickly determining and configuring the desired solutions for their customers.
- **Integrate pricing controls into quoting tools.** The integration of pricing processes into sales tools will drive consistency in price execution and reduce the risk of quoting outdated prices. This coordination will reduce revenue leakage and ensure that quotes are executed with the most accurate, intended prices.
- **Deliver price guidance with specified approval thresholds.** By tying price discounts to approval thresholds, salespeople have the option to avoid the friction of seeking discount approvals to accelerate response times. Salespeople can respond quickly to customers needing a fast response with a preapproved price and reserve the elongated discount approval process for truly exceptional cases.
- **Define coordinated price strategies.** In order to ease the burden of updating prices, rules-driven price strategies can be used. By defining price tier structures, product life-cycle strategies, and/or promotion plans, prices can be updated through automated recalculations instead of manual evaluations and uploads. Predefined price strategies will allow for easier and more frequent updates that will keep pricing better aligned with changing market conditions.
- **Seek and employ customer, sales, and pricing feedback.** Gathering data from customer-facing and sales-facing systems allows organizations to identify buying trends and behaviors. This feedback can help businesses respond to market changes with greater agility and improve personalization of the overall sales process.

Stage 3: Sales process acceleration

With the foundation of analytical capabilities in place to guide improved sales and price decision-making, organizations in Stage 3 can begin to focus on distributing these insights more directly to the point of interaction (Figure 20.7). For example, businesses in Stage 3 may have defined their price strategies, but sales teams may struggle to apply these new pricing policies (because of complicated processes or disconnected systems), or potentially even outrightly resist them due to a lack of understanding. Companies in Stage 3 will want to focus on delivering personalized price guidance and customer insights directly to sellers to accelerate and improve the quote response experience.

Stage 3 concerns:
- Administrative tasks reduce sales effectiveness
- Sales resist pricing recommendations
- Unexpected customer churn
- Stagnating growth in existing customers

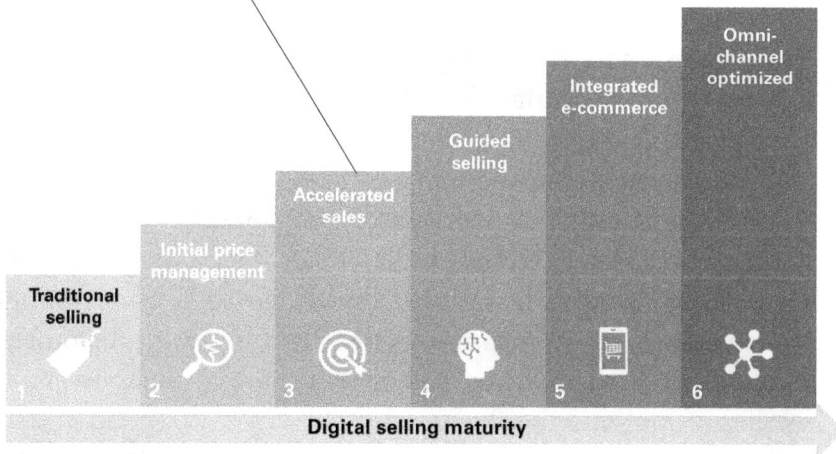

Figure 20.7. Stage 3: Accelerated sales.

Behaviors

Businesses in Stage 3 are experiencing one or more of the following:

- **Sales executives still resist pricing recommendations.** While market-segment or regional price lists have been deployed to drive adherence to a defined price strategy, sales teams continue to push back on the recommendations, expressing that the generic market prices do not adequately consider the unique needs of their customer.
- **Sales teams continue to be consumed by administrative requests.** While sales teams benefit from accelerated quote response times supported by the availability of market and revenue analytics, they continue to be tasked with responding to a wide range of customer requests and inquiries. An inability to route customers to self-serve options or automate recurring requests means that a significant portion of salespeople's time remains dedicated to administrative tasks and they are prevented from giving dedicated focus to selling.
- **Sales teams are caught off-guard by customer churn and irregular purchasing.** Focused on responding to customer needs and chasing down internal information and approvals, salespeople are unlikely to have the time to review the buying behavior of their customers. Without this review, many sales executives will be slow to see key indicators of potential churn and competitive threat such as declining spend and erratic purchases. No one wants to lose a customer, especially one that may have been preventable if sales had had earlier insight into the churn risk.
- **Growth in the existing customer base stagnates.** While penetration of products into the customer base remains relatively low, sales teams lack the insight to determine where

whitespace opportunities exist even where there are established relationships. These overlooked opportunities to grow wallet share reduce the overall potential for customer lifetime value and revenue attainment.

KEY STEPS TO DIGITAL SELLING ADVANCEMENT

To advance to Stage 4, businesses in this stage should prioritize the following initiatives:

- **Deliver prescriptive, personalized price guidance and insight.** Leverage a price optimization solution that can deliver customer-specific price recommendations and insight to salespeople at the point of interaction. Given a price optimization solution that can provide price guidance for the unique conditions of every deal, the right price can be quickly determined, accelerate sales, and improve profitability.
- **Leverage AI to provide sales insights on buyer trends.** AI-driven analysis can identify behaviors indicating the risk of customer churn, expose opportunities for upsell, and uncover buyer-specific offer recommendations. These insights are key to helping salespeople maximize their sales effectiveness by prioritizing customer retention and expansion opportunities with a high probability of uptake. The personalized recommendations and expanded wallet share help increase the stickiness and loyalty of customers.
- **Streamline the quoting process.** Investing in streamlining the configuration and quoting process can have powerful, transformative effects on the business. A streamlined solution for configuration will reduce the administrative burden of gathering disparate product configuration and pricing information, buyers will receive faster quote responses, and configuration errors will decrease. As a result, sellers will be

empowered to focus more time on selling, and sales performance will increase.

- **Optimize prices for nonnegotiated scenarios.** For digital and retail channels where there's no price negotiation, presenting the right, market-relevant price is critical to winning the sale. By leveraging AI, prices can be optimized to market context and changing demand. Advanced businesses will harmonize these nonnegotiated prices with negotiated scenarios—more on this in Stage 4.

Stage 4: Guided selling

For businesses in Stage 4 of their digital selling maturity, the core functions of the sales engine are humming. There's a centralized approach to revenue and profit analysis. Sales teams have the insights they need to deliver personalized quotes and quickly configure the offers buyers desire. And, most importantly, sellers are able to negotiate from a position of knowledge and authority—to quickly assess the potential negotiation trade-offs that protect price integrity yet still meet customer-specific needs.

With clarity on what it takes to win deals the *right way*, businesses in Stage 4 are prepared to begin fully harnessing the potential of their digital, e-commerce channels (Figure 20.8).

BEHAVIORS

Businesses in Stage 4 are experiencing one or more of the following:

- **Prices are not coordinated across channels.** Prices may be managed separately by channel with an e-commerce team setting prices for the web while another team supports pricing for contract negotiations. Without tight integration of price management across channels, there's a risk of channel conflict that may lead to customer issues. Contracted customers expect

Stage 4 concerns:
- Pricing conflicts across channels
- Sluggish adoption of e-commerce
- Limited online product information and options

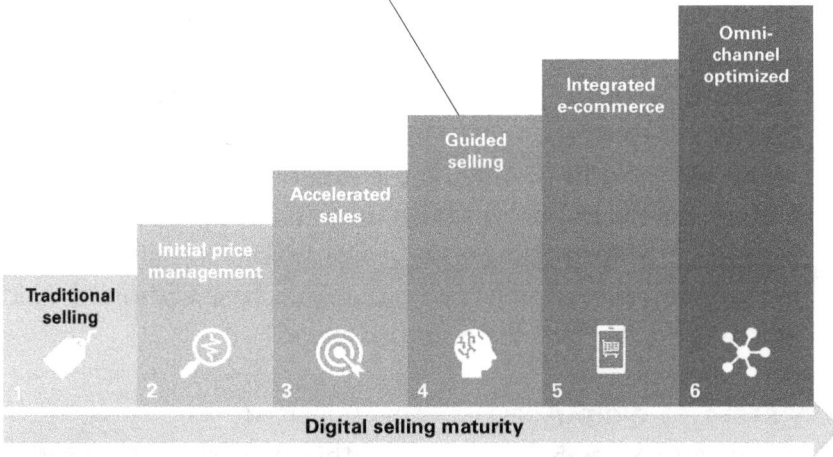

Figure 20.8. Stage 4: Guided selling.

to receive special promotional pricing for their commitment, so discovering that better or equivalent pricing may be publicly available would significantly undermine their trust in a contracted vendor.

- **Sluggish adoption of e-commerce due to limited self-serve capabilities.** While customers can choose to complete their purchases through a self-serve experience, the options for customization and configuration through an online portal may not be sufficient for the business buyer's needs at this stage. Buyers may be limited to simple, standard purchases or to product reorders. Additionally, there's limited capability to access personalized, contracted pricing when they're self-serving. For some online portals, special pricing might not be available without routing through a sales rep. For the businesses that have integrated contracted or personalized prices, many encounter limited capacity on the volume of online requests that can be handled. Slow response times to retrieve customer-specific prices can hinder the buyer experience and drive customers elsewhere to complete their purchases.

- **Limited online product information and options.** Business buyers are increasingly self-sufficient and decreasingly interested in waiting on the support of a sales executive. Unfortunately, limited visibility into the product catalog and insufficient information make it nearly impossible for buyers to autonomously complete an online purchase without the aid of a sales rep for businesses in this stage.

KEY STEPS TO DIGITAL SELLING ADVANCEMENT

To advance to Stage 5, businesses in this stage should prioritize the following initiatives:

- **Integrate all channels to a centralized pricing technology.** Sourcing pricing from a centralized platform will ensure that each delivered price is created in the context of market and customer conditions across channels.
- **Personalize pricing for self-serve experiences.** Enable customers to complete purchases online with their personalized discounts. By allowing customers to identify themselves through login criteria and retrieving their personalized prices from a centralized source, businesses can streamline purchasing by ensuring that they receive the same special pricing they would receive through any other channel. These self-serve options lower the administrative burden on salespeople to

service these clients and typically increase customer satisfaction in that it accelerates their buying process.

- **Reduce channel conflict with a coordinated channel pricing strategy.** A centralized price management platform allows businesses to analyze pricing across channels and ensure the delivery of rationality across varied purchase scenarios. Buyers may be inclined to "shop around" and pressure salespeople to provide discounts from online prices. With price strategies coordinated across channels, salespeople can be guided to discount limits harmonized with other purchase channels that maintain price consistency. While buyers may be initially disappointed to be denied an additional discount, they'll be encouraged that prices are consistent across channels and recognize that they don't have to seek out a salesperson to get the best discount in the future.

- **Optimize prices across negotiated and nonnegotiated scenarios.** AI can support businesses in determining which buying-scenario variables drive differentiation in willingness to pay across market segments and in individual customers. Whereas businesses in Stage 3 may use distinct price optimization strategies to deliver price guidance for sales negotiations and optimize online prices, businesses in Stage 4 are investing effort in harmonizing these optimization strategies across channels.

- **Invest in scalable, real-time price delivery.** Retrieving pricing from a centralized source depends on fast, reliable, and scalable pricing responses. Since many online commerce sites may display tens to hundreds of prices on a single page, near-immediate price calculation retrieval is essential. If it takes even a second to retrieve a single price, buyers will be turned off by the website's poor performance and may seek to complete their purchase through a competitive vendor.

- **Support self-service product configuration.** Allowing customers to configure their desired options without the aid of a sales rep can significantly accelerate sales while lowering costs of sale. For customers that need more than a simple, standard order, allowing them to manage their own product configuration may drive forward e-commerce adoption that was previously sluggish.

Stage 5: Integrated e-commerce

Businesses in Stage 5 have effectively equipped sales and partner teams with the pricing and customer insights that allow them to respond quickly and accurately to quote requests (Figure 20.9). E-commerce pricing and operations are integrated into the overall sales strategy, reducing the risk of channel conflict and improving the self-serve buying experience.

While companies in this stage enjoy the benefits of a series of highly effective sales channels, these channels may not be tightly integrated with their presentation to the customer. As a result, buyers may not be able to easily switch between channels without losing the context of their purchase. These disconnects may lead to lost sales when a buyer cannot easily receive sales support for the online quote request they've initiated.

Behaviors

Businesses in Stage 5 are experiencing one or more of the following:

- **Channels are performing, but buyers cannot easily switch between channels.** While businesses in this stage may have a series of highly effective sales channels, these channels may not be tightly integrated in how they present to the customer. As a result, buyers are not able to easily switch between channels without losing the context of the purchase.

Stage 5 concerns:
- Buyers cannot easily move across channels
- Sales lack real-time insights
- Scaling through partner ecosystems

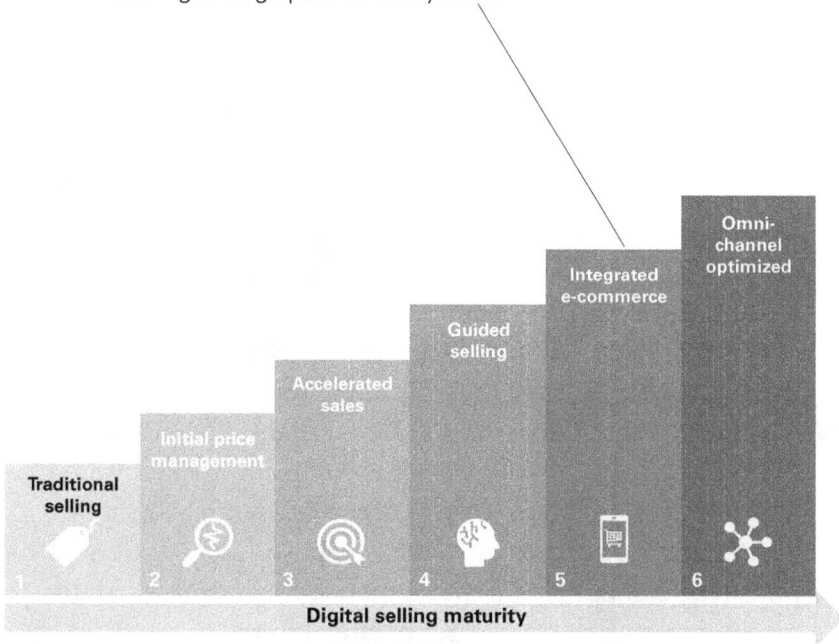

Figure 20.9. Stage 5: Integrated e-commerce.

These disconnects add friction to the buying process and hinders sales.

- **Sales teams have historical data but lack real-time info.** In this stage, salespeople are benefiting from easy access to their customers' past buying behavior; however, access to real-time information is limited. Lacking insight into updated demand and market trends may lead to the sales team leaving money on the table.

- **Partners are seeking to connect digital commerce ecosystems.** The successful growth of e-commerce for businesses in this stage has attracted partners who now want to connect into this revenue engine to amplify sales growth even further.

KEY STEPS TO DIGITAL SELLING ADVANCEMENT

To advance to the highest stage of digital selling maturity, Stage 6, businesses in this stage should prioritize the following initiatives:

- **Integrate sales technologies and processes across channels.** Allow for coordinated buyer tracking and support across channels so that customers can easily move between online, in-person, partner, and any other desired channels.
- **Advance data-gathering capabilities across channels.** Organizations in Stage 5 should focus on capturing analytics on buying behavior for each unique interaction across channels (regardless of purchase completion). Refining analytics on lost sales will help businesses identify areas of friction in the buying process. Tracking buyer-specific trends will improve personalization and enhance the business's ability to respond to market shifts with greater agility.
- **Support real-time pricing.** In highly competitive or dynamic markets, prices may need to change multiple times a day—*or even multiple times an hour.* While many companies choose to recalculate and distribute millions of potential prices in batch processes throughout the day, the most advanced businesses are choosing real-time price calculation. With real-time price calculation, high-performance price calculation engines allow for real-time data to be used in the price determination. This real-time price capability ensures that the most current market, competitive, and buyer information is used for each price response.
- **Connect all facets of the omnichannel customer experience.** Share captured data across channels to refine

buyer behavior analytics with real-time agility, ensure that emerging trends are identified early, and continuously optimize personalization for each unique customer scenario.

Stage 6: Omnichannel optimized

Stage 6 is the highest level of digital selling maturity. Companies in this stage have fully realized their ability to deliver an exceptional buyer experience (Figure 20.10).

By embracing the power of digital selling, businesses in Stage 6 enjoy improved customer loyalty, greater capabilities for personalization, and improved costs of sale. A deep understanding of their customers' buying behavior allows businesses in this stage

Stage 6 behaviors:
- Buyers easily move across channels
- Real-time insights for every channel
- Easy integration to partner ecosystems
- Agility in pricing and offer management

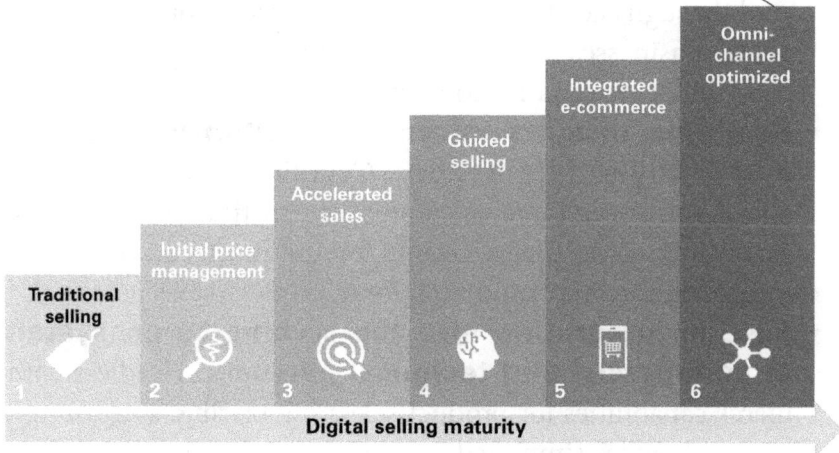

Figure 20.10. Stage 6: Omnichannel optimized.

to create a differentiated experience that competitors simply don't have the data to match. Organizations that have reached this level of maturity have a significant advantage over their competitors.

Their data-driven approach to continually refining personalization of their offers means that they'll be able to better predict customers' needs. Their capabilities to optimize prices for real-time conditions means that they'll be more likely to present a winning price that expands profits and secures capital for even further investment in improving the product offers and sales experiences.

BEHAVIORS
Businesses in Stage 6 are experiencing one or more of the following:

- **Customers value their personalized, self-serve purchase experiences.** Customers are now able to discover solution options on their own terms, evaluate configuration options, and easily switch from an online to an in-person or partner purchase channel without losing context. Data gathered through each buyer interaction (purchase or no purchase) allows businesses that have matured to this stage to continuously refine personalization for their customers.
- **Real-time insights inform and optimize offers for every buyer interaction.** Coordinated data gathering allows for prices to be calculated in real time to deliver precision in pricing that accounts for the most current market information while optimizing for maximum sales potential.
- **Ease in integrating into the commerce ecosystem of commercial and technical partners.** Headless commerce capabilities for product selection, pricing, and configuration allow for simplified integration into partner commerce

ecosystems that amplify the market reach of businesses that have matured to the highest stage of digital selling.

- **Agility in pricing and offer management.** The application of advanced analytics and AI allow organizations in this stage to stay ahead of the competition in response to marketplace shifts and disruptions. Businesses in this stage have coordinated price and catalogue capabilities that allow them to quickly adjust pricing to account for changing inventory or demand trends. Staying agile and ahead of the competition in this regard protects market share and profitability.

Leveraging continuous listening, learning, and engaging

Businesses that have reached Stage 6 have established the capabilities to respond with precision and responsiveness in offer personalization for every unique buying condition. Market volatilities may drive swings in demand, costs, and competitive conditions, but an agile and proactive pricing strategy ensures that businesses that have achieved omnichannel optimization not only will be ready to respond to shifting market conditions—they'll likely be first to take advantage of the opportunities in the new market conditions.

Is your business ready for whatever's next?

Recent years have shown us that it's impossible to predict what's next for our global, regional, or even local economies. However, it's evident that businesses that have prioritized investment in pricing agility and digital selling will be ready to adapt to whatever unpredictable market conditions come next. The ability of these companies to make swift shifts keeps them ahead as much as their ability to precisely personalize each customer offer.

While many businesses may be far from reaching a Stage 6 maturity of omnichannel optimized, most are capable of rapidly achieving Stages 4 or 5 with the application of AI and technology. With AI, insights from each customer interaction can be used to refine the personalization and pricing for every future interaction at scale. Precision in pricing at scale has measurable and impactful revenue benefits.

With the increased affordability and fast payback of price optimization technology, it's no wonder that even Gartner advises that price optimization is the number-one use case for AI in digital commerce (Shen & Linden, 2020). As shown in this chapter, building a foundation for agile pricing strategy is key to achieving success in your digital selling journey, and, for many businesses, AI and pricing technology are the essential components to getting pricing right at scale with responsiveness and precision.

References

Anthony, S, D., Viguerie, S. P., Schwartz, E. I., & Van Landeghem, J. (2017, November). 2018 corporate longevity forecast survey of 300 executives: Creative destruction is accelerating. *Innosight*. www.innosight.com/insight/creative-destruction/

The Enterprisers Project. (2016). What is digital transformation? enterprisersproject.com/what-is-digital-transformation

Martin, J.-F. (2018). Unlocking success in digital transformations. *McKinsey & Company*, October. www.mckinsey .com/~/media/McKinsey/Business%20Functions/Organization/Our%20Insights/Unlocking%20success%20in%20

digital%20transformations/Unlocking-success-in-digi-
tal-transformations.ashx

Shen, S., & Linden, A. (2020). Infographic: Artificial intelligence
use case prism for digital commerce. *Gartner, Inc.,* September 29, www.gartner.com/en/documents/3991090
/infographic-artificial-intelligence-use-case-prism-for-d

Verdino, G. (2015). What is digital transformation, really?
GregVerdino, March 5.
www.gregverdino.com/digital-transformation-definition/

The authors

John Bruno is Vice President of Commerce Strategy and an industry thought leader in the areas of digital transformation, digital experience, and e-commerce. Before joining PROS, Bruno was the head of product for Elastic Path Software, a Vancouver-based SaaS e-commerce platform, where he was responsible for product management, engineering, and user experience. Before Elastic Path, Bruno led the e-commerce research practice, specializing in B2B e-commerce, at Forrester Research. There he authored definitive works, including the B2B eCommerce Playbook and the Forrester Waves on B2B and B2C eCommerce Suites. He has spoken and written widely, with expertise featured in the *Wall Street Journal, Adweek, Forbes, Business Insider,* and more.

Valerie Howard, Solution Strategy Director at PROS, manages the go-to-market strategy for the PROS pricing solution portfolio and oversees the PROS industry marketing strategy. As a former pricing leader at Continental Airlines and BMC Software, she has firsthand experience in the transformative benefits and competitive advantages that can be realized through PROS solutions.

Valerie earned an MBA from the McCombs School of Business at the University of Texas and a BS in Electrical Engineering through a scholarship at the Cooper Union for the Advancement of Science and Art. She is a frequent speaker at pricing conferences and has written for *Digital Commerce 360, Top Business Tech,* and others.

21

Digital Transformation, Commercial Excellence, and Pricing

Gabriel Smith, Chief Evangelist, Pricefx

Introduction

BEFORE WE GET INTO digital transformation and its impact on pricing and commercial excellence, let's begin by defining what we mean by digital transformation, or DX for short: according to George Westerman, MIT scientist and co-author of *Leading Digital: Turning Technology into Business Transformation* (2014), DX "marks a radical rethinking of how an organization **uses**

technology, people and processes to fundamentally change business performance."

This change has been sought by more and more companies over the last decade. According to the *IDC Worldwide Digital Transformation Spending Guide* (2000), global spending on digital transformation was forecast to grow 10.4 percent in 2020 to $1.3 trillion.

While, according to the same report, COVID-19 has decreased DX spending by more than $500 million and slowed growth from 17.9 percent in 2019 to 10.4 percent in 2020, it still grew despite COVID-19 (Figure 21.1).

However, this growth has not been proportionate in pricing and configure, price, quote (CPQ). Despite the fact that pricing is companies' most powerful profit lever, and that it can radically improve business performance from 0.5 to 4 percent or more of revenue, according to studies by Gartner et al., according to Gartner's CPQ Magic Quadrant, spending on CPQ is less than $1.42 billion, and in 2019 grew by 15.5 percent, lagging behind the 17.4 percent increase in DX spending. Spending on price optimization

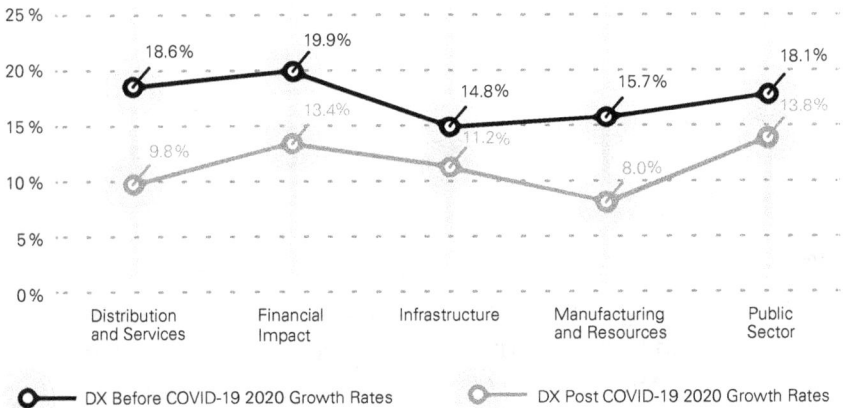

Figure 21.1. WW DX by sector: Before and after COVID-19 impact.

and management (PO&M) in B2B was less than $450 million in 2019—although it did grow at 21 percent, a greater increase than DX spending as a whole—but still a small fraction of DX spending considering its impact on the bottom line (Figure 21.1). The pandemic has awakened many companies to this need. For example, in the first six weeks after COVID-19 hit, G2 Crowd pricing software searches increased by 75 percent, quote to cash software by 48 percent, and CPQ by 22 percent (Kennedy, 2020). That said, according to Gartner, as of the end of 2019 fewer than 1,400 companies had deployed PO&M software, even though over 10,000 companies could benefit from it. Based on my own research, I estimate this number to be higher, at about 60,000 companies making more than $100 million in annual revenue that could benefit from a robust PO&M or CPQ digital transformation project.

Whatever story you take away from the numbers, one thing is clear: no modern company of any size or sophistication would dream of conducting their order management, accounting, or manufacturing with Excel or homegrown tools, yet over 54 percent of firms rely on Excel as their primary pricing tool, and 66 percent rely on either Excel or homegrown solutions (Figure 21.2)!

Where's the disconnect? While investments in digital commerce and CPQ are increasing, PO&M is sometimes getting overlooked. This is, in part, because these software solutions have until recently been quite expensive to license and implement, with only companies earning $1 billion-plus revenue having the resources to do so.

The purpose of this book is to educate executives investing in DX to make pricing, revenue management, and quote to cash a priority in their future investments. In fact, it's more than just pricing we're talking about here, it's really about achieving commercial excellence through digital transformation of revenue management and quote to cash as it relates to

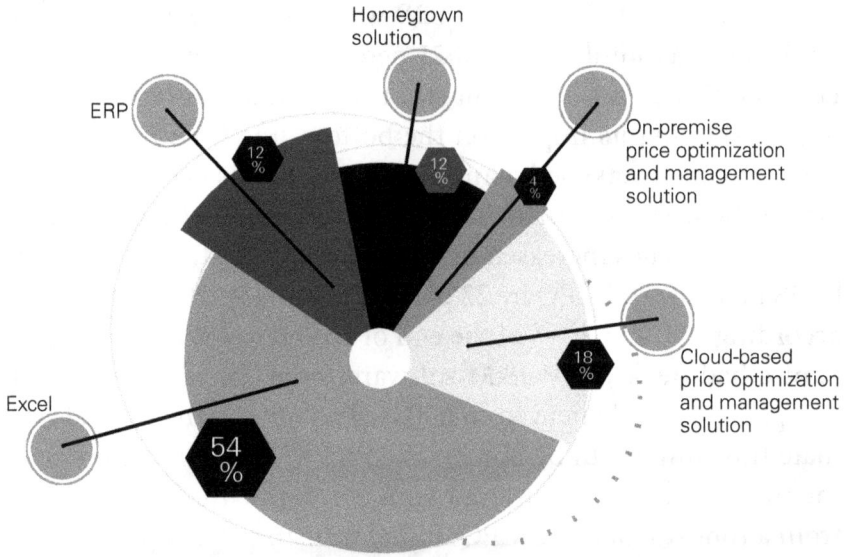

Figure 21.2. What do you currently use to manage pricing?

1 how quotes are configured, priced, and delivered to customers,
2 how that customer pricing flows into the order management system, and
3 how off-invoice incentives (rebates and promotional programs) are set and managed.

The future of commerce

Before we take a deeper dive on these areas, let's first understand what factors are influencing the future of commerce and the drive toward digital transformation of quote to order.

The "new normal." The impact of COVID-19 on how business is done will be felt for many years. In many respects, this has just accelerated trends that were already starting to be felt.

Teams will be more diverse and distributed, and there will be fewer in-person meetings, and hopefully fewer meetings overall. This means that data-driven decisions will be more key than ever, as will collaborative tools that enable groups of people to make better decisions collectively.

Direct to consumer. 2020 was the year of direct to consumer (DTC), with DTC spending topping $18 billion for the year and finally being tracked on its own. The pandemic has accelerated the DTC trends that were already taking hold in many industries, and it will put further pressure on manufacturers to seek higher-profit channels and on distributors to add more value to their customers than a single manufacturer can, whether through breadth of selection, speed of delivery, ease of doing business, or other value-added areas (Figures 21.3 and 21.4).

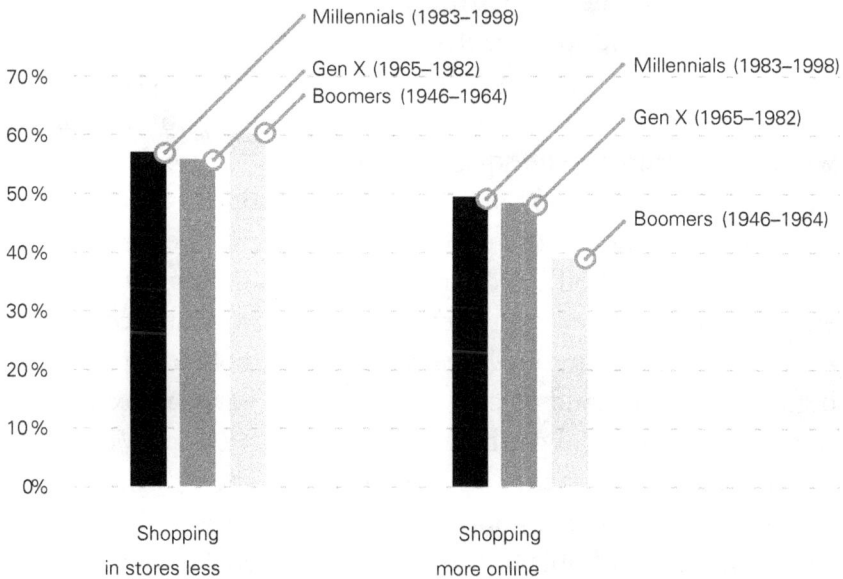

Figure 21.3. How, if at all, are you changing your shopping behavior as a result of COVID-19? (Oct. 2020)

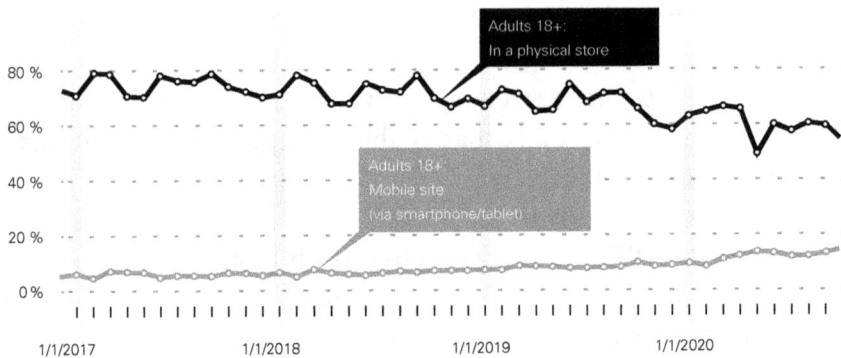

Figure 21.4. In the past 30 days, how have you shopped for household supplies? (cleaning, laundry, paper products, etc.)

B2C influence in B2B and DTC.

B2C influence in B2B and DTC. Amazon Business launched in 2015 and reached $1 billion in sales in its first year, and to $10 billion in B2B sales in 2019, a growth rate of 60 percent from 2018 to 2019. How did they do it? To a large extent, they have taken what works in B2C and applied it to B2B: customer-centricity, good prices, managing price perception with no contractual needs, large assortment, fast fulfillment, and being easy to do business with. This is putting the squeeze on more and more distributors, who will have to focus on providing unique value to their customers by understanding them better and fostering better relationships. Watsco, a $4 billion distributor of HVAC supplies, is a great example of this. They sold over $1.5 billion in digital commerce in 2020 and have invested heavily in their mobile applications, digital commerce, and pricing capabilities. As a small example of this, they have a flashlight built into their mobile app. Why would a user need that when they already can access the flashlight on the phone? Because HVAC contractors are in dark and tight spaces and they need to be able to take pictures of model numbers, serial numbers, and so forth so that they can order new equipment. This type of understanding of the customer and ability to meet their needs is how distributors can add more value than Amazon or of manufacturers in some cases.

Omnichannel (disruption). Related to DTC is an increased need for omnichannel fulfillment, strategy, and tactics, especially with regard to pricing. I was part of the project team for a high-tech manufacturer in 2014 that launched their pricing project when the CEO heard from the CEO of a customer who was supposed to have the lowest prices in the market as part of their contract. Their procurement team had found a lower-priced piece of equipment on the manufacturer's website than they were buying it for under contract, which, as you can imagine, was one of their largest customers. In an omnichannel world, having a rational and consistent pricing strategy and tactics is key.

CPQ + digital commerce convergence. The role of sales is changing from taking orders to providing value and solution selling. The order-taker sales rep roles are disappearing. Why? Because the process to configure, price, and quote an order to a customer is being automated, as is the ability to place the order. Moreover, millennial buyers prefer to order online rather than call someone and would prefer not to have to enter into a contract. This means that you need to get the price right the first time you interact with a prospective customer.

Machine intelligence. The use of AI and machine learning in price optimization CPQ and product recommendations is one of the most proven and valuable uses of this technology that exists in 2021. Machine intelligence has been used in price optimization since the 1980s, but recent advances in cloud computing power, memory, and data volume handling have brought these capabilities to the point where almost any company can use them, whereas until about 10 years ago only the largest enterprise companies had the access and wherewithal required. Machine intelligence can automate the process of getting the right price to a customer or prospect to win the business while optimizing margin for your business.

Augmented and virtual reality + 5G. As of the publication of this book, these technologies have not yet impacted commerce in a meaningful way, as the technology has not "crossed the chasm," to use Michael Moore's term. But make no mistake: the combination of augmented reality with 5G will be an absolute game-changer for how business is done and will be highly disruptive in accelerating the changing face of commerce; it might even end price tags as we know them as we transition to a much more personalized pricing and promotion optimization when combined with machine intelligence.

Subscription economy. In a 2011 *Wall Street Journal* article, Marc Andreessen famously wrote that "software is eating the world." In 2021 you might say that "subscriptions are eating the world." Everywhere you look there are subscriptions, from software to hardware to delivery to dirt. That's right: I was at a pricing conference where a dirt company had created an offer whereby their customers could bypass the line if they paid a subscription fee. Think about that for a minute: there are companies subscribing to dirt right now. This move fundamentally changes the sales motion, commercial, and customer experience. I was part of a tiger team for a high-tech hardware company in the early 2000s, exploring the implications of moving to subscriptions at that time; it truly is a fundamental change to the way business is done, and it can have huge impacts where it's deployed against new use cases. It moves you from a transactional to a relationship business, which is huge if you focus on the customer experience, value, and expectations. It also gives a business the unique opportunity to have a fresh look at the value metrics: in other words, which metrics most accurately measure the value your customers get from your offer. The dirt company realized after talking to customers that they valued the time waiting in line more than anything, as it held up their entire operation, so they allowed customers to pay more for what they valued. Many times, like in this case, this will entail moving away from selling units and into a service level. For example, at a former company, our customer was a lighting manufacturer that moved from selling light fixtures and bulbs to a subscription for lighted buildings or parking lots with a percentage of lighted coverage and uptime for a monthly fee. All the hardware, software, and services were wrapped into this, and if they did it right it was a win-win: they made higher margins and had a more predictable revenue stream, and the customer had what they valued for a predictable expense.

The future work of pricing teams

In addition to the forces shaping the future of commerce, several factors are influencing the future of work and, in particular, pricing and commercial teams. These can be summed up in the four D's: distributed, diverse, digital, and data-driven. Let's quickly touch on each one.

Distributed. The pandemic has clearly accelerated the move to remote work that was already common in the knowledge and software industries, but it will also have lasting impacts once employers realize that much work can be done as effectively, or even more effectively, in a remote setting. Many people are actually working more hours, and productivity has increased, as has job satisfaction and work/life balance, because of the elimination of commute times and the added flexibility in many cases. That said, in other cases people are less satisfied and productive. The right mix is a personal decision, but I believe the days of mandated in-office time are over for many industries except for jobs that can't be done remotely.

Diverse. The world and workforce are becoming more diverse, and the distributed nature of the workforce going forward will reinforce this. I'm talking not just about diversity in the sense of race, gender, or sexual orientation but in how media is consumed: there are many more points of view represented. Everyone consumes media in vastly different ways that change their perspective and make a common narrative more difficult to come by. This means that companies and managers have to be more thoughtful about how information is presented and be open to different ideas. Those that can foster diversity have and will continue to outperform those that do not.

Digital. The millennials are taking over more and more job roles, and they are digital first. They expect processes to be digital, to be automated, and to be work like their consumer applications. Analog processes represent activation energy and are not in focus for digital natives. Even Gen-Xers like myself feel this way about many of the consulted analog processes that still exist in the world.

Data-driven. The availability of data and the tools to analyze and act on these data to make better decisions increases every day and will become increasingly important going forward. According to a recent Harvard Business School post, companies making data-driven decisions outperform those that do not, and they're more proactive, confident in their decisions, and efficient (Stobierski, 2019).

Keys to pricing and commercial excellence

In this environment, there are several keys to commercial excellence around revenue management, pricing, and quote to cash.

An **omnichannel** approach and platform enables the strategy and execution in a cohesive manner across all the channels in which you go to market and allows for changes. The right omnichannel strategy might see the same price across all channels in some industries, but in many, you will be differentiating the price of your offer depending on the channel and situation. For example, if a customer is willing to wait a bit, they'll pay a lower price; if they need something immediately, they'll pay a higher one.

Customer-centric pricing strategy and tactics allow you to understand the unique value your solution brings to customers, how it is differentiated among them and from your competition. This works together with the omnichannel strategy, which also entails that you understand the buyer journey and what customers are willing to pay in different channels. For example, I'm willing to pay more for a bottle of water in a hotel room than in an airport and to pay more for that same bottle in an airport than in a grocery store.

In a **collaborative** approach, the process for setting, negotiating, and realizing price in the market is cross-functional across sales, customers, partners, marketing, and finance. You need to think of this as a collaborative process and instill that mindset in your commercial team instead of an antagonistic culture between finance or pricing and sales that still exists at many companies today. You also need the tools that enable this collaboration quickly and efficiently across the organization.

Agility, the ability to adjust your pricing strategy and tactics as the market changes, incorporate new data into it, see what's working and what's not, and update as needed, is a key competitive advantage in more markets and industries every year. Pricing is becoming more dynamic each year, and the ability to respond to changing market conditions, whether from cost, supply chain, or competition, is key to outperforming the market and your competition going forward.

Pricing analytics and optimization should be **integrated** into everyday business processes, not in a standalone BI tool or Excel. The analytics should help your team make better decisions where they are being made, driving workflow and approvals, and so forth. This is true in any industry, but especially in B2B, where customer-specific pricing decisions are made with high frequency and impact.

AI/machine-learning. One of the most tested and valuable applications of machine intelligence today is in price optimization. Companies began using these techniques in the 1980s, and they've gained sophistication, ease of use, and scale since. It's simply impossible to compete with this using people and spreadsheets unless you want to employ a small army of analysts to do so, and even then, the results won't be as good, fast, or precise.

What can you learn from Amazon?

Amazon excels at price optimization and managing the perception of pricing, meaning they're not always the lowest-priced provider but are on the key value items and categories that people pay attention to. But more fundamentally, what are the keys to the success of Amazon and other digital-native, next-generation companies?

Customer-centricity. Jeff Bezos said, "We are not competitor obsessed; we are customer obsessed. We start with the customer and work backwards." This idea should be applied to every part of your business but rings especially true in pricing and commercial processes, where some of the most important customer touchpoints lie.

Day 1 Principle. Always think like a startup no matter how big you get. According to Bezos, "Day 2 is stasis. Followed by irrelevance. Followed by excruciating, painful decline. Followed by death. And that is why it is always Day 1."

Seventy percent rule. Make decisions with 70 percent certainty: don't wait for more than that, embrace trends quickly. If it doesn't work, fail fast and try something new. Focus on results, not process.

Disruption. Channel and business model disruption: Amazon Prime is a good example of this; subscription models are still difficult for many retailers or distributors to embrace, but Walmart recently tried to create one, which is a huge shift for them away from everyday low pricing.

Machine learning and AI. This is an area where Amazon excels in pricing, recommendations, and customer interaction. This allows them to experiment, test, learn, and adjust very quickly, especially when combined with the other principles above.

How will you compete with a company like this if you're pricing, quoting, and managing revenue in Excel? The answer is simple: you won't. I've seen this firsthand because we have customers competing directly with Amazon in several markets.

Top pain points addressed through DX of pricing, commerce, and QTC

Pricefx conducted a survey in 2020 that revealed some interesting things about pain points and key capabilities. The survey is still underway as of this writing, but some of the initial results with a sample of 58 respondents are shared in Figures 21.5, 21.6, and 21.7.

Key performance indicators (KPIs)

Now that we've covered the top pain points and key capabilities associated with DX in this area, you might be wondering what

What best describes
your role?

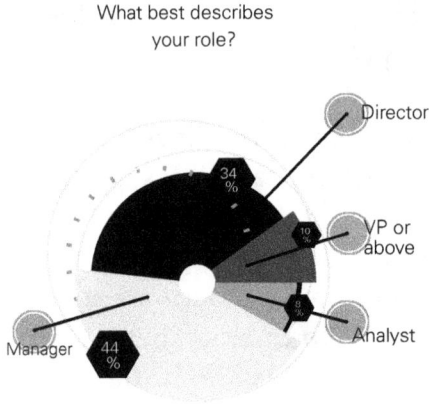

- Two-thirds rely on Excel or a homegrown solution to manage pricing.
- Nearly three-quarters of respondents are worried about at least one of the following:
  - Price transparency (74%)
  - Cost volatility (84%)
  - Decreased volume (88%)
- 98% reported losing deals and/or leaving money on the table because of "pricing that's off the mark and/or hard to defend."

What do you currently
use to manage pricing?

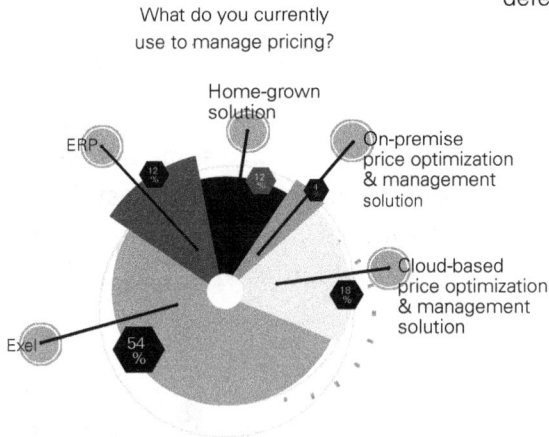

Figure 21.5. The industry is talking…we're listening. © Pricefx, Inc. 2021.

"Poor visibility into true profit drivers by product and customer segment."

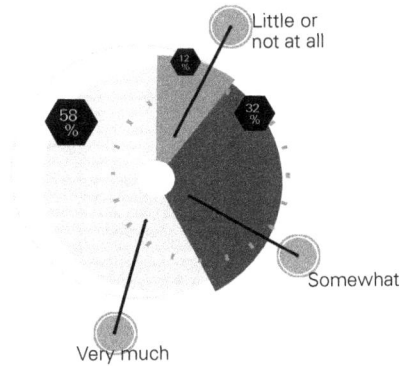

Little or not at all — 12%

58%

32% — Somewhat

Very much

"Price realization and deal profitability varies widely across the sales team."

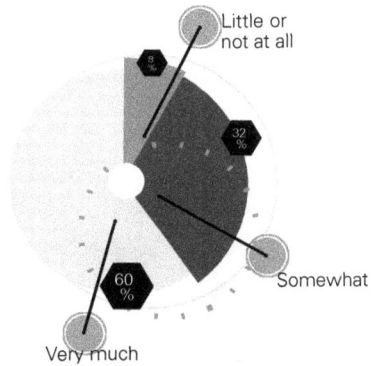

Little or not at all — 8%

32% — Somewhat

60% — Very much

"Difficulty managing pricing strategy, rules and guidelines."

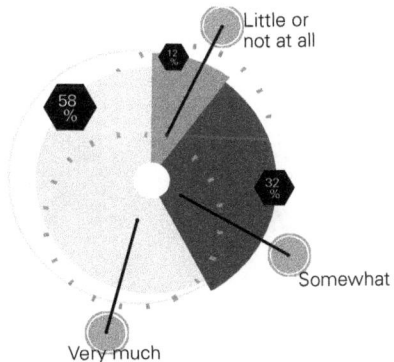

Little or not at all — 12%

58%

32% — Somewhat

Very much

Figure 21.6. Most acute pain points. © Pricefx, Inc. 2021.

"Uncovering opportunities for immediate margin improvement."

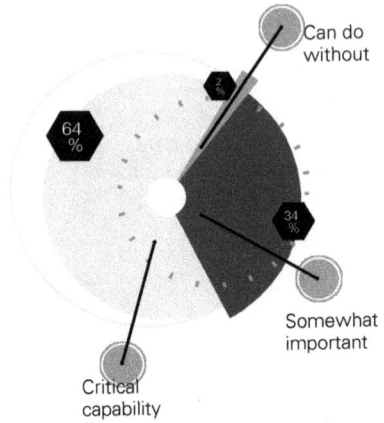

"Arming sales with target pricing and deal guidance they can stand behind."

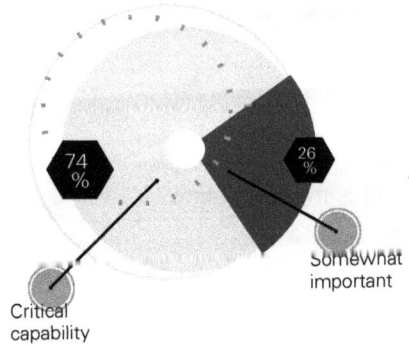

"Making it easier for my team to manage complex pricing strategies."

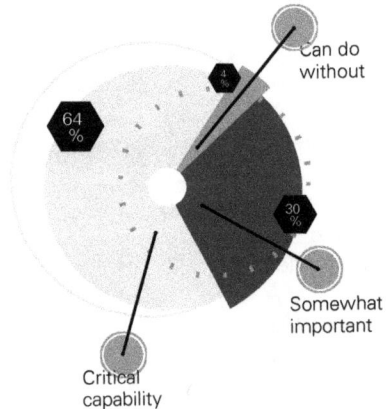

Figure 21.7. Most important capabilities.

KPIs will move through a digital transformation effort in revenue management, pricing a quote to cash.

Increased profit. Four percent to 5 percent of revenue in improved profit is not uncommon. It seems a bit unreal at first, but if you think of getting 1 percent better at price, selling something for $101 instead of $100 on average, it seems much more achievable. That 1 percent of revenue is $10 million per year for a $1 billion company. With the advances in technology and the disruptive nature of the cloud and AI, the investments generally pay for themselves in less than 12 months, though Generation 2, cloud-native software providers are much quicker than Generation 1 software providers, taking, on average, 40 percent less time to achieve ROI payback, according to G2 Crowd.

Increased margin percentage. By seeing all the items that affect the margin percentage for a customer, product, or deal, you can account for items that cause margin leakage, such as off-invoice incentives, payment terms, or freight. Also, you can reduce margin compression as suppliers change their prices to you by reacting quickly and intelligently to pass these increases through to your customers or use market data to push back on pricing with your suppliers.

Faster quote cycle times. Getting a quote to a customer with the right price should be almost instant today. If a lower price than the guidance provided is needed, automated workflows should route this to the approvers, who can approve from anywhere and any device. Once the pricing is approved, it should be orderable immediately. This sort of optimal pricing guidance and automation significantly reduces quote cycles times; in some cases I've seen average reductions of over 55 percent.

Increased win rates. By reducing quote cycle times and being first to provide a price, you'll improve your win rates. Several studies have shown statistical correlation between win rates and cycle times, and it makes sense that if you get a good price out there first, customers are more likely to go with you instead of waiting around for pricing from your competitors.

More deals per rep. By spending less time getting pricing approved and quotations out to customers, sales reps can spend more time with customers and handle more deals at a time.

Increase deal sizes and revenue per customer. Some modern pricing and CPQ solutions have recommendation engines built in that can suggest cross-sell and upsell opportunities for customers to increase the size of the deals, break into new categories, and so forth.

Increased customer satisfaction. Getting a price and ordering shouldn't be a chore for your customers or your employees. Streamlining this process and recommending the right price makes you more money and makes customers and employees happier.

Key considerations in digital transformation projects

To quote Bain Partner Chuck Davenport, "Before embarking on the transformation, define and share your intended destination, your north star. Every step of the journey should move the company forward toward the north star." This means deciding early on which key outcomes you're driving toward and using this as a guideline for what to prioritize, focus on, and invest in. Does it move the needle in the direction you're aiming for, and is it worth the effort/resources needed to achieve the result? If yes, go for it; if not, pass on it for now.

Prioritize, start small, prove success, and then expand. Don't try to do too much at once. I've seen many digital transformation efforts falter because they tried to do too much too quickly. Ambitious plans are great, but you should be realistic about what your organization can implement and digest in any given period.

Find champions. This is especially true in the sales organization, where change management in quote to cash can be a real challenge if not handled well. The best project I ever saw from a pricing and quoting perspective was done so well that the project lead had sales teams lined up and begging to get priority to implement the new CPQ solution. How did he do it? By taking the time to understand their needs, how they did things in the past, and investing a significant amount of the project budget to address those items, even if they weren't moving his pricing KPIs. In addition, building out the minimum viable product (MVP) and letting users know that you'll let them test drive it but that you want their input on which features to add will foster a sense of collaboration and partnership that pays off in both the final product and its adoption in the field (Figure 21.8).

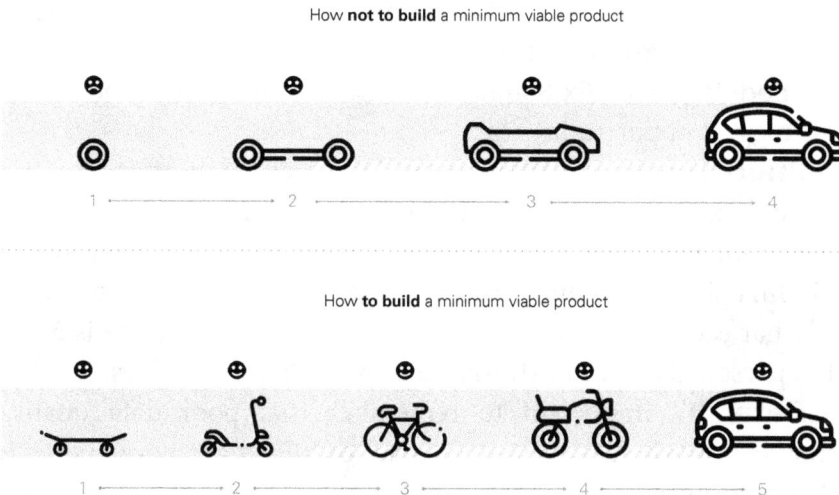

Figure 21.8. Minimum viable product.

How to get your organization ready

Pricing maturity. Understanding your organization's pricing maturity is a good starting point for identifying opportunities to improve your people, process, and systems. This is a separate topic that requires its own chapter, but there's a methodology that we and our consulting partners use that can help you access this and identify areas for improvement.

People. Hiring the right people and developing a culture that's dynamic and agile and that embraces change is key across organizations that outperform. Even more key is having people who are change agents and who will drive this change into the organization, which can be tough and politically challenging, especially in large organizations. Support these change agents and help them break down the barriers to such changes; realize that they might not be the most popular people in the company but that they are absolutely vital to your organization's continued success.

Process. All your quote to cash, pricing, and revenue management processes should be examined for inefficiencies, redundancies, and areas that aren't adding value. I suggest using a methodology like Six Sigma to do this and to understand where the biggest opportunities lie.

Prioritize. After you understand the areas to go after, have the same people assess the effort required at a high level to address the opportunities. You don't need super precise estimates, just like "T-shirt sizes: medium, large, extra-large," with clear definitions of what each mean in terms of effort. For example: large is 50 to 100 person-days, and extra-large is over 100 person-days.

Data. It's important to remember that poor data quality should *never* be an excuse for inaction. Data are never perfect; they can always get better, and often initiatives like this drive better practices around data collection, automation, and transformation. While a baseline level of data is required to successfully drive the analysis, optimization, and automation associated with DX in these areas, I've personally never seen an organization that doesn't have enough data in their ERP and DW/BI systems to make meaningful performance improvements in their business— and I've seen "under the hood" in dozens of organizations over the last 20 years.

Systems. A modern ERP, CRM, and pricing platform are generally all being used by best-in-class companies, though they're not required. The key is connecting the processes for pricing, quoting, and ordering together and enabling the right level of analysis within them to make better decisions.

Key takeaways for executives

Digital transformation of revenue management, pricing, commerce, and quote to cash processes is becoming table stakes in more and more industries. In B2C industries, DX in this arena is now fairly common, followed by distribution, but more manufacturers are investing in the solutions to become more dynamic and agile in their pricing and commercial processes. Companies that aren't investing in this area will find it increasingly difficult to compete against those that are. Companies that do invest in this area will continue to outperform their industry peers and competitors primarily through three areas.

Increasing business agility. Allow sales teams, marketing, and finance organizations to change strategy and tactics without needing IT to make changes to enable these shifts. This agility also helps reduce margin compression, especially in highly competitive markets like distribution and retail, but also in manufacturing companies, particularly those selling more commoditized products or ones that are highly dependent on commodity markets like process and chemicals.

Driving profitable growth. Understanding all the factors that contribute to profit from a given customer, product, or transaction is the starting point (Figure 21.9). Then, providing sales optimized pricing guidance, based on rules, data, and AI, allows them to stop leaving money on the table. Last, providing recommendations to the sales team and to customers about where there are opportunities to sell more or to break into new categories, and alerting them to customer health and trends they can act on, are all meaningful ways to grow revenue and profits.

Reduce effort and risk. By streamlining data flows and manual processes around analytics, price-setting, and price getting, you can significantly reduce the effort required to perform these tasks, increase the quality of decision-making, and reduce risk associated with mistakes, improper payments, and credits.

Although an entire book could be written on this subject, I hope you found this condensed chapter useful. For more information, listen to episodes 4 and 5 of Pricefx's *Pricing Matters* podcast for a detailed discussion on this topic with Bain Partners Chuck

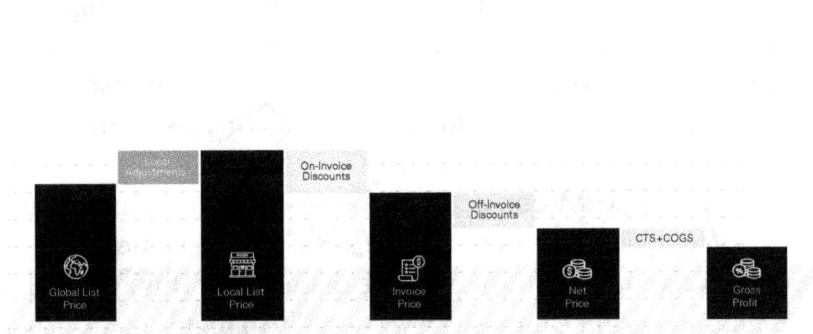

Figure 21.9. Illustration of a pricing and profitability waterfall.
© Pricefx, Inc. 2021.

Davenport and Paco Jiminez. I also did a webinar with PPS on this topic that I'm happy to share with you. For this or any other discussion you'd like to have on this topic or pricing, CPQ, or commercial excellence, email me at gabriel.smith@pricefx.com, or contact me on Twitter @swevangelist or at LinkedIn @gabesmith.

References

Andreesen, M. (2011). Why software is eating the world. *Wall Street Journal,* August 20. www.wsj.com/articles /SB10001424053111903480904576512250915629460

IDC. (2000). *Worldwide Digital Transformation Spending Guide.*

Kennedy, K. (2020). The right configure, price, quote tools can help you sell smarter in the age of COVID-19. *Research Hub,* April 30. research.g2.com/insights/configure-price-quote-covid-19

Stobierski, T. (2019). The advantages of data-driven decision-making. *Harvard Business School Online,* August 26. online.hbs.edu/blog/post/data-driven-decision-making

Westerman, G., Bonnet, D., & McAfee, A. (2014). *Leading digital: Turning technology into business transformation.* Boston, MA: Harvard Business Review Press.

The author

Gabriel Smith has over 20 years of experience in quote to cash, pricing, promotions, consulting, product management and marketing, sales, and management. He has worked on price optimization products and projects for the last 14 years at leading companies across industries, partners, and software solutions. He began his career implementing one of the first large-scale CPQ platforms at Cisco Systems, and his experience includes companies like 3M,

CertainTeed, Dell, Emerson, IBM, Iron Mountain, Praxair, Seagate, and Smith's Group and partnering with top management consulting firms. Gabe is currently the Chief Evangelist and VP of Innovation for Pricefx; he holds an Interdisciplinary Studies degree from UC Berkeley after deciding he would rather architect software solutions than buildings. He is a father of two, lives in San Jose, California, and enjoys cooking, sailing, golfing, basketball, snowboarding, and travel.

Conclusion:
The Next Frontier
of the Pricing Profession

Kevin Mitchell, President,
Professional Pricing Society

Introduction

OVER THE PAST 50 years, pricing has evolved from a topic related purely to economics and academic research to a highly practical and powerful instrument for driving firm profitability. The pricing function has also evolved, especially in the last two decades with the development of a strong marketing discipline and the creation of the four P's in which price, the only "P" that is not an initial marketing expense, plays a critical role. Today, as pricing becomes a more widely published topic in economics, marketing, and management literature, we're also experiencing some barriers to making the pricing function and the profession as a whole a true managerial discipline. Compared with disciplines such as innovation, continuous improvement, and supply chain management, the pricing function isn't fully breaking through to the next level. Post COVID-19, the pricing discipline stands at an existential crossroads. Trade organizations, such as the Professional Pricing Society, and academics have been strong and passionate contributors to bringing the pricing discipline to the forefront of the marketing and finance field, but these groups cannot do this work alone.

In this concluding chapter, we reflect on where we come from as a profession and where we need to go to bring pricing where it deserves to be. It's important to explain to members of the C-suite what pricing is, where it comes from, and what critical changes it will bring to the future of the business world. We also examine the next frontier of pricing and call for much innovation in the pricing field to generate excitement and interest for the discipline and profession. Only through innovations and professionalization can we convince the C-suite to take this discipline seriously and to invest in its development.

Where we come from

The pricing discipline has come a long way. A series of evolutionary changes have occurred in the last few decades. The most critical change has been the role of pricing within the firm: from what was a "gut decision" made by a vocal senior manager in marketing or finance, to a more specific clerical or bookkeeping function that maintained a written price list (strictly on a "cost-plus" basis, most likely), to finally a more strategic function with decisions made at the highest level of the organization, including chief pricing officers, chief value officers, or chief revenue officers.

Pricing as a clerical function

An early pricing practitioner might not have even known that they were exercising the pricing function or in charge of pricing activities in their firm. Perhaps this person was an outcast in the marketing or accounting department with limited upward mobility or gravitas within their company. As no pricing-specific classes were offered in colleges and universities beyond perhaps a few chapters in introductory marketing courses, skill sets and training were difficult to define or locate. Limited power and limited information would mean that our proto-practitioner's work would exist only at the mercy of a cross-functional menagerie that likely had very different goals and ideas. Corporate desires for market share or sales volume targets would (and often still do) greatly outweigh aims to improve specific margins or profits, so pricing goals would have been nebulous. Our proto-practitioner would quickly learn about situations where higher-ups decided that big deals would not be lost because of price.

This administrative employee probably had very little interaction with customer purchasing departments and would have been at a supreme disadvantage in the rare situations when there was customer contact. Then (and now, to a smaller extent) buyers would have had better data, better systems, stronger motivations, and better training at a minimum. If price became a sticking point, a customer could rely on the sales department to pull rank and make the deal outside of pricing targets.

One evolutionary step: Becoming tactical

Increased focus on pricing's potential as a profit lever for the firm led to greater knowledge of and emphasis on our practitioner's goals. Those within the pricing discipline were gaining a framework of the importance of their jobs and had opportunities to increase their skill sets. Pricing managers could block some unprofitable deals (leading to the common joke of the pricing department being the "sales prevention department") and perhaps even had options to move up in their firms, although still lacking the career progression of more glamorous fields. Some industries had pricing software options available to further level the field in dealings with customers' purchasers. Marketing research used tools like conjoint analysis to provide better data and estimate elasticity. There were even whole textbooks (Monroe, 1990; Nagle & Holden, 2002) on pricing—first and foremost, not just subsets within other marketing books.

As the pricing discipline advanced, practitioners learned the value of their daily tasks and could communicate gains made by advising senior management about bottom-line gains. Consulting companies created pricing practices whose primary concern was to help clients improve their pricing structure and processes. Eric Mitchell began publishing *The Pricing Advisor* newsletter in 1984 and *The Journal of Professional Pricing* in 1991. Pricing conferences, networking options, and literature began to grow and flourish.

Pricing as a strategic function

Further advances came as corporations looked to leverage pricing power and value propositions to improve profitability. Many companies expanded pricing departments and created vice president–level positions in pricing. Some practitioners (Reid, 2010) have called for the further expansion of the CPO—chief pricing officer—position, and Wall Street analysts began to look beyond same-store sales and other volume measures in favor of pricing metrics. In 2010 billionaire investor Warren Buffett even placed pricing power above management acumen in evaluating the worth of a company. Along with management focus, special pricing projects and longer-term corporate goals became commonplace, and organization charts and reporting structures elevated pricing's status within the firm (Survey of the Pricing Professional, 2009).

Several top business schools (Wharton, Stanford, University of Chicago, and others) have made pricing education a cornerstone of their executive education programs, and some business schools (notably, University of Rochester) have developed concentrations in pricing. Advanced training options and professional designations, such as the Certified Pricing Professional, have allowed pricing practitioners to escalate their skills and demonstrate extra learning within the discipline. Pricing has become a topic of discussion in many boardrooms, executives' suites, and team meetings in medium and large enterprises.

So, pricing has made some great progress in becoming a function that's accepted more and more in the organizational fabrics of firms. The last 25 years, pricing has been placed on the map and has demonstrated its potential impact with best-in-class marketing organizations. But where do we go from here? How do we bring pricing to the next level and to reach its next frontier?

The next frontier

Over the past five to 10 years, significant changes have occurred in the business worlds. We've experienced severe forces of disruption of various kinds and levels of intensity. The COVID-19 health crisis has also changed the game. Most consulting companies have written about the new world, or what they call "the next normal." What's certain is that pricing has a great future as both a discipline and a function. Our reflections at PPS have led to the identification of five critical elements for the future of the pricing profession.

Greater adoption and presence in the C-suite

The next normal focuses on profitable growth and rapid recovery of lost sales. The past year has been challenging for many sectors, with depressed demand levels and margin erosion. Many executives report that this crisis has set their business back by five years. Stephan Liozu reports in the introduction of this book that the adoption of pricing in large organizations is increasing. We project an increased presence of pricing in the C-suite through the chief revenue officer or chief growth officer. We come from very far, but we're making great progress. But more executives need to take pricing more seriously as a lever of growth and profit. The next normal will be more diversified, more digital, more self-service, more connected, and very fast. Competitive intensity will only increase from where we are today. Therefore, we anticipate much wider adoption of pricing systems and pricing tools as part of digital transformation investments as reported by many contributors in this book.

Greater use of technology

As with other professions, pricing is benefiting from great advances in technology. From powerful computers to the more advanced versions of analytical software, the pricing function has gained in analytical skills, speed of execution, and quality of team interactions. Pricing decisions are taken with more scientific support, more automated processes, more team interactions via video conference or other collaboration tools, and a greater ability to be tested in the field with customers. Feedback and data can be received in real time via ERP, CRM, or other cloud-based platforms. In short, it's just the beginning. The technological developments we've witnessed in the last few years can only offer immense possibilities for pricing experts. Working closely with IT and digital departments, pricers can have access to the best communication and analytical tools to make the best decisions in real time and quickly.

The increasing importance of pricing software

Over the past 10 years, we've witnessed the emergence of robust and modern pricing software that allows firms to systematize and optimize their pricing activities. These software platforms have made great inroads with Fortune 500 companies and are relevant in the pricing sphere. The next generation of pricing software is being created as we speak. The cloud computing environment offers many opportunities for smaller firms to benefit from pricing software at a fraction of the costs without a long and difficult implementation process. AI-based pricing startups are popping up around the world to enable small and large firms to mine their data and improve pricing decisions. Companies will be able to rely on proven, systematic, and robust platforms instead of Excel-based, internally designed, static tools and methods. The increased adoption of software also benefits the pricing profession, as skills and competencies can be transferred from firm to firm, creating opportunities for advancement.

The democratization of pricing in the mid-market segment

Who manages pricing in the millions of small and medium businesses around the world? The Small Business Administration reports that 99 percent of businesses are small and create the vast majority of GDP. As a profession, how do we carry the pricing and value messages to the millions of marketing, sales, and finance professionals involved in pricing strategies and tactics? Size doesn't matter in pricing. With the emergence of cloud-based and right-sized pricing technology, small and medium businesses (SMBs) can now afford to buy a nimble and simple pricing software suite. The cost barrier of enterprise software acquisition and implementation has disappeared. It offers SMBs and startups an opportunity to start right away with a CPQ solution or a pricing analytics engine. Specialist companies have appeared offering pricing research at the click of a button for a fraction of the cost and within a few days. This is good news. There's no longer any excuse not to adopt these technologies and begin making an impact on the bottom line.

The skills of the future

Last but not least, we project that the pricing skills of the future will evolve. With the advent of pricing software and greater access to technology, pricing professionals will have to show a combination of hard and soft skills. Pricers will be required to gain organizational and behavioral skills to accompany firms through their transformational activities. Soft skills such as change management, emotional intelligence, and communication intelligence will be increasingly needed. How, then, do we equip pricing professionals with these skills? Firms will have to create more balanced profiles in order to be able to speak with computers and software for data analysis but also to lead humans through tough and sometimes tenuous transformational journeys.

Conclusions

The pricing profession has evolved and continues to do so with the increased role of technology and a much greater presence in the C-suite. In 2010 the PPS reported that only 10 percent of global Fortune 500 companies had a pricing team. That share is now 22 percent (Liozu, 2019)! We hope this figure will continue to grow over the next 10 years with the support of CEOs, CFOs, and CMOs. The Professional Pricing Society is staying ahead by embracing mega trends and by preparing the way for the next transformational steps. We're planning for the future by embracing technology in our training programs but also during our numerous industry meetings. We're embracing academic research and have welcomed thought leaders in our future thinking. The road ahead is bright and challenging. We can achieve great things as a profession as long as we all work together and lead the profession to reach this new frontier. Join us in this journey!

References

Liozu, S. M. (2019). Penetration of the pricing function among Global Fortune 500 firms. *Journal of Revenue and Pricing Management,* doi.org/10.1057/s41272–019–00209–2, 1–8.

Monroe, K. (1990). *Pricing: Making profitable decisions.* New York, NY: McGraw-Hill.

Nagle, T., & Holden, R. (2002). *The strategy and tactics of pricing: A guide to profitable decision making.* Upper Saddle River, NJ: Prentice-Hall.

Reid, W. (2010). Consider this—Why companies need a chief pricing officer. *Industry Week,* August 12. www.industryweek.com/finance/software-systems/article/21940258/consider-this-why-companies-need-a-chief-pricing-officer

The author

Kevin Mitchell is President of the Professional Pricing Society (www.pricingsociety.com/), located in Atlanta, Georgia, in the

US. He is the publisher of *The Pricing Advisor* newsletter and *The Journal of Professional Pricing*. PPS is the preeminent international association for pricing professionals and offers resources to help you enhance your knowledge and connect to peers all over the world. Organizations and their leaders have the ability to stay current with pricing trends and best practices, network with other professionals, and invest in their future. Kevin can be reached via email at kevin@pricingsociety.com or through LinkedIn.

The Editor

Stephan M. Liozu is a pricing evangelist who has widely promoted pricing for the past ten years. He is the Founder of Value Innoruption Advisors (www.valueinnoruption.com), a consulting boutique specializing in industrial, digital, and value-based pricing. He is also an Adjunct Professor and Research Fellow at the Case Western Research University Weatherhead School of Management. Stephan holds a PhD in Management from Case Western Reserve University (2013), an MS in Innovation Management from Toulouse School of Management (2005), and an MBA in Marketing from Cleveland State University (1991).

Stephan holds the following certifications:

Certified Platform Design Toolkit Facilitator (PDT, 2020)

Certified IoT Professional (IoT-Inc., 2019)

Certified Black Hat Coach (Thales, 2018)

Certified Pricing-to-Win Shipley Instructor (2017)

Business Model Innovation Coach (Strategyzer, 2016)

Certified Innovation Leader—GIMI/IXL (2014)

Master Customer Value Modeler (CVM®, 2013)

Prosci® Change Management Certification (2013)

ThinkBuzan® Licenced Instructor—iMindMap® (2012)

Certified Pricing Professional (CPP) (2009)

Certified Facilitator for DDI Learning Systems (2009)

Breakthrough Thinking (Gap International ECC 2007)

Six Sigma Green Belt (2007)

Over the past few years, Stephan has published academic articles in the *Journal of Revenue and Pricing Management, Business Horizons, MIT Sloan Management Review,* and *Industrial Marketing Management.* He has also written many articles on strategic pricing issues for the *Journal of Professional Pricing.* Stephan sits on the Advisory Board of Professional Pricing Society and Leverage-Point Innovation.

Over the past ten years, Stephan has edited or published ten other pricing books:

B2G Pricing: Best Practices in Business-to-Government Pricing Strategies (VIA Publishing, 2020)

Pricing Strategy Implementation: Translating Pricing Strategy into Results (Routledge, 2019)

Monetizing Data (VIA Publishing, 2018)

Value Mindset (VIA Publishing, 2017)

Dollarizing Differentiation Value (VIA Publishing, 2016)

The Pricing Journey (Stanford University Press, 2015)

Pricing and Human Capital (Routledge, 2015)

The ROI of Pricing (Routledge, 2014)

Pricing and the Sales Force (Routledge, 2015)

Innovation in Pricing: Contemporary Theories and Best Practices (Routledge, 2012 & 2017)

All books are available on Amazon.com. Please connect on LinkedIn or contact through the website at stephanliozu.com.

www.ingramcontent.com/pod-product-compliance
Lightning Source LLC
Chambersburg PA
CBHW060112200326
41518CB00008B/807

9 781945 815089